Unruly Gods

Unruly Gods

Divinity and Society
in China

EDITED BY
Meir Shahar and Robert P. Weller

UNIVERSITY OF HAWAI'I PRESS, HONOLULU

Library of Congress Cataloging-in-Publication Data
Unruly gods : divinity and society in China / edited by Meir Shahar
and Robert P. Weller.
p.   cm.
Includes bibliographical references and index.
ISBN 0–8248–1724–9 (alk. paper)
1. China—Religion. 2. China—Religious life and customs.
3. Gods, Chinese. I. Shahar, Meir. II. Weller, Robert P. (Robert
Paul), 1953– .
BL1802.U67   1996
299'.51—dc20   96–5144
CIP

Book design by Kenneth Miyamoto

Contents

Acknowledgments

THIS BOOK grew out of a double-session panel entitled "Chinese Gods beyond the Bureaucracy" at the 1992 annual meeting of the Association for Asian Studies. The original participants in this panel were: Ursula-Angelika Cedzich, Robert Hymes, Paul Katz, P. Steven Sangren, Meir Shahar, and Robert Weller. (Cedzich had by then already committed her paper for publication elsewhere.) We are grateful to the two discussants at the panel, David Johnson and James L. Watson, for their useful comments and suggestions. The manuscript benefited from the comments of anonymous readers for University of Hawai'i Press as well as suggestions made by Stephen F. Teiser. We are grateful to them all. Finally, we would like to express our thanks to our editor at the University of Hawai'i Press, Patricia Crosby.

MEIR SHAHAR
ROBERT P. WELLER

Unruly Gods

Introduction: Gods and Society in China

Meir Shahar and Robert P. Weller

The religious landscape of China is complex. Scholars usually distinguish among at least four Chinese religious traditions: the popular religion, Buddhism, Daoism, and Confucianism. The popular religion is sometimes referred to as the "diffused" religion or the "lay" religion of China, while the latter three are commonly designated the "institutional" or "clerical" Chinese religions. The idea of Chinese popular religion includes religious beliefs and practices that were shared by the overwhelming majority of the Chinese laity in late imperial times, commoners and elite alike. It has continued unchecked in Hong Kong, Taiwan, and overseas Chinese communities, and has surged again in the People's Republic of China after decades of discouragement. This popular religion has no canonical scriptures. Its heterogeneous beliefs, myths, and values have been transmitted, to a large extent, by popular lore (fiction, drama, and visual arts) and by symbol and ritual. Similarly, popular religion by and large lacks religious institutions independent of secular organizations, such as the family, the clan, and the guild. Thus, it does not exist as an entity independent of Chinese society and culture, and for this very reason it has no name. Western scholars coined the phrase "Chinese popular religion." Villagers in Taiwan are apt to say that they have no "religion" at all, even though they burn incense daily to various gods and ancestors. Here they are contrasting their daily practice with institutionalized systems featuring clergy, core texts, and formal membership. Still others simply have never heard the term *religion (zongjiao)*; it is a recent word in Chinese. By contrast, China's three main institutional religions had canonical scriptures and professional clergies, which were aware of their own distinct religious identities. The case of Confucianism is further complicated. Scholars have some-

1

times reserved this name for the moral and spiritual dimension of this tradition, referring to the rituals performed by Confucian scholars in their capacity as officials by the term "state religion"; we will maintain this distinction.[1]

These four traditions were of course intimately related to each other, as mutual competition encouraged mutual borrowings. Erik Zürcher introduced the influential metaphor of the pyramid to describe the relationship between the institutional religions of China and the popular religion. The institutional religions, he suggested, resemble peaks that emerge from the same mountain base. At the top —the level of learned clergy, the authors of canonical scriptures— these peaks appear far apart. But at the bottom—at the level of lay praxis and beliefs—they "merge into a much less differentiated lay religion" (Zürcher 1980:146).[2] Historians, whose access to the lay religion has been limited by the paucity of written documents, have until recently tended to view the Chinese religious landscape from the peaks. Thus, their studies are inclined to highlight the differences between China's religious traditions. By contrast, anthropologists, whose field work focuses on the praxis of religion in daily life, tend to emphasize areas of congruence.

One area of congruence is the supernatural. The state religion, Daoism, Buddhism, and the popular religion are all polytheistic. Beginning in ancient times state officials worshiped a large pantheon of deities arranged in a hierarchical bureaucratic structure at the apex of which stood Heaven (Tian). The Daoist clergy venerated their own divine bureaucracy as well as a rambunctious group of unruly deities known as immortals (xian). Buddhism enriched the Chinese supernatural with a host of its own religious characters, including buddhas (who have escaped the wheel of incarnation) and bodhisattvas (who choose to remain in this world until all others are saved). Finally there is the pantheon of the amorphous popular religion, which has been the richest and most diverse of all. The Chinese laity worship a plethora of supernatural figures, ranging from local guardian saints to national deities, from deities of popular origins to gods of Daoist or Buddhist descent.

For lack of a better term in English, we will follow common practice by referring to all these spirits as "gods." Such use should be taken to imply not the omniscience and omnipotence of the Abrahamic god, but something more akin to Catholic saints: spirits of dead worthies who can respond to requests from the living. Even this comparison risks obscuring the range of such spirits in China, from personified nature spirits (foxes, monkeys, stones, constellations) to subdued bandits to moral exemplars. The key Chinese term is *shen* (as in the common terms *guishen,* "ghosts and gods," or *shenfo,* "gods and Buddhas"), which refers abstractly to vital force and concretely to gods.

At least four types of gods—Daoist, Buddhist, state, and popular —thus exist in China. Yet these four groups are by no means distinct. Gods are mutually borrowed and sometimes are shared by two, three, or all four religions. The popular religion inherited many of its deities from Daoist and Buddhist mythology, and the supernatural bureaucracy of the imperial state was administered by deities of popular descent. Likewise, under the laity's pressure, the Daoist and Buddhist clergies sanctioned local cults and adopted popular deities into their supernatural realms. In the process deities' images were changed. Imperial state officials attempted to Confucianize local cults, and Daoist and Buddhist clergy clothed borrowed deities in their respective religious terminologies.[3]

This volume begins a systematic reexamination of the rich and complex world of Chinese gods. Drawing on recent research, it challenges some previously held notions regarding the Chinese supernatural. The seven essays that follow survey a large number of gods of varying sorts: local deities who rose to national prominence, deities who figure primarily in spirit-medium cults, and others in whose honor large temples have been built. The essays cover a lengthy time period from the Southern Song to the present.

Two sets of questions underlie this volume. First, what is the relationship between the Chinese supernatural and the Chinese social and political order? Do the Chinese heavens mirror the social and political landscape of late imperial China, or do they turn it upside down? How are they the products and producers of relations of power and identity? Western scholars have pointed out significant similarities between the Chinese supernatural and the bureaucratic structure of the Chinese state; they have thus tended to describe Chinese deities as bureaucratic and their relationship to society as a metaphor (e.g., Ahern 1981, Wolf 1974a). The following chapters, however, show that the bureaucratic idea applies only to one segment of the Chinese supernatural. Indeed, these essays reveal that the Chinese heavens were neither a passive metaphor for China's political order nor a simple reification of its social hierarchy. Rather, the heavens expressed and negotiated the tensions within society. Chinese gods did mirror the existing order in some ways, but they also shaped it, compensated for it, and changed it. They participated in the dynamics of power and struggles over identity that characterized China as much as any other society. These essays begin to suggest the historical, geographical, social, and cultural patterns that reverberated with the images of Chinese deities.

The second set of questions concerns the transmission of gods' cults. How were the diverse images of the gods disseminated, both geographically across regional and linguistic boundaries and temporally from one generation to the next? This is especially pertinent to the popular religion, which, unlike the institutional religions of China, has neither religious organizations nor canonical scriptures.[4] Here the volume addresses the question of unity and diversity in Chinese culture. To what extent, if at all, is one popular religion shared throughout the vast Chinese state? How are shared images transmitted, and how do they interact with local variations? How did the pressures toward a unified cosmology contend with the centrifugal forces of diversity?

Deities as Bureaucrats

Chinese gods often resemble earthly bureaucrats in many ways. In Max Weber's definition, a bureaucrat derives authority from his legally defined post, not from his person (Weber 1968), and many Chinese deities are known to their believers by their posts only. They are defined by their functions and not as individuals. Henri Maspero noted that in China "divinity is a responsibility like a public function: the title endures but those who hold it succeed one another ... These are functionary gods who receive a position, who lose it, who are promoted or demoted" (Maspero 1981:87).[5] The conception of gods as functionaries is especially apparent in the case of territorial deities, whose jurisdiction is defined geographically. The two notable examples are the gods of the locality *(tudi shen)*, who are typically responsible for a village or neighborhood, and the city gods *(chenghuang shen)* (literally "wall-and-moat gods"), whose jurisdiction parallels that of a magistrate in late imperial times. These deities serve given terms of office and are then promoted or demoted according to their performances (Wolf 1974a:134–145; Hansen 1993:75,108).

Hierarchy that stipulates the jurisdiction of each office and provides for the supervision of lower offices by higher ones characterizes every bureaucracy (Weber 1968:956–957). Such a hierarchy is clearly apparent in the pantheon of the Chinese state religion. Already during the second millennium B.C.E. the Shang theocrats conceived of the heavens as an elaborate hierarchy of ancestors, each with his specific jurisdiction (Keightley 1978). State bureaucrats in later generations likewise conceived of the heavens in hierarchical terms, downplaying the association of Shang gods with ancestors. The state enhanced this idea in local cults by assigning popular deities to specific positions in a celestial hierarchy, fashioned after its own bureaucratic structure.[6] It is noteworthy that the divine bureaucrats thus appointed were subject to the authority of their earthly counterparts, who had assigned them their positions in the first place. State officials—most notably the emperor himself—could revoke deities' titles, demote them, or even physically punish them if they failed to perform their duties (Cohen 1978, Seidel 1989–1990:255–256, Ebrey and Gregory 1993:7–8).

Daoist clergy, like Confucian officials, envisioned the heavens as a vast hierarchical bureaucracy. As early as the fifth century C.E., the Daoist mystic Tao Hongjing (456–536) "made strenuous efforts to fit the Daoist gods of all the various traditions into one orderly flow chart" (Seidel 1989–1990:255). Daoists of later generations supplemented his efforts by devising an entire system of divine ministries, each complete with a presiding officer, assistants of all sorts, and an army of subordinates (Maspero 1981:92). A celestial bureaucracy also figures in the pantheon of the popular religion, though less prominently than in Daoism and the state religion. Its lowest ranking official is the Stove God (Zaojun), who ascends on New Year's eve to heaven to report to his ultimate superior, the Jade Emperor (Yuhuang Dadi), on each family's behavior.[7] The netherworld, as depicted in the popular religion, is likewise bureaucratic. By the tenth century at the latest, the Chinese laity conceived of purgatory as a series of tribunals fashioned after earthly courts and staffed by fearsome bureaucrats (Goodrich 1981, Teiser 1993).

The bureaucratic image applies not only to the structure of the Chinese heavens but also to the rules by which they operate. David Keightley has suggested that already during the Shang period Chinese religion was permeated by the optimistic belief that the heavens operate according to decipherable and stable rules—rules that, according to Weber (1968:958), are the preconditions for bureaucratic government. These rules were evident in a routinized system of sacrifices, specifying which gods were entitled to which offerings in anticipation of or thanks for specific favors (Keightley 1978:214–216). The primary means of bureaucratic communication is the written document (Weber 1968:957), and, interestingly, Chinese ritual has made extensive usage of the written language since ancient times. Some paleographers maintain that the earliest Chinese ideograms, discovered on Shang oracle bones and tortoise shells, were invented to communicate with deities.[8] Han officials, like their descendants throughout the imperial area, used identical written documents to communicate with human colleagues and with gods (Seidel 1989–1990:255–256).

Written communication with the divine characterizes not only state rites but also Daoist ritual. The offering of texts is the most common form of Daoist sacrifice. Memorials "couched in . . . administrative jargon" (Seidel 1989–1990:255) are burned, whereupon they materialize in the divine courts to which they have been addressed (Schipper 1982:122–125, 1985:34). The centrality of the written document in Daoist ritual reflects the symbolic significance of the Chinese script in Daoist mysticism. The Daoist priest perceives in a character's graphic form the essence of the thing it represents. He thus considers the script a key for the understanding, and hence the taming, of the forces underlying reality (Seidel 1989–1990:251–254; Robinet 1991:128; Schipper 1982:124). In the popular religion written documents likewise figure prominently. Charms *(fu),* for example, are bureaucratic writs, which subdue demons by the superior authority of the gods. Whether written by Daoist priests or by the ritual specialists of the popular religion (mediums or diviners), they use administrative terminology. Like other official documents, charms are valid only when sealed. They therefore invariably carry the seal of the god in whose name they were issued. Emily Ahern noted that the application of the English term *charm* to such written communiqués with the supernatural is in one sense misleading. The word *charm,* like the related word *magic,* implies the application of extraordinary forces. However, these written messages to the supernatural are supposed to operate exactly like written messages to humans (Ahern 1981:24–30).

Thus, the Chinese heavens in this context resemble the bureaucratic Chinese state in their complex hierarchy and their largely bureaucratic modes of communication, both clearly related to their secular equivalents. Furthermore, many deities share emblems of power with earthly bureaucrats. Their temples resemble magistrates' yamens and like them are surrounded by a bevy of clerks, runners, and soldiers (Ahern 1981:2). Deities, like officials, are carried in sedan-chairs during yearly inspection tours, and when officiating in court they carry the same trappings of judicial authority. Even the instruments of torture employed in the courts of the netherworld resemble those once used in earthly courts. These are often depicted in stirring detail in murals and paintings exhorting the faithful to behave morally (Maspero 1981:185, Goodrich 1981:43–57, Teiser 1988, Teiser 1993:129–130, Vidor 1984). In addition, anthropologists have often reported that people will explicitly liken deities to secular bureaucrats, for instance comparing the Earth God to a policeman or the Jade Emperor to the president (e.g., Wolf 1974a, Jordan 1972).[9]

Why are the Chinese heavens envisioned, at least to an important extent, in bureaucratic terms? This question can be answered from several vantage points, and we will present only a few here. First, in the eyes of Chinese commoners state bureaucrats wield power so overwhelming that bureaucratic terms offer a clear way to understand any power, even divine power. Indeed, the bureaucratization of the Chinese heavens may lead us to reassess the degree to which the state penetrated and influenced local society. Historians and political scientists have revealed the limitations of the Chinese state in reaching the local level. The general bureaucratization of the heavens, however, reflects a long-range impact of the state on the peasantry (Wolf 1974a:145). In more general terms, these images of transcendent power speak to basic processes of Chinese socialization, family, and local life, all of which encourage images of what Steven Sangren (1991) calls "alienated" power.

Second, bureaucratic heavens certainly can serve the interests of a bureaucratic state. In imperial times state officials in their capacity as priests of the state religion promoted a conception of the heavens as a mirror image of their own bureaucracy.[10] Such heavens could have encouraged the population to accept the existing sociopolitical order as natural. They precluded the introduction of a new system of government and prevented the questioning of official authority. The bureaucratized supernatural "did not open the possibility of a radically different kind of world" (Ahern 1981:83). It therefore enhanced the hegemonic position of the ruling Confucian elite, at least insofar as it successfully dominated other possible interpretations.

Yet we should also note that an image of the heavens fashioned after the existing political order did not necessarily serve only those who ruled. It could have benefited subjects as well. Ahern has suggested that Chinese ritual, which was modeled so closely after the bureaucratic procedures of the Chinese state, served as a learning game, teaching peasants "how to analyze (and so manipulate) the political system that governed them" (Ahern 1981:92). In her view, Chinese ritual procedures teach people how to obtain power, how to obtain access to those in power, and how to limit those with power. Chinese god-bureaucrats are not simple tools of power, but rather terms through which power could be negotiated and fought over.

Last, we need to be careful not to interpret the bureaucratic dimension of the Chinese supernatural reductively, as a tool consciously or unconsciously designed to benefit one or another social group. The bureaucratic image serves intellectual goals as well as political ends. It enables the classification of natural phenomena and the ordering of reality. The primary concern of the imperial bureaucratic religious mentality might have been, as Anna Seidel has suggested, "not *Realpolitik* and domination, but the integration of absolutely everything into one coherent system" (Seidel 1989–1990: 256). Thus, it is entirely possible that the heavenly bureaucracy influenced the earthly one as much as mirrored it. Keightley has suggested that the bureaucratic mentality of Shang religion informed the bureaucratic structure of the Shang state: "The habits of an optimistic, manipulating, and prognosticating religious logic endowed the order and structure of ranks and hierarchies, jurisdictions, contracts, and stipulated criteria which were emerging in Shang secular administration with special worth" (Keightley 1978:224). Seidel has similarly concluded that "the Chinese supernatural bureaucracy does not, after all, seem to be a copy of social conditions; it is the other way around. The Han administrative structure was itself based on a pre-existing religious model" (Seidel 1989–1990:256). Recognizing that the significance of the bureaucratic image of gods goes well beyond the reinforcement of secular politics also helps explain why Daoists should so actively promote the idea of a heavenly bureaucracy (as seen especially in Robert Hymes' essay in this volume): they are more interested in asserting an ordering control over the world than in promoting the civil bureaucracy. It also helps us focus more broadly on how the gods speak to general processes of power in China.

Deities beyond the Bureaucracy

The studies in this volume both build on and move beyond this discovery of the bureaucratic facet of the Chinese supernatural, suggesting that many deities are not conceived in simple bureaucratic terms and that the parallels between Chinese religion and politics are only partially revealing. Some of the most popular gods do not carry the trappings of office, and their power is not imagined in bureaucratic terms. They do not belong to a celestial bureaucracy. Their devotees address them in a personal language rather than in an administrative jargon. While the bureaucratic idea clearly dominates in the state religion, in the popular religion it is but one of several ways to think about the supernatural. Even in Daoism an exquisitely constructed bureaucratic order coexists with an ideal of self-perfection toward immortality that owes nothing to bureaucratic hierarchy.

Much recent scholarship reminds us of the dangers in too simple a Durkheimian reduction of religion to social structure or in too simple a Marxian one of religion to the interests of the ruling class. Moving beyond the metaphor of gods as bureaucrats helps us to focus on areas of contention and creativity, to reveal more complex evocations of the heavens, and to see the relationships between the production of identity and deity. Such an analysis relies on a more nuanced picture of the meaning of gods and also on a fuller understanding of various kinds of secular power in China. Several earlier works pointed the way in this direction. Ahern (1981), for example, had addressed the apparent lapses in the way the heavenly world modeled secular bureaucrats and argued that they helped empower worshipers with knowledge of the system. Sangren's work brought our attention to nonpolitical kinds of power. He discussed how female deities—by definition not plausible bureaucrats—revealed tensions in the position of women (Sangren 1983). Later, he argued for a much more general conception of power and hierarchy through an idea of spiritual efficacy *(ling)* that does not rely on the secular political order (Sangren 1987). At about the same time, Hill Gates and Robert Weller (1987) urged a more thorough rooting of Chinese religion in the experience of daily life and in the struggle to impose (and resist) particular interpretations. This argument attempted to move beyond seeing god-officials as unproblematic reinforcers of secular politics. Finally, Stephan Feuchtwang (1992) emphasized the level of raw violence that underlay many ideas about the heavenly order.

The most obvious examples of nonbureaucratic deities come from the Buddhist pantheon. Deities of Buddhist descent figure prominently in the pantheon of the popular religion, and they are anything but bureaucrats. Yet this does not diminish their powers in the least. In this respect it is enlightening to read the sixteenth-century novel *Journey to the West (Xiyou Ji),* where Monkey (Sun Wukong), himself a deity, rebels against the entire celestial bureaucracy. When the Jade Emperor fails to subdue this mischievous simian, the Tathāgata Buddha is called in for the rescue and with a snap of his fingers imprisons Monkey under a magic mountain (Yu 1977–1983:170–175). The Buddha does not belong to the celestial bureaucracy, and he has agreed to quell the rebellious Monkey as a personal favor to the Jade Emperor. Nonetheless in the author's eyes the Buddha is much stronger than the Jade Emperor.[11]

One of the most prominent Buddhist deities is the Bodhisattva Guanyin, who in China took on a female form. Guanyin, like other Chinese goddesses, does not belong to a celestial bureaucracy. Chinese female deities, whether of Buddhist, Daoist, or popular descent, usually bear no iconographic resemblance to bureaucrats. For the most part they favor personal appeals over bureaucratic communiqués, and in some cases—notably that of the Queen Mother of the West (Xi Wang Mu)—their communication with mortals may even assume an amorous and sexual tone (Cahill 1993). Despite their nonbureaucratic characteristics, female deities occupy prominent positions in the pantheon of the popular religion. In Taiwan, for example, Guanyin ranks second in number of temples, and the goddess Mazu ranks third (Qiu 1985:103,214). Goddesses upset the gender hierarchy of late imperial China, which placed men above women. Thus they testify that Chinese religion is "more than a sterile reification of the social order" (Sangren 1983:25). Furthermore, many of them defy the Confucian ethos of late imperial times by refusing to marry. Guanyin, incarnated as Princess Miaoshan, refused to be wed despite her father's explicit order (Dudbridge 1978:85–98). Mazu and Wusheng Laomu (the Eternal Mother) likewise declined to marry. These goddesses remind us of how much power lies outside politics, in the ability to recreate families and nurture children, but also to threaten male ideas of patrilineal unity.

Even some Daoist deities are anything but bureaucrats. The Daoist heavens feature, side by side with the celestial bureaucracy, a group of carefree immortals *(xian),* whose power is not envisioned in bureaucratic terms. The immortals achieved their blissful state by withdrawing from worldly politics, and they do not resemble earthly officials (Seidel 1989–1990:248). Daoist scriptures sometimes describe them as saints in disguise, holy fools hiding their true natures behind a simpleton's façade (Strickmann 1984). Some Daoist immortals have been incorporated into the pantheon of the popular religion, where their eccentric traits have been accentuated. Paul Katz notes, elsewhere in this volume, that the celebrated Eight Immortals (Ba Xian) are often depicted in vernacular novels and plays as lascivious drunkards. Here the move beyond bureaucracy glorifies another sort of power, a kind of creative urge at the margins of formal order. Daoism constructed its detailed bureaucratic arrangement only to transcend it through meditative unity with the transcendent Dao and to tease it with a celebration of eccentric immortality. This is a specific example of the more general case where ordered hierarchy generates a kind of creative counterpower at its margins.

Thus, the bureaucratic image applies only to some Chinese deities, and then often only partially. Even where bureaucratic emblems serve to illustrate a deity's power, the deity in question may be far removed from the typical bureaucrats of late imperial times. The personalities, careers, and educational backgrounds of numerous deities who occupy positions in the celestial bureaucracy often differ markedly from the appropriate background of officeholders in late imperial China. In other words, the Chinese supernatural may reflect the Chinese political structure at the same time that it upsets its underlying social order. The Stove God is a case in point. Oral folktales, unlike Daoist scriptures, often describe this heavenly bureaucrat in an unflattering light. According to one tradition he is a voyeur who enjoys watching women disrobe in front of the stove; according to another he was originally a gossipy old woman (Chard 1990:173). Even the Stove God's ultimate superior, the Jade Emperor, emerges from oral folktales as a figure strikingly different from the learned Confucian scholars of the earthly bureaucracy. According to one tradition he is a trickster and imposter, who has achieved his exalted position by sheer luck (Feng 1936:247–248). In another tradition, the Jade Emperor represents a threat of apocalyptic violence just underneath the surface of those imperial robes—perhaps showing the power of a real emperor but certainly not that of a bureaucrat (Feuchtwang 1992).

The Stove God and the Jade Emperor occupy positions in the celestial bureaucracy. Yet in oral literature they deviate from the Confucian ethos, according to which morally upright literati are to assume the responsibility of governance. Other heavenly bureaucrats likewise defy accepted social norms, and their dubious backgrounds are reflected in their ghostly origins. Ghosts are usually the departed souls of people who died prematurely, leaving no descendant kin behind to provide for them in the netherworld. They have thus no choice but to pester the living for offerings. It is even said that they sometimes attempt to escape their ghostly fate by killing someone, who will then substitute for them. Arthur Wolf, who saw in Chinese gods a symbol of earthly officials, argued that there is a sharp difference between them and ghosts: while gods are respected, ghosts are despised; while gods are worshiped, ghosts are merely propitiated (Wolf 1974a:169–174). We are becoming increasingly aware, however, that no clear line separates gods from ghosts (Yü Kuang-hong 1990). Many gods, perhaps even most, share the kinds of premature and violent deaths, often by suicide, that typify malevolent ghosts, and like the latter, they have no descendants to worship them. Barend Ter Haar, for example, has suggested that popular deities in Fujian "have evolved from what were originally (considered to be) vengeful hungry ghosts—feared and worshiped for this very reason" (Ter Haar 1990:349).[12] The ghostly roots of so many deities again speak to kinds of power in China well beyond the imperial state and its bureaucrats. While many of these gods have a bureaucratic side, they also draw on the power of the margins, of death, and of the outside (where both the lowliest ghosts and the highest gods are worshiped). Donald Sutton's essay in this volume reminds us that the term *enfeoffment* itself (typically used for the appointment of gods) is not bureaucratic; instead, it implies a recognition of the power of foreign princes—an attempt to internalize external power.

Oral literature and written fiction in the vernacular often highlight the ghostly origins of gods. According to an oral tradition from Jiangsu, the Stove Gods—here described as the composite of several deities—were foreign soldiers who had been stationed in the houses of local Chinese as spies. Their hosts murdered them and, fearing revenge from their ghosts, appointed them as gods of the stove (Chard 1990:174). Even such prominent deities as Guangong and Zhenwu encountered untimely and violent deaths; the fourteenth-century novel *Three Kingdoms (Sanguo Yanyi)* describes in detail the violent death of Guangong, who was beheaded by his enemies (Luo 1986:619–623). Zhenwu, according to one version of his myth, was a butcher who committed suicide by cutting out his own bowels (Seaman 1987:2). Several of the deities discussed in this volume were likewise victims of murder or violent accidents. Some (Nazha, Zhong Kui, and members of the Infernal Generals [Jiajiang] group) committed suicide, and one (Mazu) willed herself to death. Most of these deities had national significance, and many serve as patrons of community cults.

The ghostly and even demonic origins of some deities continue to lurk behind their respectable appearances. Some deities may be just as dangerous to the community within which they live as ghosts are. For example, the Wangye spirits, who cure diseases, are also the demonic perpetrators of these same diseases. Their modern cult in Taiwan reflects their dual nature; the believers simultaneously worship and exorcise them. Even as people make offerings to the Wangye, they place these deities' images in a boat that is sent adrift at sea or burned (Katz 1987:197–215). A similar situation occurred with the Gods of the Five Paths to Wealth (Wulu Caishen), whose cult was prevalent in seventeenth-century Jiangnan. These five deities were derived from diabolical mountain spirits called *shanxiao*, one-legged fiends notorious for hurling rocks at lone travelers and leading them astray. The Gods of the Five Paths to Wealth continued to betray their noxious origins by seducing young girls and debauching wives. Like the Wangye spirits, these devilish deities were simultaneously exorcised and worshiped, sometimes through female mediums who claimed to have had sexual intercourse with them (Glahn 1991, Cedzich 1995).

Thus the Chinese supernatural is neither a mere tool of China's political system nor a simple reification of its social hierarchy. We know now that the bureaucratic facet of the pantheon is but one of many. While some deities are described in bureaucratic terms, belong to a celestial bureaucracy, and receive communications through administrative documents, others are different. Furthermore, even where popular deities are arranged in a bureaucratic hierarchy, their social and cultural backgrounds are often radically different from those of earthly bureaucrats. Thus, at least in some cases, the supernatural simultaneously mirrors the administrative structure of the state and defies its underlying social reality. The bureaucratic image coexists with social defiance and social deviance within the images of the gods themselves.

Most of the deities examined in the following chapters do not fit the bureaucratic model of the pantheon, and the few who do occupy celestial bureaucratic posts are still radically different from the typical officeholders of late imperial times, the Confucian literati. Hymes examines a Song-period cult, prevalent in Jiangxi, of three deities known as the Three Lords of Mount Huagai (Huagai San Zhenjun). The Three Lords did not belong to the celestial bureaucracy, and their authority was inherent in their person. Similarly, interactions with them were not patterned after bureaucratic modes of communication. Instead, the believers appealed to them in a personal language. Hymes suggests that the laity's interaction with the divine is often marked by a personal vocabulary, while a bureaucratic language characterizes Daoist communication with the supernatural. He contrasts the Three Lords with the extraordinarily bureaucratic mechanisms of Tianxin Daoism (which was very popular at the time), and he concludes by showing how the more modern Stove God is open to both bureaucratic readings (as the Jade Emperor's agent) and personalistic ones (as a household guest). Katz discusses another nonbureaucratic cult that emerged during the Song, that of the immortal Lü Dongbin. Varying social and religious groups understood Lü's image differently over time. While Daoist clergy promoted him primarily as a master of internal alchemy, the laity conceived of him as a miracle-worker, an exorcist, and, above all, a member of the rambunctious group of deities known as the Eight Immortals. Some novels and folktales even elaborate upon Lü's misadventures with prostitutes. Katz qualifies Hymes' suggestion that the clergy promoted a bureaucratic view of gods by pointing out that immortals like Lü were never bureaucrats, even for professional Daoists. Bureaucratic and nonbureaucratic images coexist even within the clerical traditions.

The subject of Brigitte Baptandier's paper is a female deity, Lady Linshui (Linshui Furen), whose cult is prevalent in Fujian and Taiwan. Like other female deities, such as Mazu and Guanyin (Princess Miaoshan), Lady Linshui defied the social ethos of late imperial times by refusing to marry. Like them too she blurs the distinctions between god and ghost: she died young and left no descendants. Lady Linshui's persona is complex, with both benevolent and malevolent aspects. Her alter-ego and nemesis is a snake demon whom she subdues following a series of battles, in which she heads the celestial army of *yin* forces *(yinbing)*. Her iconic image reflects her dual nature: she sits on the serpent's head.

Sangren analyzes the myths of three deities, Nazha, Guanyin (Miaoshan), and Mulian, none of whom is a celestial bureaucrat. Sangren refers to them instead as "family-relationship gods," because their myths, as narrated in vernacular fiction and drama, express key tensions inherent in the Chinese family. Nazha is an Oedipal son who attempts (unsuccessfully) to kill his father. Miaoshan refuses her father's explicit order that she marry and is executed by him (only to be reborn and reunited with him). Mulian undertakes heroic exploits on behalf of his mother. Sangren suggests that these myths enjoy immense popularity exactly because they express feelings, frustrations, and tensions that are repressed in the normative and self-conscious self-representations of Chinese culture. They are the emotion-laden results of the production of gendered identity in China.

Meir Shahar examines the images of popular deities as reflected in vernacular works of fiction. He surveys a large number of gods, which he classifies into three categories: female (such as Guanyin and Mazu), eccentric and rebellious (such as the drunken monk Jigong and the mischievous monkey Sun Wukong), and martial (such as Guangong and Zhenwu). He points out that none of these groups belonged to the male-dominated literati elite of late imperial times. Shahar suggests that the colorful and humorous pantheon, as depicted in vernacular fiction, offered literati and commoners alike liberation and relief from accepted social and cultural norms, thus functioning much like carnival in medieval Europe. His essay not only shows the alternative power of women, or of outsiders more generally, but also indicates how state power can generate its own antithesis, a power of resistance or escape through reversal.

Sutton studies a group of devilish demon-quellers known as the Infernal Generals (Jiajiang), whose cult is prevalent in today's Taiwan. The Infernal Generals originated as "ghostlike creatures in bad deaths or bad lives." They appear in the form of face-painted amateur performers prone to possession. The Infernal Generals perform a ritual exorcistic dance, which is variously influenced by Daoist, shamanic, and operatic traditions. Sutton examines the history of this cult since its appearance in eighteenth-century Fuzhou. He argues that icon and gesture have played a greater role than text in the transmission of these deities' cult, that performance is more important than myth, and that practice outweighs ideology in shaping their role.

Finally, Weller examines two cases in which spirits of questionable Confucian morality have risen to popular prominence that rivaled that of more properly bureaucratic gods: east-central Guangxi in the 1840s and Taiwan in the 1980s. Both cases witnessed a growth in the popularity of deities known more for sex, drunkenness, gambling, and murder than for dedication to bureaucratic order. In the former, a matricidal deity named King Gan rose to prominence, while in the latter, humble ghosts, some those of known criminals, became the object of widespread cults. The most popular of these reverses regular ritual procedures: worship is performed at night and features cigarette offerings instead of incense oblation. Weller suggests that the rebellious facet of the pantheon has always existed side by side with its bureaucratic and orderly dimension. However, this upside-down facet of the supernatural comes to the fore in those cases where the bureaucratic state loses control over religion.

Most of the deities described in this volume do not fit the bureaucratic model of the supernatural, or else fit it only partially. In addition, many of them belong to marginal social groups, and they often deviate from accepted social and cultural norms. Yet as several of the authors point out, the popular conception of a deity often differs significantly from its image in the eyes of Buddhist monks, Daoist priests, or imperial scholar-officials. Vernacular fiction (both oral and written) and drama often present the mischievous, rebellious, and antinomian aspect of a deity. The same deity, however, may emerge from other literary genres in a completely different light. Katz shows that novels and folktales highlight Lü Dongbin's lustfulness, while Daoist scriptures generally portray him as a respectable master of internal alchemy. Shahar notes that members of the Unity Sect (Yiguan Dao) downplay Jigong's love of wine, while novels invariably portray this eccentric monk as a drunkard. In some cases state officials and religious professionals consciously attempt to reform popular deities. Prasenjit Duara has shown, for example, that the state bureaucracy attempted to mitigate the rebellious aspect of Guangong's personality. State-sponsored literature depicted this martial deity as a filial son and a scholar well versed in the Confucian classics (Duara 1988). In other cases members of the laity, who were seeking government sponsorship for a deity, themselves cleansed him of all dubious traits. In this manner the noxious Wutong goblins were transformed during the twelfth century into the venerable Wuxian deities (Glahn 1991, Cedzich 1995).[13]

Kenneth Dean (1993:131–171) has shown that Guo Shengwang, possibly the most important local deity in Fujian, is understood differently by various social groups. While popular legends highlight this deity's lowly social origins and his struggle to establish a lineage of his own, Confucian literati praise his filial piety. Guo Shengwang's cult, like his legend, takes different forms in different social milieus. He is currently the object of Confucian rites performed for reasons of social prestige by one lineage, and he figures simultaneously in Daoist rituals shared by larger segments of Fujianese society. James Watson has similarly shown that the goddess Mazu is interpreted in diametrically opposed ways by different social groups. While government officials promoted her cult along China's southern shores as a symbol of state hegemony, "Taiwanese people accepted her as the embodiment of their own independence" (Watson 1985:302). The Taiwanese therefore largely avoid Mazu in state-controlled temples and appeal to her only in temples they themselves constructed. Contradictory images of this goddess coexist also in Hong Kong's New Territories, where leaders of prominent lineages conceive of Mazu as a symbol of lineage domination and have coerced satellite villages to participate in her festivals so as to express this domination. For their part, however, members of the satellite villages regard Mazu as their own patron deity, who would never deign to assist the dominant lineage (Watson 1985:311–313,315–320).[14]

It is thus clear that bureaucratic gods do not stand opposed to another set of female, marginal, or outcast deities. Instead, the bureaucrat and the vagabond, the mother and the suicide, intertwine, inextricably linked in the person of many gods. One voice spoke more loudly than the others at times, and interested groups fostered one reading over another, but all the possibilities are typically present. Like the god-kings of Polynesia or of some classical Western societies, the power of many Chinese deities "is typically founded on an act of barbarism—murder, incest, or both . . . Power reveals and defines itself as the rupture of the people's own moral order" (Sahlins 1985:79). Power, in other words, always appears to be external and alien. And yet it is the king's own power. Only slightly altered for Chinese deities, we see upright bureaucrats and nurturing mothers with ghostly roots in breaches of accepted kinship and political structures, insiders and outsiders at the same time. Chinese deities thus form part of a complex web of different kinds of power that draws on bureaucracy and violence, filial piety and self-destruction. These various dimensions of power, often combined in versions of a single deity, allow us to focus on how religion allowed people to contend and coexist, to impose and resist interpretations.

Deities and Social Dynamics

The essays in this volume show that the Chinese supernatural features a rich gallery of nonbureaucratic deities alongside a heavenly bureaucracy and that channels of direct and personal appeals to the divine exist alongside bureaucratic communication. Furthermore, these essays reveal that even where gods are arranged in a bureaucratic hierarchy and carry bureaucratic emblems of power, their personalities and careers are often radically different from those of idealized officeholders in late imperial times. What types of tensions within Chinese society does the Chinese supernatural reveal? What dynamics produce these deities and make them sensible? Under what circumstances—economic, social, historical—do eccentric and rebel-

lious deities, which have always coexisted with the heavenly bureaucracy, come to the fore? Where and when does a personal language
overshadow bureaucratic vocabulary in communicating with the
divine?

First, the difference between bureaucratic and personal communication with the divine is related, at least in some cases, to the difference between clerical and lay religions in China, between institutionalized and domestic religious practice. Hymes' essay on the
Song-period cult of the Three Lords of Mount Huagai reveals that
laypersons, unlike Daoist priests, used a personal vocabulary to
address these deities. Hymes suggests that the interaction of the laity
(including the elite) with the divine is often characterized by a personal language, while a bureaucratic vocabulary marks Daoist communication with the supernatural. He argues that one use of personal
vocabulary might be to distinguish an individual's own relationship
to the divine and experience of divine authority from those of religious professionals (by which he means Daoist, not Buddhist,
priests). This case shows how the institutionalization of meaning
under Daoist professionals helped promote a particular reading of
gods; it also reminds us strongly of the limits on institutionalized religion in China, and thus of the limits on the ability of Daoists (or anyone else) to solidify a unified interpretation across the entire population. Lay and professional interpretations always pushed against
each other in China, as both Hymes and Katz make clear in their
essays.

Second, the nonbureaucratic and rebellious facet of the Chinese
supernatural clearly relates to political tensions. State officials bureaucratized local deities by granting them posts in the celestial hierarchy
and, in some cases, Confucianized them by mitigating their socially
dubious traits. Nonbureaucratic deities, as well as gods who carry
the bureaucratic trappings of office but deviate from accepted social
norms, may rise to prominence in those times and places where the
state loses control over religion. When the state fails to project its
own bureaucratic image into the heavens, nonbureaucratic cults have
the opportunity to become dominant. This theme is developed in
Weller's essay, which highlights the role of the Chinese supernatural
in the political struggle between state and local society, between state
bureaucrats and local elites. Weller suggests that local elites tend to
promote the cults of antinomian deities, who deviate from the Confucian ethos, in those cases where their interests conflict with the
state's. He shows that the rise of ghostly deities in Guangxi of the
1840s paralleled the collapse of state control over the region. The
Guangxi cult of the matricidal King Gan thrived when the faltering
state encouraged local elites to act as strongmen instead of aspiring

officials.[15] Hymes similarly argues that the Southern Song elite of Fuzhou Prefecture tended to favor a personal, rather than bureaucratic, vocabulary in negotiating the world of the gods at a period when local gentlemen conceived of themselves primarily as powerful and benevolent local patrons rather than as potential bureaucrats (Hymes 1986:177–199). Such gods make arguments for local versions of alternate power; they do not just reflect the political landscape or enforce a hegemonic control.

More broadly, the inversions apparent in the Chinese supernatural world may be interpreted as a (largely unconscious) attempt to balance the Confucian ethos that guided late imperial society and politics. This theme is developed in Shahar's essay, which applies Bakhtin's interpretation of the European medieval carnival to the Chinese supernatural. According to Bakhtin, carnival offered medieval people a humorous respite from the austere and hierarchical ethos that governed their daily lives (Bakhtin 1984). Shahar similarly suggests that the colorful and humorous aspect of Chinese deities offers literati and commoners alike liberation and relief from accepted social and cultural norms. The female, martial, and eccentric gods he discusses all defy the official ideology of late imperial times, which placed men above women, learning above physical heroism, and etiquette above spontaneity. Shahar suggests that like the European carnival, the upside-down aspect of the Chinese heavens functioned as a safety valve, allowing society to let off steam. But again, as with carnival, given the right historical circumstances, defiant gods could also provide the necessary symbolic resources for rebellion. Where political control is powerful, humor may be the only option for escape or resistance, with the humor itself providing the best defense from accusations of immorality. At the same time, the ludic aspect of many deities added greatly to their broad appeal.

The political dimension of nonbureaucratic deities is especially evident in periods of social and political unrest. It has long been recognized that female (hence nonbureaucratic) deities, rather than male gods, often occupied central places in the millenarian movements that sometimes threatened the Chinese state (Sangren 1987:166–186). Thus, for example, the White Lotus rebels of 1774 were firm devotees of the Eternal Mother (Wusheng Laomu) (Naquin 1981). Similarly, many rebellious and eccentric gods figured in the pantheon of the Boxer uprising of 1900. The Boxers were often possessed, for example, by the mischievous deity Sun Wukong, who had attempted to dethrone the Jade Emperor himself (Esherick 1987). Millenarian rebellions often originated in poor and underdeveloped areas, defined by G. W. Skinner as the peripheries of China's macroeconomic regions (Skinner 1977). We have at present very little data on the geographic distribution of cults in late imperial times. However, Weller's research suggests that Skinner's distinction between cores and peripheries may be useful to the understanding of the spread of nonbureaucratic cults. He suggests that nonbureaucratic deities figured primarily in peripheral areas, where government control was limited and local elites did not necessarily collaborate with state officials. In such areas it was relatively hard for state officials to control religious life by bureaucratizing and Confucianizing local deities. Often, tensions between state and locality remain in earlier layers of a cult, even in core areas. Thus, Lady Linshui sits on the snake she conquered (see Baptandier's essay, elsewhere in this volume), a New Territories Mazu image is built around the stone image of an earlier deity she has "eaten" (Watson 1985:310), and Taiwanese worship the ghostly Lord of the Foundations (Diji Zhu), who preceded their residence. A history of conflict, and an image of power as both autochthonous and externally imposed, often remain in myth and image even in the most central cults.

Third, the way the Chinese supernatural joins in economic discourse creates another area of dynamism. Weller's essay demonstrates that in Taiwan of the 1980s the growing popularity of mischievous and ghostly deities paralleled an increase in speculative investment—in the volatile stock market and the illegal lottery system alike. Weller suggests that when profit appears less as a product of hard work than as a result of luck, greed, and insider connections, playful deities who do not heed moral principles come to the fore. Such capricious deities match the fickle nature of profit itself. Thus, in the rapidly expanding and yet unstable economy of the 1980s Taiwan witnessed significant growth in the popularity of eccentric deities, such as Jigong, Nazha, and Sun Wukong, as well as a growing cult of ghosts. Sutton's essay also shows the close connection between market and religion, explaining both the shared core of Jiajiang performance and its tremendous innovation and rapid evolution as responses to competition for business. During roughly the same period when Weller documents the increased popularity of ghostly gods in Taiwan, Sutton shows the sudden success of new types of Jiajiang performance based on spectacular self-mortification of possessed mediums.

Richard von Glahn's study of the Gods of the Five Paths to Wealth in seventeenth-century Jiangnan suggests a similar correlation between a fast growing, precarious money economy and the prominence of mischievous and even demonic deities. The inflation and economic instability that accompanied the growth of the money economy in late Ming Jiangnan "gave rise to a conception of wealth as a dispensation from inconstant and demonic forces" (Glahn 1991: 713). It was under such conditions that the noxious Wutong spirits, notorious for raping women, came to be worshiped—under the name Gods of the Five Paths to Wealth—as gods of riches. China has long had a commodity-based side to its economy, which rested uneasily with the Confucian authority of the state. It should come as no surprise that this tension showed up as well in religious practice.

Fourth, the Chinese supernatural interacts with the strains inherent in the structure of the Chinese family. Chinese gods articulate the frustrations felt by females and males alike within the patrilineal and patriarchal Chinese family system. The heavens do not merely mirror the Confucian-sanctioned Chinese family, they also compensate for it. This theme is developed in Sangren's essay, which examines three deities whose myths express discords intrinsic to the Chinese kinship and marriage system: Nazha's attempted patricide, Miaoshan's refusal to marry, and Mulian's heroic exploits on behalf of his mother. All three deviate from accepted social norms by their refusal to marry, and the first two also explicitly defy patriarchal authority. Sangren suggests that these deities' myths show the cost in unfulfilled or unfulfillable desires paid by Chinese individuals as gendered members of their society.

Baptandier analyzes family tensions in the myth of Lady Linshui, another female deity who refused to wed. Lady Linshui did eventually submit to patriarchal authority and married, only to abort her fetus and die of a hemorrhage following a successful fertility ritual she performed on behalf of the community. Her myth is typical of many female deities, who, even though they serve as fertility goddesses, never acted as real mothers themselves. Baptandier notes that Lady Linshui's failure to produce a son is a breach of contract with the patriline. Similarly many of the deities discussed in this volume, females and males alike, died young and childless. Their premature deaths are strictly speaking unfilial, for these deities abandoned aged parents, and, more significantly, broke a chain of ancestors and descendants meant to be infinite.[16] Unfilial behavior as well as other manifestations of social defiance on the part of Chinese deities are, as Sangren suggests, expressions of unachievable desires borne of Chinese social institutions. Yet given the right historical circumstances, these deities may serve as behavioral models. For example, Guanyin (Miaoshan) served as the patron deity of marriage-resistance cults in nineteenth-century Guangdong (Topley 1975).

A Chinese Religion?

These essays thus document an ordered diversity in the images of gods, which both grows from and helps constitute the structural tensions in Chinese society. This evidence poses anew the old problem of cultural variation in China. How far do social and historical differences create genuine cultural diversity? To what extent do Chinese share a unified culture? The problem was first introduced into the study of Chinese religion in the classic debate between Maurice Freedman and Arthur Wolf (Freedman 1974, Wolf 1974b). Freedman believed in a kind of shared Chinese cultural essence and argued for the assumption that "a Chinese religion exists" (Freedman 1974:20). Wolf argued the opposite: "We should begin by reconstructing the beliefs of people who viewed the Chinese social landscape from different perspectives . . . The fact that an idea was shared by people with such very different perspectives would suggest to me that it was relatively insignificant or that it was easily invested with very different meanings" (Wolf 1974b:9). While the debate has been greatly refined in the two decades since then, the basic question remains as vexed as ever.

The material in this volume clearly moves away from one aspect of Wolf's work on religion, or at least from typical readings of his work. We no longer see the Chinese supernatural as a mere reflection of China's social hierarchy and political structure. The image of gods as bureaucrats and nothing more (if such was ever Wolf's intention), as each of these essays shows, loses sight of many of their most interesting features. Yet at a deeper level these cases force us toward some position like Wolf's: that Chinese religious interpretation moves hand in hand with social experience. The difference from Wolf is less in fundamental outlook than in the clearer view we now have of the tensions and pressures inherent in both Chinese society and religion, and of the ways in which interested parties might actively promote and resist particular interpretations. Religion is not a reflex of Chinese social structure, or even of class, gender, or geographical position. It is instead part of an ongoing dialogue of interpretations, sometimes competing and sometimes cooperating.

This need not imply diverse and multiple religions in China, as opposed to Freedman's notion of a unitary one. Indeed, however odd these deities are in relation to a set bureaucratic idea, and however rooted in local history, they would still seem familiar to Chinese anywhere. After all, the complex social tensions that intertwine with these deities occurred across China: the undercurrents of competition and jealousy in the ideally harmonious family, the political and even military control held by local elites beneath the state, and markets and individual profit motives in a system that officially frowned on merchants. When we consider as well the absence of effective, unified control over religious interpretation, we should not be surprised that a fairly uniform undercurrent flowed through Chinese religion everywhere. From seductive fox fairies to patricidal sons, breaches of Confucian morality ran all through the cracks of a religion that claimed to worship upright officials.[17]

China thus clearly had a kind of unified religion, in the sense that even the wildest variations drew on a set of general themes, shared ambiguities, and common tensions. The bureaucratic image did not dominate at all times or in all places, but everyone recognized it. The set of alternatives, contradictions, and inconsistencies also spread widely. Dead virgins, parent killers, and unidentified corpses occur over and over, and spring from the dynamics inherent in real family and political relationships that the metaphor of gods as bureaucrats covers up.

Seeing gods as a metaphor for bureaucrats is thus not wrong, but it reduces them in two ways: Chinese deities are not just bureaucrats, and they are not simply a metaphor. Gods are both products and producers of social power. This enables them to function as a way of speaking about secular political power, as a metaphor for bureaucracy, but it also clarifies their much broader significance for other realms of power in family life, gender relations, and even the most general process of defining otherness.

What people shared was not the set of ruling ideas that Freedman expected, but instead a set of unruly ideas built around related social experiences of power, a disorganized palette of possibilities that was always ready to break out in different directions. While this is not the kind of neat structuralist unity of simple transformations out of a consistent base that Freedman expected, it is nevertheless a remarkable achievement in a country as diverse as China, and one with such weak mechanisms of religious orthodoxy. This brings us to the second major theme of this volume, the problem of what mechanisms could have transmitted these ideas across China.

Transmission

The Chinese supernatural displays regional diversity. Some deities are worshiped only in specific localities, with followings limited to provinces, districts, river basins, towns, or even individual villages. Four of the essays included in this volume are concerned with what are essentially local gods. Hymes studies three deities whose cult was prevalent in Song-period Jiangxi, and Weller examines local cults in nineteenth-century Guangxi and twentieth-century Taiwan. Both Sutton and Baptandier study deities who figure primarily (though not only) in Fujian and its neighbor Taiwan.[18] Nonetheless, the pantheon of the popular religion also displays many deities shared throughout China. Thus, the other three essays in this volume examine cults that are prevalent throughout China or at least through large areas of it.

Lü Dongbin, studied by Katz; Nazha, Guanyin (Miaoshan), and Mulian, whose myths are analyzed by Sangren; and the large array of deities surveyed by Shahar all figure through vast areas of China. How were their cults transmitted, both geographically across regional (and linguistic) barriers and temporally from one generation to the next? What processes allowed a deity to be shared across such a diverse country, especially in the absence of strong institutions of religious control?

The problem of the pantheon's transmission can be divided into two closely related questions: first, which social, religious, or political groups sponsor a deity's cult? Who are the people who pronounce the efficacy of worshiping a certain deity, transmit the god's cult from one region to another, build temples in the god's honor, and finance the rituals conducted therein? The second question concerns the shaping of a deity's image. Which media—literary, dramatic, or visual—transmit the gods' myths and their visual images? How do the devotees learn of the personal identity—the appearance and the biography—of the deity they worship? These questions pertain not only to deities who are worshiped throughout China, but even to those we have termed "local." Chinese "localities" are sometimes large indeed. Some provinces are as large as, or larger than, certain European countries. Thus it is difficult to explain how cults are transmitted even within such "localities." How, for example, did the deities studied by Hymes rise to prominence in Song-period Jiangxi? Which mechanisms spread the cult of the Infernal Generals, studied by Sutton, throughout Taiwan?

A comparison to the spread of Buddhist and Daoist deities can illustrate the difficulties posed by the dissemination of popular cults. Buddhism and Daoism have religious institutions and a professional clergy, which sponsored gods' cults. Both religions also have canonical scriptures, where the deities in question are described. Thus, for example, the Buddhist image of Guanyin and the Daoist conception of Lü Dongbin are transmitted primarily through canonical scriptures, which circulated among the Buddhist and the Daoist clergy. By contrast, the amorphous popular religion has neither canonical scriptures nor a religious establishment. How are its cults transmitted? And which media shape the popular conception of the gods, including those who figure also in the Buddhist and Daoist pantheons? Which mechanisms, for example, shape the laity's conception of Guanyin as Princess Miaoshan, and which literary genres transmit the popular image of Lü Dongbin as a lascivious drunk?

Travelers of various sorts contributed significantly to the spread of gods' cults. As Ter Haar pointed out, "for a cult to spread beyond the immediate boundaries of a village and/or district, it was necessary that there should be a group of traveling people to transmit it" (Ter Haar 1990:373). The travelers in question were often merchants. Valerie Hansen has noted that local cults, such as that of Mazu, spread during the Southern Song from specific localities to large areas comprising several provinces. She correlated the expansion of regional cults to the Southern Song's economic growth and suggested that merchants played a crucial role in the transmission of cults across regional boundaries (Hansen 1990:164–166). David Johnson has similarly argued that the spread of the City God's cult during the late Tang and Song was related to the economic revolution of the period and that the mercantile elite played a crucial role in this cult's transmission (Johnson 1985:417–424). Other groups of travelers that played an important role in the dissemination of gods' cults included officials, who were stationed away from their home provinces, and migrants (Hansen 1990:164–166, Ter Haar 1990:387–388). The latter group contributed to the transmission of two cults discussed in this volume. Lady Linshui and the Infernal Generals, discussed by Baptandier and Sutton respectively, were brought to Taiwan by immigrants from Fujian.

Another group of travelers that contributes to the transmission of gods' cults is pilgrims. Pilgrimage sites enhance the prestige of the deities with which they are associated, just as the gods have endowed them with sanctity in the first place. Yü Chün-fang has shown that the growth of Guanyin's cult corresponded to the emergence of pilgrimage sites associated with her name, such as Xiangshan in Henan and Putuo island off the Zhejiang coast. She suggested that "only when Guanyin became associated with certain sites and when people began to make pilgrimages to these places did the cult of Guanyin really take root in China" (Yü Chün-fang 1992:191–192). Pilgrimages are often related to the *fenxiang* (literally "incense division") network of affiliated temples. When a new temple is constructed, its incense burner is usually filled with ashes brought from the incense burner of an existing temple for the same deity. This founding rite is ideally followed by yearly pilgrimages on the part of the affiliated group to the senior temple. In this volume Baptandier examines the *fenxiang* network of Lady Linshui, thereby tracing the spread of her cult. Kristofer Schipper has argued that some communities joined the *fenxiang* network because they were interested in the economic, social, and even military ties it offered them. He suggested that at least in some cases deities' cults spread due to the communication networks offered by the *fenxiang* system, rather than because of these deities' own intrinsic qualities (Schipper 1990:410,414; see also Dean 1993:83–93).

In addition to travelers of various sorts, the state bureaucracy also contributed to the transmission of the pantheon. The state granted divine titles to popular gods and in some cases built temples in their honor. Thus it attempted to capitalize on these gods' prestige at the same time that it further enhanced their cults. As James Watson has pointed out, "the state both led the masses and responded to popular pressure; it both promoted and coopted deities" (Watson 1985:323). One god in whose cult the state played an important role is Zhenwu. The Yongle Emperor (reigned 1403–1424) attributed his success in the usurpation of the throne to this martial deity (Seaman 1987:23–26). Once in power he embarked upon a massive construction effort on behalf of his divine patron. A large number of temples dedicated to Zhenwu were erected on Wudang Mountain (in Hubei Province), which was transformed into a national pilgrimage center. Ongoing sponsorship on the part of the Ming court, combined with a steady stream of pilgrims to Wudang Mountain, transformed Zhenwu into "the object of one of the few truly 'national' cults, involving all levels of society" (Lagerwey 1992:293).

Thus, various groups of travelers—merchants, officials, migrants, and pilgrims—have been as important as the state in the transmission of deities' cults. Cults spread along commerce and migration routes, and temples are interconnected through the *fenxiang* pilgrimage network. But this does not address the problem of how people come to understand the particular personality of a deity. How are the gods' images conveyed to the devotees? It appears that in many cases oral literature was the earliest genre that shaped a deity's image. Devotees extolled their local gods by narrating miracles, which testified to these gods' efficacy *(ling)*. Such stories, still told by believers today, were also narrated by professional storytellers, who spread them along the same commerce routes traveled by merchants, officials, and migrants. Thus, for example, Shahar's essay in this volume points out that Hangzhou storytellers transmitted the earliest legends about the eccentric god Jigong. Where the majority of the population was illiterate, oral fiction reached wider audiences than written literature. Shahar notes that Qing-period literati were keenly aware of the role of oral literature in the transmission of religious beliefs. Some oral folktales were transcribed and published in the early twentieth century, and others are still available to the fieldworker. Baptandier in her essay draws on contemporary oral traditions regarding Lady Linshui, and Robert Chard's study of the Stove God is partially based on published folktales (Chard 1990:167–182).

Sutton's essay in this volume also focuses our attention on iconography, procession, and ritual. The historical record often makes these physical means of transmission difficult to retrieve, but the history of the Infernal Generals in Taiwan is recent enough for Sutton to trace their development. In the case of the Generals, oral and written forms were clearly secondary to dance, makeup, and performance. Practice may be just as important as speech, even though it may be more difficult to recover historically.

Another medium that plays an important role in the dissemination of myth is drama. The significance of the Chinese theater in the shaping of social norms and religious beliefs has been noted by many scholars (e.g., Schipper 1966, van der Loon 1977, Ward 1979, and Johnson 1989). This volume highlights the role of drama in the dissemination of gods' cults. Indeed most of the deities discussed in these essays are the subject of plays. Katz, for example, compares the portrayal of Lü Dongbin in Yuan-period *zaju* plays to his image in Daoist scriptures, and the three deities Sangren examines are all the subjects of dramatic representations. Likewise, the gods surveyed by Shahar figure in the theater, as does even a local deity such as Lady Linshui, the subject of Baptandier's paper. Gods' lives are celebrated in a large variety of regional dramatic styles, including various forms of the puppet theater: hand puppet, rod puppet, shadow puppet, and marionette. Drama reaches a wide audience because, like oral literature, it is not limited to the literate elite. Troupes of traveling actors brought gods' lives to all segments of society, thereby enhancing these deities' cults and shaping their images.

In the modern period gods' lives have also been celebrated in movies and television serials, which may be animated, enacted, or—in the Taiwanese case—played by televised puppets. Thus, for example, the Eighteen Lords, studied by Weller, have been the subject of a movie as well as a television serial. Both capitalize on the Eighteen Lords' popularity at the same time that they further enhance their cult. Likewise, most of the deities discussed by Sangren, Shahar, and Baptandier have been celebrated in movies and television series. These mass-media productions testify to the close relationship between drama and ritual, which still characterizes Chinese religion. Shahar points out that the actors portraying Jigong on television serials wear exactly the same colorful clown garb as do his possessed spirit-mediums, and both enact exactly the same character.

It is noteworthy in this respect that the religious content of many traditional plays is often matched by the ritual function of their performance. Most forms of regional drama, including puppet theater, are performed on religious occasions, such as festivals. Many plays have an exorcistic function, and most are considered an offering to the gods, who are invited to watch them. Plays are usually performed in temple courtyards, with the stage facing the altar (although they now also take place in theaters and television studios). The gods watch the plays, of which they are often the protagonists, alongside the human audience. In some cases plays include dances, which convey the gods' appearances and bearings rather than their myths. Sutton points out that the Infernal Generals' cult has been transmitted by performative troupes of exorcistic festival dancers, influenced in part by operatic traditions. His evidence shows how little influence written texts can sometimes have and how much myth can bend to follow performance. The demon-quelling Zhong Kui, who performs an acrobatic exorcism at the end of the annual ghost festival, is similarly performed by a member of the operatic troupe in full makeup (Weller 1987:71). The line between ritual and drama could be very fine.

Oral fiction and drama reached the unlettered masses because understanding these forms does not require literacy. But for this very reason their power to transmit religious beliefs across regional and temporal barriers is limited. Oral fiction, narrated in the local dialect, is by definition regional, and most plays, performed in local dialects, are not written down. Thus, with rare exceptions, neither oral fiction nor drama can shape a deity's cult throughout China. Neither can they guarantee the continuity of religious tradition across generations. Similarly, much domestic ritual and iconography (like the carving of god images) rests in the hands of local experts with no broader institutional mechanism that could guarantee unity of practice. Here lies the importance of another medium that has played a crucial role in the dissemination of gods' myths: written fiction in the vernacular. Forty years ago Willem Grootaers noted the significance of the late Ming novel *Journey to the North (Beiyou Ji)* in the dissemination of Zhenwu's cult (Grootaers 1952, Seaman 1987). In this volume, the majority of deities discussed by Katz, Sangren, Baptandier, and Shahar are also the subject of novels. Shahar discusses in general terms the role of fiction in the transmission of the pantheon. He points out that almost every single god whose cult has been widespread through vast areas of China is celebrated in a novel. Many of the novels in question were written during the late Ming, and their significance in the dissemination of religious values was noted by Qing literati.

Some novels on the supernatural—the *Journey to the West (Xiyou Ji)* and the *Enfeoffment of the Gods (Fengshen Yanyi)* are two examples—portray an enormous cast of supernatural characters. Others celebrate the career of one deity only. Both types generally appear rather late in the history of the deities they describe. In many cases myths were first transmitted by oral literature and drama, and perhaps by ritual (as Sutton points out). Only later were they written down in the form of a novel. Written novels can control the growth and variation of the oral, dramatic, and ritual traditions. These novels often serve as a unifying source for oral literature and drama across regional, linguistic, and temporal barriers. Shahar argues that the written vernacular plays an important role in the pantheon's transmission because of its relationship to oral literature and drama. The novels reached every segment of late imperial society because they served as sources for storytellers and playwrights. Thus, those who could not read the *Journey to the West* heard Sun Wukong's adventures as narrated by storytellers or saw them enacted on stage. Often deriving from oral literature and drama in the first place, novels would in turn influence oral and dramatic performances.

Some novels are related to another literary genre that played a role in the dissemination of gods' cults: *baojuan* (Precious Scrolls). For example, a late Ming novel celebrating Guanyin was influenced by a *baojuan* text (Dudbridge 1978:44–50, 56–58).[19] Temples sometimes distribute *baojuan* as proselytizing literature, and in some cases they publish novels as well. Shahar notes that a seventeenth-century novel about Jigong has been distributed in Taiwanese temples with a commentary attributed to Jigong himself, written in the automatic spirit-writing technique of the stylus on a planchette. Ursula Cedzich points out that at least one modern edition of the *Journey to the South (Nanyou Ji),* describing Huaguang's supernatural career, was commissioned by a temple, also in Taiwan (Cedzich 1995:141, n. 8).

While novels and precious scrolls disseminate the gods' myths, statues, murals, paintings, and various forms of folk art, such as prints and papercuts, transmit their visual images. Stephen Teiser suggested that as early as the medieval period visual representations—murals, paintings, and illustrations—played a crucial role in shaping Chinese ideas of the netherworld. Some of these illustrations were used in "mortuary rituals performed by families to assist the spirit of the deceased in its journey through the chambers of the nether world" (Teiser 1988:459). The artists who created visual images of hell were sometimes believed to have gone there themselves and come back. Their depictions of the netherworld were therefore considered accurate (Teiser 1988). As late as the first half of the twentieth century, graphic depictions of the tortures awaiting sinners in hell exhorted the believers to behave morally. Thus, for example, the Beijing Temple of the Eighteen Hells contained lifelike statues of the officers of the netherworld tormenting their hapless victims (Goodrich 1981:43–57), and painted scrolls in Taiwan still depict in detail the judicial proceedings awaiting evildoers in purgatory (Vidor 1984).

Visual representations of the gods are found both in temples and inside the laity's homes, where they usually take the form of colorful prints. Since the late Ming period, woodblock prints of the gods have been mass-produced by a simple process, utilizing one block for the outline and one block for each added color. By the early twentieth century they could be purchased for less than a cent, and thus they found their way into practically every home, in villages and cities alike. Such paper gods are either placed inside the home as objects of domestic worship or pasted on the doors to ward off evil spirits. When burned they serve as horses transporting the deities to heaven, for which reason they are known as *zhima* (paper horses).[20] By far the most ubiquitous among these paper deities is the Stove God, whose image is burned on the twenty-third of the last lunar month, when he is sent to heaven to present his report on the family's behavior. He is welcomed back from his trip early on New Year's day, when a new image of him is pasted on the kitchen wall (Day 1940, Goodrich 1991, Po Sung-nien and Johnson 1992).

Some prints depict not only a deity's image but also scenes from his divine career. Other forms of visual art likewise narrate the gods' biographies. Grootaers has noted the significance of frescoes depicting Zhenwu's life in the dissemination of this deity's myth. In a survey of two rural counties in northern Hebei, he found no fewer than forty temples containing such frescoes (Grootaers 1952:163–181). In this volume Katz examines the portrayal of Lü Dongbin's career in Yuan-period murals preserved in the Daoist temple Yongle Gong in Shanxi. The origins of such visual narratives vary. Grootaers suggests that most of the frescoes in rural Hebei mirror oral traditions, though some may have been influenced by the hagiographic novel *Journey to the North*. Katz sees in the Yongle Gong murals the dual influence of Daoist scriptures and local traditions, always open to multiple interpretations. Baptandier argues that Fujianese and Taiwanese bas-reliefs celebrating Lady Linshui's life faithfully follow novels, although the source of their authenticity seems to float back and forth across the Taiwan strait.

Drama as a form of visual art contributes to the shaping of deities' appearances, as well as playing a significant role in the dissemination of their myths. The costumes and makeup of performers enacting the gods on stage are often identical to the deities' iconic representation. Thus actors (and puppets), dancers, and spirit-mediums convey the gods' likenesses to devotees. It is noteworthy that at least in some cases the believers recognize a deity's appearance but are not aware of the god's myth. In this volume Sutton points out that even some of the Infernal Generals' performers identify only these deities' appearances and gestures, and not their myths, which probably derived from iconic images in the first place. In contrast to the essays that concentrate on fictional sources (especially those of Sangren and Shahar in this volume), Sutton argues against the central importance of written texts in the transmission of the Infernal Generals' cult. He reminds us that meaning lies as much in action as in words, as much in ritual as in text.

The significance of oral and written fiction, ritual, and folk art in the dissemination of deities' myths and images highlights the importance of interdisciplinary research for the study of Chinese religious tradition. The body of religious beliefs and practices now variously called "Chinese religion" and "Chinese popular religion" is inseparable from the fiction, drama, and popular arts that served as vehicles for its transmission.

Conclusion

Religion defines values and shapes identity. As a result, it forms a natural part of the negotiation of power and self, from the level of the family to that of the nation as a whole. Religious variation interacts with broader social variation because religion both makes sense of the world and actively shapes it. Religion does not simply mirror the existing social order. Yet not all religions appear to have as clear a dialogue with social variation as the Chinese popular religion. The key to its great flexibility has been the lack of central institutions capable of controlling religious interpretation. Much of the mechanism of interpretive control in Christianity, Judaism, or Islam has been absent in China. The social relations of religious interpretation in China appear to have been so loose that a wide set of alternative possibilities lay dormant in the system even under the strongest state control, allowing an easy transition to new sorts of gods when circumstances changed. The meaning of a complex ritual or of a god would always be up for grabs.

The essays in this volume show that the Buddhist and Daoist establishments exercise only limited influence on the spread of deities' cults and the shaping of their images. Members of the laity play a role as important as Buddhist and Daoist clerics in the construction of the supernatural. Merchants, migrants, and pilgrims spread gods' fame; storytellers, novelists, actors, and artisans portrayed gods' images. The power of the state to control religious interpretation, like that of the Buddhist and Daoist clergies, has been limited. The state made every effort to promote its version of a bureaucratic and Confucian heaven. Nonetheless, even deities such as Guangong and Mazu, whose cults had been sponsored by the state, were understood differently by diverse religious, social, and political groups (see Watson 1985, Duara 1988). Even when the state was strong and apparently successful in promoting a bureaucratic understanding of gods, alternative interpretations waited in the shadows.

The result for China has been the lack of either a shared ortho-doxy or a consistent and unified system of ruling ideas. The unman-ageable nature of this set of ideas has given Chinese popular religion the power to adjust to radically new kinds of social conditions. In contrast to the old state cult, which naturally died with the old state, change without transformation has been easy for popular religion largely because the lack of tight controls on interpretation and the creative tension inherent in Chinese gods kept the doors open. This allows the disorganized unity of Chinese religion to continue, vital and familiar, under social systems as radically different as late impe-rial China, capitalist Taiwan, and the socialist People's Republic of China.

Notes

1. The distinction between the "diffused" and the "institutional" Chinese religions was introduced by Yang 1961. On the relations between the various Chinese religious traditions, see also Maspero 1981:77–88, Ebrey and Gregory 1993:11–18, Naquin and Yü 1992:9–10; also Zhang and Lin 1992.

2. See also Ebrey and Gregory 1993:12.

3. See Dean 1993:154–159 for an example of systematic elite attempts to put a Confucian gloss on a local god by emphasizing the deity's filial piety over his less upright characteristics.

4. Sectarian movements, which emerge from the amorphous popular religion, do have religious institutions and scriptures, although not on the scale of Bud-dhism or Daoism. Partly for that reason, we have a clearer understanding of their dissemination (see, among other studies, Overmyer 1976, Naquin 1981, Jordan and Overmyer 1986, Ter Haar 1992). Although we will refer to these sects in passing, we do not undertake their systematic study in this volume. Their deities in general are open to the same kinds of analysis we attempt here.

5. See also Levi 1989:203.

6. On the granting of divine titles during the Song, see Hansen 1990:79–104.

7. On the Stove God, known also as the Kitchen God, see among others Wolf 1974a:133–134,138–139; Sangren 1987:162–165; and Chard 1990. On the bu-reaucratic facet of the popular religion in general, see also Jordan 1972, Feucht-wang 1974 and 1992.

8. See the summary of relevant studies in Seidel 1989–1990:251–252.

9. We will not address the question of why so much imperial political imagery remains salient in the late twentieth century. Clearly it survives in part for the reasons most informants would state: things have always been done this way and cannot be changed simply because officials now wear neckties instead of peacock feathers. More fundamentally, bureaucratic government has not faded at all dur-ing the twentieth century, but instead has expanded still further. To the extent that the pantheon is a commentary on power itself, perhaps little has changed. Even so, there have been some changes, such as rumors that "Jade Emperor" is

simply the name of an office whose incumbent rotates or the spirit-medium transcript of a panel discussion involving the main deities of five world religions, moderated by Guan Gong (Shengxian 1978). They urge respect for the Constitution and filial piety.

10. See Duara 1991 and Weller 1994:176–180 on the inability of the modernizing state to influence religion in the ways the imperial state could.

11. See also Weller 1987:110–124, who argues for fundamental differences between the Buddhist and all other Chinese cosmologies, especially in their refusal of the bureaucratic metaphor.

12. See also Schipper 1982:58 and Yü Kuang-hong 1990. Anthropological studies conducted in Taiwan more than two decades ago had already shown that ghosts can undergo a process of deification (Harrell 1974).

13. Regarding multiple meanings of the same deity or ghost, see also Katz 1990:194,206; and Weller 1987.

14. Similarly, Weller 1987 analyzes conflicting images of ghosts evident in the annual ghost festival.

15. Even deities who occupy positions in the celestial bureaucracy sometimes support local claims against the state. The god of agriculture (Shennong) denounced plans for the Taiwanese state-owned oil company to build a new refinery in Gaoxiong on the grounds that the pollution threatened the local community (Shoudu Wanbao, 6 May 1990).

16. It is noteworthy that it is generally considered inauspicious to bury an unwed woman in her natal family's burial ground. Taiwanese families sometimes rid themselves of an unmarried daughter by depositing her ashes in what is known as a guniang miao (maiden temple). These small shrines are sometimes visited by prostitutes "who take the collective soul [of unwed girls] as a kind of patron deity" (Wolf 1974a:150).

17. The authors in this volume also show no simple unity of opinion on this issue. Sangren in particular tends to emphasize the shared images of alienated power throughout China, which leads him to a position closer to Freedman than to Wolf.

18. See also Dean 1993 on local cults in Fujian.

19. Baojuan literature played an important role not only in the transmission of myths but also in the shaping of religious and moral values; see Overmyer 1985.

20. Since they were usually replaced on New Year's day, they were also known as nianhua ([New] Year's pictures).

Literature Cited

Ahern, Emily Martin. 1981. Chinese Ritual and Politics. Cambridge: Cambridge University Press.

Bakhtin, Mikhail. 1984. Rabelais and His World. Translated by Hélène Iswolsky. Bloomington: Indiana University Press.

Cahill, Suzanne E. 1993. Transcendence and Divine Passion: The Queen Mother of the West in Medieval China. Stanford: Stanford University Press.

Cedzich, Ursula Angelika. 1995. "The Cult of the Wu-t'ung/Wu-hsien in History and Fiction: The Religious Roots of the Journey to the South." In Ritual and Scripture in Chinese Popular Religion: Five Studies. Publications of the

Chinese Popular Culture Project, no. 3. Berkeley: Institute for East Asian Studies.

Chard, Robert L. 1990. "Folktales of the God of the Stove." *Hanxue Yanjiu (Chinese Studies)* 8(1):183–219.

Cohen, Alvin P. 1978. "Coercing the Rain Deities in Ancient China." *History of Religions* 17(3–4):244–264.

Day, Clarence Burton. 1940. *Chinese Peasant Cults, Being A Study of Chinese Paper Gods.* Shanghai: Kelly and Walsh.

Dean, Kenneth. 1993. *Daoist Ritual and Popular Cults of Southeast China.* Princeton: Princeton University Press.

Duara, Prasenjit. 1988. "Superscribing Symbols: The Myth of Guandi, Chinese God of War." *Journal of Asian Studies* 47(4):778–795.

———. 1991. "Knowledge and Power in the Discourse of Modernity: The Campaigns against Popular Religion in Early Twentieth-Century China." *Journal of Asian Studies* 50(1):67–83.

Dudbridge, Glen. 1978. *The Legend of Miao-shan.* Oxford Oriental Monographs 1. London: Ithaca Press.

Ebrey, Patricia Buckley, and Peter N. Gregory. 1993. "The Religious and Historical Landscape." In *Religion and Society in T'ang and Sung China,* edited by Patricia Buckley Ebrey and Peter N. Gregory, 1–44. Honolulu: University of Hawai'i Press.

Esherick, Joseph W. 1987. *The Origins of the Boxer Uprising.* Berkeley: University of California Press.

Feng, H. Y. 1936. "The Origin of Yü Huang." *Harvard Journal of Asiatic Studies* 1(2):242–250.

Feuchtwang, Stephan. 1974. "Domestic and Communal Worship in Taiwan." In *Religion and Ritual in Chinese Society,* edited by Arthur P. Wolf, 105–129. Stanford: Stanford University Press.

———. 1992. *The Imperial Metaphor: Popular Religion in China.* London: Routledge.

Freedman, Maurice. 1974. "On the Sociological Study of Chinese Religion." In *Religion and Ritual in Chinese Society,* edited by Arthur P. Wolf, 19–41. Stanford: Stanford University Press.

Gates, Hill, and Robert P. Weller. 1987. "Hegemony and Chinese Folk Ideologies." *Modern China* 13(1):1–16.

Glahn, Richard von. 1991. "The Enchantment of Wealth: The God Wutong in the Social History of Jiangnan." *Harvard Journal of Asiatic Studies* 51(2): 651–714.

Goodrich, Anne Swann. 1981. *Chinese Hells: The Peking Temple of Eighteen Hells and Chinese Conceptions of Hell.* St. Augustin: Monumenta Serica.

———. 1991. *Peking Paper Gods: A Look at Home Worship.* Monumenta Serica Monograph Series 23. Nettetal: Steyler Verlag.

Grootaers, Willem A. 1952. "The Hagiography of the Chinese God Chen-Wu." *Folklore Studies* 11(2):139–181.

Hansen, Valerie. 1990. *Changing Gods in Medieval China, 1127–1276.* Princeton: Princeton University Press.

———. 1993. "Gods on Walls: A Case of Indian Influence on Chinese Lay Religion?" In *Religion and Society in T'ang and Sung China,* edited by Patricia

Buckley Ebrey and Peter N. Gregory, 75–113. Honolulu: University of Hawai'i Press.

Harrell, C. Stevan. 1974. "When a Ghost Becomes a God." In *Religion and Ritual in Chinese Society,* edited by Arthur P. Wolf, 193–206. Stanford: Stanford University Press.

Hymes, Robert P. 1986. *Statesmen and Gentlemen: The Elite of Fu-Chou, Chiang-Hsi, in Northern and Southern Sung.* Cambridge: Cambridge University Press.

Johnson, David. 1985. "The City-God Cults of T'ang and Sung China." *Harvard Journal of Asiatic Studies* 45:363–457.

———. 1989. "Actions Speak Louder than Words: The Cultural Significance of Chinese Ritual Opera." In *Ritual Opera and Operatic Ritual: "Mu-lien Rescues His Mother" in Chinese Popular Culture,* edited by David Johnson, 1–45. Publications of the Chinese Popular Culture Project 1. Berkeley: Institute of East Asian Studies.

Jordan, David K. 1972. *Gods, Ghosts, and Ancestors: The Folk Religion of a Taiwanese Village.* Berkeley: University of California Press.

Jordan, David K., and Daniel L. Overmyer. 1986. *The Flying Phoenix: Aspects of Chinese Sectarianism in Taiwan.* Princeton: Princeton University Press.

Katz, Paul. 1987. "Demon or Deities? The Wangye of Taiwan." *Asian Folklore Studies* 46:197–215.

———. 1990. "Wen Ch'iung—The God of Many Faces." *Hanxue yanjiu (Chinese Studies)* 8(1):183–219.

Keightley, David. 1978. "The Religious Commitment: Shang Theology and the Genesis of Chinese Political Culture." *History of Religions* 17:211–225.

Lagerwey, John. 1992. "The Pilgrimage to Wu-tang Shan." In *Pilgrims and Sacred Sites in China,* edited by Susan Naquin and Yü Chün-fang, 293–332. Berkeley: University of California Press.

Levi, Jean. 1989. *Les fonctionnnaires divins.* Paris: Seuil.

Loon, Piet van der. 1977. "Les origines rituelles du théâtre chinois." *Journal asiatique* 265 (1–2):141–168.

Luo Guanzhong. 1986. *Sanguo Yanyi.* Taipei: Lianjing Chuban Shiye.

Maspero, Henri. 1981. "The Mythology of Modern China." In *Taoism and Chinese Religion,* translated by Frank A. Kierman, Jr., 75–196. Amherst: University of Massachusetts Press.

Naquin, Susan. 1981. *Shantung Rebellion: The Wang Lun Uprising of 1774.* New Haven: Yale University Press.

Naquin, Susan, and Yü Chün-fang. 1992. "Introduction: Pilgrimage in China." In *Pilgrims and Sacred Sites in China,* edited by Susan Naquin and Yü Chün-fang. Berkeley: University of California Press.

Overmyer, Daniel L. 1976. *Folk Buddhist Religion: Dissenting Sects in Late Traditional China.* Cambridge: Harvard University Press.

———. 1985. "Values in Chinese Sectarian Literature: Ming and Ch'ing *Paochüan.*" In *Popular Culture in Late Imperial China,* edited by David Johnson, Andrew J. Nathan, and Evelyn S. Rawski. Berkeley: University of California Press.

Po Sung-nien and David Johnson. 1992. *Domesticated Deities and Auspicious Emblems: The Iconography of Everyday Life in Village China.* Publications of the Chinese Popular Culture Project 2. Berkeley: IEAS.

Qiu Dezai. 1985. *Taiwan Miaoshen Zhuan (The Story of Taiwan's Temples and Gods)*. Taipei: Xintong Shuju.

Robinet, Isabelle. 1991. *Histoire du Taoïsm des origines au XIVe siècle*. Paris: Cerf.

Sahlins, Marshall. 1985. *Islands of History*. Chicago: University of Chicago Press.

Sangren, P. Steven. 1983. "Female Gender in Chinese Religious Symbols: Kuan Yin, Ma Tsu, and the 'Eternal Mother'." *Signs* 9:4–25.

———. 1987. *History and Magical Power in a Chinese Community*. Stanford: Stanford University Press.

———. 1991. "Dialectics of Alienation: Individuals and Collectivities in Chinese Religion." *Man* 26:67–86.

Schipper, Kristofer. 1966. "The Divine Jester, Some Remarks on the Gods of the Chinese Marionette Theater." *Bulletin of the Institute of Ethnology, Academia Sinica* 21:81–96.

———. 1982. *Le corps taoïst*. Paris: Fayard.

———. 1985. "Vernacular and Classical Ritual in Taoism." *Journal of Asian Studies* 45(1):21–57.

———. 1990. "The Cult of Pao-sheng Ta-ti and Its Spread to Taiwan—A Case Study of *Fen-hsiang*." In *Development and Decline of Fukien Province in the 17th and 18th Centuries*, edited by E. B. Vermeer. Leiden: Brill.

Seaman, Gary. 1987. *Journey to the North*. Berkeley: University of California Press.

Seidel, Anna. 1989–1990. "Chronicle of Taoist Studies in the West, 1950–1990." *Cahiers d'Extrême-Asie* 5:223–347.

Shengxian Tang. 1978. "Xiudao Zhinan" (Guide to the Cultivation of the Dao). Taichung: Shengxian Tang.

Skinner, G. W. 1977. "Regional Urbanization in Nineteenth-Century China." In *The City in Late Imperial China*, edited by G. W. Skinner. Stanford: Stanford University Press.

Strickmann, Michel. 1984. "Holy Fools." Davis Lecture, presented at Oxford University.

Teiser, Stephen F. 1988. " 'Having Once Died and Returned to Life': Representations of Hell in Medieval China." *Harvard Journal of Asiatic Studies* 48(2): 433–464.

———. 1993. "The Growth of Purgatory." In *Religion and Society in T'ang and Sung China*, edited by Patricia Buckley Ebrey and Peter N. Gregory, 115–145. Honolulu: University of Hawai'i Press.

Ter Haar, Barend J. 1990. "The Genesis and Spread of Temple Cults in Fukien." In *Development and Decline of Fukien Province in the 17th and 18th Centuries*, edited by E. B. Vermeer. Leiden: Brill.

———. 1992. *The White Lotus Teachings in Chinese Religious History*. Leiden: Brill.

Topley, Marjorie. 1975. "Marriage Resistance in Rural Kwangtung." In *Women in Chinese Society*, edited by Margery Wolf and Roxanne Witke, 67–88. Stanford: Stanford University Press.

Vidor, Paul. 1984. *Ten Kings of Hades: The Vidor Collection*. Exhibition catalogue. Taipei: National Museum of History.

Ward, Barbara. 1979. "Not Merely Players: Drama, Act and Ritual in Traditional China." *Man* 14(1):18–39.

Watson, James L. 1985. "Standardizing the Gods: The Promotion of T'ien Hou ('Empress of Heaven') along the South China Coast, 960–1960." In *Popular Culture in Late Imperial China,* edited by David Johnson, Andrew J. Nathan, and Evelyn S. Rawski, 292–324. Berkeley: University of California Press.

Weber, Max. 1968. "Bureaucracy." In *Economy and Society: An Outline of Interpreteive Sociology,* edited by Günther Roth and Claus Witich, 956–1005. New York: Bedminster Press.

Weller, Robert P. 1987. *Unities and Diversities in Chinese Religion.* Seattle: University of Washington Press.

———. 1994. *Resistance, Chaos and Control in China: Taiping Rebels, Taiwanese Ghosts and Tiananmen.* Seattle: University of Washington Press.

Wolf, Arthur P. 1974a. "Gods, Ghosts, and Ancestors." In *Religion and Ritual in Chinese Society,* edited by Arthur P. Wolf, 131–182. Stanford: Stanford University Press.

———. 1974b. "Introduction." In *Religion and Ritual in Chinese Society,* edited by Arthur P. Wolf, 1–18. Stanford: Stanford University Press.

Yang, C. K. 1961. *Religion in Chinese Society.* Berkeley: University of California Press.

Yu, Anthony C., trans. and ed. 1977–1983. *The Journey to the West.* 4 vols. Chicago: University of Chicago Press.

Yü Chün-fang. 1992. "P'u-t'o Shan: Pilgrimage and the Creation of the Chinese Potalaka." In *Pilgrims and Sacred Sites in China,* edited by Susan Naquin and Yü Chün-fang. Berkeley: University of California Press.

Yü Kuang-hong. 1990. "Making a Malefactor a Benefactor: Ghost Worship in Taiwan." *Bulletin of the Institute of Ethnology, Academia Sinica* 70:39–66.

Zhang Maogui and Lin Benxuan. 1992. "Zongjiao de Shehui Yixiang—yige Zhishi Shehuixue de Keti" (The Social Image of Religion—A Problem in the Sociology of Knowledge). Paper presented to the Conference on the Psychology and Behavior of the Chinese, Institute of Ethnology, Academia Sinica, Nankang.

Zürcher, Erik. 1980. "Buddhist Influence on Early Taoism: A Survey of Scriptural Evidence." *T'oung Pao* 66(1–3):84–147.

Personal Relations and Bureaucratic Hierarchy in Chinese Religion: Evidence from the Song Dynasty

ROBERT HYMES

THE CHINESE have seen their gods in many ways. That they did not
—contrary to a view that had been well established in the field—see
them always or only as bureaucrats is becoming more and more
clear, and was becoming clear through the work of Emily Martin
Ahern, Robert Weller, and Steven Sangren, among others, even
before the studies in the present volume were undertaken. But it
seems to me that we have not yet found adequate ways of conceiving
how bureaucratic notions of divinity in China interact with other
notions, and just what those other notions may be. In this essay I will
try to place the bureaucratic "vocabulary" of gods and divine-human
relations in relation to a second, quite different vocabulary. Using
materials drawn largely from research on a Daoist immortals' cult of
the Song dynasty but also from recent ethnography, I will examine
the ways in which the two may compete or intertwine.

Let me begin with two stories, both from south China in middle
Southern Song. The stories make a nice pair because although very
different they are in certain ways closely parallel. Both are tales of
divine punishment for misconduct during a ritual. The first comes
from the milieu of the professional religious practitioner and tells of
the transgression of a man who in every way but technical ordination
is a Daoist priest.

A certain Rite-Master Wang, from inside the Yongjin Gate in
Lin'an, daily practiced the rites of Celestial Heart, conducted *jiao*
to present memorials [to Heaven] on others' behalf, and wore the
ritual vestments; but he was not a *Daoshi*. He was much employed
by the common people because his fees were one-third less than
those of an ordained Daoist priest. He regularly used his neighbor

Mr. Li to write the memorial and the Azure Petition [*qing ci*] [for the *jiao*]. In the second year of the Qingyuan period [1196], on the fifteenth day of the first month, a rich family invited him to hold a *jiao* for Preservation of Peace [*baoan jiao*] on the occasion of the festival of the first full moon. Mr. Li had gone out with his friends the previous night to watch the lamps and had drunk wine and eaten meat. Now he said nothing, but took up his brush while [still] drunk; the characters he drew and the seal he affixed were neither fine nor elegant.

When the *jiao* was finished, Wang dreamed that two red-shirted clerks sought him out and escorted him before the court of an Officer of Heaven. The Officer of Heaven sat upright in fine clothing, with his attendants all proper and decorous. The clerks led Wang to stand before him. Suddenly a number of soldiers led a prisoner in: it was Mr. Li. The Officer of Heaven was fearfully angry and asked him: "As to the Azure Plaint you wrote recently: how dare you write it after drinking wine and eating meat?" He had them force him to sit and bare his feet, and pronounced a sentence of over a hundred blows.

After this he questioned Wang, blaming him in the same way. Wang replied: "I was simply superintending a *jiao* site to administer high merit; I had no previous knowledge of this transgression by staff member What's-his-name." [The Officer] shouted an order and withdrew. One of the soldiers raised the stick he was holding and pounded [Wang] in the chest, saying: "Go!" He awakened in terror with an unbearable pain in his chest.

Before he had had a chance to talk with anyone, he heard someone calling urgently outside his gate and sent a boy to check on it. It was Li's wife. She said, "My husband has suddenly fallen sick. It's very serious. He's asking for the Rite Master to rescue him." Wang bore with his pain and went to their house, where Li kowtowed to him from a certain distance and said: "I have just received my beating; my suffering is to have no limit. You, sir, are seeing it right now. There is nothing more to be said. I would wish that on account of my long service with pen and ink you might give me three thousand cash to buy my coffin." In grief and distress Wang answered: "All right." At this, Li died. As to Wang, from then on his chest throbbed and ached more and more, and later he began to vomit blood, till at the end of the fourth month he died. (Hong 1981:*zhiwu* 6:1101)

Here with all its apparatus is the "bureaucratic model" of religious authority that we know is central to the professional Daoist world view and ritual practice, as much today as in the Song.

The clerks who summon Wang, the court with its attendants and soldiers, the heavenly judicial process that is the crux of the story, and indeed the memorial and Azure Petition themselves, which lie at the heart of the primary Daoist rite, the *jiao* or Offering: all recall the institutions and procedures of an earthly Chinese state. Rite-Master Wang himself gives the model rich new content by acting like any good bureaucrat brought before a tribunal: he denies not only his own responsibility but all knowledge of the crime or even the guilty subordinate's name. But the reader knows, and Rite-Master Wang learns, that this is mere evasion. As a bureaucratic officer performing an official function, he is responsible for the misconduct of his direct subordinate, and he must suffer punishment along with him. (This is, after all, an *ideal* bureaucracy.)

Rite-Master Wang practiced Celestial Heart Daoism. This practice, as Judith Boltz and others have shown, gave particularly elaborate scope to bureaucratic and judicial images of the divine in its texts and liturgies, and this is reflected in the great many stories of Celestial Heart practitioners that Hong Mai preserves in his *Yijian Zhi* (Boltz 1985). The Celestial Heart sect claimed its origin in a textual revelation at a mountain in eastern Jiangxi circuit, Mount Huagai.[1] The same mountain was the center, especially in Southern Song and after, of a cult devoted to three Daoist immortals, the lord Fuqiu and his two disciples Wang and Guo. My second story comes from a collection of miracle tales in a text celebrating these Three Perfected Lords. Again, a subordinate misbehaves before a ritual. Here the milieu is not that of the religious professional, but that of the lay (but elite) devotee and worshiper.

> Chen Cao, or Weiming, a man of Caoping, during the Qiandao period [1165–1173] would frequently visit [*chao*] the mountain in the spring and stay there overnight. He would order twenty-odd tenant-dependents [*dianbin*] to prepare his sedan-chair, baggage, and such. All who were scheduled to go would fast and purify themselves. Among these was one, a certain Yan Yatuier, whose family that day had bought a pig's head and put it on to boil. His father said: "You are to be taken up the mountain by Inspector-General Chen. You ought not to eat meat." The son said: "It's the master himself who's going up the mountain; what's that got to do with me?" After he had sucked and chewed on it he went up the mountain as usual. When the *jiao* was finished, they headed back, but when they were midway, suddenly he was gone. Chen Cao said: "I think that servant was following along behind; he is bound to come, isn't he?" By nightfall he still hadn't arrived. The next morning they sent people up the mountain to search. When they

came below Blood-tree Hollow, suddenly they found a bamboo
hat. There was the barest little path down to Halfway Ridge,
where they further found a head-wrapping. After a while they also
found some baggage. They did not move farther, but by lots chose
another servant to go back and look everywhere for him. Suddenly,
near a place north of the mountain called Zhiwan Gully, there he
was, monkey-hanging in the air before the three gates. They untied
him and stood him upon the ground; he was unconscious. When
evening came they brought him back and used the warmth of a fire
to bring him to his senses. He could not speak until the next day.
They questioned him, and he said: "When I had come about halfway down the mountain, I suddenly saw four strong men dressed
in red, who pulled me down. I did not know how I had come here.
I vowed at once to cleanse my guilt and begged forgiveness; only
then was I allowed to awaken." Such was the warning. (HGS 5:
15a–16a)

The parallels to the previous story, I think, make the contrast in
their meaning striking. Carnivorous tenant Yan, like drunken petition writer Li, is the subordinate of the leading figure in an act of
ritual: here, a yearly worship-journey up Mount Huagai, probably in
fulfillment of an earlier vow, and the *jiao* or offering to the Three
Perfected Lords that such a journey often entails. Like Li, Yan gives
in to sensual enjoyment when he ought to maintain ritual purity. Like
Li, he does so without his employer's knowledge. Like Li, he is punished. But here the differences begin; and the differences, I am arguing, freight this story with a very different picture of divine authority
and of the relation of the human to the divine. First of all, the
bureaucratic trappings of the first story are simply missing. This
seems to me most striking where the imagery of the second in fact
nearly matches the first: with the four red-shirted men who carry out
the Three Immortals' response to Yan's impiety. As a matter of cultural etymology, as it were, I have no doubt that these are the descendants of the "red-shirted clerks" who bring Rite-Master Wang before
the divine court and who appear in many another Song Daoist tale.
But the point is that here they are represented not as clerks but
simply as "four strong men dressed in red," who do not apprehend
Yan legally but simply subdue him physically; they take him before
no court, but presumably are responsible for leaving him hanging in
midair before the gates. If they are reminiscent of anything beyond
what they are said to be, it is perhaps the hired toughs whom just
such a master as Inspector-General Chen might employ to deal with
misbehaving dependents. In contrast to Celestial Heart authority,
which operates through the mediation of bureaucratic procedures,

the punitive authority of the Three Perfected Lords here has an informal and ad hoc cast, right down to the rather comic punishment itself.

If this is in a way informal authority, authority without official trappings, it is also personal. Drunken Li's misconduct incriminates his employer Rite-Master Wang along with himself. When we read the story, we know Rite-Master Wang is lying when he pretends not to know his "staff member's" name; but the story suggests that it does not matter whether he does or not. As a ritual practitioner he is a celestial official: he is responsible for the communications and ritual documents that proceed from his office, regardless of whose hand actually draws them. Inspector-General Chen, on the other hand, suffers no punishment for his dependent's desecration of the rite. This is because his journey up the mountain brings him into a personal and individual, not bureaucratic or even complexly hierarchical, relationship with the Three Lords. His tenant sees this in part when he says, "It's the master himself that's going up the mountain; what's that got to do with me?" "Going up the mountain" here clearly has more than its literal sense, for Yan is indeed going up the mountain; here as elsewhere in the Huagai texts "going up the mountain" refers to the ritual act of pilgrimage and worship that those who literally go up are often engaged in. The point again is that this is an individual and personal act, often dictated by a personal vow; it need not include others and so need not be affected by their misconduct. Though Chen is an official on earth, in his relationship to the divine he is not a bureaucratic practitioner with a staff of underlings to govern. Tenant Yan understands that Chen is, rather, a lone worshiper with a retinue of personal dependents. What Yan does not see is that he himself, by even the literal act of "going up" the mountain, is treading on the Three Lords' own precincts and so is entering into his own personal relationship with them. He will be held personally responsible, as his master will not, for his own misconduct in their presence—and entering their presence with meat in his stomach is misconduct. His master offers no act of atonement for the desecration, and as far as the story is concerned need offer none, while Yan properly reacts to his punishment by making his own personal vow to "cleanse his guilt."

It is probably important to bear in mind that the cult of the Huagai Immortals, at least as represented in surviving texts, is very much an elite cult, honored and promoted by members of the *shidafu* stratum. This may help to account for the fact that, though few of the miracle stories in the collection deal with punishments, those that do invariably show the Lords punishing men of low status, not just commoners, but relatively lowly ones: here a tenant and personal ser-

vant, in another story a cook, in another, six dog-eating brothers
"from a remote and insignificant village." The parallel I have suggested between Yan's relationship to the Immortals and his relationship to his own master is, from the point of view of these texts, not
an idle one. But I will not pursue this here, as my immediate concern
lies elsewhere. In brief, the texts of the Huagai Immortals' cult consistently offer just the personal and relatively informal view of the
Three Lords' authority that the story of tenant Yan conveys. Though
bureaucratic imagery is not absolutely missing from the texts, it has
only a tiny part to play, and it is virtually absent from the miracle
stories that tell of the Lords' intervention in the world in the present
day or the recent past. Never, in any part of the Three Lords materials, are the Three treated as mediators or intercessors to higher
authority. The texts also usually represent their interaction with worshipers as direct and unmediated.[2] By this I mean something more
specific than broader uses of the word *mediation* may have accustomed us to: I mean that no person (human or godly) stands between
the worshipers or beneficiaries of the Immortals and the Immortals
themselves. This in itself is an important further point of difference
with bureaucratic models, and indeed with the actual practice of
professional practitioners, who of course claimed that they themselves mediated between human worshipers or appellants and divine
powers.

Now since Martin's (1981:98–108), Weller's (1987), and Sangren's
(1987) work it should not surprise us to find a Chinese divinity, or
his or her authority, represented in terms other than bureaucratic. Yet
for two reasons it seems to me worth exploring what the Three Perfected Lords cult can tell us about nonbureaucratic authority in Chinese representations of the divine. One is that the cult does not, I
think, fit well into Sangren's and Weller's pictures of nonbureaucratic
authority among Chinese gods. In particular, although the Three
Lords frequently grant personal favors to those who pray to them—
heirs to the childless, cures for the sick, and so on—they are not
female, and they are not marginal or lowly deities: they are represented and treated by their worshipers as very high gods indeed.
How without any bureaucratic imagery they can be represented as
higher than other regionally important deities—how hierarchy is pic-
tured if not bureaucratically—is a point I will return to. I do not have
the data to show whether the cult to the Three is technically a "territorial cult" according to Sangren's definition (whether the Three are
the object of regular *communal* sacrifice), though I strongly suspect
that it is, since sacrifices by county or prefectural authorities at times
of particular crisis are a matter of clear record. There is no doubt
that the Three Lords' authority is represented as extending over a

very large region—much of Jiangxi—and no doubt that they are represented as concerned for and beneficent to the regional community as a whole. Yet their frequent interventions on behalf of particular individuals are never treated, as Sangren suggests, as instances of bribery or under-the-table favors, or in any other way as departures from their normal practice of community-minded beneficence, even when they seem to disadvantage other members of the community.

In the first place, then, this seems a different sort of cult than we find in Weller's or Sangren's work. But in the second place, it seems to me that—despite the work of Martin, Sangren, and Weller—the possible range of content and meaning of nonbureaucratic divine authority, or more specifically of personal or direct relations or connections between humans and gods, has not yet been adequately explored. As such authority and such relations are richly represented in the cult of the Three Lords, it is worth examining the Three Lords miracle stories in somewhat greater depth. I will go on to argue that the notions of *personal relations* with the divine, and of divine authority that is itself *personal and inherent,* constitute for the Chinese a cultural vocabulary of potentially equivalent weight to the notions of hierarchical mediation and derived authority that inform bureaucratic vocabularies. I will also argue that certain Chinese religious phenomena are usefully conceived in terms of competition, interaction, or changing balance between the two.

I will treat the material in the Three Lords miracle stories under three general categories: direct appeal, visitations, and vows.

Direct Appeal

The miracle stories concerning the Three Lords typically show their worshipers calling on them directly, with no mediation by any third party, and sometimes even without the mediation of writing.

> At a place near the mountain, called Qifu, there was a country commoner, whose name I have foolishly forgotten, whose family had offered sacrifices to the Three Immortals for generations. During the Shaoxing period [1131–1162], suddenly a mountain fell down—what the local people call "the roar of the mountain." In front, in back, and to the left and right of where he lived, everything collapsed at once. The entire family, in a single voice, recited the sage-names of the great Immortals in hope of rescue. Outside the house all was a deep pit. This one family alone remained, as if on a high platform: there was no ground to spare. Thus they were saved alive. Afterward they moved their residence, and [what had been] their ground too collapsed. (*HGS* 5:15a)

In some cases this kind of direct appeal leads to a meeting with the Immortals in the flesh. In the following story it seems to be Wang and Guo themselves, often treated as a pair (the Two Immortals) apart from their master Fuqiu, who respond in person to the entreaties of a drowning devotee:

> Below Mount Huagai, at a place called Bifu, there was a tenant [*ke*], a certain Chen Four, whom the people of the neighborhood called Flowery Fourthling. His family had prayed to the Immortals very diligently. His eldest son went to Gaoyou Prefecture [in Huai-nan East circuit] to trade. The boat sank on the way, and everyone else was drowned. This son alone called out the Sagely Appella-tions of the Great Immortals, and floated downstream hugging the mast for a day and a night, not knowing where he was. In some rushes near the shore were two old men rowing a small boat. They came to his rescue, pulled him out onto the bank, revived him with a fire, and fed him rice-gruel. Within two or three days he had regained his senses and was lively and healthy. The two old men had nothing at all in their boat; they gave him their extra provi-sions and took their leave, saying: "There are no people living for some forty or fifty *li* from here. If you go straight ahead in that direction, you are sure to reach the place where you live." He did as they said and headed forward, and just as they had said came upon a path and went home. His family, thinking him already dead, had provided full filial rites; they had completed seven fasts, and the monks were just finishing, when they saw an emaciated form, utterly dissipated, arrive at the gate. The whole family sus-pected he was something ghostly; not for some time did they believe him. Only then did they ask what had happened to him, and he said: "At the moment of peril, through my merit in reciting the sage-names of the Three Immortals of Huagai in hope of res-cue, I was allowed to live again." (*HGS* 5:14a–b)

In only two cases in the miracle stories do we learn explicitly that believers are communicating with the Three Lords in writing (*HGS* 5:10a–b, 5:10b–11b). More often we read simply that they "prayed," and the nature of the prayers is left unclear. But even where the prayers are written, they are represented as the petitioner's own act: we are never told that a religious professional or any other third party mediates the communication.

The notion of direct personal appeal by individuals is a central theme of the Three Lords cult. It can make the difference between life and death for different members of the community.

> Below Dafou Mountain there was a certain Yanxian; I foolishly forget his surname. In the *jihai* year of the Qunxi period [1179],

there was suddenly a noise behind his house. He rushed to look. It was an avalanche, with a force certain to crush the whole household with all its members. The ground shook so that there was no sure place to hold on to. So he gathered the whole family, and they looked toward Dafou Mountain and appealed to the Three Immortals of Huagai to save them, vowing [to hold] a *jiao* to pay reverence at the mountain. Their appeals were most pitiable. Suddenly the avalanche stopped, and the whole family was saved. To this day the break [in the earth] is still there. The clear response in this case is particularly manifest. Within half a *li* of Yanxian's house, there was one Zhang Bangchang, whose family encountered the same avalanche, and half of them were crushed to death. Ah! When Yanxian, who appealed to the Immortals, receives good fortune in this way, while Bangchang, who had not appealed, receives ill fortune in *that* way, how can the people of this age not reverently serve the Immortal Perfected? (*HGS* 6:1b–2a)

Now this is strange in a way. Zhang Bangchang, as far as we can see, has done nothing positively wrong; he is not being punished for misbehavior; he simply has not appealed to the Immortals and so is not rescued. We have seen something like this with the man saved from drowning, but there we cannot be sure that those who drown are from the same region, since the accident happens on the way to a distant prefecture. But Zhang Bangchang is Yanxian's neighbor. Don't the Three Lords, as high, beneficent gods whose sway extends over a broad territory, care equally for all the inhabitants of the region? The answer seems to be that they do, *potentially*. The oldest stratum of the Huagai texts, an account written in early Northern Song, tells us that "when the prefecture or county met with bad harvest or disaster from insects, when men were in grief, distress, or difficult straits, if they paid a visit to the altar and prayed to them, none ever went unanswered. Consequently the people of the four directions were led to come to them without regard to distance" (*HGS* 2:10b). The conditional is significant: one must ask for help to receive it. The life story of the Two Immortals, whose ascent to heaven followed that of their master Fuqiu by some years, tells us that when an emperor offered them positions at court, they refused with the words: "We live on the mountain and are to bring fortune and benefit to the people"—surely a commitment to the welfare of the regional community (*HGS* 2:9a). But the same account tells us that just before their ascent, "they gave these parting words to the men of the locality: 'After we are gone, if you meet with disaster from insects, with drought or flood, with sickness or suffering, if you are pressed by difficulty in carrying on your line, pray at this place, and we shall answer you with good fortune and benefit' "

(*HGS* 2:9b). Again, those who seek aid are expected to ask for it, and boons to single individuals, such as heirs for the childless or cures for the sick, are treated on the same plane as beneficence on a commu-nitywide or regional scale, such as relief from drought, flood, or locusts. Take note as well that the Immortals' words are represented as addressed directly to the "men of the locality" and as "parting words": they symbolize the personal relationship of the Two to the local populace. Even sacrifices offered by administrators on behalf of their jurisdictions are presented as the acts of individual officials, taken on their own:

> In Yuanfu 2 [1099] Hongzhou had no rain in the summer, and the people had worried faces. The court official Wang [Gong?]heng, as Fiscal Intendant, was acting manager of the prefecture and heard how responsive the Three Lords were; so he fasted, purified himself, and sent the Chongren County registrar, Ye Zuwen, to pay his respects at the shrine and escort the Perfected's images to the prefectural city, where he led his subordinates in welcoming them outside the city gates, and lodged them in the Tianqing Abbey. Clouds came in their wake. He burned incense and prayed humbly for rain; it then poured for three days before clearing, and the grain shot up. The people of the prefecture in their joy cried out and sighed that there had never before been [such a thing]; all credited him [official Wang] for the boon. (*HGS* 1:8a)

This image of ad hoc grants of favors in response to direct individual appeals runs throughout the Huagai materials. It is consistent with a notion of personal authority exercised informally by powerful figures beneficently interested but not at every moment actively involved in the affairs of their region. It would square far less well with the idea of a celestial bureaucrat assigned to a jurisdiction and responsible to higher authorities for whatever happens there. To establish a personal connection of sorts to the Three Lords was not difficult—one had only to pray to them. Of Flowery Fourthling's drowning son and the nameless family in the first avalanche story we are told that they had long worshiped the Three; their connection was an old one. But there is no sign of this with Yanxian in the second avalanche story. One did not have to be a long-term client, with the Three Lords as one's established patrons. But one did have to establish a connection, individually, to receive the Three Lords' boon, whether for oneself or for those one cared for.

The notion and practice of personal appeal to divinities is important in understanding the larger social-religious context within which professionals like the Celestial Heart practitioner operated. Religious and occult stories from all viewpoints in Song make it clear that people commonly offered their own prayers to as many gods as they could. In fact, they sometimes only turned to professionals after their own direct appeals had failed.

In Chenzhou, because it had not rained for six months, *they had prayed everywhere with no response.* The elders went to the prefectural administrator, saying that it was already too severe a drought, and that no one but Vice-Prefect Lu would be able to bring rain. (Hong 1981:*sanzhi* 8:1362–1363)

                    *   *   *

The wife of the younger brother of the Judicial Intendant Wang So-and-so became ill and was possessed by some entity, so that she cursed Mr. Wang's name and cried out and scolded, never falling silent. This went on for over a year, and *there was no place so far that they did not go there to pray and make sacrifices,* but she was not healed in the least. They heard Sun's [Shimo's] name and sent to invite him. Sun asked that the whole house fast and cleanse for seven days; only then would he cap and belt himself, burn the incense, and personally draft a petition and deposit it at the Hall of the Celestial Pivot. (Hong 1981:*ding* 2:549–550)

In each of these two stories the superiority of the professional's skills to mere personal appeals will be shown in the end by his success where family prayers to gods had failed. But in another story a practitioner himself suggests that personal prayers may in some cases have force when professional rites are unequal to the problem. The daughter of one Administrator Bi is possessed, and the Rite-Master called in learns by spirit interrogations that her dead sister is taking just revenge for grievances suffered in life. "Mr. Lu thought deeply for a long time, then said: 'Her case is a strong one.' He looked back at Administrator Bi and said, 'Your honor ought himself to use the strength of his goodness to pray for forgiveness for her; this is not something that can be controlled by [my] rites'" (Hong 1981:*yi* 7:237).

We know from many stories that different practitioners, and practitioners of different sorts, competed with each other to offer services to ordinary people in search of divine aid. But we need to think of the services that ordinary people could provide themselves, by direct appeal to gods, as posing similar competition to the services that professionals (Daoist and otherwise) offered. The idea of direct personal contact with gods likewise stood in competition with the Daoist practitioner's claim to mediate between person and divinity.

Visitations

If the worshipers of the Three Immortals must appeal directly and personally to them, the Three usually respond directly as well.[3] Unlike the bureaucratic authorities of Celestial Heart Daoism—who, when they deal with humans in person, summon them (in dreams and visions) to their own official turf, in court in heaven—the Three Lords are more likely to come to their beneficiaries (sometimes in the flesh) than to bring their beneficiaries to them. We have already seen the Two Lords apparently manifesting themselves as harmless old men to the nearly drowned son of Flowery Fourthling. To a man in Hubei one of them appears in mortal guise so convincing that it takes some time to sort the mystery out:

> During the Qiandao period [1165–1173] in Hubei there was a local strongman whose family property was vast in quantity. His household was infected by a seasonal epidemic. One day there suddenly appeared a man of the Way, who came to the gate to teach and convert. A servant waved his hand and pointed, saying: "Daoist, you go away! We have nothing! The master's whole house is unhealthy." The man of the Way said: "What sickness is it they are suffering from?" The servant answered: "It is a current outbreak of plague [wenyi]." The man of the Way said: "I can enchant [zhou] the water and make the illness better at once." The servant said: "If this is so, the master will find out what you want and supply you as you command. Now wait until I come back." He reported to his master, who when he heard could not contain his joy. He sent the servant to transmit his words, asking the man of the Way to stay and sit, and immediately drew some water for the man of the Way to enchant. When the man of the Way got the water he sucked it into his mouth and washed and rinsed his mouth several times, then had the servant take it in and give it to the master to consume: if everyone from adults to children drank it, their illness would get better in less than a full day. The servant took the water in, the master knocked his teeth and drank it, and they distributed it to all the household. Their pains cleared and cooled, and they felt strong and healthy at once. Then he most urgently sent the servant to transmit his words to the man of the Way: that they did not know his high surname. The man of the Way said: "I am surnamed Guo." When asked where he lived, he said, "I live in Chongren County in Fuzhou." "At what place?" "In a thatched hut below Huagai Mountain." When the master learned his surname and residence, he at once had a room made ready in his house, rice cooked and noodles made to serve him; he wanted him to stay. The man of

the Way said: "I am just stopping by here. I knew there was trouble in the house, so I came to offer aid. Now that the sickness is cured, I had already promised a friend of the Way to go on to a famous mountain; I cannot stay long." The master said: "You may live in my poor household; even a year or two would not be too much. Why do you go?" The man of the Way said: "I will come back in two days. You need not detain me." He did not stay, but left. The master waited for him for days, months, years, but never saw him return. At this he sent men bearing pledges and generous gifts of money to below the mountain, where they searched everywhere for the hut of the man of the Way, Guo. For days they could not find him. The fuel gatherers and local elders summoned them and said: "There has never been a Way-man Guo's hut below the mountain. Was it not Perfected Lord Guo of the mountaintop, who is well known to transform himself in this way? You should go quickly, offer incense and paper [money], and hold repeated *jiao* of thanks." The men did as they said, ascended the mountain, and thanked him. They returned to their county and told all their acquaintances. Ah! So well known is the numinous responsiveness of the Perfected Immortals. (*HGS* 5:8a–9a)

More commonly, however, the Three appear to their believers in dreams.

Zhou Xian of Luling, in the *xuwu* year of Baoyou [1258], had a woman in his family who became pregnant. He felt apprehension but had business [that called him away]. He wanted to leave, and was about to go, but hesitated; he expressed his thoughts in reverent prayer to the Three Perfected. That night he dreamed that two Daoists [literally "feather-shirts"] were in his house performing a *jiao*. Xian said to the two Daoists: "I have business and have not the leisure to keep you company; is it all right if I go off to take care of my affairs?" The Daoists answered: "Do not do harm to your business; if something should happen, we will handle it ourselves." He awoke from the dream. [He left, and] after several days received a letter from home reporting the birth of a son, and that the delivery had been very difficult . . . Again in the *yichou* year of Xianqun, in the spring, [Xian's] middle sons Wenqing and Wengui, while at home, were plagued one after the other by pox-pustules and for several days did not eat or rise. The whole family wore worried faces. Xian burned incense and from far away called upon the Three Perfected, praying that what his sons were plagued by would not grow serious. Subsequently the elder, Wenqing, dreamed that three Daoists came to the house and told him to let them examine his hands. When their examination was finished they told him that the illness would do no harm. The son then woke from the dream. When he had finished telling about it, before long he dreamed again that the Daoists from before came once more, examined him, gave him medicine, and left. Within a few days the sons were eating and drinking freely. Their symptoms vanished and they were entirely cleansed [*jing jin*]; thus they were returned to life. They carefully carved a board [*kan ban*] and placed it above the Cavern of Purple Tenuity [*zi xuan dong*] to broaden the transmission [of the story] as a response to the bestowal of grace. (*HGS* 6:14a–b)

The story is typical: the Three come to worshipers in dreams in thirteen of the twenty-six miracle stories, sometimes calling at the door of their house, sometimes simply entering their bedroom. In each case they interact in a matter-of-fact and personal way with the dreamer, answering questions or granting favors asked for in earlier prayers.

Vows

We have already seen in the story of Tenant Yan's retribution that he responded to his punishment by vowing, immediately and either orally or in his thoughts, to "cleanse my guilt." He credits this for his revival. We have seen another sudden vow in the story of Yanxian and his family and their rescue from avalanche: "they looked toward Dafou Mountain and appealed to the Three Immortals of Huagai to save them, vowing [to hold] a *jiao* to pay reverence at the mountain." Vows, and the process of exchange between human and divine that they establish, are clearly central to the Huagai cult, appearing in about one-third of the miracle stories.

There was a certain Wang, an Administrative Officer of the Department of Ministries who, on a visit to Huagai, came to the county seat and happened to meet with me.[4] Our talk touched on the scenery of Huagai Mountain. Suddenly Wang said, "Have you, my Master, ever heard of the Old Man from South of the Mountain?" I said I didn't know of him, and asked him why he had spoken of this. He said, "He was my former self." I asked him to explain, and he said, "My late father had no heir. He prayed everywhere [*bian dao*], without response. When he inquired of those of age and experience, they said: 'If you want a successor, your only course is to disregard all distance and seek at Huagai.' He then fasted and purified himself and set out on his journey. After several days he reached the very peak and told the yellow-hats [Daoists] to hold a *jiao*. He burned a prayer [*fen ci*], promising that he would pay one visit each year until he had a son and would then hold a great and splendid affair to repay the boon of the Immortals. In the third year, on the night of his stay at the mountain, he suddenly dreamed that three Daoists saluted him and said: 'Thank you for coming so far. Originally you were to have no son; we now send you the Old Man from South of the Mountain as your heir.' When their words were finished, he awoke from the dream and found himself wrapped in his bedclothes, and nothing more. He considered the meaning carefully and was greatly delighted. Without waiting for dawn he cleansed himself, ascended the hall, and made a hundred obeisances of thanks. On the day he returned home his wife was pregnant. When her term was full she bore, just as promised, a son. From then on he fulfilled his pledge by making renovations and holding *jiao* at the mountain in thanks for the favor. He never missed a year. When I grew older he would bring me along as well, to join him in the visit and obeisances. Later I came alone. I presently have five sons. How can I ever repay in balancing measure [*baocheng*] the boon I have borne from the Immortals?" I heard these words myself and so have reverently written them down. (*HGS* 5:10b–11b)

Here the father's vow of yearly visits grows into a continuing annual pilgrimage of gratitude even after his son is born. Such yearly, semiyearly, or biyearly journeys seem to have been common; we have already seen the pattern in the story of Tenant Yan, whose master goes up the mountain every spring. It is very likely that even where a vow is not explicitly mentioned, it lies behind the regularity of pilgrimage. A relatively explicit example survives in a poem by Zeng Jili, who received his *jinshi* degree in 1132. The poem records his own visit to Mount Linggu in Linchuan County, an outlying center of Huagai Immortal worship, and ends with the couplet: "I only hope my feet are strong and healthy / That year after year I may here renew my covenant [*xun meng*]" (Li 1983, v. 2:1227). When the high official Zhou Bida, in his travel diary from 1163, writes of the Nanfeng County man Huang Yue, who "every year in the ninth month goes to the back of the mountain and climbs to the Altar of the Three Immortals," pulling himself up with his hands by the vines on the mountainside, we have reason to imagine a "covenant" like Zeng's. We may imagine the same when Chen Yuanjin, a *jinshi* in 1211 and later a circuit intendant, tells us that he climbs Mount Huagai every other year, particularly when we learn elsewhere that his son was still an active worshiper thirty or more years later.[5] Vows, then, may commonly have established a tie that would last. But of course they need not do so; the family of Yanxian simply vows one *jiao*, not a yearly one, and this happens in other stories as well:

Huagai is always being visited and honored; there is not an empty
day in a year. In the cold of winter and in the height of summer the
clouds and mist abound; this is the rule. On the very summit, in
cold or in heat, however unseasonably, there are devout worshipers. A whirling, sweeping fog then rises to the sun. In a recent
year Wu Cheng of Jingxiang, seeking blessings for his kinsmen,
made a vow to visit the Immortals' peak. After a time, in accordance with his vow, he went to the mountain and gave thanks
there. For days in succession there had been thick rain. When he
reached an inn he burned incense, and from far off saw the Three
Perfected. So he prayed for it to clear. The next day it was just as
he had prayed. He went and came back at ease. Accordingly he
intoned a poem to recount the matter:

> A damp week, freezing rain, the road become mud,
> At all hours, filling the sky, the snow and sleet flew.
> Thank the Perfected: the wind is held, the shadows screened
>   away;
> The myriad peaks' summits spout a clearing brilliance upward.
> (HGS 6:12a–b)

There is no evidence here that Wu Cheng's vow committed him to
continuing pilgrimages. What is important about vows, rather, is
their construction of a relationship of personal exchange—if the
Immortals do such-and-such for me, I will do such-and-such for
them—and, once again, their unmediated character. Depending on
the magnitude of the favor from the Immortals and probably on the
resources of the beneficiary, the exchange relationship may seem to
extend indefinitely—Mr. Wang, above, asks how he may "ever repay
in balancing measure" what the Immortals have done for him—or it
may stand as a one-time bargain. There is nothing crass about such
bargains as they are represented in the Huagai texts. Those who
make vows are shown as entirely sincere in their belief in the Three
Lords and in their gratitude for the benefits they have received; they
do not haggle. But the process of making and keeping the vow does
have an immediacy and a flavor of face-to-face exchange about it
that make any conceivable mediation superfluous. I have never seen
a Song source—counting here not only the Huagai materials but also
the innumerable miracle stories and tales of sacrifices, visitations,
and so on in Hong Mai's *Yijian Zhi*—that treats a vow as passing
through some third party before reaching a god, or as passing
through one god's hands on the way to another's.

Now the institution of the vow is extremely well known to students of saints' cults and gods' cults elsewhere than China. It has
been most thoroughly studied in Catholic Europe, both medieval and

modern, but is present also in Orthodox Europe, in Latin America, in Islamic practice in the Middle East and in India, and in deity cults in India and Southeast Asia as well.[6] Typically, in all these societies, a worshiper seeking a favor promises some gift to the saint or god if the favor is granted. More often than not the gift is a religious ceremony in the saint's or god's honor (in Europe, a mass; in China, as we have seen, a *jiao*), though there are other possibilities. Some scholars have argued that the structures of reciprocity established by vows should be considered chiefly in relation to the secular structures of patronage—or alternatively the patterns of bargaining and reciprocity among equals—that obtain on the ground among human beings in each specific society in question (Wilson 1983:21).

Examination of Chinese vows to saints and deities in this light is made much more difficult by the lack, as far as I can discover, of any scholarship on the place and role of vows or promises in secular Chinese life at any period. Still, one may certainly say that the vows one sees in the Three Lords cult are *not* interactions between equals. In my own view, it would be just as hard to argue that they are modeled on human patronage relations, since I see no evidence that there was any such thing as stable, dyadic patronage or clientage in the relatively developed rural areas of south China in Song and after. In any case, the rather striking parallels and recurrences in vows to saints or gods and their surrounding practices between societies that have differed dramatically in their secular social relations suggest to me that single-case explanations of these kinds face serious problems. If structures of secular patronage and the role of secular promises are not the same in the societies where religious vows are prominent, yet vows themselves and the practices surrounding them show striking similarity, are there other similarities among such different societies that can help us understand the vow?

What strikes me as a crucial common feature in all these cases is the presence of a professional religious class with a well-defined and highly developed theology and cosmology, within which the saints or gods that lay people usually pray to are secondary, subordinate, marginal, or in some cases even unrecognized figures, and with a liturgy that places its own members at the node of communication between humans and the divine. In this context, in all these societies, vows appear to serve—even when they are offered in the setting or at the time of larger, clerically managed rituals[7]—as an alternative channel of direct communication and exchange for a lay population, a way of establishing contact that works around, or at the very least supplements, the liturgies and the interventions of professionals. Thus Pierre Sanchis tells us of modern Portuguese *romarias:* "Involved in the whole practice of vows . . . there is a 'popular' movement of independence, of resistance to the clergy's religious monopoly, and a demand for autonomy so far as relations with the sacred are concerned" (Sanchis 1983:270). For William Christian, dealing with sixteenth-century Spain, "the vow and similar prayers to the saints were forms of direct engagement between the Christian and the divine, with no inquisitive or costly middleman" (Christian 1981:32). Jill Dubisch finds Christian's analysis applicable to Orthodox pilgrimages in present-day Greece (Dubisch 1990:126). Similarly Marc Gaborieau tells of the suspicion in which individual prayers to Islamic saints, notably including vows, have been held by clerical reformers in India and Nepal, who find the notion of direct prayer to anyone but God idolatrous (Gaborieau 1983:299). It seems to me that we might well consider Chinese vows to gods and saints in similar light.

Inter-deity Relations

In examining direct appeals by worshipers, visitations by the Immortals, and vows, I have been dealing only with relations between deities and humans. It is worth saying at least a bit about relations among divinities themselves. Bureaucratic vocabulary allows religious professionals and lay people alike to model inter-deity relations in clear and comprehensible ways, to sort what might be a confusing multiplicity of gods into a single hierarchy—with the stress on *hierarchy*. I have said that the Huagai texts treat the Three Lords as high gods, but what can this mean—and how can one tell—in the absence of a bureaucratic picture? A short answer would be that the Huagai texts have very little to say of other divinities and that one can tell they are gods of stature by the geographic extent of their authority, by the nature of the services they provide—relief from flood or drought for whole prefectures, for example—and by the fact that local and regional governmental authorities repeatedly choose them as objects of sacrifice in times of crisis. But this answer would be incomplete.

There are two passages in the Huagai miracle stories that relate the Three to other divinities. Both manage to establish hierarchy and to place the Three (or one of their members, in one story) above the others, without bureaucratic vocabulary. In one story, worshipers of another group of Immortals, the Four Immortals of Mount Ba, are climbing their own mountain to place and dedicate a set of images of the Four. Along with them they plan to enshrine as subsidiary figures the Three Perfected Lords of Huagai and a group of twelve other immortals from a mountain in Hongzhou to the northwest. But when the figures are arranged, with the Four in the center, thunder and lightning burst out, and when it does not stop, the worshipers are convinced they have done something wrong. They perform several divinations and finally learn that the Four Immortals are objecting to being placed in the center when their *jiaozhu* (literally their "sect-chief") Lord Fuqiu is also present. He, it turns out, must have the central position instead (*HGS* 5:11b–12b). Fuqiu, of course, is the first among the Three Immortals of Huagai. A *jiaozhu,* in Buddhist but also more general Chinese religious terms, is a sort of patriarch, founder of a sect or teaching. At bottom, such a figure is precisely a teacher to those who follow him. By calling Fuqiu their *jiaozhu* and giving him pride of place, the Four Immortals of Mount Ba are subordinating themselves to the head of the Three, but by way of a relationship—the teacher-student or master-disciple tie—that, while clearly hierarchical, is also profoundly personal and individual. It is largely in terms of the student-teacher tie, too, that Fuqiu's relationship to his followers Wang and Guo is articulated in the Huagai texts.

The second passage is briefer and perhaps more obscure. One of the pieces in the miracle story collection, more in the nature of a topographic description than a real story, tells us of some of the marvelous features of Mount Longyuan, an auxiliary center of Huagai worship. One of the sites described is the "Money Storehouse" *(qian cang):* "this is where the Perfected Lords have employed [*yi*] the god[s] of the earth [*dishen*] to yield up money to aid those in poverty and distress." Here again the Three appear as the superiors of other divinities. But the text does not tell us, for instance, that they "ordered" *(ling)* the earth gods to perform this service; nor does it use any other clearly bureaucratic or official language. The term it does use, *yi,* "to cause to work," "to employ," is ambiguous, but in Song usage most often occurs where someone hires a laborer or employs a dependent, such as a tenant or a servant, to perform some recurrent or regular service. A Song reader would probably picture the earth gods as working for the Three in some unspecified but personal capacity.

Personal Relations vs. Bureaucracy

Direct appeals, visitations, and vows in the relations between humans and gods, and master-disciple and master-servant or employer-employee ties in the relations between gods themselves, I am arguing, are all elements of a vocabulary and repertoire of personal or direct relations that provide a powerful alternative to the vocabulary of bureaucracy for Song (and later) Chinese in talking about, writing about, and negotiating the world of gods. There may be other such elements, missing from these materials, but the Huagai texts, especially the miracle stories that tell of the Three Lords' recent interventions, do articulate and develop this vocabulary in a particularly consistent and organized form. I have argued elsewhere that for this particular cult, in a Southern Song, southeastern, and elite context, this way of approaching things divine serves to exalt a sort of authority and forms of relationship that the local elite of Fuzhou Prefecture and the surrounding region can see as parallel to their own authority and role, or the authority they imagine themselves wielding and the role they imagine themselves playing, in their own locality. That is, local gentlemen who no longer prefer—or who can no longer afford—to conceive of themselves chiefly as officeholders or potential officeholders now address gods whom they picture as something other than bureaucrats: in effect, as the inherently powerful, beneficent, and reliable personal patrons they would like to imagine themselves to be.

But the vocabulary of personal relations could have many other purposes, and once one has a clear sense of its possible elements one may begin to recognize them, and to investigate those purposes, in other contexts. As I have already suggested in connection with vows, one ready use of personal vocabulary could be precisely to distinguish one's own relationship to the divine, and one's own experience of divine authority, from those characteristic of religious professionals. That is, a division not between popular and elite religion, whatever those might be, but between *clerical* and *lay* religion may be articulated in the competing vocabularies of bureaucracy on the one hand and personal relations on the other. This could work in either direction. It is striking that when stories celebrating Celestial Heart masters or other practitioners deal with personal relations between the human and divine worlds, they very commonly focus on ties that are illegitimate, licentious, or a distortion of proper relations. The common Chinese motif of the ghost lover appears in two stories about Celestial Heart masters:

> Liu Cai, whose courtesy name was Muzhong, was the younger brother of my [Hong Mai's] wife's mother. When he was young he studied rites and registers under a Daoist, and later went with his wife's father to [the latter's] magistracy in Gusu [County], where he traveled with the other members of his family to the Lingyan Monastery. He stayed overnight in the monks' dwelling, and heard far off in the mountains the call, "Second *guanren* Liu!" As time went on the sound gradually grew nearer. The other people in the dwelling were also awake, and he asked them, "Did you hear that sound?" They all laughed and said: "You have received the Correct

Rites of Celestial Heart; you should act accordingly." The next day, Cai subpoenaed the God of the Locality [*tudi shen*], saying: "I have performed my rites with the utmost sincerity, and have never been warned of having violated any prohibition; how can the mountain ghosts harass me?" That evening, he dreamed that a spirit/god told him: "We have instructed our attendant clerks to search out [the offender], and it turned out to be a flower-spirit who had done it, not the mountain ghosts. We will take action to suppress it." When Cai returned home, he dreamed that his former concubine Qin Nu came to him and said: "The one who called to you behind the monastery was only me. If you have not forgotten me, do not let the monastery guardians hurry me [away] [*ji wo*]." Cai drew up another dispatch, like a secular delivery form, and sent someone to deposit it at [a/the] shrine. After a few days he dreamed again that the concubine came to him and took her leave, saying: "As you have already deposited the form, I dare not stay any longer." Weeping, she left. This Qin Nu was a woman of the capital [Kaifeng], who had died in Lin'an some six years before this. (Hong 1981:19:347)

Here Liu's bureaucratic duty as a Celestial Heart functionary wins out over his personal relationship to his former concubine. Another man first acquires his Celestial Heart skills as a means of escape from a dangerous tie to the other world:

The imperial lineage member Zhao Ziju, whose courtesy name was Shengzhi, lost his wife in the prime of life, and his heart pined after her without cease. In his house he decorated her little room and served her as if she were alive. He was spending the night alone one night when he sensed that something had opened the door and come out of the room. In fear he called for his servants, but after a servant-girl had answered and gone back to bed, within a moment [the person] was before his bed, pulling back the curtains and speaking softly: "Don't be afraid; don't be afraid; it's I who have come." Now his spirit was suddenly clouded, and he knew not the boundary between the living and the dead. So he shared his bed with her and was as happy as when she had been alive. From then on she came every day, and whenever he ate and drank they were always across the table from each other. When his servants and concubines watched from the side, they saw nothing, but on the dishes was always something that looked like someone's leftovers. As the attachment lasted, he became troubled in his thoughts, gradually losing his liking for food, and his steps and words grew weaker. But he never spoke of it to anyone. There was a man of the Way who stopped at his gate to beg for food and happened to see him. he sighed and said: "You are willingly consorting with a ghost; how can you take no account of your own life! I can perform the Correct Rites of Celestial Heart; I will hand them on to you. If you work hard at them, the ghost will retire on its own even if unattacked." Ziju came to his senses in a rush, then made repeated obeisances and received the transmission. He painted images of the six[th] *jia* and the six[th] *ding,* fasted and purified himself, and offered service most diligently. His wife continued just as before, but was somewhat unhappy, and from time to time would give long sighs, like someone who was not getting her wish. After another half year, she took her leave, weeping, saying: "If I stay, I fear I will do injury to your rites. I will leave." After that she never came again. From then on Ziju performed his rites with increased force, treating illnesses for others with immediate effect. (Hong 1981:*yi* 6:235–236)

Here not only the practitioner but the ghost-wife herself understands that Zhao's standing as a Celestial Heart practitioner and his personal relationship to a dweller in the world of gods and ghosts are in conflict. To be sure, in both these stories the personal tie that must be rejected is to a ghost, not a god. But in another story a god, or his family, tries to engage a mortal woman in a personal tie of particular importance: the tie of marriage. The story is told by the Celestial Heart master who, with some difficulty, intervened:

Recently I passed through the villages of Yanzhou and stopped in at my old friends the Fang family's house. I stayed to drink and enjoy their hospitality for a day and an evening, and the local powerful family of the Ye came via my host's introduction to say: "Our young daughter, not yet married, has been disturbed by a demon, and all those who come with their rites are at once defeated and go away. We venture to make a reverent request of your honor." Though I had been affected by the wine, I could not be excused from performing my rites, and so went to the Yes', and called on the daughter to come out. When she came out, she was extraordinarily beautiful, and I was secretly startled and admiring, thinking her such as I had never gazed on before. The woman suddenly lurched forward, as if driven or pressed forward by others. Disconcerted, I paled, and rushed into the Buddha-hall. The woman pursued me, but turned back when she reached the gate. I found myself harassed by a ghost; I sought from her family a place of repose, where I would draft a memorial to Heaven. My host led me to a lone hall in a small garden on the west side [of the house], with enormous bamboo before and behind, and distant from the residence,[8] and he said: "This place is the purest." I took red cinnabar and my talisman brushes and such from my bag and placed them on the table, but before I had a moment to lift a brush, suddenly I was lost in a blind confusion. I shut my eyes and listened closely, and felt that my body was in empty air, and the spot I sat in was now shaking, now still, never settling . . . After a moment, I had returned to my former spot, to find that the table and windows were all covered with filth and disarranged and could not be [used].[9] Reckoning that I could not match this, I quickly called my servant to bear my sedan-chair away. I went more than ten *li*, and came upon a Daoist abbey, where I stayed for the night. With my spirit somewhat calmed, I hastened into the hall, faced the Dipper, burned incense, bowed a hundred times confessing my faults, then withdrew and burned my memorial text. I stayed two nights, and when it seemed a bit as if there might have been some effect, I sent one of the Daoists to go to the Yes' and find out. He returned saying: "A fire arose yesterday from the hall in the garden, burning the whole bamboo grove, spreading to the tall forest behind the hill, and several tens of buildings were burned, along with a little *tudi* shrine." I knew that my appeal had been granted, and went back myself to ask about it. The whole family, young and old, congratulated me, saying: "Our daughter had known no one for a whole year, and today is as if returned to her senses. She said, 'Last year, in my chamber, I was visited by an old man who came as a go-between. He came and went several times, and after another several days he brought several boxes of gold, pearls, and silks, then soon after escorted in a young man, who was to become man and wife with me. The next day he took me back to visit his father and mother, and ten or so others who were said to be his brothers. The old man was very old, and said to the crowd: "My family has received the Yes' incense-fire for several generations; now if you juniors commit an impropriety, the disaster will surely touch me; why not choose one from somewhere else?" The young man said: "Here we have relied on a matchmaker and given [bride]wealth to obtain her; the marriage ritual is clear and correct; what have we to fear?" Afterward I heard several times that gentlemen of skills had come, but [the god's family] would always join forces to resist them, and again and again they would give up. When Perfected Officer Lu came, the old man again called upon the crowd: "I have heard Perfected Officer Lu's rites are of divine strength, beyond compare with ordinary men's; we surely cannot escape." The crowd too was much afraid. Suddenly someone called me, saying, "The Perfected Officer is calling for you." I went forth, and the crowd followed behind me, heading for the academy, when suddenly they cried out with laughter, saying: "The Perfected Officer praises your fineness; why don't you go to him?" Then they pressed me forward. When I withdrew, the old man asked me the situation, then sighed and said: "Now that matters have come to this, it would have been best if we had managed to kill him; the disaster is almost upon us." Just as we were assembling to eat, a fire suddenly arose within the gate, the smoke and flames rose to heaven. The old man beat his breast and wept pitiably, saying: "The disaster has come!" He pushed me out with his hand, saying: "We have destroyed our family for you!" Then I was able to return.' " When the fire had somewhat died down, all the buildings that had normally stood there had left no trace. The one who was said to have come as a go-between was the *tudi*. This is how fearful this matter was from beginning to end; I almost came to grief from it. (Hong 1981:*ding* 18:684–685)

Here the god reaches improperly, through direct personal contact, into the world of the living for a daughter-in-law and is vanquished by the practitioner, who appeals through bureaucratic channels to divine authorities more powerful than he. The following story from Hong Mai, clearly from a context of Celestial Heart practice, similarly concerns a human and a god, but the relationship is very different:

In Fenghua County the households of the great surnames have generally built, next to their dwellings, small buildings for worshiping a god whom they call "Three Halls." They say that if one sacrifices to it with real sincerity it can make one prosperous. But after long years it can also do harm.

A rich man of Xiashe Village in that county, Chen Bing, served this god with especial diligence, and in every third year without fail killed an ox, a sheep, and a pig and rendered rich sacrifices. When the sacrifice was over he would gather all his kin and neighbors and drink to good fortune and partake of the sacrificial meat, just as if it were a wedding ceremony. Bing died in the prime of his life.

In the month of the end of mourning, which happened to be the same as the time for sacrifices to the god, [Chen's] concubine, one Aquan, was suddenly possessed. She spoke in her master's voice to his sons:

"I was not originally meant to die yet; for Three Halls improperly checked my name off and forced me to become his servant. Every day I have shouldered his falcon and gone off into the wilderness; at night I have passed through the marketplaces causing apparitions and making bizarre mischief. For two years I had not had a moment's rest; I could not bear the hardship, and finally asked for a leave and so was able to go and bring suit to the Eastern Mount.

"It happened that the Lord of the Mount had gone out traveling. I stopped in before a small palace and called to the attendant to invite me to enter; I told him everything. He said, 'This need not be handled here; the Bureau for Expelling Perverse Forces would do.' I bowed and pleaded: 'I am but a lowly ghost. How would I know where the Bureau for Expelling Perverse Forces is?' The attendant sent an azure-shirted guard along to guide me. We ascended gradually into the air for a hundred or so *li,* till we reached a grand palace gateway, whose golden rays filled Heaven. Two mailed warriors, very grand, stood at the gate. I told them the situation, and they led me into a long corridor that stretched on and on, with no one around, and then we came to the palace and made repeated obeisances. I was facing a hanging screen, with a brilliant glow of five colors behind it, too bright to look at straight on; but from time to time I could hear a sound of pendants jingling from a girdle.

"Suddenly the screen was rolled up, and someone called out: 'On what business does Chen Bing come here?' I then told the whole story of my abuse by Three Halls. In a moment a piece of paper flew out from within, and in the blink of an eye the god was brought before the court. I could not see that he was bound, but he hobbled and held his breath, and his pleading and wailing were most acute. Then another piece of paper flew out, revolved around the god's body several times, then turned into searing flames and burned him. In a moment he was ashes. I bowed my thanks and withdrew. You should tell all the local people that from now on they should cease this improper worship."

His words had gradually grown faint, and Aquan now revived. (Hong n.d.:*bu* 15:1693–1694)

Here again there are personal relations between god and human, and once again it is precisely those relations that are illegitimate: the god forces the man to serve, not as his clerk, not as his guardsman, not as his staff member, but as his personal servant, bearing his falcon and doing his little mischief. It is the forces of divine bureaucracy (with clerks, guardsmen, palaces, buck-passing among agencies, and flying paperwork) that properly dissolve the tie of personal dependence that the god has improperly established. The story can be read not only as an assertion of Celestial Heart authority over a god of the lay populace—more broadly, as an elevation of clerical above lay religion—but as a proclamation of the superiority of bureaucratic to personal relations.

From the other side, once again, Hong Mai tells a very different sort of story:

The registrar of Jinqi County in Fuzhou, Wu Shiliang, when his term was completed, housed his family in the Dragon-Head Temple in a nearby village. In the night someone threw a stone against his window, and he thought it was the monks of the temple who had done it, so in the morning he scolded them. The monks were reluctant to respond, but with cautious words said: "The gods of this county called the Three Worthies are very well known; it must be that they have been offended." Wu did not believe them. The next day, all through the building, tiles and shards fell from the sky, all helter-skelter, with no ceasing. It happened to be snowing at that time, yet the thrown objects were all dry, almost like things found in an ancient tomb. Now Wu grew alarmed, and summoned the monks to recite sutras and offer prayers of apology, but the marvel continued, till the flying stones filled the air. His father picked up a brick and inscribed a message on it, then threw it, with the prayer: "If we have indeed offended the Three Sages, let this come back." In a moment it was back again, with the inscribed part unchanged. When they were unable to stop it, they moved from the east suburbs to the west to escape [the gods'] anger. Before their luggage was even put away, the disturbance was back again. So he moved the entire household into the county town, and lodged at the Magical Sounds Daoist Monastery. The marvel was still severe, so he called the Daoists to set up a *jiao* to offer reverence, but this did not stop it for a moment. Wu grew angry, called out the gods' names, and cursed them, saying: "You are gods; you should be intelligent and upright. Why would you commit such outrages against me? From now on, I will fear you no more!" When his words were finished, all sounds ceased. (Hong 1981:*ding* B3:555)

Wu tries the mediation of two different kinds of religious professionals, who fail. Only when he calls on the gods directly and in personal terms does his torment end. Unlike the previous story (but like Rite-Master Lu's advice to Mr. Wang, above) this one suggests the superiority of personal contact to hierarchical mediation. Similarly, the gentlemen who worshiped the Huagai Immortals, accustomed to exercising informal power or ambitious to do so, surely preferred to see themselves as capable of dealing with divine authority directly, without the mediation of mere specialist practitioners.

The two vocabularies need not always compete: they may even appear in the utterances of the same person or text. Weller has already pointed out, for modern Taiwan, that the same Daoists who describe the divine world in bureaucratic terms characterize their own ties to their earthly teachers and disciples as personal relations

(Weller 1987:100). But it is not only earthly ties that Daoists, at least in the Song, treat as personal. Among Celestial Heart and similar practitioners, where the bureaucratic vocabulary is so powerfully articulated that one might expect to find nothing else, there are still moments of personal contact and interaction with higher divine figures, particularly at times of revelation or first "conversion." In a Song text recording a dialogue between the Five Thunders Daoist master Wang Wenqing (d. 1153) and a disciple, Wang tells how he first received the secrets of his arts:

> The Imperial Attendant said: "Of old I traveled the famous mountains, visiting more than two hundred sites. Once I came to the Cavern of Pure Perfection in Jinling. This was the place where, in Tang, the Heavenly Master Ye had cultivated his Perfection. In early evening there was no sign of human or habitation to avail myself of. I looked far off into the mountains, when suddenly there appeared the light of a lamp. So I hurried in the direction of the lamplight and came to a thatched hut. Inside it was lonely and abandoned; there was no one. My heart was greatly alarmed. Under the lamp, on a table, there was a piece of writing. I opened and looked at it: its title was 'Writings on Exhaling Wind and Rain.' I thought this must be the dwelling of the thunder; now my heart was set at ease. I took brush and ink and used wooden slips to copy the text. When the copying was nearly done I suddenly heard the sound of a cock's crow, and in an instant an old lady emerged. I asked her surname. The old lady said, 'I have no surname. This is the place where the thunderclaps dwell. One may not tarry here long.' I asked how it was that there was a cock's crow here, and the old lady said: 'That was the crow of the golden cock within the earth.' I understood, and left. After a few steps I turned back to look, and could not see the thatched hut. Less than a *li* farther on I reached the cavern-heaven. It was at the Cavern of Pure Perfection that I first received a thunder text." (*Chongxu . . .:* 1a–1b)

Notice how little suggestion there is here of anything bureaucratic. Wang enters a humble thatched hut, not a palace or government bureau. He suspects it is the "dwelling" of the thunder—again, not the thunder's office or site of administration. The old woman, when she appears, confirms this: "This is the place where thunderclaps *dwell*" (emphasis mine). She herself lacks not only title but surname as well. Wang receives his arts not by some decree or order but simply by copying a text he finds open—and there is no suggestion that this is an official document. The image is of a man stealing into another's home and surreptitiously copying from his valuable books. Of course we are not to suppose—and this becomes clearer through

the disciple's interpretation of Wang's story, further on in the dialogue—that Wang could do this if he did not in some sense have the
permission or acquiescence of those to whom the text belongs: the
old woman herself partly plays this authorizing role in the story. But
the passage does not represent the implicit permission as something
official or in any way formal.

This is entirely typical of Daoist representations of the transmission of Daoist knowledge and status: again and again one finds the
practitioner or practitioner-to-be wandering into the hills or the
woods, where he meets, hidden away in a rustic hut or sitting at a
table in the open, a mysterious old man who directly and personally
hands a text over to him or teaches him secrets, and who later proves
to be some high immortal or god. It would be interesting to explore
why direct and personal communication comes to the fore at such
crucial transitional moments, even for professional Daoists. It is certainly not the only means Daoist practitioners have to represent
transmission of their power and status. A Celestial Heart ritual manual preserves a form to be submitted to Heaven by a master who is
recommending his disciple for ordination as a Celestial Heart functionary:

> From the Omnicelestial Controller of the Perverse and Demonic
> for their Return to the Correct, (insert ranks, surname, and given
> name, in full):
> This Bureau,[10] on the (Xth) day of the (present) month, is in
> receipt of the application, offered in heartfelt sincerity, of the disci-
> ple B, of (X) prefecture, county, and ward, requesting transmission
> to him of the Correct Rites of Celestial Heart of the Northern
> Bourne, in order to assist what is correct and remove what is per-
> verse, to aid Heaven in its transformations, to relieve the ills and
> sufferings of the people, and to cut short the ambitions and striv-
> ings of evil spirits. The officiant A, above, has already by himself
> drawn up an account of this matter and by memorial notified the
> Emperor on High, and has further accepted B for appointment to
> office (X), and further given him talisman-texts, lists of manual
> signs, and the printed formats of the Bureau for Expelling Perverse
> Forces, and in accordance with regulations has performed the
> transmission and ordination. This completed, the officiant A care-
> fully inscribes [this] notification to his Humane Sageliness of
> Tianqi of the Eastern Mount, begging that his sagely intelligence
> grant the favor of an order giving universal notice to the Great
> Kings of Walls and Moats [i.e., City Gods] within the Three
> Regions . . . and to all the spiritual intelligences of the Five
> Mounts, of the Four Rivers, of the mountains of renown and the

great streams, of the temples and of the altars of the soil, and of the hills and streams and numinous marshes, directing them to take notice that B has received the rites and undertaken an office, and that if in the future he may, for the sake of others, treat illness or expel perverse forces, they must assist him in his rites and capture evil spirits without falling into laziness or sloth.

The officiant A further requests that, in accordance with the precedents, there be assigned two Spirit Officers and 1,000 Spirit Troops to be despatched to the office of the new appointee, B, for him to oversee and to assist him in his rites.

Respectfully drawn up on day of month of the year (X), by (insert ranks, surname, and given name). *(Taishang* 10:5b–7a)

There is certainly no hint here that the relationship between transmitter and initiate might be a personal one: they appear simply as bureaucrats of different levels. And yet when the compiler of another edition of the same manual sat down to preface his text he was careful to name the series of teachers and disciples through whose hands the materials in the text had been transmitted: "When [Rao] ascended to Heaven he transmitted the rites to his disciple, the Abbey Superintendent Zhu, named Zhongsu; Zhongsu in turn transmitted them to You Daoshou; Daoshou in turn transmitted them to the *tongzhilang* Zou Fen; Zou Fen transmitted them to my first teacher, Rite-Master Fu, named Tianxin. With me the transmission has reached the present day" (Deng n.d.a:*xu*:2a).

There is not much here, to be sure, about the personal content of these relationships. But the transmission is not represented, as it might have been, as a passage of documents between celestial officials, but rather as a passage of secrets between men. And further on the author treats the transmission as incurring a specific personal debt that he can now attempt to repay: "I grieved at the decline of the Way, and cried out: having undertaken my master's instruction and personally received the secret essentials and amulet-texts of the four-graded canon-registers of the Supremely High [*taishang*], how dare I not think hard on the conveying of [these] divine treasures. Lest I turn my back ungratefully on the former sages, I have thus taken the marvelous Way I had received and have recompiled one full set of the *Correct Rites of Celestial Heart*" (Deng n.d.a:*xu*:3a).

The vocabularies of bureaucracy and of personal relations, then, appear together—or, better, separately but in the same texts—in the representations of Celestial Heart and other Song Daoist practitioners, at least when they talk about the transmission of their arts and their relationships to their own masters and disciples, whether human or divine. Their example shows that the vocabularies not only compete but also, in some contexts and settings, alternate or combine. Yet the two vocabularies, as we have seen, do also compete: they seem to be used to articulate two competing explanatory or organizing principles for the religious world. I think that to see them in this way helps shed new light on a piece of modern religious talk that has already been the subject of interpretive efforts by two major figures in the field. Arthur Wolf has told us how his informants explained why, in arranging images, they placed the Stove God in a higher ranking position than the God of the Locality, despite his formally lower bureaucratic rank: "The view of the gods as bureaucrats is so pervasive that evidence to the contrary is itself explained away in bureaucratic terms . . . I asked: 'But how is it that a little god like the Stove God can report directly to T'ien Kung [the Lord of Heaven]?' Another old man answered: 'The Stove God is not a small person like T'u Ti Kung [the God of the Locality]. He is T'ien Kung's younger brother.' The apparent departure from bureaucratic principles is thus explained away as nepotism" (Wolf 1974: 138–139).

Now Sangren, dissatisfied with Wolf's explanation here and more broadly dissatisfied (as I am, obviously) with the notion that "the gods are modeled on bureaucrats and nothing more," has offered his own alternative explanation: that the Stove God is associated with fire, and that fire is known to mediate between heaven and earth, as when incense and prayers are burned. Sangren remarks on other mediative or transformative functions of fire, such as the conversion of the raw to the cooked or (in the ancient myth of archer Yi) of wilderness into civilized ground (Sangren 1987:162–165).

I must confess that Sangren's explanation strikes me as coming a bit out of left field. As far as I know, the Stove God's association with fire is not with the fire that sends prayers and incense to heaven but with the fire that cooks the food that feeds the family. The significance of that cooking, for Chinese who speak of stoves and stove gods, is, as far as I understand it, not so much that the raw is transformed into the cooked or the natural into the cultural as that the food is provided and that the whole family eats together: the stove is preeminently the symbol of the family as a unit, of family togetherness. It is by this connection that the god of the stove can be conceived as the governor of the family and its fortunes. He is a representative of family who is not a member of the family. This only hints at my own interpretation of Wolf's conundrum. Sangren notes that "it is not bureaucratic hierarchy per se that is invoked to gloss inconsistency, but an image of nepotistic behavior attributed to celestial bureaucrats," (Sangren 1987:162) but does not build on this promising beginning. Wolf, indeed, argues as if to explain something as nepotism were to explain it on bureaucratic principles. But it is not. Nepotism, in the Chinese view as in ours, is not a simple expression of bureaucratic principles but an interaction or tension between two *different* principles: a principle of impersonal, merit-based bureaucratic hierarchy and a principle of *personal relationship,* more specifically kinship. That is, when Wolf's informants tell him that the Stove God is placed where he is because, although he governs a lower unit than the Place God, he is the son of the man at the top and so has more direct access, they are saying that in this instance, in this context, for this god, personal ties are more important than bureaucratic hierarchy.

But why might they want to see things this way? Let us return to who the Stove God is. We know, as it were, the pessimistic view of the Stove God: he is a spy in the bosom of the household, who reports the household's sins as well as its virtues to the top of the celestial government. A spy is the agent of a bureaucracy, if anyone is, and enters into personal relationships only for that bureaucracy's purposes. But there is an optimistic view of the Stove God available as well, as I understand it: the Stove God is a guest in one's home, who if treated well as a guest will treat one well in return. From this point of view, though not a family member, he stands in a personal relationship with the family he lives with. Now let us assume that ritual acts, such as the placement of images on an altar, are often to be read (as I forget who once said) not in the indicative but in the subjunctive mood: not as "it is so" but as "let it be so." Then I think it becomes easy to argue that when Chinese assert, by the placement of the Stove God and by their explanation of it, that personal ties mean more in the Stove God's case than bureaucratic principles, they are saying: "*Let* personal ties overcome bureaucratic principles; *let* the Stove God act according to a personal, not a bureaucratic model." To say this is to say implicitly, with regard to the Stove God's relations in the other direction, his relations with the family itself, "Let the Stove God be more guest than spy; let him honor his personal obligations to his hosts more than his official duties to his superiors." In sum, let him report well of us, as a loyal guest would, and protect us before heaven.

I am speculating here, and have perhaps strayed too far. But I think I have shown how a vocabulary of personal relations works itself out in the writings of a major regional cult of the Southern Song and how treating that vocabulary precisely as an independent vocabulary, articulating independent cultural principles in potential competition with the principles articulated by the bureaucratic vocabulary, may offer at least suggestive insights into other phenomena of Chinese religion.

Notes

1. See the prefaces to Deng Yougong's *Shangqing Tianxin Zhengfa* and *Shangqing Gusui Linwen Guilü* (Deng n.d.a, n.d.b).

2. The present story, in which the Three do not appear directly but act through their red-shirted thugs, is in this one respect not typical, and their mediated approach here may again reflect the lowly status of the man dealt with.

3. There are exceptions. In two cases the Three do respond through a human being we could call a mediator, or more properly a medium: they speak by "descending into a boy" at their shrine. This is shorthand for the use of a young medium, who may have been kept on hand regularly to serve in just this way.

4. The narrator is Zhang Yuanshu, compiler of the collection of miracle stories.

5. See Chen n.d.:6:6b–7a. For his son, Chen Tongzu, see *HGS* n.d.:6:13a–14a.

6. For vows to saints in Europe, see Wilson 1983, especially the introduction (especially 13, 21), as well as the articles by Robert Hertz (59–60, 90), Pierre DeLooz (208), and Pierre Sanchis (267–272); Badone 1990, especially the introduction (16–17) and the articles by Caroline Brettell (58, 66) and Jill Dubisch (120, 126); and Christian 1981:23–69 and 1989:118–135. For vows to Islamic saints in India and Nepal, see Gaborieau 1983:296, 299. For vows to Hindu deities, see Bhardwaj 1973:154–162. For what look like vows and fulfillment of vows in spirit cults in Thailand, see the treatment of *pa ba* rites in Tambiah 1970:269–270.

7. This is the case, for example, with the father who receives the "Old Man from South of the Mountain" as his son: he offers his vow at the time of a *jiao* that he has ordered *(ming)* Daoists to perform; but he offers it in his own individual prayer, which he burns himself.

8. My speculative reading: a character is missing, and the original may have meant either "near to" or "distant from" the residence.

9. *Used* again stands in for a missing character.

10. Referring to the Bureau for the Expulsion of Perverse Forces, of which the Celestial Heart master is a Commissioner.

Literature Cited

Ahern. *See* Martin.

Badone, Ellen, ed. 1990. *Religious Orthodoxy and Popular Faith in European Society.* Princeton: Princeton University Press.

Bhardwaj, Surinder Mohan. 1973. *Hindu Places of Pilgrimage in India: A Study in Cultural Geography.* Berkeley: University of California Press.

Boltz, Judith. 1985. *Taoist Rites of Exorcism.* Ph.D. diss., University of California.

Chen Yuanjin. n.d. *Yushu Leigao.* Siku Quanshu Zhenben, first collection.

Christian, William A. 1981. *Local Religion in Sixteenth-Century Spain.* Princeton: Princeton University Press.

———. 1989. *Person and God in a Spanish Valley.* Princeton: Princeton University Press.

Chongxu Tongmiao Shichen Wang Xiansheng Jiahua (The Household Talk of the Void-Soaring Mystery-Penetrating Imperial Attendant, Master Wang). Daozang 996, HY 1240.

Deng Yougong. n.d.a. *Shangqing Tianxin Zhengfa (Correct Rites of Celestial Heart of Upper Clarity).* Daozang 318–319, HY 566.

———. n.d.b. *Shangqing Gusui Lingwen Guilü (Spirit Code: Numinous Writings from the Marrow of Upper Clarity).* Daozang 203, HY 461.

Dubisch, Jill. 1990. "Pilgrimage and Popular Religion at a Greek Holy Shrine." In *Religious Orthodoxy and Popular Faith in European Society,* edited by Ellen Badone, 113–139. Princeton: Princeton University Press.

Gaborieau, Marc. 1983. "The Cult of Saints in Nepal and Southern India." In *Saints and Their Cults: Studies in Religious Sociology, Folklore, and History,* edited by Stephen Wilson, 291–308. Cambridge: Cambridge University Press.

HGS (Huagai Shan Fuqiu Wang Guo San Zhenjun Shishi) (Verities of the Three Perfected Lords Fuqiu, Wang and Guo of Mt. Huagai). n.d. Daozang 556–557, HY 777.

Hong Mai. 1981. *Yijian Zhi.* Beijing: Zhonghua Shuju.

Li, E. 1983. *Songshi Jishi.* Shanghai: Shanghai Guji Chubanshe.

Martin (Ahern), Emily. 1981. *Chinese Ritual and Politics.* Cambridge: Cambridge University Press.

Sanchis, Pierre. 1983. "The Portuguese 'Romarias.' " In *Saints and Their Cults: Studies in Religious Sociology, Folklore, and History,* edited by Stephen Wilson, 261–289. Cambridge: Cambridge University Press.

Sangren, P. Steven. 1987. *History and Magical Power in a Chinese Community.* Stanford: Stanford University Press.

Taishang Zongzhen Biyao (Secret Essentials of the Most High for Assembling the Perfected). Daozang 986–987, HY 1217.

Tambiah, Stanley. 1970. *Buddhism and the Spirit Cults in North-East Thailand.* Cambridge: Cambridge University Press.

Weller, Robert P. 1987. *Unities and Diversities in Chinese Religion.* Seattle: University of Washington Press.

Wilson, Stephen, ed. 1983. *Saints and Their Cults: Studies in Religious Sociology, Folklore, and History.* Cambridge: Cambridge University Press.

Wolf, Arthur. 1974. "Gods, Ghosts, and Ancestors." In *Religion and Ritual in Chinese Society,* edited by Arthur Wolf, 131–182. Stanford: Stanford University Press.

Enlightened Alchemist or Immoral Immortal? The Growth of Lü Dongbin's Cult in Late Imperial China

PAUL R. KATZ

WHILE THE LATE imperial Chinese pantheon featured numerous cults to nonbureaucratic deities, few were both as popular yet as complex as the cult of Lü Dongbin. Worship of this immortal, reputed to have lived during the Tang dynasty, took on a wide variety of forms after his cult arose during the Song. People who worshiped Lü saw him as an itinerant religious specialist, a patriarch of Quanzhen (Perfect Realization) Daoism, a healer and wonder-worker, a patron god of various tradespeople ranging from ink makers to prostitutes, a powerful spirit of planchette cults, and a member of that powerful yet rambunctious group of deities known as the Eight Immortals (Baxian). These various representations of Lü were the result of years of evolution among people from many different social groups of late imperial China, including scholar-officials, Daoist priests, dramatists, tradespeople, artisans, and so forth. Although scholars such as James Watson have theorized that cults undergo a process of "standardization" as they develop (Watson 1985), such a phenomenon does not appear to have occurred in the case of Lü's cult. Rather, the increasing number of Lü's worshipers led to an ever burgeoning variety of representations of this immortal.

In exploring the growth of Lü Dongbin's cult, I will attempt to answer the following questions: How did Lü's cult change over time? Who contributed to the transformations his cult underwent? How did vastly different representations of Lü coexist and interact? Finally, was one group's representation able to dominate all others? I will approach these questions by means of a case study, focusing on the Palace of Eternal Joy (Yongle Gong), a Yuan-dynasty Daoist temple dedicated to Lü. The Palace of Eternal Joy was originally located near the town of Yongle but was moved to Ruicheng in 1959 to make way for a water project. Originally a small shrine to Lü, it was rebuilt and greatly enlarged by members of the Quanzhen Daoist movement during the thirteenth century. The temple's world-famous murals, which include depictions of Lü's hagiography, were completed during the mid-fourteenth century.

To study the different representations of Lü that circulated in the area around the Palace of Eternal Joy, I will rely on hagiographical sources in the *Daoist Canon,* temple stele inscriptions, local gazetteers, the Yongle Gong murals, novels, dramas, and local folktales. Each source has its own biases of which the social historian must be aware. Works in the *Daoist Canon* clearly reflect the agenda of the Daoists who composed them, presenting Lü as a master of internal alchemy *(neidan)* who would initiate and instruct worthy disciples. The murals, being the products of Quanzhen Daoist patronage, present a similar view, though somewhat modified for popular consumption. Local gazetteers and stele inscriptions depict Lü as a well-educated literatus, conforming to the views of the scholar-officials who composed them. The Yuan-dynasty *zaju* dramas, described below, are more problematic, tending to reflect the world view of classically educated scholars who for one reason or another had not been able to pass the exams and/or assume an official post. They emphasize both Lü's Confucian and his Daoist learning, while also describing his willingness to convert others and the joys of immortality a successful adept could experience. Copiously illustrated novels, such as the *Journey to the East (Dongyou Ji),* circulating in cheap and poorly edited editions that could be purchased or rented, were intended for a literate but not highly educated audience (perhaps a third of the male populace if one accepts Rawski's estimates [Rawski 1979:1–23]). These works, as well as collections of folktales, tended to present more popular representations of a deity (though the stories the novels contain were often edited by commercial publishers we know very little about, and some collections of folktales fail to present faithful transcriptions or data on the people who tell them). Such works emphasize Lü's miraculous powers, while occasionally presenting humorous and sometimes even ribald stories about him and his associates, the Eight Immortals.

Such a broad and problematic body of sources, each with its own particular bias, might seem to present one with an impenetrable maze of data. These "biases" are also of great value, however, in that they reflect the realities of the social and religious landscape of late imperial China. Therefore, in examining these sources I will pay close attention to the identity of their authors, as well as of their intended and actual audiences (Johnson 1985:34–72). Such a method will allow us to see how members of different classes attempted to spread their respective representations of Lü Dongbin and how far their efforts succeeded.

I will pay special attention to the Yongle Gong murals because they and other works of art like them have not been adequately used as sources in the study of Chinese hagiography (with the exception of Grootaers 1952). This emphasis on the importance of artworks accords with David Johnson's conclusion that "de-emphasizing words, abstract formulations, definitions, and the like in favor of central scenes or *images,* whether ritual or operatic, that are embedded in well-known narrative or religious matrices, in the attempt to identify those cultural elements that make the Chinese Chinese, begins to make a certain amount of sense" (Johnson 1990:54–55, my emphasis).

During my postdoctoral fellowship at the Chinese Popular Culture Project in 1990–1991, my colleagues and I conducted research on popular art, including dedicatory Buddhist steles, temple murals, and New Year's prints *(nianhua)*. It is important to note, however, that although all these works were created for and viewed by a mass audience, their contents may not necessarily have been "popular" in the sense of reflecting representations widespread at any particular place or time. This is particularly true in the case of religious art, which was usually didactic and designed to reflect the agenda of the patrons who sponsored it, whether religious specialists and/or members of the elite (Katz 1993). The evidence presented below reveals that the murals in the Yongle Gong, sponsored by Quanzhen Daoist priests, attempted to communicate Daoist values that were not always appreciated by the pilgrims who viewed them.

Lü's Cult at Yongle

Most hagiographical accounts agree that Lü was born on the fourteenth day of the fourth lunar month in 798 C.E. in the town of Yongle. His given name was Lü Yan, but he later adopted the stylename Dongbin. After becoming a Daoist he used the Daoist name Chunyang (meaning "Purified Yang"). He is said to have been the son of Lü Rang and the grandson of Lü Wei, a Vice-minister of Rites. Although these two men are historical figures, I have not been able to find data on Lü Yan in any Tang historical or biographical source. Some hagiographical accounts maintain that Lü had passed the *jinshi* examination during the Huichang (841–846) or Xiantong (860–874) reigns, but an examination of Xu Song's list of 3,326 successful Tang examination candidates, entitled *Dengke Jikao* (1838), did not uncover anyone named Lü Yan (the text *does* include Lü Rang and Lü Wei). There may have been a historical Lü Dongbin, just as Anna Seidel and Wong Siu Hon have demonstrated that one or more individuals claiming to be Zhang Sanfeng may have existed during the Ming (Seidel 1970, Wong 1988), but this must at present remain a tentative hypothesis pending the discovery of further evidence.

We do not encounter comprehensive hagiographies of Lü (as opposed to occasional brief references to him) until the end of the Northern Song. Three different versions took shape during that time, the first two centering on Lü's cult at Yueyang (or Yuezhou) in Hunan and the third on Lü's cult at Yongle.[1] Lü's hagiography at Yongle was composed in 1222 by the late Jin dynasty *jinshi*-turned-hermit named Yuan Congyi and preserved at the Yongle Gong on a stele that was carved in 1228 (recarved in 1252 and 1324). A partial translation follows:

> Over one hundred paces northeast of Yongle town is a place called Summoning Worthies Village (Zhaoxian Li). If one takes a path further north from there one arrives at the former residence of Lord Lü of the Tang who attained the Dao. The locals admired his virtue, and turned it into a temple, reverently making offerings there on an annual basis. . . . The perfected man *(zhenren)* [Lü] was named Yan, and took the style name Dongbin and the Daoist name Chunyang. The Vice-minister of Rites Lü Wei was his grandfather. In the year 825 he passed the highest level of the *jinshi* exam. Before being assigned a post he spent the spring wandering near the Feng River (in Shaanxi) where he encountered the Han hermit Lord Zhongli [Quan]. Lord Zhongli perceived that Lü was of uncommon make,[2] and enticed him to study the way of immortals. . . . He orally transmitted to Lü secret instructions for internal alchemy *(neidan bizhi)* as well as the Heaven-Concealing Sword Technique *(tiandun jianfa)*. Lord Lü thereupon broke off all ties with the mortal world, building a hut of grass on Lu Shan . . . where he later attained a position among the immortals. (Chen Yuan et al. 1988:447–448)

This hagiography differs markedly from the Yueyang versions in claiming that Lü had *passed* the *jinshi* examination in 825. Why did this change occur? Perhaps because some of Lü's worshipers at Yongle found it difficult to accept a hagiography that claimed their deity had failed as a traditional scholar. Yet folktales cited below indicate that other worshipers there saw Lü as a poor scholar who had not passed the exams.

A Brief History of the Yongle Gong

According to Yuan Congyi's inscription, the Palace of Eternal Joy was located at the site of Lü's former residence.[3] The text does not give the date when his shrine was founded, but I would speculate that this did not occur until the Five Dynasties at the earliest, and probably not until the Northern Song. We know that this shrine was converted into a Daoist monastery during the Jin dynasty (again the exact date is not given), but no information is given as to which sect's priests were in charge of it. During the turbulent years of the Mongol conquest of north China, the temple fell into disrepair and ended up being destroyed by a fire in 1244. Shortly thereafter, in 1252, the Mongol court appointed Pan Dechong (1191–1256), a disciple of the renowned Quanzhen master Qiu Chuji (1148–1227), to take charge of a large-scale reconstruction and enlargement project. By 1252 most of the temple buildings had been finished. This indicates a rapid rate of construction, considering that many contemporary temples took up to twenty years to build or even rebuild (Su 1962:82,84,86; major temple construction projects in Taiwan can sometimes last up to a decade as well). The speed at which the temple was completed probably reflects the degree of support the project had from the Mongol court, local officials (both Han and non-Han), and the local populace. The temple was renamed the Purified Yang Palace of Limitless Longevity (Chunyang Wanshou Gong) and was also referred to as the Yongle Gong. The murals were not completed until the fourteenth century, the delay probably resulting from a drop in Quanzhen support at the Yuan court following the disastrous Daoist-Buddhist debates of 1281 (Jagchid 1982:61–98; Kubo 1968:39–61; Rossabi 1988:37–43,141–147,203–205; Thiel 1961:1–81).

Daoist temples like the Yongle Gong served the needs of both Daoist priests and the surrounding community. On the one hand, they functioned as a site where Quanzhen Daoists could perform rituals and practice self-cultivation. On the other hand, they resembled the great cathedrals of Europe, drawing thousands of pilgrims to worship the images or relics of popular deities on their holy days.[4] The popular nature of the Yongle Gong may be seen in this account written by a Shanxi native now residing in Taiwan:

> Whenever there was a temple fair or religious celebration [such as Lü Dongbin's birthday], devout worshippers from all the surrounding villages and towns would continuously flock to the temple to make offerings. People living on the southern banks of the Yellow River from as far away as Tongguan [in Shaanxi] and Shouxiang [in Henan] would cross the river to worship. The atmosphere was extremely lively [renao]. (Li Xianzhou 1983:104)

What did the average pilgrim see as he or she walked inside the enormous temple complex, which covered an area of more than 8,600 square meters? I visited the site at Ruicheng during the summer of 1991, and the following description is based on my field-work there. One entered through the temple gate, constructed during the Qing dynasty. From there, one passed along a path nearly 80 meters long flanked by columns of stelae, the earliest surviving of which dated back to the Jin dynasty (Katz 1995a), until reaching the Gate of the Limitless Ultimate (Wuji Men), completed in 1294. Here one saw the first temple murals, featuring heavenly soldiers and heavenly generals.

From the Gate of the Limitless Ultimate one walked 80 meters farther past two huge stelae (dating from 1262 and 1689) to the Hall of the Three Pure Ones (Sanqing Dian), which was completed in 1262. This was the largest hall of the entire complex, covering an area of more than 430 square meters (28.44 m x 15.28 m). Statues of the Three Pure Ones sat inside the hall,[5] surrounded by murals depicting 290 members of the Daoist pantheon conducting an audience with them (Jing 1993). This massive work, known as the *Audience with the [Three] Primordials (Chaoyuan Tu)* covered an area of more than 402 square meters, the deities featured being as tall as 2 meters and the murals covering 4 meters from top to bottom. These murals were completed in 1325 by the Luoyang artisan *(huagong)* Ma Junxiang and his disciples. A comparison of the Wuji Men and Sanqing Dian murals with contemporary Daoist liturgical texts reveals that the deities featured were not merely decorations but also the objects of worship at Daoist rituals regularly held at the temple (Katz 1993).

Forty meters beyond the Sanqing Dian lies the Hall of Purified Yang (Chunyang Dian) in which Lü is worshiped. This hall was completed in the same year as the Sanqing Dian, but on a much smaller scale, covering just over 300 square meters (20.35 m x 14.35 m). The murals depicting Lü's life, entitled *The Illustrated Divine Travels and Immortal Transformations of the Lord Emperor of Purified Yang (Chunyang Dijun Shenyou Xianhua Tu),* were also smaller, being only 3.6 meters high and covering just over 200 square meters of wall space surrounding a statue of Lü. Completed in 1358, they were painted by students of the Yuan-dynasty mural painter Zhu Haogu.[6] Most of the fifty-two scenes from Lü's hagiography presented in the murals are accompanied by a cartouche *(tiji)* describing the story portrayed. Nearly two-thirds of these texts (thirty-seven in all) are direct quotations from a work in the *Daoist Canon* entitled *The Record of Divine Transformations and Miraculous Powers of the Lord Emperor of Purified Yang (Chunyang Dijun Shenhua Miaotong Ji),* hereafter referred to as *Miaotong Ji (MTJ).* This work was written by the Quanzhen Daoist master Miao Shanshi (fl. 1288–1324), a native of Nanjing. Many of these stories can also be found in later Daoist compilations such as the *Record of the Patriarch Lü (Lüzu*

Zhi, 1601) and the *Complete Writings of the Patriarch Lü* (*Lüzu Quanshu,* 1846) (Jing 1995, Mori 1992:31–47).[7]

Twenty meters farther behind the Chunyang Dian lies the Hall of Redoubled Yang (Chongyang Dian). Chongyang was the Daoist name of the Quanzhen movement's founder Wang Zhe (1112–1170), who is enshrined in the temple along with his seven leading disciples. A total of forty-nine murals depicting scenes from Wang's life decorated the walls of this temple, but unfortunately more than one-third of these have been partially or totally destroyed. It is not clear who painted the murals, but they appear to have been completed around 1368, shortly after the Chunyang Dian murals (Wang Chang-an 1963a:40–43).

Apart from these main halls, several other temples made up the entire Yongle Gong complex, the most important of which was the Shrine to Patriarch Lü (Lüzu Ci), the significance of which I have discussed in detail elsewhere, as the site for popular worship of Lü at Yongle (Katz 1994). Two smaller palaces flanked the Chongyang Dian (almost all of the rest of the buildings described below no longer exist), and behind it lay a temple dedicated to Qiu Chuji. To the west of the main halls lay two temples in which were enshrined images of the two Quanzhen Daoists responsible for the thirteenth-century construction of the temple: Pan Dechong and Song Defang (1183–1247). There were also other temples, including one for the Jade Emperor and one for the City God, as well as an academy, shops, kitchens, a pilgrim's hostel, and so forth. There was even a ginkgo tree supposedly planted by Lü, as well as the reputed site of his grave.

Although members of various social groups ranging from local officials to commoners played a role in the reconstruction of Lü's shrine, members of the Quanzhen sect were mainly responsible for initiating, organizing, and carrying out this massive project. As early as 1240 Song Defang had visited Lü's shrine on a pilgrimage and been greatly dismayed by the disrepair it had fallen into. He reported this state of affairs to Quanzhen leaders Yin Zhiping (1169–1251) and Li Zhichang (1193–1256), who in turn petitioned the court to give its support to a massive reconstruction project. Their efforts resulted in Pan Dechong being placed in charge of just such a project in 1246. Song, Pan, and their disciples played the most important role in the building of the Yongle Gong, not only organizing and directing construction efforts but even contributing their own funds to the project (Chen Yuan et al. 1988:491–493,546–549,554–556, 613–614; Li and Lin 1986:303–316). Why did members of the Quanzhen movement devote so much effort and such a large amount of resources to a small shrine located hundreds of miles away from the Mongol center of power at Dadu (Yuan Beijing)? This was largely because the sect adopted Lü as one of its fictive patriarchs in order to enhance its prestige at the Yuan court, a process I have discussed in detail elsewhere (Katz 1994).

Because of Lü's critical place in the "historical" lineage the Quanzhen movement presented of itself, the preservation and expansion of his temple was of paramount concern to the movement's leaders. This can be seen in Song Defang's statement to his fellow Daoists: "The fact that our patriarch's home has fallen into this state is our responsibility... We should rebuild this shrine as a palace in order to display our patriarch's virtue and enlighten future generations" (Chen Yuan et al. 1988:613,617–618).

The Mongol rulers of north China and the officials who served them also took great interest in the reconstruction of Lü's shrine, although not necessarily because they cared about the role Lü had allegedly played in the history of Quanzhen Daoism. These men tended to support the building project because they viewed Lü's temple as a site of great spiritual power where rituals for the state could be successfully performed. This can be seen in a series of memorials dated 1246, which were carved onto a stele at the temple in 1262. Each memorial opens with a statement reading: "It is respectfully requested that the great teacher Pan Dechong be placed in charge of the Chunyang Palace at Yongle... in order to burn incense and engage in self-cultivation on behalf of the state, as well as perform rites for the limitless longevity of our sage sovereign" (Chen Yuan et al. 1988:491–493). The Yongle Gong was also a site for rituals performed for the deities of mountains and rivers by Li Zhichang to mark the ascent of the emperor Möngke to the throne in 1252 (Chen Yuan et al. 1988:555).

Although work on most of the temple buildings was completed in the 1250s and 1260s, except for the Wuji Men which was finished in 1294, the murals in the Sanqing Dian were not done until 1325, those in the Chunyang and Chongyang halls taking thirty more years to complete. The Buddhist-Daoist debates of the 1280s, mentioned above, appear to have been the major cause of this delay. Work did continue during the 1290s and early 1300s, but at a much slower pace than before (Chen Yuan et al. 1988:708). By the early fourteenth century, however, many new temple and mural projects were undertaken throughout Shanxi province (Steinhardt 1987:13–14). Why such a flurry of activity? In the case of Quanzhen temples, the cause seems to have been the efforts of a new generation of leaders who found favor with the Yuan emperors, especially Miao Daoyi (fl. 1310s–1320s). All Quanzhen sect patriarchs were promoted and awarded new titles (of "lord emperor," *dijun*) in 1310, and following

years witnessed an outpouring of imperial edicts warning local officials and members of other religions (especially Buddhists) not to
interfere in the management of Quanzhen temples. There followed a
new frenzy of temple building, as well as the mural projects mentioned above (Chen Yuan et al. 1988:727–733,786–787; Jing 1993).

In the case of the Yongle Gong, this new wave of imperial support
provided a major impetus to new construction and mural projects.
The imperial edicts recounting the promotion of sect patriarchs were
all carved on steles erected in the temple complex in 1317, perhaps as
a symbolic statement of the Quanzhen movement's new-found influence at court (Katz 1995a). These stelae also provide further data on
the social history of the Yongle Gong, as they list both the Daoists
and lay leaders of ritual associations *(huishou)* who supported it.
One stele of 1317 even describes the size of temple lands and lists
other local temples as well as Daoist priests, monks, and nuns who
had established connections with the Yongle Gong (Chen Yuan et al.
1988:728,733,792–795). There are also three edicts, dated 1327,
1332, and 1339, that reaffirm the temple's tax-exempt status and
warn all officials and members of other religions not to abuse temple
property (Chen Yuan et al. 1988:781–782,804–805, Katz 1995a).

From the 1320s to 1350s two major construction projects in addition to the murals were undertaken. The first was a temple to the
Tang official Cui Yu, popularly known as Lord Cui (Cui Fujun),
which was completed in 1326 (Chen Yuan et al. 1988:776–777). The
second was a temple to the Emperor of the Eastern Peak, which was
completed in 1349 (Chen Yuan et al. 1988:807). In both cases,
money for the construction projects was raised by the leaders of
ritual associations that supported the Yongle Gong, as well as the
Daoists who managed the temple itself. These two groups mobilized
the villagers and local merchants to support such projects, not only
during the fourteenth century but in later centuries as well (Chen
Yuan et al. 1988:1301–1302,1308–1311; Su 1963:55–60).

Patrons and Artisans: The Creation of the
Chunyang Dian Murals

The history of the Yongle Gong presented above reveals that the
growth of Lü Dongbin's cult at Yongle, and the expansion of the
temple complex itself, was due to the efforts of people from many
different social classes, including Daoist priests, scholar-officials,
merchants, and local villagers. We shall see that each group embraced strikingly different representations of Lü, which are presented
in the different source materials I have utilized. Which group's representation of Lü appears most clearly in the Chunyang Dian murals?

A close examination of their contents and the circumstances behind their creation reveals that they were intended to present and spread the Quanzhen Daoist representation of Lü to a mass audience.[8]

A cartouche of 1358 on the walls of the Chunyang Dian lists the names of some forty individuals who paid for the creation of the murals (Wang Chang-an 1963b:73).[9] Of these, thirty-eight were Quanzhen Daoists (eleven lived at the Yongle Gong, the rest at neighboring Quanzhen temples and monasteries), while the other two were local officials. The cartouche also lists the amounts they donated, either in cash (paper money) or in kind (grain). We can see from this inscription that the men who paid for the murals shared the same backgrounds as those who organized the drive for the temple's expansion and reconstruction: almost all were Quanzhen Daoist masters with a vested interest in promoting the cult of one of their sect's main patriarchs, Lü Dongbin.

I have not been able to find much biographical data concerning those Daoists who sponsored the murals. The only information I have about their activities at the Yongle Gong is that one man named Liang Daocong helped organize efforts to build the temple to the Emperor of the Eastern Peak, while another named Du Dechun donated money for repairing pillars in the Sanqing Dian in 1365 (Chen Yuan et al. 1988:728,792,805,807; Su 1963:57). We do know that those Daoists who managed the Yongle Gong throughout the Yuan (and later dynasties) were all members of the Quanzhen movement (Katz 1991). Those responsible for the construction projects during the thirteenth and fourteenth centuries were mostly disciples of Pan Dechong and Song Defang, both of whom were renowned disciples of Qiu Chuji. The Daoist names of these men follow the sect poem *(paishi)* of the Longmen branch of Quanzhen Daoism, the first line of which reads *"daode tongxuan jing."* Accordingly, the Daoists who ran the Yongle Gong during the Yuan all had the characters *dao* and *de* as the second character of their names (Yoshioka 1979:229–231, Igarashi 1938:61–108).

Most of the Daoists associated with the Yongle Gong were given the titles of superintendent *(tidian)* or supervisor *(tiju)*, the two titles being largely interchangeable. Such positions were created during the Song dynasty and became largely a sinecure for retired officials. Supervisors and superintendents managed not only temples but also granaries, irrigation projects, the salt and tea monopolies, and so forth (Hucker 1985:494,497).[10] In the Daoist temple bureaucracy, the posts of supervisor and superintendent were given to retired officials and to members of a particular Daoist movement. For example, the biography of a superintendent named Zhang Zhide (fl. 1300–1320) states that he was a peasant who joined the Quanzhen movement at age twenty-five following the death of his wife. He resided at the Shengshou Gong in Jizhou (Shandong), where apart from engaging in self-cultivation he also studied medicine and gained great popularity among the populace for his healing skills. He initially managed temple affairs on behalf of his master and was officially appointed to the post of superintendent by the Quanzhen leader Sun Deyi in 1316. According to his biography, his primary duties as a superintendent were "to raise money for the expansion of the temple complex" (Chen Yuan et al. 1988:745).

What sort of representation of Lü did the Daoists at the Yongle Gong embrace? Although almost no biographical data exist on these men or other fourteenth-century Daoists living at the Yongle Gong, we can attempt to understand their beliefs by examining other contemporary Quanzhen materials about Lü (which I have done in detail in Katz 1994; see also Ang 1993, 1995). Of greatest relevance is Miao Shanshi's *Miaotong Ji*, the source for most of the murals in the Chunyang Dian. I will compare individual tales to the murals below, but here I wish to present a portion of Miao's preface to the text, which perhaps best reveals Quanzhen representations of Lü during the late Yuan. The overwhelming emphasis of this text is on Lü's role as a teacher who can instruct his followers—especially Daoists—in techniques to attain immortality.[11] In his preface to the *Miaotong Ji,* Miao Shanshi specifically states that he compiled this work to help his fellow Daoists who shared the goal of attaining immortality through self-cultivation and internal alchemy:

> Our Dao employs divine powers to guide and help the masses, while also using medicinal arts to rescue the good. It smoothly proceeds on its winding way, following the natural course of events. Its benevolence and power of transformation unite the myriad sects as having originated from one source . . . [Those who follow the Dao] can be enlightened about the perpetual emptiness of all things, and can grasp the mysteries of primeval forces . . . I have collected records [of Lü Dongbin] from Tang and Song sources, editing out superficial aspects, and compiled a record of 120 stories which I have named the *Record of Divine Transformations and Miraculous Powers*. I have done this in order to help those scholars who share my ideas . . . to see heaven's signs, silently merge the mysterious and clear aspects of the Dao, penetrate the great mysteries of the limitless ultimate, grasp the abstruseness of [Lü] Chunyang, thoroughly comprehend the ultimate Tao, and wholly attain the purity of the prior heavens.

Despite the difficult and often abstruse language of this preface, we can see that Miao's primary concern in compiling these stories

about Lü Dongbin was to aid fellow Daoists in practicing self-cultivation. Miao was a member of the southern branch of Quanzhen
Daoism, which emphasized the importance of the master-disciple
relationship and the necessity of pursuing a path of intensive self-
cultivation through internal alchemy to gain enlightenment (Boltz
1987:179–184, Chen Bing 1986:66–80).[12] Miao's concern with these
issues might explain why the overwhelming majority of stories in
Miaotong Ji deal with the themes of recognition *(shi)* and conversion
(du). The ability to recognize an immortal in disguise was considered
an important step on the path to immortality and a sign that one was
ready to have an immortal as one's master.

How popular were such representations of Lü? Although the
Quanzhen movement did attract a mass following during the Jin and
Yuan dynasties, it is difficult to determine how widely the representations of Quanzhen Daoists could have spread (Katz 1994). The Chunyang Dian murals present an even more complex problem, as the
Quanzhen Daoists at Yongle who sponsored them had to rely on the
aid of artisans who specialized in painting religious murals in order
to present their images of Lü. We know nothing of the seven students
of Zhu Haogu who worked on the Chunyang Dian murals except
their names, that they came from different parts of Shanxi (including
Ruicheng and other sites near Yongle), and that they specialized in
painting Buddhist and Daoist subjects (Guo 1991:61,67,68,74,83;
Guo 1992:51–52; Zeng 1989:44–48).

An important change in the social status of the muralists appears
to have occurred during the Tang and Song dynasties. Before the
Song, most of the famous painters of religious art were members of
the aristocracy; quite a few were Daoist priests or Buddhist monks.
Wu Daozi, for example, had served as chief of civil servants in a sub-
prefectural post in Yanzhou (Shandong) before being summoned to
the court by the Tang emperor Xuanzong. By the Song dynasty, however, most literati artists had begun to devote their efforts to landscape painting, considering religious art as unworthy of attention.
Even those muralists who ended up serving as court painters do not
appear to have been members of the gentry class. Renowned Song
artists who painted religious subjects, such as Wang Zhuo and Wang
Guan, were commoners before being commissioned by the court to
paint murals for imperially sponsored temple projects. The one exception was Wu Zongyuan, who came from a gentry family and had
served as a civil official before becoming a court painter (Qin
1960:5–6, Yu 1958:131–138, Zhai 1987:109–111). It is not clear
why such a drastic change in elite attitudes toward religious art
occurred, but this shift meant that religious art (including murals)
became the realm of a group of semiliterate professionals, many of

whom passed on their skills not only to apprentices but also to their sons. For example, the artisan Ma Junxiang worked on the Sanqing Dian murals alongside both his apprentices and four of his sons.

Many of the artisans whose names appear in the inscriptions are listed under the title *daizhao,* which Hucker translates as "Editorial Assistant." Such a title was usually only given to lowly compilers in the imperial bureaucracy during the Song and Qing dynasties. However, the title *daizhao* was also used as an informal form of address toward artisans and tradespeople in late imperial times, including barbers, doctors, diviners, and muralists. Therefore, we should consider the men who painted the Chunyang Dian murals to have been not people of rank serving in the imperial bureaucracy but merely professional artisans who plied their trade in the temples of north China.

There is no indication as to who wrote the cartouches in the Chunyang Dian, but it is worth noting that these works contain many incorrectly written characters and faulty transcriptions of passages in the *Daoist Canon.* For example, in the first cartouche the character *zhen*(1) of the regnal year Zhenyuan (785–805) is written as *zhen*(2), while in the second cartouche the Tang emperor Xianzong (r. 806–820) is erroneously listed as Lingzong. In mural YLG 15 the character *gong*(1) is written as *shang,* while in YLG 45 the character *weng* is written as *gong*(2). In YLG 46, the year 1108 is said to have occurred during the Zhenghe reign (1111–1117), when it actually occurred during the Daguan reign (1107–1110), and the entire text appears fragmentary and incoherent. These errors suggest that the cartouches were either based on a faulty version of Miao's text or, more likely, were written down by semiliterate artisans. Many of the New Year's prints that circulated in late imperial China also contain such errors, similarly a result of the social status and educational background of those who created them (Bo 1986: 66–74).

The Daoists at the Yongle Gong were able to hire highly skilled (though not highly educated) artisans because Yongle itself was near the area of southern Shanxi famous for its temple murals, including those of the Guangsheng Si in Zhaocheng County and the Xinghua Si in Jishan County (Guo 1992:50–52; Steinhardt 1987:11–16; White 1940:37,39–48). The Shanxi area had long been a home for many of China's best-known muralists, the most famous of whom was Wu Daozi. Although none of Wu's murals has survived, his influence continued to flourish in north China through the efforts of artists like Wang Guan, Wang Zhuo, and Wu Zongyuan. These men and their disciples created a style of religious art that served as a model for those artisans who painted the Yongle Gong murals (Yu 1958:108–

164, Qin 1958:59–60). The religious murals of Shanxi Province that have survived appear to belong to one particular genre, whether they portray Buddhist or Daoist deities. They share stylistic features, pigments, such conventions as the use of buildings or natural objects to frame a particular scene, and so forth (Pan 1958:61–62, Qin 1960: 5–7, Steinhardt 1987:13–16, Wang Chang-an 1963a:40–41, White 1940:39–48).

There is some evidence to indicate that the murals in the Sanqing Dian follow the influence of Wu Zongyuan, who was in turn following in Wu Daozi's footsteps. One sketchbook *(fuben)* attributed to Wu Zongyuan that still exists, entitled the *Immortal Procession for an Audience with the [Three] Primordials (Chaoyuan Xianzhang Tu)*, shows a procession of deities that resembles the one shown on the Sanqing Dian murals. In addition, a second sketchbook attributed to Wu Zongyuan, entitled *The Eighty-seven Divine Immortals (Bashiqi Shenxian Tu)*, also resembles the Sanqing Dian murals (Pan 1958:61, Xu 1956:57–58). We cannot be sure whether any of the artisans who worked on the Yongle Gong murals ever saw the works of the above-mentioned artists. It is clear, however, that such traditions of mural painting were passed on from one generation to another.

One way aspiring young muralists could learn from a master was to visit a temple and gaze on its walls. Both Wang Guan and Wu Zongyuan studied the works of Wu Daozi in this way. Wang's biography states that "his family was extremely poor, so there was no money to support his travels in search of a master. Therefore he went to the Laozi temple at Beimang Shan [near Luoyang] to look at [Wu Daozi's] works . . . He frequently went to gaze on these murals, no matter how cold the temperature or how deep the snow in winter" *(Shanxi Tongzhi* 1892:158:20a). According to mainland Chinese art historians Bo Songnian and Wang Shucun, artisans who made popular prints often watched dramatic performances as a source of inspiration for their work. It is not clear whether Yuan-dynasty artisans working on murals did this, but such a practice might explain why the two largest murals in the Chunyang Dian appear to portray scenes from dramas (see below; Bo 1986:84–86, Wang Shucun 1991).

The more common way for an artisan to learn his trade was to study under a master and receive training from him. Masters passed their secrets on to their disciples through two sources: first, through sketchbooks, variously known as *diben, fenben, fuben,* or *xiaoben;* second, through secret formulas known as *huajue*. After three years of training the apprentice could become a master himself, assuming his own master had allowed him to see all his sketchbooks and memorize all the essential formulas. Many masters jealously guarded their trade secrets, and such knowledge appears rarely to have been transmitted intact from one generation to another (Bo 1986:65–75, Wang Shucun 1982:4–5).

A sketchbook for the Yongle Gong murals existed as late as the early twentieth century, only to be lost during the Japanese occupation. Such a work may have been used by those disciples of Zhu Haogu who had created the murals, although it is also possible that it was used by artisans who restored the murals during the Ming-Qing era. According to the field report written by the scholars who first rediscovered the Yongle Gong, modern artisans used this work as the basis for making repairs and restorations to damaged murals.[13] We are less certain, however, whether a sketchbook of the murals was first presented to the Daoists for their approval before the murals were painted.

The evidence available at present does not help us in determining the degree to which the Daoists were able to direct the artisans in their creation of the murals. We have no records of contracts or other written agreements, which in the case of fifteenth-century Italy clearly stated what the patron required of the artist he hired (Baxandall 1972:3–14). However, there is good reason to suspect that—like Titian and Bellini, who worked for the Franciscans (Goffen 1986:73–106), or like the artisans who adorned medieval French cathedrals (Duby 1981:9,77–78,94–135)—the Yongle Gong artisans attempted to transform the agenda of their patrons into the visual medium.

The Image of Lü Dongbin in the Chunyang Dian Murals

The series of fifty-two hagiographical murals about Lü Dongbin, located in the Chunyang Dian, occupies just over half the available wall space. I have described each mural and its links to other versions of Lü's hagiography in a separate essay (Katz 1991). Therefore, I shall use only a few murals as examples to support the arguments presented in this essay. In addition to the murals of Lü's hagiography, two others show Daoist fast (zhai) and offering (jiao) rituals being performed, possibly in the same way as those held at the Yongle Gong. Two tree spirits Lü converted are also portrayed on the walls directly behind Lü's statue, as are two other murals featuring Lü but not part of the series of fifty-two. The first shows Lü receiving instruction from his master Zhongli Quan, while the second depicts Lü and the other members of the Eight Immortals crossing the ocean (Baxian guohai), a popular theme featured in late imperial (and modern) popular fiction, drama, and art.

The murals portraying Lü's hagiography begin on the eastern wall of the Chunyang Dian and proceed all the way to the northeastern corner of the hall; the story continues along the western wall to the

Interior of the Hall of Purified Yang (Chunyang Dian), Yongle Gong, as it appeared in the 1950s. Since then the statue of Lü Dongbin in the hall's center has been restored, but damage to the murals has yet to be repaired. Note that many of the cartouches are well above the ground, making it difficult even for those worshipers who could read to make out their contents. (From *Yongle Gong Bihua Xuanji* [Beijing, 1958])

northwestern corner (see figure). Each scene is set in a frame consisting of buildings, bridges, rivers, mountains, and so forth, the story moving from top to bottom and right to left along the wall in the same way as Chinese characters were read along the traditional written or printed page. Apart from providing a source for the study of Daoist iconography and hagiography, the murals are an invaluable tool for the social historian in that they depict the people, costumes, buildings, and activities of Yuan daily life.

While Quanzhen Daoists attempted to use the murals to transmit their representation of Lü Dongbin, they were also aware that he was popularly worshiped as a deity famed for his exorcistic and healing powers. As for the artisans who created the Chunyang Dian murals, although they had to cater to the needs of their patrons, they also appear to have been strongly influenced by popular beliefs.[14] This may explain why the images of Lü presented in the Chunyang Dian murals often fail to correspond exactly to the text they were based on (see below). Such a phenomenon, which in fact indicates the prominence of popular representations of Lü, may be seen in the table, where I have divided the contents of the Chunyang Dian murals into four types: (1) accounts of Lü Dongbin's life; (2) tales showing Lü converting others *(du),* including the tree spirits and other members of the Eight Immortals, such as He Xiangu; (3) tales depicting those who fail to recognize *(shi)* Lü and therefore fail to attain salvation (such as the story of Hou Yonghui, presented below); and (4) tales stressing Lü's miraculous powers. More than 40 percent of the stories in the *Miaotong Ji* focus on the theme of recognition, as do nearly one-third of the murals. Both sources place equal emphasis on the theme of conversion. The most striking difference between the murals and the *Miaotong Ji* concerns Lü's miraculous powers. Stories describing these take up less than 20 percent of the *Miaotong Ji,* while representing nearly one-third of the contents of the murals. Furthermore, 40 percent of those murals not based on the *Miaotong Ji* but drawn from local folktales portray Lü as a wonder-worker. In the miracle stories in particular, we see Lü responding to direct appeals from his worshipers, much like the Three Lords of Mount Huagai discussed by Robert Hymes in this volume.

Even with this apparent concession to the "hegemony" of popular beliefs however, there is reason to doubt whether the Daoists were actually able to use the murals to transmit their representation of Lü to their intended and actual audience, the masses of pilgrims and local worshipers that flocked to the temple. Recent hermeneutical studies of paintings and other works of art indicate that such objects can provoke a wide range of emotional responses, and not always those their creators or patrons had intended (Freedberg 1989:xix–xxv,1– 27; Fyfe and Law 1988:1–14). This is apparent in the Chunyang Dian

Themes in the the *Miaotong Ji* and the Murals at Yongle Gong[15]

	MTJ		YLG		YLG		YLG	
	#	%	#	%	#	%	#	%
Biography	8	9	5	10	5	14	0	0
Conversion	29	30	15	29	11	29.5	4	26.7
Recognition	41	43	16	30.5	11	29.5	5	33.3
Miracles	17	18	16	30.5	10	27	6	40
Total	95	100	52	100	37	100	15	100

murals. Even in those cases where the murals are based on sources from the *Daoist Canon,* the image of Lü presented in the murals does not always correspond to that expressed in the text. This is particularly true for stories in the *Miaotong Ji,* which stress Lü's mastery of internal alchemy. In the murals Lü appears not as an alchemist but as a powerful miracle-working deity.

One example of this involves Lü's encounter with the Daoist Hou Yonghui (YLG 13, *MTJ* 52; see figure). In this account, Hou is intrigued by what he considers to be the exorcistic powers of Lü's

Lü Dongbin's encounter with Hou Yonghui. In this mural (YLG 13), Lü enters Hou's residence and goes flying off into the heavens after his sword as an astonished Hou looks on. (From *Yongle Gong Bihua Xuanji* [Beijing, 1958])

sword, while Lü attempts to explain its function as cutting off the chaotic thoughts in one's heart that prevent successful Daoist self-cultivation. Finally, perceiving that Hou has not grasped the significance of his instruction, Lü throws his sword into the air and flies away with it. While the *Miaotong Ji* and the cartouche explore the issue of how best to engage in self-cultivation, such a lesson may have been lost on most people who visited the Chunyang Dian. Those unable to read the cartouche (or unable to see it clearly because it was 2 meters off the ground) simply saw Lü flying into the heavens with his sword. Most might have unknowingly agreed with Hou's interpretation of the power of Lü's sword, based on what we know of popular novels like Wu Yuantai's (fl. 1522–1565) *Journey to the East* and Deng Zhimo's (fl. 1566–1618) *Record of the Immortal Lü's Flying Sword (Lüxian Feijian Ji)*. The latter work not only mentions Lü's sword in its title but also portrays him as a powerful exorcist (Baldrian-Hussein 1986:139–145, Ono 1968:52–69).

Such a contrast is also apparent in another mural (YLG 18, *MTJ* 34) showing Lü's encounter with the Neo-Confucian scholar Shao Yong (see figure). Shao predicts Lü's arrival using a divinatory technique from the *Book of Changes,* thereupon setting up a tablet to worship him. The account of this meeting in the *Miaotong Ji* contains a long and complex discussion of Daoist and Confucian doctrine, including allusions to *Mencius.* None of this appears in the cartouche, however, and it was probably of little interest to those worshipers who gazed on the murals. All they saw was a Confucian scholar respectfully welcoming Lü and worshiping his tablet, much as pilgrims and Daoists worshiped tablets that were set up in the Yongle Gong (Chen Yuan et al. 1988:1308,1310).

Two scenes on the northwestern wall of the Chunyang Dian also treat Lü's relations with scholar-officials, in both cases featuring intense discussions about Quanzhen doctrine and internal alchemy (YLG 49, *MTJ* 73; YLG 52, *MTJ* 81). Stories like these reflected an important factor in the spread of Quanzhen Daoism: the ability of the sect's leaders (many of whom had been officials or members of the gentry themselves before converting to Daoism) to bring many of their Jin and Yuan peers into the sect as their disciples (Zheng 1987: 73,75,88,95,98–101,107–108; Ren 1990:441,449–450). The terminology of internal alchemy is again absent from the cartouches, and it is unclear whether Lü's worshipers were interested in Quanzhen conversions of important scholar-officials. Nevertheless, most people would have been duly impressed at seeing Lü in the company of, or even instructing, such people.

Another highly significant aspect of the murals is the way they depict Lü Dongbin himself. While the cartouches follow the *Miao-*

Lü Dongbin encounters the scholar Shao Yong. This mural (YLG 18) shows Lü being welcomed by a servant (bottom) and engaged in an animated discussion with Shao (right). Note the spirit-tablet Shao erected in honor of Lü, which is housed inside a shrine in the background. (From *Yongle Gong Bihua Xuanji* [Beijing, 1958])

tong Ji in describing Lü disguising himself as an ugly and filthy beggar, the murals consistently depict him as a well-clad and attractive Daoist. No revulsion can be seen on any of the faces of the people who encounter him; rather, their expressions are often of reverential awe.

Lü Dongbin in the teashop. In this mural (YLG 7), crowds of guests enter and leave the shop (bottom), while Lü sits inside, being waited on by the serving girl he will later bless with longevity. Although the cartouche describes Lü as a filthy beggar, in the mural he appears as a well-clad Daoist priest. (From *Yongle Gong Bihua Xuanji* [Beijing, 1958])

We see this in the seventh scene of the Chunyang Dian murals (YLG 7, *MTJ* 11), a story in which Lü disguises himself as a diseased beggar and asks for alms at a teashop (see figure). According to the written versions of this story, only one young girl is not disgusted by his appearance, and she proves willing to serve him, even drinking down the dregs from Lü's cup. Lü rewards her by allowing her to become a servant in an imperial family and to live to the ripe old age of 135. While the cartouche follows the *Miaotong Ji* in describing Lü's ugliness and filth *(yifu lanlou, xuerou gouwu),* the murals show him well dressed and handsome. No one in the teashop appears revolted by his appearance as he is being served by the young girl.

This aspect of Lü's iconography at the Yongle Gong may indicate an important change that had taken place in Lü's iconography over time. Although many Song-dynasty paintings tend to portray Lü as a more slovenly and unkempt individual (Toshio 1981:189–197, Liu Wensan 1981:139–140), this does not occur in later iconography, even though late imperial sources and modern folktales frequently describe him as a beggar or mendicant Daoist (Baldrian-Hussein 1986: 154–155,164; Lin 1933:13–15,45–46). This iconographical transformation may be due to the influence of Quanzhen Daoists: as they attempted to gain favor at the imperial court and enhance the overall prestige of their movement, they appear to have tried to avoid presenting one of their main patriarchs in an unflattering light.

Another factor behind this iconographical transformation involves the issue of "decorum," a concept Martin Powers borrowed from Ernst Gombrich in his work on Han-dynasty tomb art. In imperial China the importance of decorum (perhaps best translated as *li*) meant that those sponsoring or designing works of art were careful to ensure that the images depicted would be "normal and proper" for the environment and/or occasion (Powers 1991:62–65). It would therefore have been considered inappropriate to depict Lü as a beggar in a sacred site at the reputed place of his birth. This also explains why none of the five stories of his relationships with prostitutes in the *Miaotong Ji* was painted in the Chunyang Dian, even though in these versions he always resists sexual temptation and sometimes even converts the women in question to Daoism—as opposed to the popular stories below in which he sleeps with prostitutes and even attempts to seduce the Bodhisattva Guanyin!

The Interaction between Quanzhen and Local Representations of Lü

It is clear from the evidence presented above that the Quanzhen Daoists at the Yongle Gong actively attempted to promote their representations of Lü Dongbin, even while allowing imagery from the local popular traditions to enter the murals. I have also given examples indicating that not all worshipers may have "gotten the message," based on what they saw in the murals, as opposed to what a few might have been able to read in the cartouches. Further evidence that Quanzhen representations of Lü did not necessarily dominate others may be found in examining dramas, novels, and local folktales.

Most Song- and Jin-dynasty hagiographies of Lü Dongbin described above, including Yuan Congyi's stele at the Yongle Gong, maintained that Lü was converted to Daoism by an immortal, usually named as Zhongli Quan. Yuan's stele differs from other hagiographies, however, in stating that Zhongli Quan converted Lü after the latter had passed his *jinshi* exams. Early Quanzhen hagiographical works, such as Qin Zhian's *Jinlian Zhengzong Ji* (1241) (*TT* 75–76, *H-Y* 173), though they do not copy Yuan's stele verbatim, do follow his inscription in recording that Lü had passed his exams before encountering Zhongli Quan (1:5b–9a). However, by the time Miao Shanshi had begun to compose the *Miaotong Ji*, the story of Lü's conversion to Daoism had undergone a significant transformation, with new versions claiming that Zhongli Quan had used a dream to convert Lü. These new stories are known by the title *The Yellow Millet Dream (Huangliang Meng)*.

The Yellow Millet Dream is the second scene portrayed in the Chunyang Dian murals, the cartouche being an abbreviated version of the second story by that name in Miao Shanshi's *Miaotong Ji* (*H-Y* 305:1:5a–6b).[16] According to the cartouche:

> In the year 810, our lord emperor stayed at an inn while journeying to Changan to take part in the examinations. There he met a strange-looking man, who attempted to entice him to become a Daoist. [Lü] replied: "Let me first earn an official post and bring honor to my family. After that, it won't be too late to follow you." [Lü] then felt sleepy, and the immortal gave him a pillow to rest his head on. [Lü dreamed] that he had attained the top rank in the exams and become an official, enjoying wealth and fame for forty years. Later however he ended up [being disgraced and] losing his wealth and family. At that point he awoke, only to find the man laughing beside him, saying: "The millet is not done and you have already dreamed a lifetime." [Lü] bowed to the man and asked his name. He replied: "The immortal Zhongli Quan, style-name Yunfang," and promptly flew away. Lü returned home in a state of great disappointment.

The third through eighth stories of the *Miaotong Ji* go on to describe how Zhongli Quan revealed himself to Lü a second time and accepted him as his disciple. He then took Lü into the mountains with him, instructing him in internal alchemy and subjecting him to a series of five tests (some later versions maintain there were ten tests), which Lü was able to pass and become an immortal. Some of these stories are included in the fourth and twenty-first scenes of the Chunyang Dian murals. The overall popularity of the *Yellow Millet Dream* story may be determined by the fact that later *Daoist Canon* accounts, as well as Ming-dynasty novels, invariably associate Lü's enlightenment with a dream, regardless of whether he is said to have passed the examinations or not.[17]

What could account for this transformation of Lü's hagiography? It appears that this occurred because people began to confuse Lü Dongbin with the character Old Man Lü (Lü Weng) from the late Tang story "The World inside a Pillow" *(Zhenzhong Ji)* composed by Shen Jiji (Katz 1994). The confusion as to whether Lü had passed or failed his examinations and whether he had been enlightened through a dream persisted throughout late imperial times. For example, the 1629, 1734, and 1892 editions of the Shanxi provincial gazetteer *(Shanxi Tongzhi)* state that Lü failed the examinations; yet the latter two editions also list him among those who had passed the examinations during the Tang![18] The biography of Lü in the Puzhou prefectural gazetteer *(Puzhou Fuzhi)* does state that he had passed the examinations, yet his name is not listed with those who had.[19] In addition to this, the late Ming Daoist work entitled *The Record of the Patriarch Lü (Lüzu Zhi)* contains *both* Shen Jiji's story and a description of Lü's having been converted by Zhongli Quan following a dream (H-Y 1473:1:3b–4b,15a–16a).

It is likely that this version of Lü's hagiography became more popular following the publication and, more important, the performance of the *Yellow Millet Dream* drama (in the *zaju* form), which was written by Ma Zhiyuan (1260–1325) (Yang 1958:3–10). As Ma and Miao were contemporaries, it is difficult to state with certainty which work influenced the other, or whether they were written independently based on a third version of the story that was already circulating widely. Be that as it may, both their versions of Lü's hagiography represent an important change in representations of Lü that took place during the Yuan dynasty.

A total of six Yuan *zaju* featuring Lü Dongbin have survived; they form part of a class of operas referred to by scholars such as David Hawkes as "deliverance plays" (Hawkes 1981:153–170). Such dramas were frequently performed during festivals on stages that were part of a temple complex (Liao 1989:82–95, Liu Nianci 1973:58–65). As just such a stage was located on the northern side of the Wuji Men (facing the temples inside), it is highly likely that dramas like Ma Zhiyuan's *Yellow Millet Dream* were performed at the Yongle Gong on Lü's birthday or other Daoist holidays.

The description of Lü's encounter with Zhongli Quan in this drama is similar to that in the *Miaotong Ji,* though the former places more emphasis on the joys of immortality, while the latter stresses knowledge of internal alchemy. Take, for example, this passage of Ma's *Yellow Millet Dream:*

> [Zhongli Quan to Lü:] There are many ways to enjoy life. Listen to the pleasures we immortals relish. [Sings] We pick our own flowers and make our own wines. With a cup in my hand, I face the green mountains alone. And at leisure I ride my red-crowned crane soaring high and low. When I am drunk, I return home—my robes brushing past the pine branches along the way. The moon is high, the breeze free, and notes from my iron flute scatter the clouds. Renounce the world and follow me.[20]

Despite the potential popularity of representations of deities presented in dramatic performances, if we examine folktales about Lü that circulated at Yongle, we find that *none* of the stories describing Lü's conversion by means of a dream appears to have had a significant influence on local representations of him. Yongle was located in Puzhou Prefecture, so the fact that Lü's hagiography in the 1754 edition of the Puzhou gazetteer follows Yuan Congyi's stele inscription might reflect the persistence of that version, at least among literate members of the local populace. However, I believe it would be best not to overestimate the influence of Yuan's stele on the majority of the populace in light of the two local folktales I will now describe.

The first folktale differs sharply from all the hagiographies discussed above in presenting Lü as a poor scholar who tried to steal food for his wife so that she might replenish her strength after giving birth to a son; this, despite the fact that all the sources mentioned above state that Lü was single, while in some Daoist versions he even refuses to marry. The text of the folktale is as follows:

> The immortal Lü Dongbin was a poor scholar. One year, his son was born. Lü thought to himself: "My wife is taking her one-month recuperation period [literally "sitting for a month" *(zuo yuezi)*], yet we can't afford to buy eggs. It would be nice to buy some sauces to flavor our food, but we can't afford those either. What should I do? Buy some? No money. Borrow money? I'd never be able to pay it back." The more he thought the more powerless he felt. To have his wife eat their usual poor fare made him deeply ashamed . . . [Lü then comes up with the idea of stealing some sauces from his wealthy neighbor.]

... That night, Lü dug a hole [to the neighbor's storehouse], entered, and lifted the lid of one of the jars. He dipped his gourd in when he suddenly heard a "Crack!" which scared him half to death. He pulled back his hand only to find that the top of the gourd had been cut off, leaving only the bottom half. Oh no! He had been discovered! Lü felt both scared and ashamed, his face turning a bright red. It turned out that his neighbor had heard him digging the tunnel, and waited for him with knife in hand [which he used to slice up the gourd]. Happily his neighbor didn't scold him, thus saving him some face. But, Lü thought: "Even if he hasn't scolded me can he help talking about it? ... How will I dare show my face again?" The more he thought things over, the more he felt he couldn't stay at home. He made up his mind to go away and wander in the world [literally "rivers and lakes" *(jianghu)*]. [The story goes on to tell how Lü's son passed the exams. Lü went home to see him, but the son didn't recognize the father. Lü then wrote a poem revealing his identity and left for good.][21]

The second folktale, told by Lü himself (disguised as a Daoist) to a worshiper whose elderly friend he heals, reveals a different representation of Lü as a married man. As the Daoist (Lü) states:

Dongbin originally had the surname Li and given name Qiong, style name Boyu. In his later years he devoted himself to studying the Dao, abandoning his four children and taking his wife (whose family name was Jin) to lead a spiritual life together.[22] The two of them lived in a mountain cave. Because they had two mouths to feed, Li changed his name to Lü [because the character is composed of two mouth radicals] and his style name to Dongbin [literally "guest in a cave"]. Later his wife died, leaving Lü all alone. He then assumed the Daoist name Chunyang (Lu et al. 1987:73).

Guides inform visitors to the Yongle Gong today that Lü cultivated the Dao in the mountains with his wife at his side, and that the surname Lü is a pun on the expression "newly married couple" (*xiao liangkou,* literally "two little mouths"; Zhang 1984:277). The Yongle people's belief that Lü had a wife may have had a historical basis, because the grave at the Yongle Gong said to house Lü's remains actually contains the bones of a man and a woman, whom archaeologists assume to have been husband and wife (Li Fengshan 1960:25). The question of whether these two are Lü and his wife will probably remain an unsolved mystery.

It is important to note that both these folktales resolve an important issue that is largely ignored by Daoist compilers of Lü's hagiography: filial piety. In all *Daoist Canon* works, Lü is said to have refused to marry and father descendants for his family. The sources do not mention whether or not he was an only son, but in any case his actions went against the traditional Chinese view that the most unfilial of all acts was to be childless. Many of the deities in this volume, such as those described by Steven Sangren and Brigitte Baptandier, also failed to live up to this ideal. In Lü's case, some of his worshipers resolved this conflict in folktales by endowing him with a wife and children.

However, Lü never became a fully "orthodox" deity. There were also stories circulating in the area around the Yongle Gong describing Lü's misadventures with prostitutes. The *Miaotong Ji* contains five stories in which Lü encounters prostitutes, but in these he resembles a latter-day Vimalakirti, resisting the temptations of the flesh and sometimes even being able to convert the prostitute who attempts to seduce him. Quite a different view of Lü's relationship with members of the opposite sex emerges in Ming popular novels, however, particularly in stories describing his affair with the courtesan Bai Mudan. Both the *Record of the Flying Sword* (Deng 1987: 312–315) and the *Journey to the East* (Wu 1985:42–44) contain this story, which states that one day Lü saw Bai Mudan and was struck by her beauty, transforming himself into a scholar and subsequently seducing her. As an adept of the arts of the bedchamber *(fangzhong shu)*, he refrained from ejaculating while being able to absorb Bai's *yin* essence, enabling him to absorb her *yin* and replenish his *yang* *(caiyin buyang)*. After many such encounters Bai grew progressively weaker until learning that she could make Lü ejaculate by tickling him during intercourse. Bai thereupon used this method to force Lü to ejaculate, which in turn prompted him to realize his error in seducing her and return to the path of self-cultivation. The Bai Mudan stories closely resemble accounts about the sexual encounters of the eccentric Buddhist monk Jigong, discussed by Meir Shahar in this volume. Lü's romantic misadventures do not merely extend to prostitutes: other stories even portray him as attempting (unsuccessfully) to seduce the Bodhisattva Guanyin (Lin 1933:62–64)!

The sexual aspects of the Bai Mudan story seem to have been edited out of more recent versions. A comic strip in the 1984 edition of the journal *Shanxi Minjian Wenxue* portrays Lü as flirting with Bai in order to convince her to steal a pin from her mistress the Queen Mother of the West, which Lü uses to exorcise a mountain demon. A novelette found near Ruicheng also recounts this and other heroic exploits of Lü and Bai. It describes them as having a close but generally platonic friendship and does not deal with the sexual nature of their relationship (Lu 1987:163–224).

There is, however, a more negative side to Lü Dongbin as a dashing young immortal: his jealousy of young lovers, which stems from his "failures" with Guanyin and Bai Mudan. Even in modern-day Taiwan, few couples dare to visit the Zhinan Gong (also known as the Xiangong Miao), a very popular temple to Lü located in the mountains south of Taipei. The reason for this is their fear that Lü will cause their relationship to fall apart. Even among those people who do not appear to know the story of Lü and Bai, a belief persists that Lü is a deity who is not fond of happy lovers.

These humorous and irreverent depictions of Lü contrast sharply with hagiographies in the *Daoist Canon,* which consistently portray him as an intent and serious immortal. Even in the stories where he gets drunk or behaves eccentrically, he is said to have done so in order to test a certain individual before enlightening him; such acts are not viewed as a sign of inadequacies in Lü's self-cultivation. The novels and folktales described here show Lü in quite a different light. In these tales he makes mistakes, gets into trouble, but also has fun. He is a more fallible character, but at the same time appears more human and endearing. Take, for example, this story recorded by Lin Lan, which describes how Lü and another member of the Eight Immortals, Li Tieguai, attempted to trick a clever mooch named Li Guangda, who always drank with others but never paid his share of the bill. Lü and Tieguai drank with Li, but then ordered a bowl of broth and proposed that each person should contribute to making a bowl of soup. Tieguai promptly cut off his nose and added it to the broth, whereupon Lü sliced off his ears. When it came to be Li Guangda's turn however, he merely pulled out three of his hairs and threw them in the bowl, saying that they would make up the noodles in the soup. The two immortals had nothing for it but quickly to eat up and leave (Lin 1933:56–59).

Folktales and novels are a particularly valuable source for understanding the late imperial cult of Lü Dongbin because they present a view of him rarely found in sources such as the *Daoist Canon,* stele inscriptions, or local gazetteers. Those sources never show Lü or any of the other Eight Immortals in a humorous or fallible light, perhaps due to the authors' own sense of "decorum." In contrast, folktales and novels like the *Journey to the East* portray Lü and the Eight Immortals as a rollicking, fun-loving bunch. Such a range of representations also appears to have characterized the cult of Jigong, as Buddhist monks and members of sectarian groups tended to downplay eccentricities that are emphasized in the popular tradition.

Conclusion

The various stories about Lü Dongbin presented above reveal that *more than one* Lü Dongbin existed in the minds of the late imperial Chinese. As a result, different representations were able to coexist and interact, in a process I have referred to elsewhere as reverberation *(Katz 1990, 1994, 1995b).* Some groups, such as Quanzhen Daoist priests, were more active in promoting the representations they embraced, but even the use of the visual medium, accessible to all Chinese, which the Chunyang Dian murals provided did not guarantee that their representations would gain widespread acceptance.

Although in this essay I have stressed the differences between various representations of Lü Dongbin, it is important to realize that they all share one thing: the nonbureaucratic metaphor. This might come as a surprise to those who view the Daoist pantheon as a supernatural bureaucracy. It is certainly true that nobody who has witnessed a Daoist ritual, with its stacks of memorials being sent off to deities governing all manner of celestial and infernal posts, could possibly overlook the importance of the bureaucratic metaphor in Daoist religion. Yet there are other facets of Daoism besides the supernatural bureaucracy and elaborate hierarchies of spiritual beings, one of the most ancient and perhaps most important being the cults to the immortals.

The Chinese people were worshiping feathered beings called immortals long before the Daoist religion developed at the end of the Han dynasty. Such spirits are described in an ancient collection of legends entitled the *Biographies of the Immortals* (*Liexian Zhuan*, translated by Max Kaltenmark), which dates back to the Han dynasty as well. Legends concerning immortals have appeared throughout Chinese history, from the "esoteric biographies" *(neizhuan)* of the Shangqing sect composed during the Six Dynasties, to the poems Tang literati wrote about Elder Mao (Mao Xianweng), to the sources on Lü described above. It is also important to note that many immortals, inlcuding Elder Mao, Lü Dongbin, and later Zhang Sanfeng, were both literary figures and also the objects of popular worship.[23]

The late Anna Seidel has pointed out that cults to immortals "may help us *not* to extend the very helpful insight into the bureaucratic character of the Chinese supernatural world beyond its proper limits" (Seidel 1989–1990:248). She has further speculated that "perhaps one function of the immortals was to counterbalance [the Chinese] obsession with rank and all-inclusive hierarchies" (Seidel 1989–1990:258). While further research is needed to determine whether immortals like Lü Dongbin actually served as some sort of religious counterweight, Seidel is certainly correct in emphasizing that cults to immortals reveal that the Chinese supernatural world, like Chinese society itself, was highly diverse and complex, and cannot be encompassed by a single metaphor.

Such a conclusion can also help us better comprehend the interaction between Daoist and popular representations of Lü Dongbin.

Although Hymes' distinction between "clerical" and "lay" is of great value in studying Chinese religion, the representations these groups embrace may not always be distinguished based on competing vocabularies of bureaucracy and personal relations, as he argues elsewhere in this volume. In the first place, more than one "lay vocabulary" of Lü existed, as is apparent in the differing representations of him presented in gazetteers, stelae, dramas, and folktales. More important, no story about Lü—including those in the *Daoist Canon*—portrays him as a bureaucrat or as part of a supernatural bureaucracy. Al-though numerous representations of Lü did circulate throughout late imperial China, the differences between them center instead on the circumstances of his conversion to Daoism, his spiritual powers, and his morality. Cults to deities such as Lü Dongbin or Jigong—both of whom were very popular in late imperial China and continue to be widely worshiped on Taiwan today—reveal to us the limited value of the bureaucratic metaphor in describing Chinese religion. They also show that many deities enjoyed great popularity not because they conformed to common ethical values but because they challenged them.

Notes

1. The Yueyang sources have been translated and analyzed by Farzeen Baldrian-Hussein in her article on Lü's early hagiography (1986). See also Ang 1993, 1995, Ma 1986, and Pu 1936.

2. Literally "of uncommon style and bones" *(fenggu bufan)*. In Taiwan people believe that one must have the "bones" to become a Daoist priest (Schipper 1974:311).

3. Data on the temple's history may be found in Wang Shiren 1959 and Su 1962, 1963.

4. For a comparative perspective, consult Brown 1981, Duby 1981, Mitchell 1968, and Wilson 1983.

5. All statues referred to were destroyed during the Japanese occupation of north China, but have been rebuilt in recent years.

6. For more on Zhu's career and works, see Steinhardt 1987.

7. The *Miaotong Ji (MTJ)* can be found in *TT* 159, H-Y 305. For the *Record of the Patriarch Lü*, see: *TT* 1112–1113, H-Y 1473.

8. I would like to thank Martin Powers of the University of Michigan for introducing me to some important works on patronage, including his own prize-winning book. See Baxandall 1972, Goffen 1986, and Powers 1991.

9. This inscription was written on the day the murals were completed, the ninth day of the ninth lunar month, which is also the date of the Double Yang (Chongyang) festival. The murals may have been scheduled to be completed on this date not only because of its significance in the Chinese festival calendar, but also because Chongyang was the Daoist name of the Quanzhen sect founder Wang Zhe. Sacred works of art were often completed on holidays.

10. These titles are also included in the Ming Daoist encyclopedia entitled *The Jade Fascicles of Taiqing on the Ultimate Dao of the Celestial Sovereign (Tianhuang Zhidao Taiqing Yuce; TT* 1109–1111; *H-Y* 1472), which was composed by Zhu Quan (1378–1448) in 1444. This work lists *tidian* and *tiju* as being middle-ranking officials in Daoist temples, ranking just below the abbot (*guanzhu;* see *juan* 4).

11. Quanzhen beliefs and practices relating to the pursuit of immortality have been masterfully analyzed in Eskildsen 1989.

12. Some of Miao's sermons were recorded by his disciple Wang Zhidao in the *Great Case Studies in the Teachings of Profundity (Xuanjiao Da Gongan; TT* 734; *H-Y* 1057). See *juan xia* 15a–16a, for comments by Miao on Lü's success in self-cultivation using internal alchemy.

13. See the field report in *Wenwu Cankao Ziliao* 11 (1954):72.

14. For more on the relationship between patrons and artists in China, see Powers 1991:27–29,304–308,316–317,352.

15. Column 1 represents the 95 stories preserved in the *Miaotong Ji;* column 2, the 52 Chunyang Dian murals; column 3, the 37 murals based on the *Miaotong Ji;* and column 4, the 15 murals for which the source is unknown or not in the *Miaotong Ji*.

16. Unfortunately, much of this scene has been badly damaged, making its contents impossible to determine.

17. See, for example, *Supplemental Folios of a Comprehensive Mirror on Successive Generations of Perfected Transcendants and Those Who Embody the Dao (Lishi Zhenxian Tidao Tongjian Xubian; TT* 149, *H-Y* 297), 45:1a–3b; *The Scripture of Carefree Wandering and Emptiness (Xiaoyao Xujing; TT* 1081, *H-Y* 1453), 1a–2a; and *Lüzu Zhi,* 1:3b–4b, 15a–b. For the story in novels, see Wu 1985:36–37 and Deng 1987:294–295.

18. See *Shanxi Tongzhi* (1629), 26:20b; *Shanxi Tongzhi* (1734), 15:15b and 160:5a–13a; and *Shanxi Tongzhi* (1892), 14:14a and 160:19b–20a.

19. See *Puzhou Fuzhi* (1754), 14:18b–19b.

20. The entire drama was translated into English by Yen Yuan-shu for a special double issue on the Eight Immortals in the Taiwan magazine *Echo* 5(2–3) (1975):13–23,94. The passage I have translated is on p. 14.

21. See *Shanxi Minjian Wenxue* 3 (1984):12. There is also a story in the same journal depicting the Eight Immortals as thieves! See 29 (1986):24–26. The story of Lü caught stealing may also be found in the *Complete Collection of Chinese Folktales (Zhongguo Minjian Gushi Quanji* 1989:269–272).

22. The text uses the term for becoming a monk or nun, *chujia* (literally "leaving the family"), indicating that Lü and his wife maintained a celibate lifestyle.

23. For an overview of research on Daoist immortals, see Seidel 1989–1990:246–248.

Literature Cited

Ang, Isabelle. 1993. *Le culte du Lü Dongbin des origines jusqu'au début du XIVe siècle: Caractéristiques et transformations d'un saint immortel dans la Chine pré-moderne.* Ph.D. diss., University of Paris.

———. 1995. "Du taoïste-lettré itinérant au Saint immortel: Sources pour l'élaboration d'une hagiographie de Lü Dongbin." Paper presented at international conference on The Cult of Saints and the Cult of Sites: Sources of Chinese Local History and Hagiography. Paris, May 29–June 1.

Baldrian-Hussein, Farzeen. 1986. "Lü Tung-pin in Northern Sung Literature."
    Cahiers d'Extrême Asie 2:133–169.
Baxandall, Michael. 1972. *Painting and Experience in Fifteenth-Century Italy.*
    Oxford and New York: Oxford University Press.
Boltz, Judith. 1987. *A Survey of Taoist Literature: Tenth to Seventeenth Centu-*
    ries. Berkeley: Institute of East Asian Studies.
Bo Songnian. 1986. *Zhongguo Nianhua Shi (A History of Chinese New Year's*
    Prints). Shenyang: Liaoning Meishu Chubanshe.
Brown, Peter. 1981. *The Cult of the Saints.* Chicago: University of Chicago
    Press.
Chen Bing. 1986. "Yuandai Jiangnan Daojiao" (Daoism in South China during
    the Yuan Dynasty). *Shijie Zongjiao Yanjiu (Research on World Religions)* 2:
    66–80.
Chen Yuan et al., eds. 1988. *Daojia Jinshi Lue (Abbreviated Collection of Daoist*
    Epigraphy). Beijing: Wenwu Chubanshe.
Deng Zhimo (fl. 1566–1618). 1987. *Lüxian Feijian Ji (Record of the Immortal*
    Lü's Flying Sword). In *Baxian Quanshu (Compendium of the Eight Immor-*
    tals). Shenyang: Chunfeng Wenyi Chubanshe.
Duby, Georges. 1981. *The Age of the Cathedrals: Art and Society, 980–1420.*
    Translated by Eleanor Levieux and Barbara Thompson. Chicago: University
    of Chicago Press.
Eskildsen, Stephen E. 1989. *The Beliefs and Practices of Early Ch'üan-chen Tao-*
    ism. M.A. thesis, University of British Columbia.
Freedberg, David. 1989. *The Power of Images: Studies in the History and*
    Theory of Response. Chicago: University of Chicago Press.
Fyfe, Gordon, and John Law. 1988. *Picturing Power: Visual Depiction and*
    Social Relations. London: Routledge.
Goffen, Rona. 1986. *Piety and Patronage in Renaissance Florence: Bellini,*
    Titian, and the Franciscans. New Haven: Yale University Press.
Grootaers, Willem A. 1952. "The Hagiography of the Chinese God Chen-wu."
    Folklore Studies 11(2):139–181.
Guo Rongsheng. 1991 and 1992. "Lidai Shanxi Shuhuajia" (Painters and Callig-
    raphers in Shanxi's History). *Shanxi Wenxian* (Shanxi Historical Docu-
    ments) 38:61–90 and 39:38–65.
Hawkes, David. 1981. "Quanzhen Plays and Quanzhen Masters." *Bulletin de*
    l'Ecole Française d'Extrême Orient 69:153–170.
Hucker, Charles O. 1985. *A Dictionary of Official Titles in Imperial China.*
    Stanford: Stanford University Press.
Igarashi Kenryu. 1938. *Dōkyō sōrin Taiseigu shi (Gazetteer of the Daoist Public*
    Monastery Taiqing Palace). Reprinted 1986. Tokyo: Kokusho Kankokai.
Jagchid, Sechin. 1982. "Chinese Buddhism and Taoism during the Mongolian
    Rule of China." *Mongolian Studies* 6:61–98.
Jing Anning. 1993. *Yongle Palace: The Transformation of the Daoist Pantheon*
    during the Yuan Dynasty (1260–1368). Ph.D. diss., Princeton University.
———. 1995. "A Pictorial Hagiography of Lü Dongbin." Paper presented at
    international conference on the Cult of Saints and the Cult of Sites: Sources
    of Chinese Local History and Hagiography. Paris, May 29–June 1.
Johnson, David. 1985. "Communication, Class and Consciousness in Late Impe-
    rial China." In *Popular Culture in Late Imperial China,* edited by David

Johnson, Andrew Nathan, and Evelyn Rawski, 34–72. Berkeley: University of California Press.

———. 1990. "Scripted Performances in Chinese Culture: An Approach to the Analysis of Popular Literature." *Hanxue yanjiu (Chinese Studies)* 8(1): 37–55.

Katz, Paul. 1990. "Wen Ch'iung—The God of Many Faces." *Hanxue yanjiu* 8(1):183–219.

———. 1991. "Images of the Immortal: Lü Tung-pin in the Yung-lo Kung Murals." Paper presented at the Chinese Popular Culture Project Spring Regional Seminar. Berkeley, Ca., May 11.

———. 1993. "The Religious Function of Temple Murals in Imperial China— The Case of the Yung-lo Kung." *Journal of Chinese Religions* 21:45–68.

———. 1994. "The Interaction between Ch'üan-chen Taoism and Local Cults: A Case Study of the Yung-lo Kung." In *Proceedings of the International Conference on Popular Beliefs and Chinese Culture,* 201–250. Taipei: Center for Chinese Studies.

———. 1995a. "Text and Textuality: Temple Inscriptions in the Study of Chinese Local Cults." Paper presented at international conference on The Cult of Saints and the Cult of Sites: Sources of Chinese Local History and Hagiography. Paris, May 29–June 1.

———. 1995b. *Demon Hordes and Burning Boats. The Cult of Marshal Wen in Late Imperial Chekiang.* Albany: SUNY Press.

Kubo Noritada. 1968. "Prolegomena on the Study of the Controversies between Buddhists and Taoists in the Yuan Period." *Memoirs of the Research Department of the Tōyō Bunko* 26:39–61.

Liao Ben. 1989. "Song-Yuan Xitai Yiji" (Remains of Song-Yuan Stages). *Wenwu (Cultural Artifacts)* 7:82–95.

Li Fengshan. 1960. "Shanxi Ruicheng Yongle Gong Jiuzhi Song Defang, Pan Dechong he "Lüzu" Mu Fajue Baogao" (Excavation Report of the Graves of Song Defang, Pan Dechong, and "Patriarch Lü" from the Former Site of the Yongle Palace [now at] Ruicheng, Shanxi). *Kaogu (Archaeology)* 8:22–25.

Li Mengcun and Lin Hongyao. 1986. "Yongle Gong yu Quanzhen Jiao" (The Yongle Palace and Quanzhen Daoism). In *Chin Tai Yu Fanggu (In Search of Ancient Relics of North China)* 303–316. Taiyuan: Shanxi Renmin Wenxue Chubanshe.

Lin Lan. 1933. *Lü Dongbin de Gushi (Folktales about Lü Dongbin).* Shanghai: Beixin Shuju.

Liu Nianci. 1973. "Cong Jianguo Hou Faxian de Yixie Wenwu Kan Jin-Yuan Zaju Zai Pingyang Diqu de Fazhan" (The Growth of Jin-Yuan *Zaju* in Pingyang as Seen in Artifacts Discovered after 1949). *Wenwu* 3:58–65.

Liu Wensan. 1981. *Taiwan Shenxiang Yishu (Iconography of Taiwan's Deities).* Taipei: Yishujia Chubanshe.

Li Xianzhou. 1983. "Yongji Gumiao—Yongle Gong" (Yongji's Ancient Temple —The Yongle Palace). *Shanxi Wenxian (Shanxi Historical Documents)* 22: 101–105.

Lu Shizheng et al., eds. 1987. *Yongle Gong de Chuanshuo (Legends of the Yongle Palace).* Ruicheng: Zhongguo Luyou Chubanshe.

Ma Xiaohong. 1986. "Lü Dongbin Xinyang Shuoyuan" (The Origins of the Cult of Lü Dongbin). *Shijie Zongjiao Yanjiu (Research on World Religions)* 3: 79–95.

Mitchell, Ann. 1968. *Cathedrals of Europe.* Middlesex: Hamlyn Publishing Group.

Mori Yuria. 1992. "*Junyō teikun shinka myōtō ki* ni mieru Zenshinkyō na tokuchō ni tsuite." (Special Features of Quanzhen Daoism as Seen in *The Divine Transformations and Miraculous Powers of the Lord Emperor of Purified Yang). Tōyō no Shisō to Shūkyō (Thought and Religion of the East)* 9:31–47.

Ono Shihei. 1968. "Ro Dōhin densetsu ni tsuite" (A Study of Legends about Lü Dongbin). *Tōhō shūkyō (Eastern Religions)* 32:52–69.

Pan Xiezi. 1958. "Yongle Gong Yuandai Bihua Yishu" (Yuan Dynasty Mural Art as Seen in the Yongle Palace). *Zhongguo Hua (Chinese Painting)* 2:61–62.

Powers, Martin J. 1991. *Art and Political Expression in Early China.* New Haven: Yale University Press.

Pu Jiangqing. 1936. "Baxian Kao" (An Examination of the Eight Immortals). *Qinghua Xuebao (Qinghua Journal of Chinese Studies)* 11(1):89–136.

Puzhou Fuzhi (Puzhou Prefectural Gazetteer). 1754 edition.

Qin Lingyun. 1958. "Yongle Gong Wuji Men Bihua Tansuo." (An Examination of the Wuji Men Murals at the Yongle Palace). *Zhongguo Hua* 2:59–60.

———. 1960. *Zhongguo Bihua Yishu (Chinese Mural Art).* Beijing: Renmin Meishu Chubanshe.

Rawski, Evelyn. 1979. *Education and Popular Literacy in Ch'ing China.* Ann Arbor: University of Michigan Press.

Ren Jiyu, ed. 1990. *Zhongguo Daojiao Shi (History of Chinese Daoism).* Shanghai: Shanghai Renmin Chubanshe.

Rossabi, Morris. 1988. *Khubilai Khan: His Life and Times.* Berkeley: University of California Press.

Schipper, Kristofer. 1974. "The Written Memorial in Taoist Ceremonies." In *Religion and Ritual in Chinese Society,* edited by Arthur Wolf, 309–324. Stanford: Stanford University Press.

Seidel, Anna. 1970. "A Taoist Immortal of the Ming Dynasty: Chang San-feng." In *Self and Society in Ming Thought,* edited by William Theodore deBary, 483–531. New York: Columbia University Press.

———. 1989–1990. "Chronicle of Taoist Studies in the West, 1950–1990." *Cahiers d'Extrême Asie* 5:223–347.

Shanxi Tongzhi (Shanxi Provincial Gazetteer). 1629, 1734, and 1892 editions.

Steinhardt, Nancy S. 1987. "Zhu Haogu Reconsidered: A New Date for the ROM (Royal Ontario Museum) Painting and the Southern Shanxi Buddhist-Taoist Style." *Artibus Asiae* 48(1/2):11–16.

Su Bai. 1962. "Yongle Gong Chuangjian Shiliao Nianbian" (Chronicle of Historical Materials on the Construction of the Yongle Palace). *Wenwu* 4(5): 80–87.

———. 1963. "Yongle Gong Diaocha Riji" (Diary of Field Investigations at the Yongle Palace). *Wenwu* 8:53–64.

Thiel, Joseph. 1961. "Der Streit der Buddhisten und Taoisten zur Mongolenzeit." *Monumenta Serica* 20:1–81.

Toshio Ebine. 1981. "Iconographic Problems on the Group of Figure Compositions Titled Lü Tung-pin." In *International Symposium on the Conservation and Restoration of Cultural Property: Interregional Influences in East Asian Art History,* 189–197. Tokyo: Tokyo National Research Institute of Cultural Properties.

Wang Chang-an. 1963a. "Chunyang, Chongyang Dian de Bihua" (The Murals of the Chunyang and Chongyang Halls). *Wenwu* 8:40–43.

———. 1963b. "Yongle Gong Bihua Tiji Luwen" (Transcriptions of the Cartouches on the Yongle Palace Murals). *Wenwu* 8:66–78.

Wang Shiren. 1959. "Yongle Gong de Yuandai Jianzhu he Bihua" (Yuan Dynasty Architecture and Murals at the Yongle Palace). *Wenwu Cankao Ziliao (Reference Materials on Cultural Artifacts)* 9:32–33.

Wang Shucun. 1982. *Zhongguo Minjian Huajue (Chinese Folk Painting Formulas)*. Shanghai: Renmin meishu chubanshe.

———. 1991. *Xichu Nianhua (New Year's Prints about Dramas)*. Taipei: Hansheng chubanshe.

Watson, James. 1985. "Standardizing the Gods: The Promotion of T'ien Hou ('Empress of Heaven') along the South China Coast, 960–1960." In *Popular Culture in Late Imperial China,* edited by David Johnson, Andrew Nathan, and Evelyn Rawski, 292–324. Berkeley: University of California Press.

White, William C. 1940. *Chinese Temple Frescoes*. Toronto: University of Toronto Press.

Wilson, Stephen. 1983. "Cults of Saints in the Churches of Central Paris." In *Saints and Their Cults,* edited by Stephen Wilson, pp. 233–260. Cambridge: Cambridge University Press.

Wong Siu Hon. 1988. *Mingdai Daoshi Zhang Sanfeng (Zhang Sanfeng: A Ming Dynasty Daoist)*. Taipei: Xuesheng Shuju.

Wu Yuan-tai (fl. 1522–1565). 1985. *Dongyou Ji (Journey to the East)*. In *Siyou Ji (The Four Journeys)*. Harbin: Beifang Wenxue Chubanshe.

Xu Bangda. 1956. "Cong Bihua Fuben Xiaoyang Shuo Dao Liang Juan Song Hua—*Chaoyuan Xianzhang Tu*" (A Discussion of Two Scrolls of the *Chaoyuan Xianzhang Tu* Based on a Mural Sketchbook). *Wenwu Cankao Ziliao* 2:57–58.

Yang, Richard L. S. 1958. "A Study of the Origin of the Legend of the Eight Immortals." *Oriens Extremis* 5(1):1–22.

Yoshioka Yoshitoyo. 1979. "Taoist Monastic Life." In *Facets of Taoism,* edited by Holmes Welch and Anna Seidel, 229–252. New Haven: Yale University Press.

Yu Jianhua. 1958. *Zhongguo Bihua (Chinese Murals)*. Beijing: Zhongguo Gudian Yishu Chubanshe.

Zeng Jiabao. 1989. "Yongle Gong Chunyang Dian Bihua Tiji Shiyi—Jian Ji Zhu Haogu Ziliao Buchong" (Explanations of the Meaning of the Cartouches in Yongle Palace's Chunyang Hall—With Additional Sources on Zhu Haogu). *Meishu Yanjiu (Research on Fine Arts)* 55:44–48.

Zhai Zongzhu. 1987. *Zongjiao Meishu Gailun (Introduction to Religious Art)*. Hefei: Anhui Meishu Chubanshe.

Zhang Chongyou. 1984. *Zhongguo Mingsheng Guji Quwen Lu (Interesting Tales about China's Famous Ancient Sites and Monuments)*. N.P.: Neimenggu Renmin Chubanshe, 1984.

Zheng Suchun. 1987. *Quanzhen Jiao yu Da Mengguguo Dishi (Quanzhen Daoism and the Mongol Imperial House)*. Taibei: Xuesheng shuju.

Zhongguo Minjian Gushi Quanji (Complete Collection of Chinese Folktales). 1989. Shanxi volume. Taipei: Yuanliu Chubanshe.

The Lady Linshui: How a Woman Became a Goddess

BRIGITTE BAPTANDIER

The Cult of the Lady Linshui

Sources, Origins, and Particulars

The cult of Lady Linshui, named Chen Jinggu and revered under the title *Shunyi furen*,[1] is one of the three biggest cults in Fujian.[2] She is revered there as the protecting goddess of the people, especially of women and children, and also as the mistress of the local Lüshan ritual tradition, also called Sannai. This cult extends throughout northern Fujian, and one finds it equally prevalent in southern Zhejiang. It is very active in Taiwan, where it emigrated during the eighteenth century, in Southeast Asia, and in other foreign countries.[3]

The cult goes back to the Tang dynasty. The Lady herself was once a woman—born, according to certain sources, in 766 C.E., which corresponds with the date of her base temple, constructed in 792. According to other legendary sources, she was born in 904, which is a way to associate her life with the history of the Min kingdom, to which the cult has close connections.[4] These two versions undoubtedly refer to two different stages of the same cult, a point to which I shall return. The official canonization and inscription on the Register of Sacrifices took place under the Song, between 1241 and 1253, at the request of the prefect of Fuzhou, Chen Qinsou. The cult is still very active, with its rejuvenation occurring as much in its place of origin as in Taiwan, where the biggest part of its emigrant community lives.

Three essential points thus characterize the past and present of this cult: its presentation as closely connected with the history and territory of a kingdom, its representation of a local shamanistic tradition, and its female deity, in this kingdom, mistress of this ritual tradition.

We possess various sources, as much historical as legendary, concerning the Lady and the origins of the cult. The Lady appears in the local monographs of the Min, of Fuzhou, of Gutian, and of other relevant districts, where laconic elements about the biography of a local shaman and more documented data on her later miracles and her cult are presented. Her historical existence is taken for granted by everybody. In 1993 a conference was organized by the Association of International Cultural Exchanges, the Association of Research on Civilization, and the Association of Research on Popular Literature and Arts of Fujian (Fuzhou, Gutian, and Ningde) called "Research into Chen Jinggu's Cult (Chen Jinggu wenhua yanjiu). One of its major topics was the question of how she, as a human being, became a goddess. Her most important exploits—the killing of the serpent, a ritual to bring rain, her participation in Min kingdom affairs—were not actually questioned, which obliges us to consider two periods of origin for her cult: in 766 and 904.

Apart from the monographs that I have mentioned, the life and legend of Chen Jinggu are well documented in another kind of literature. These are the mirabilia and hagiographic documents, like the various *Researches on Gods (Soushen Ji),* or the *Miscellaneous Documents on Min (Min Zaji),* or the *Monograph of the 36 Dames (36 Pojie zhi).*

The *Mindu Bieji (Historical Legends of the Min),* a collection of local legends fictionalized and compiled under the Qing, dedicates numerous chapters of its epic retelling to her. This book was reprinted in 1987. It has been a great success in North Fujian, where it immediately sold out and was quoted by everybody as a reference book on the subject.

More specifically, another kind of literature is totally dedicated to her. These are "novels," *xiaoshuo,* such as the *Linshui Pingyao* (Pacification of the Demons at Linshui) or the *Furen Quanben (Complete Works on the Lady).* They were published in Fujian as well as in Taiwan. Another novel, *Chen Shisi Qizhuan* (Strange Story of Chen Shisi), seems to be a secondhand version of the legends, published in Zhejiang (Ye 1985). These are not actually novels, that is to say, fictions. They appear as collections of the most important episodes of the legend of Chen Jinggu. They faithfully follow the mythological episodes of her life and exploits, without personal innovation from the anonymous authors. People consider them as the story of her life. Divided into *juan* and chapters *(hui),* those sequences of the epic story have been and are still used as models for wall paintings and engravings that retell her story in temples. This is the case in Fujian, where—apart from the base temple whose wall paintings were designed, and are now restored, according to this model—I was able to visit many smaller temples presenting such wall frescoes with the same division by *hui,* the same episodes and titles. This is the case in Tainan too, where the main temple has just been rebuilt (1987–1989) and where rich golden engravings have been executed according to the *Linshui Pingyao's* seventeen chapters (Berthier 1988).

As Shahar discusses elsewhere in this volume, these *xiaoshuo,* once written to be sold in markets and bookshops, are now treasured by people in the temples. I have been given several copies of the *Linshui Pingyao* in temples in Taiwan. I have myself given one copy to the temple in Gutian, on the recommendation of the man who did the engraving of the Tainan temple, because they were looking for a model, a *huaben,* to restore the wall paintings in Gutian. Considering this book as a valuable gift to keep the orthodox form of the legend in memory, some Taiwanese participants at the 1993 conference brought several copies, which they generously gave to the organizers and to me. In addition, believers in the temple of Tainan gave me, two years ago, a copy of the book that I had myself given previously to the temple of Gutian, saying that it was an important document they had just brought back from the mother temple. The book goes back and forth: it is the warrant of the memory and proper transmission and propagation of the cult.

There is also a body of pious literature *(shanshu)* emanating from the temples, such as *Danai Lingjing* (The Sacred Book of the Great Lady) and *Yulin Shunyi Dutuochan Ruozhenjing* (Authentic Book on the Abortion of Yulin Shunyi) of the Linshui temple in Gutian or the *Sannai Furen Quanshi Zhenjing* (Authentic Book of Exhortation of the Three Ladies) of the Luyuansi in Taizhong. These works tell the story of the Lady and present the characters in her pantheon. They also furnish magical formulas, talismans, and ritual elements. Those documents given to people visiting the temples are certainly also an important element of the propagation of the cult.

A song in the fashion of storytelling, the *Furen Changci* (The Ballad of the Lady), and a play with eleven scenes, the *Chen Danai Tuotai* (The Abortion of the Great Lady Chen) (Zhuan, n.d.), complete these works. The play was still performed in Fujian some years ago, and people there wish to perform it again, after a long period of prohibition. It had been forbidden because it was considered too "superstitious." This point is important. What does it mean to be "superstitious"? This was precisely one of the topics discussed at the conference in 1993. Most of the people there considered superstition to be what could not be true, that is, metaphor. Of course, for the faithful, it means that this play manifests the heart of the beliefs concerning Chen Jinggu, the foundation of her cult as a goddess, and thus what has to be transmitted about her. The play shows her apprenticeship in the shamanic arts in Lüshan, her exorcising of the demons of Min, her abortion, and her death while performing a ritual for the rain to fall. "Those are the reasons for the temples to exist," I have been told so many times. And of course, this does not fit very well the image of an orthodox, well-behaved historical character.

After this conference a book was published (1993) producing a kind of new, orthodox point of view on Chen Jinggu and her cult. Moreover, during the conference a new version of the play, more fictionalized and sometimes unfaithful to its actual meaning, was performed twice, for the first time in many years, once in Fuzhou and once in Gutian. It was a local event, which generated articles in the newspapers and attracted the presence of national television. Yet the people in both places felt that it was not the "real drama" of Chen Jinggu. Why? This was clearly shown to me by one of the shamans I know, and it was not only because of the modifications of the story. Having heard that the play was going to be performed, he came to the temple to attend it. But he saw nothing . . . because it was performed in the city theater. He was angry and disillusioned, and he told me that it was time to show me the actual play of Chen Jinggu— "the corpus of all the rituals she is able to perform as the master of the Lüshan tradition." Thus the play, the true one, is an efficacious ritual. It is impossible to perform it if you do not wish to enact what she does. In other words: the real drama of Chen Jinggu is the whole corpus of rituals of the Lüshan Sannai tradition, still performed in her name by her shamans and mediums. This is exactly what a medium of the Lady often told me, asking me: "What do you think I am doing? trance? theater? playing mad? I am Chen Jinggu." The texts of these rituals are, of course most precious to us to understand the process of her "civilization," to keep the Chinese term.[5]

The play is also part of the repertory of at least one theater group in Gaoxiong, Taiwan. A television series on Chen Jinggu also ran there during the 1980s, presenting a fictionalized version of her story, which, like the new play in Fujian, was not much appreciated by her shamans and mediums, even if many people watched it.

All these documents, of different epochs and different natures, give detailed access to the cult's life, its role in the society of imperial China (especially in the Min kingdom), through the character of this female shaman, Chen Jinggu.

Chen Jinggu's Story

Let me now introduce a brief synopsis of the legend of Chen Jinggu. The version of the legend that I give here follows the one given by her novels, which is also engraved on the walls of her temples and on the steles in front of them. It includes the short versions of the *Soushen Ji* and of the local monographs. Of course, it also follows the oral tradition, as transmitted to me (1980–1993) by people in both Fujian and Taiwan. It is in harmony with the play and ritual texts, too. The story of Chen Jinggu does not present major contradictions in its different versions. They just have more or fewer episodes and more or fewer glosses surrounding them. The contradictory features are rather to be found through the different aspects intrinsic to her own character, as we shall see. I present here the heart of her story, in order to expand on it below. It begins with the episode of the construction of the Wanan Bridge, which is built across an arm of the sea called Loyang, near the city of Quanzhou. It was actually built by the prefect Cai Xiang between 1054 and 1060, which indicates that this episode of the legend corresponds to a late period. It is nonetheless always mentioned as the origin. We can only conclude that the metaphoric elements here included are structurally indispensable to the modern cult.

It is said in the legend that when the prefect despaired of success in building the bridge, the goddess Guanyin decided to help him. She appeared on the waves of the arm of the indomitable sea, in a marvelous boat, rowed by none other than the local earth god. Anyone who could succeed in touching her by throwing a piece of money could marry her. The crowd filled the riverbanks, and money accumulated in the boat as people tried to reach this woman offered on the water in a game of nuptial penny-toss. A vegetable merchant touched her on the hair with a silver powder, under the good advice of Lü Dongbin, who had come to his aid. Like a mirage, it seemed to him, she disappeared. Horrified at this treason, the man threw himself in the water and drowned. But Guanyin sent his soul to be reincarnated at Gutian, where he became Liu Qi, a young literatus and magistrate. Then she bit her finger and spat a drop of blood in the water. Following mysterious paths in the water of the Min where it sailed, this drop arrived at the Lower Ford (Xiadu) at Fuzhou. A woman, Lady Ge, was doing her wash there. Wife of a magistrate, she was no longer young but nevertheless had not yet conceived children. Along the banks of the Min, in the tumultuous waters, this small red pearl—resembling, it is said, a small strawberry or prune—drifted in the water toward this woman with her sterile womb. Attracted and absent-minded, she took and swallowed this blood—the blood of Guanyin. Chen Jinggu was born from this, to Lady Ge, in the Chen family of Xiadu.

The hair of Guanyin, which the man had hit, turned white and fell in the water. This was hardly wasted either. It became a white serpent, a female python. It is said that Guanyin bore Chen Jinggu to dominate this serpent at the expense of her own life, in a premonition of the misdoings of this demon, animated itself by the desires of the future Liu Qi. Blood and hair of Guanyin, woman and demon serpent, marriage and desire, they were both ready to marry, in their own manner, Liu Qi.

Chen Jinggu grew up in Xiadu as a model child. But when she was about fifteen or seventeen, she refused to marry Liu Qi. She was taken by Liangnü, servant of Guanyin, to Mount Lü (Lüshan), to learn the magical arts. She stayed there for three years and was taught by Xu Zhenjun. She learned everything but the art of protecting childbirth, still persisting in her refusal to marry. Then she returned to Fuzhou. During the two years following her return, she acted as a shaman, exorcising the kingdom of Min of its demons and creating her own shamanic community of ancient demons she had tamed and Daoist/shaman friends she met during her trips. These included her two sworn sisters, Lin Jiuniang and Li Sanniang.

During her life Chen Jinggu battled the demon serpent three times, with each battle corresponding to the king giving her a new title. The first time, she cut the serpent in three pieces on the bed of the king, where it had taken the human appearance of the queen and eaten the consorts. She put one part of it in the well of the Kaiyuan Si in Fuzhou, the second part in the Min River, and the third in the well of the seven stars of the Dipper Constellation in Fuzhou. The second time was to save Liu Qi, who had been raped by the serpent's head, which had escaped from its jail and transformed itself into a beautiful woman to marry him against his will. The last time was during a ritual to make rain, when they died together as they were born.

Chen Jinggu finally had to marry Liu Qi and became pregnant. At that moment she was required to perform a ritual for the rain to fall, to save the Min kingdom from a severe drought. This is why she had to "abort" the fetus while acting as a shaman, taking the child out of her womb and hiding it in her mother's house. She died of a hemorrhage while dancing on the river's waters, because her double, the white serpent, which had found its way to Chen Jinggu's house, had just swallowed her embryo, in a cannibal act to "feed its life" (yangsheng). She had just enough strength left to kill the serpent, while riding on its head, both flying to the Gutian Linshui temple, where they are still represented together. It is said that Chen Jinggu's body was mummified, while the serpent is kept under her seat, in a small cave that is still visible in the Gutian temple.

After her death, she returned to Lüshan to learn the secrets of pregnancy. She took back the soul of her child by performing a ritual to transform it into a child god named San Sheren, the Third Secretary, or Qilin Sansheren, the Third Secretary Who Rides the Unicorn.

A cult was then offered to her, and later she was officially canonized as a goddess.

The Base Temples in Fujian and Taiwan

The Linshui Mother Temple in Daqiao, Gutian

The base temple of the cult in Fujian can be found in the village of
Daqiao, in Gutian, at a place called Linshui. It was constructed in
792, under the Tang. Much later (1341–1348), the temple was embellished and aggrandized, and it was the occasion for a *jiao* ritual of
installation. This was financed by the community of worshipers of
the whole province and, without doubt, by newly gained imperial
subsidies, if one believes the sources, notably the report of Zhang
Yining (1301–1370), which was based on a stele written by the prefect Hong Tianxi (1225–1228).[6] The temple was restored after being
burned by a careless beggar under the Qing, during the first year of
the Guangxu era (1875). The statues were broken in 1950 during the
campaign against superstitions, and they suffered further damage
during the Cultural Revolution, though they were not completely
demolished.

Since 1980 the keeper has undertaken the restoration of the
temple and has also worked to revive the cult community. At this
local level, the restoration has not been without conflict. There was a
rivalry with a female medium of the Lady who had the same intention and wanted to be the main player. She finally withdrew, building
another Linshui temple and taking part in the restoration of the old
Chenghuang temple in Gutian, the temple of the city god. This local
anecdote is strongly suggestive about the formation of the cult communities that weave the texture of these networks, and about their
discords. I will have occasion to mention other, similar anecdotes.
Since 1991 the State Bureau of Religions has taken charge of the official restoration of the temple. A Quanzhen-tradition Daoist from the
Baiyun Guan in Beijing has taken on the role of manager. The temple
is now under the control of the Baiyun Guan and of the local administration. This latest development seems to me quite traditional, in
looking at the history of the temple and at the different metaphors
for the strata of society and of Daoism that it raises. This will
become more evident, I hope, in the rest of this essay. The conference
in 1993 was held partly in Fuzhou and partly at the nearby temple at
Linshui, in a new hotel constructed by a Taiwanese believer for the
pilgrims and overseas Chinese visitors, whose numbers are increasing
and for whom the small bedrooms at the side of the temple no longer
sufficed.

The temple was constructed on the site of a cave in Linshui, where
there had been another, earlier cult of a demon serpent to which, it is

said, two children were sacrificed every year.[7] Later, according to this legend, this other white demon serpent challenged the Lady, who killed it.[8] The Lady, according to legend, her body mummified, sits upon the head of the vanquished serpent invisible in a small cave under her throne. It is said that the first temple was constructed by the queen of the Min (or by a queen of the Tang) who had dreamed of the Lady after her death. This fact holds significance for the relations between the cult and the state. The temple looks like a palace, with an official reception room, in the back of which the Lady is dressed as an empress. There are also galleries on the aisle of the main hall and a floor with other altars and a pavilion for makeup, theatrical performances, and processions. In the principal hall a theater stage, which was restored and used for a performance in 1991,[9] faces the ritual area; the two spaces are separated by a sunken courtyard. Perhaps one can see here a ritual mountainous Daoist structure, like that of the temple of Baosheng Dadi in Xiamen, described by Kristofer Schipper (1990) and Kenneth Dean (1993). There is thus a temple, an imperial palace for Daoist rituals, nothing but banalities. But the characters who appear in the temple, like its origin, tell another story.

In the place of honor are the Sannai—Chen Jinggu, Lin Jiuniang, and Li Sanniang—the three shamans who use the ritual techniques of Lüshan. All three of them died violent deaths through abortion or suicide. At their sides are the Lady Tigress (Jiang Hupo) and the Ladies Stone-Press (Shijia Furen), repented demons who have become shamans under the orders of Chen Jinggu. The galleries are occupied by the Ladies of Thirty-six Palaces, the consorts of the king of the Min (Wang Yanjun, fl. 928–935), whom the white serpent reduced to a state of blanched bones. They have become the nurturers and protectors of children, and this is how their statues in the temple show them. Their names are posted with a mention of the origin of each one, so that, as people say, "you don't make a mistake when invoking them." This may refer to previous local cults, later subjugated to the Lady. This is the case for one of them, at least: the smallpox goddess, coming from Fuqing, mother of twin brothers, sons of a serpent god. The aborted son, Liu Cong, is also present in these galleries of the royal consorts. He is represented mounted on a chimera or a unicorn (qilin).

It is a curious palace, where one also finds the queen of the Min, reigning as she should, over the royal concubines in the galleries of the temple.[10] The generals Wang and Yang, of the celestial army of the five directions (yinbing), whom the Lady commands as the shaman of Lüshan, are also there, ready to assist her. In a room at the entrance to the temple also stand the two Taibao—the two guardian protectors, the *bendi shen,* local divinities—showing a cult community that preceded Chen Jinggu's. The walls of their small room are decorated with paintings illustrating episodes of the tales of the Three Kingdoms, while at the floor, in the makeup pavilion, where there is an articulated statue of the Lady for processions, the walls are covered in paintings illustrating her myths, following the *Furen Zhuan.* The mother of the Lady is also present at the floor, together with the two gods in charge of the Bridge of One Hundred Flowers, the heavenly region over which she reigns. An Earth God altar once flanked the temple, and it is said that there was an altar to Guangong. The State Bureau of Religions has rebuilt the Earth God altar and wants to construct a room for the Three Pure Ones, which may better suit the patronage of the Baiyun Guan and the claimed orthodoxy of the cult. There is also a large tree at the source of the turtle and the dragon, signs of *fengshui,* affirming the correct local geomancy.

We can see how the bureaucratic metaphor of an official palace, Daoist lineages, the implications of royal structures, and shamanistic and cosmic values mix intimately into the history of this woman, Chen Jinggu. All of this is engraved in the very structure of the temple. Thus, to "read" the temple is to gain access to the whole mythological and sociological story of the cult.

The Temple in Tainan

The founding temple in Taiwan, at Tainan, was conceived on the same principle, with some mythological variations. Constructed in 1736, it originated from a temple in Fuzhou and is the neighbor of the temple of Koxinga. It has been expanded and embellished at great cost. The *jiao* ritual of construction and the ritual for the reopening of the doors took place in 1987–1989. Officials of the town hierarchy were also present, as well as the newspapers and television. The cult community of the whole island is active and prosperous. In recent years many pilgrims have returned to Gutian to renew their communities' ties. Such is the case of the Linshui temple in Taipei, whose director is one of the most important benefactors of the Gutian temple. The director, a native of Fuzhou, was present at the conference in 1993. The mother temple in Tainan also envisages making a pilgrimage. The reconstruction of the temple, again, saw its share of dissension among the different economic groups of worshipers. Here as well, a privileged medium of the Lady has chosen to construct her own temple and hopes to go and make allegiance, "divide incense" *(fenxiang),* directly in Gutian. The temple in Taiwan was built on the same official model as the one in Gutian: an audience room and galleries occupied by the royal concubines and nurturers of the cult occur here as well. Performances take place in front of the temple. The Earth God is present inside, but on the other hand, neither Jiang Hupo nor the Shijia Furen are present. There is, however, an altar to the monkey Danxia Dasheng, the Great Sage of the Cinnabar Fumes, a demon castrated by Chen Jinggu. The Lady's mother is missing, but there are Zhusheng Niangniang, the Lady who Registers All Births, and a couple of gardeners of the Bridge of One Hundred Flowers (Huagong Huapo), over which Chen Jinggu watches and which one finds materialized in the Daqiao, in Fujian, standing in the front of the temple. Her son, Liu Cong, is also missing, but the white serpent is said to be there, invisible. The myths of the Lady are sculpted in gold-plated bas-relief, modeled after the *Linshui Pingyao,* just as in Gutian.

One can make some very interesting comparisons among the numerous temples of the network, but this is not my objective here. We can see well enough, through these two examples, how revealing these paradoxes (bureaucratic metaphor and shamanistic structure, diachronic and syncretic representations) are about the cult, a point to which I shall return in presenting various facets of the character of Chen Jinggu herself.

Every year, between the New Year and the fifteenth of the first lunar month, during the days of the festival of the Lady in both Fujian and Taiwan, pilgrims flood the mother temple, coming from all the points of the *fenxiang* network, accompanied by their shamans. The names of the communities that visit are conscientiously recorded and their gifts entered in the temple registry. At both temples, new steles have recently been chiseled, showing the affiliated members from all regions. Other steles tell the story of the Lady, the foundation myth. Those steles are considered to be the warrant of the orthodoxy of the cult, to be transmitted to the pilgrims.

We can then see two important aspects of the cult: the networks of affiliation *(fenxiang)* and their economic function in the real world, and the vertical ties of the state bureaucracy. These functions are orchestrated in ritual performance by the *fashi,* "masters of the magic methods," the shamans who act in the name of Chen Jinggu. This reveals a particular aspect of the land: an economic network of affiliations animated by the shamans who appeal to this woman, the mistress of the Lüshan Sannai line. *Fashi* of the Lüshan lineage officiate over these different temples. In Fujian they come principally to present incense *(jinxiang),* to divide incense to renew community ties and affiliations *(fenxiang),* and also to present people's personal wishes or to demand an oracle. In Taiwan they also carry out other rituals at the temple, always in the name of the Lady. In Fujian these same rituals are usually completed in the houses of the patients.[11]

Lüshan and the Tradition of the Sannai

One of the particularities of this cult is its association with a certain ritual tradition, the Lüshan, Sannai tradition. This fact certainly played a great role in the transmission of the cult through the ages.

Yiwu Lüshan, Mount Lü of the Healing Shamans, is actually located in Beizhen, in the Liaoning district of Manchuria. This high place of shamanism was already well known in Min country, as certified by the master Daoist of Fujian, Po Yuchan (1209–1224).[12] According to both written and oral legendary traditions, Mount Lü was "imported" to Fujian, after a fashion, in the form of a mythological mountain where the procedural rituals of shamanistic Daoism were taught. Finally, this mountain, whose calm was troubled by the affluence of the disciples, was immersed upside-down *(fan)* in the waters of the Min at Fuzhou, at the place called Longtan Jiao, at Shangdu, the upper ford of the island of Nantai. Only those who truly have the proper destiny, after a "boat journey" that I consider shamanistic, can successfully find the entrance to the cave where the master spreads his teachings. Perhaps one can see in this transposition of Mount Lü a sign of affiliation with a tradition coming from elsewhere.

A whole pantheon accompanies these beliefs, and the *fashi* of Lüshan possess ritual paintings that represent it. These include their Treasure of the Magic Method *(fabao)*. It is composed of three painted scrolls, always present on the altar, closed, when they perform rituals. They are opened only in cases of extreme importance, and many offerings must be presented. The first scroll represents the celestial soldiers, the spirits who have submitted to the shaman. The second represents the twelve "original bodies" *(benshen)*, the twelve masters of the *fashi*. Finally, the third scroll is a talisman of investiture from Lüshan. In addition, the *fashi* usually use ritual paintings, which they hang to create the sacred area. Those paintings show different mythological episodes of Chen Jinggu's life, well known to all the faithful. The magical treasure of the *fashi* includes, besides paintings and ritual texts, a body of written healing talismans for exorcism and protection, transmitted through the generations. These appear sometimes to be true scriptural rituals, meant to express a specific vision of the world, like a chart of the universe with its paradises, pantheons, and mythologies (Baptandier Berthier 1994a). The masters of Lüshan are equally celebrated for their mudras, gestures of magical value, reputed to be very efficacious. This fact recalls the practices of the magical arts of thunder *(leifa)*. This is a kind of bodily theater where every gesture tells a whole story and keeps it alive in the memory of the shamans, as associated with secret mantras.

Daoist masters from different lineages, like Zhengyi, also possess paintings of this pantheon, which serve to construct a ritual area as they conduct the Sannai rituals. In reality, the different traditions often blend in Fujian, and masters easily perform rituals that come from neighboring sects. One can thus see a Zhengyi Daoist, wearing his black headdress, temporarily put the traditional red headdress of Lüshan over it, when he completes a rite of this sect.

In effect, the current Sannai Lüshan tradition is molded from elements of shamanistic and neighboring Daoist traditions, added to its own specific foundation (Baptandier Berthier 1994b). One can clearly see that the Sannai Lüshan tradition constitutes a local case, founded on an ancient shamanistic tradition, supplemented across the ages and especially since the Song by borrowing from other traditions, leaving its origin uncertain. The ritual substrata of the line are rites of curing and of exorcism, including rites of calling the souls of the living, like *shoujing* (collecting frights). In any case, going beyond the orthodoxies, the masters of one tradition and the shamans of the other can perhaps be seen as "the first Chinese psychoanalysts," as Judith Boltz (1987) said in looking at their practices.

One of the most important rituals is the one for rain and for the reestablishment of cosmic harmony that Chen Jinggu herself performed. There are also the exorcism of terrestrial evils and of the white tiger *(xietu)* and the rituals for women and children. These shamans also perform community rites *(jinxiang, fenxiang)* and the seasonal rites of passage. The ritual *liandu*, a kind of after-death curing ritual that certain shamans adopted, can also be added. Note that in parts of Taiwan, *fashi* of the Lüshan tradition also carry out funeral ritual *(chaodu)*. Spiritual administration to the living and the dead is in all ways a shamanistic task. The presence in the ritual corpus of the voyage rite called *guo luguan* confirms the *fashi* in this role.

The *fashi* perform these rituals at the head of the celestial troops, the soldiers of the five directions, appealing to the Sannai, the Three Ladies. These shamans are men, but to practice the rituals of this tradition they must wear the ritual clothing of Chen Jinggu, notably her skirt. They are thus transformed into this woman, and they dance and act like her.[13] It is remarkable and strange to observe all these men dressed as female shamans, giving the impression of a collective ritual of transsexuality, especially during the festival of the Lady, as the crowd invades the temple. The *fashi*, however, are generally married men and well integrated in the local society. Perhaps one can see in this transsexual ritual a memory of its origin, since the tradition was female. Thus the very body of the shaman, as well as the ritual dress and attitudes, is also a support for the transmission of the tradition and its metaphors. This is the interpretation of the shamans themselves. One can also see the application, as if in a dramatic act, of the Daoist precept of cultivating femininity inside oneself, as the way of nourishing life, *yangsheng*. This also establishes an equality between femininity and ritual activity, to which I will return later. Or perhaps it is merely a pure theatricalization of the rituals, based on the myths.

There are also a number of female mediums of Chen Jinggu who act in her name, in trance, dispensing curing rites and talismans, generally less elaborately. The ritual virtue is placed here on trance and on direct contact with the goddess. The transformation is not the same as that of the *fashi*. One transforms ritualistically, the other is possessed; one proceeds more by metaphor, the other by metonymy. In both cases, it is the shaman Chen Jinggu whom we continue to observe everywhere.

Who Is Chen Jinggu?
The Fundamental Destiny: Where a Woman Appears like a Landscape Chart

According to the legends as painted in the temples and as told up to the present, Chen Jinggu's origin was Guanyin—the promiser of marriage, alliance, and descendants—at Quanzhou during the construction of the Bridge (see the short synopsis, above).

Here, then, is the original destiny *(benming)* of Chen Jinggu, the future Linshui Furen, Lady at the Edge of the Water. She is the blood of a goddess, offered to the desire of humans, in order to construct a bridge; the daughter of an old woman, who nevertheless conceived as she washed her laundry in the river water, where by a miracle she found the fertile blood; and also the future shaman, the exorcist of the female demon serpent. It is no surprise at all to see the Buddhist divinity Guanyin so integrated into the legend of this cult, an additional marker of the general syncretism. Moreover, Buddhism was favored in the land of Min throughout the time of Wang Shenzhi (898–925). His successors did not imitate him. They tended to favor Daoism and the shamanistic cults. Some trace perhaps remains through this "descent line" of Chen Jinggu.

This is also a commentary on femininity and on the social role of women, which appears between the lines. The French anthropologist Yvonne Verdier (1979) has clearly shown the relationship between the traditional feminine activity of washing and a double passage: of the newborn toward the world of the living and of the dead toward the world beyond. During each of these two steps, there is a ritual washing, which task is incumbent upon women. The woman who accomplishes this often also helps to give birth. This is the later role of Chen Jinggu, after she has become a goddess, and also the role of Zhusheng Niangniang at the temple in Tainan. Here, Lady Ge washes and conceives at the same time, by eating the fruit of maternity. This also shows the passage from the prior world *(qianshi)* before birth to the present life of Chen Jinggu, the incarnation of a vow of marriage and, in this patrilineal society, of conception. One can also detect an archaic vein of representations of female generations, following a female lineage of miracle making/receiving that constitutes Guanyin, who promises to marry and then disappears by transforming herself; Lady Ge, aged and sterile, who conceives outside the patrilineage, by the grace of Guanyin's blood; and Chen Jinggu, future goddess and protector of women and children, who dies in the middle of an abortion. Her destiny as a shaman is already presented in this "retro-image" of her original destiny: she is born to tame the serpent demon, as we shall see.

The scenes in Fuzhou where her conception/birth took place, which remain basically the same today, serve as landmarks for the memory of the beliefs, of the practices, and of the past communities; they gleam in the water of the river of Longtan Jiao, "where Lüshan can still be seen," say current believers. This is a construction in a mirror: Xiadu, the lower ford, the place of birth, and Shangdu, the upper ford, the place of mortal combat, one on each side of the bridge in Fuzhou, itself the contemporary of the bridge in Quanzhou, place of her original destiny. Perhaps one can also see in the legendary passage of the fertile blood from Quanzhou to Fuzhou an interpretable sign as to the local rate of natality or to the exchange of populations.[14] In any case, in this epoch of the creation of the cult, when maritime commerce and water transportation were flourishing, all these spots were certainly vital points: fords, marketplaces, places of exchange of all sorts, places of passage. This is again the case today, when temples and their life appear once more as the face of the market.

Other sites also serve as important landmarks in this story. The micro-environment of the temple at Gutian, for example, is very revealing about the relations between the different communities, notably between Gutian and Fuzhou. Curiously, the old village of Gutian has been submerged by a dammed lake. Near the temple of the Lady at Linshui, in the village called Daqiao (Great Bridge), there is a local market. There, two other bridges determine the surroundings of the temple. One is the Baihua Bridge, the Bridge of One Hundred Flowers, named after the celestial place the Lady runs, the place of all human reincarnations. Terrestrial and celestial places seem here to mix with one another in a troubling manner. This bridge was con-

Chen Jinggu and her husband Liu Qi at the temple in Zhongcun village. (Author photograph)

structed and decorated with images of celestial scenery by the female medium who was in rivalry for the restoration of the mother temple and who represents a community of worshipers in Gutian. But on the other side of the tiny river, in the village of Zhongcun, another female medium, from Fuzhou this time, has constructed a small temple to the Lady with the help of her followers. Here the goddess is represented sitting with her husband, Liu Qi (see figure). Both personify, even today, the alliance of a woman of Fuzhou and a man of Gutian. A little farther away, in a neighboring hamlet, sits the second bridge: Shuchuang (Hairbrush). It was cut during the war with Japan (1931), which proves that it was important. It also represents the place of the last exorcism accomplished by the Lady, who, with Lin Jiuniang, raptured the Demon of the Big Crevice by using a long hair.[15] The usual landmarks of this demon are found in Fuzhou, on the island of Nantai, at Zhangan Shan, under Shangdu. But at the bridge of Shuchuang, one can also see a gap by the waterside, where he was vanquished, associating the two places, which people say are in communication. On the flanks of the mountain between these villages, named the Mountain of the Lady (Furen Shan), one can find the base Linshui temple. This is also where the old road ran, which crossed these bridges. An ancient stele, standing at the entrance to the mountain, attests to it. Today, pilgrims attending the goddess festival at the base temple and about to rebuild their own temple come here to do a kind of sociological enquiry, studying every detail of the landscape—natural as well as built—to be able to follow the right model in their own village.

This sketch follows the Min and its tributaries, landmarked by bridges, which indicate the mythological distance covered both by this female shaman between the two vital points of her cult, Gutian and Fuzhou, and, without doubt, by those communities that have adopted her as a tutelary divinity in their exchanges and processions. Witness the local proverb: "The serpent of Fuzhou does not have a head, it is found in Gutian." This is a reference to the myth, where part of the serpent was cut off by Chen Jinggu and taken prisoner to Fuzhou, while she sits upon its head at the temple in Gutian. The processions of local worshipers take this same road even today.

The main temple in Fuzhou, which was situated near the place considered to be the original birth house of the Lady, in Nantai, does not exist anymore. It is now a hospital. Thus, unfortunately, it is impossible to analyze the current relations between the two temples nowadays. Another Linshui temple is being rebuilt in the same surroundings. This will perhaps allow a further study at some future date.

The Shaman of the Min Kingdom

An Interesting Genealogy: Where State, Religion, and Cult Communities Become Associated

Despite appearances, Chen Jinggu is presented as a "daughter of good family," well placed in the masculine hierarchy of official Confucianism and religion. Her grandfather is said to have been a shaman named Chen Yu. Her father, Chen Chang, was a censor and had received the title of Great Master of the Second Defense. Her cousin, Chen Shouyuan, was the official *daoshi* of the kingdom. His historical existence is certified, as well as his relationship with the founder of the Tianxin Zhengfa tradition of Daoism.[16] Her husband, Liu Qi, became an inspector in Loyuan. It is interesting to see the different hierarchies: Confucian and Daoist, then Daoist and shamanistic, spontaneously mixing, without opposing or excluding one another. Lady Linshui was daughter and wife of magistrates, granddaughter and sister of a shaman and Daoist, mother of a divine infant, itself shaman and celestial magistrate.

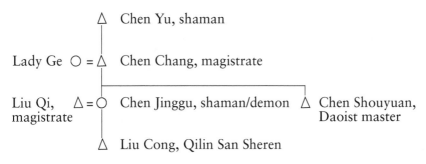

Another point also merits attention. The Daoist (Tianshi sect) cousin Chen Shouyuan was, the legend tells, too poor to marry. He kept at his house a young actor, who played female roles in a Suzhou troupe. This young man was vampirized by the white serpent and saved by Chen Jinggu at the same time as her husband Liu Qi. Chen Shouyuan thus kept at his house a victim of the white serpent, "in place of a wife," says the *Linshui Pingyao*. Chen Jinggu, at the same time, saved Liu Qi from her alter-ego, the white serpent, and married him. These are odd marriages. . . . Moreover, the actor who plays the female roles curiously reminds us of the *fashi,* the shamans of Lüshan, who play female roles as they transform themselves into women (more precisely, into Chen Jinggu herself) for ritual purposes. Femininity, ritual, and theater find themselves, this time, strictly associated.

Chen Shouyuan, △ = △ / ○   ○ / □ = △   Magistrate,
Daoist   actor   Chen Jinggu   Liu Qi
                        (man/wife)   (woman/demon)

This double scheme of alliance and this genealogy, once again, show an image of relations among the state, religion, and the cult community that weaves together the social structure in all its complexity and was undoubtedly constructed to confirm them. It is a picture that suits the Min kingdom at this historical epoch. Moreover, we should note that the entire family of Chen Jinggu would have received official titles after her death, in memory of the merits of this female shaman. We can also see that while the bureaucratic metaphor emerges at this moment, it is only one part of the story. We need only look at the steles in front of the temples to see the inverse, where the names of the officials are shown without any particular distinction, considered as simple members of the cult community.

The current situation seems to be very much the same. A Daoist of the Baiyun Guan has managed the temple since 1991, under the direction of the State Bureau of Religion. Today, shamans and mediums perform the rituals, while drama is enacted. During the 1993 conference, officials of the local government hierarchy and intellectuals analyzed the exploits and the life of Chen Jinggu for a kind of new "canonization" as an orthodox, Daoist, nonsuperstitious cult, suitable to be shown to the overseas Chinese and even to foreigners.

The Warrior: Where the World Appears as a Shamanistic Battlefield

Chen Jinggu, like most of her sister shamans or goddesses in this context, is a warrior. The Lüshan sect is governed by the symbolism of the five elements, with their cycles of mutual creation and destruction, seen metaphorically as the five camps. Chen Jinggu commands a celestial army, the *yinbing* (soldiers of yin). Two chief generals are under her orders, Wang and Yang. She herself, an expert in martial arts, possesses weapons: the Sword of Ursa Major and a whip whose handle is a serpent. Her dress as a magician is also for combat: the crown placed on her undone hair is that of a general and her long skirt, which is worn by the present shamans of her line, can be hitched up when she jumps over rivers, mounts a horse, or engages in hand-to-hand combat. Modern shamans enact these same gestures during their rituals. Several statues represent her in this role (see figure).[17]

Chen Jinggu's legendary history thus makes her an active participant in the wars of the kingdom. At the head of the *yinbing* and also of an army of women—shamans, tamed demons, and even the queen and her consorts—she succeeded in ending a historical siege of Fuzhou, which had been led by the king's brother, assisted by a "perverse" initiate of the rival Maoshan sect.[18] Thus, the historical rivalries of the royal clans and of the Daoist/shamanistic traditions are again intimately mixed, alongside the battle of the sexes. Chen Jinggu takes part, she is implicated, she fights. Or in other words, her character is being manipulated to reveal this situation.

This theme of warrior-goddesses is widespread in China. To take only one example, a repertory opera of the Min tells of such a siege ended by a woman; it is called the *City of the Lady (Furen Cheng)*. Warrior-shamans disguised as women for ritual reasons, and women becoming warriors themselves, use this metaphor in ways that may evoke the relations between the sexes through these elements of transsexuality. One can see a kind of alternation, as in the proceed-

Chen Jinggu next to her horse on the altar of the Linshui temple. (Author photograph)

ings of "nourishing life" through the exchange of yin and yang. Let us recall that in the arts of the bedchamber, sexual vampirism exercised by one of the deviant partners is called "grasping in combat."

It would be wrong to think that the modern world has seen the end of this martial virtue. During fieldwork (1991), a medium of Cai Furen, another goddess close to Chen Jinggu, who herself died fighting the enemies of her father's city, assured me that the divine sisters had taken part in the Vietnam War and indeed in the Gulf War, which was then raging. "They are going to help," she explained to me, "they can't stay indifferent when people are being oppressed." This is perhaps the expression of a latent despair from seeing the intervention of other terrestrial structures.

The Different Strata of the Cult: Where a Local Shaman Becomes the Favorable and Just Lady Linshui

An Exceptional Character: Where Her Transgression of Norms Earns Her a Cult

Chen Jinggu's birth was no less exceptional than her conception. While perfumes suffused the air, celestial music was heard. From her birth, she gave signs of being exceptional. There is no ritual text, no legendary narrative that does not begin with the following verse: "At one and two years old, she was very intelligent, at three and four, very clairvoyant. From five and six years old, she learned to embroider. At seven, she learned to read and did it to perfection. She was wise and knowing, no one could rival her. Vegetarian since her infancy, she offered a cult to Guanyin. At fifteen years old, she went to Lüshan with the Lady of the Perfumed Pearl, to learn the magic of Ursa Major and save the people."[19] This is a summary description, quite standard and ordinary for immortals and future divinities, and close enough to the female precepts and proprieties of the *Nüjie*.[20] Other descriptions are less polished and come closer to the more archaic strata of the cult of a healing shaman and to oracle powers. Chen Jinggu is presented as the knowing mistress of the cycles of nature and of animals, as well as of her own body. Beyond norms and social laws—notably those of filial piety—her very short life is like a flash, one deserving of a cult:

> According to the *Fengjing Zalu,* there was a girl of the Chen family who lived in the prefecture of Gutian in the land of Min, during the Dali era (766–779). From her birth, she could predict the future and her predictions were correct. For playing, she liked to cut out paper butterflies and hawks and other animals on which she would breathe charmed water, and they would then know how to fly and dance. She made a wand with her teeth, about as long as a foot, with which she could make the cows moo and the horses whinny; she could also make them run and stop at her will. When she felt like eating, she could reach the bottom of a barrel of food, but she could also fast for several days if this pleased her. She stunned the whole world, and even her parents had no power over her. She had not yet attained the age of an adult when she died. This is why she possessed a medium in order to communicate. The people of the country addressed her on the occasions of drought and other calamities and each time her works are effective. A temple was

founded for her, and the Song dynasty canonized her as the Favorable and Just Lady, Shunyi. Her numerous miracles survived the ages. Today [1607] her cult is spread throughout the country of Bamin [that is, the Fujian region]. (*Soushen Ji* [1607] 6:6b–7a [Xu Daozang, no. 1476], Biography of Shunyi Furen)

This portrait brings her together with her present mediums. Some of them explain their destiny, strange even to themselves, as if the components of their horoscope *(benming)* went against the destiny of ordinary people, and of their families in particular, so that they risked being "struck" *(chong)* and "striking" others. Like Chen Jinggu, they are thought to have only a rather short life span, which only possession by the divinity—occurring as a cult—can prolong. Again like Chen Jinggu, they are consulted for both people and animals, which are considered a part of the family wealth. But they are also expert in affecting harvests and the seasons, and in predicting the future. They have unusual powers over their own bodies, which allows them, while in trance, to hurt themselves without acknowledged danger and without durable marks.

The "Face" of the Cult: Where Its Different Strata Appear like the Serpent's Successive Sloughings

The most interesting exorcism of Chen Jinggu, the heart of the cult, is her exorcism of the serpent, which gives access to the various strata of the cult's existence. This again reveals a theme already emphasized: the serpent-bond, associated with the creation of the territory. In effect, an attested cult was formerly dedicated to a demon serpent, in the cave of Linshui. This serpent was mastered, according to the different versions, by either Chen Jinggu or her brother (or cousin) Chen. This serpent, managing to escape death, is associated in the legend with the constellation of the serpent. This is probably the expression of a stellar stage—the constellation of the serpent—of the cult and as a manifestation of the Chinese belief in baleful stars (the constellation of the serpent is one). This could also correspond to the first construction of the temple in 792.[21] I actually know of at least one temple dedicated to the Lady in Fujian, where this stratum of the cult is figured by the statues of its protagonists. Moreover, the oral tradition continues to echo this phase of the cult: in the neighboring village of the Linshui temple, at Gutian, people volunteer a tale of the sacrifice of the two infants to the serpent.

The exorcism of the demon white serpent corresponds to another stage during the Min kingdom. Presented nowadays in almost all the temples, it is also echoed in the novels *Linshui Pingyao, Furen*

Zhuan, and *Mindu Bieji,* and in the rituals. The white serpent, the hair of Guanyin, was also the master of the cave of Linshui, at Gutian, from which Chen Jinggu expelled it.

Two stages thus appear in relation to this theme of the serpent. In one, the poisonous serpent, devourer of children, is ritually mastered by the shaman who removes its venom and reestablishes order in the country "by offering incense," says the legend. Since she cannot actually kill it, she offers a cult to "transform" it. In the second stage, the shaman kills the female python, while she creates the affiliation networks of the *fenxiang* by taming the other demons of the kingdom—or, in other words, by incorporating the older cult communities: it is the *pingyao* (pacification of demons) that transformed her into the benefactor of the kingdom. She then created an order by conquering in high combat the first occupants of the place, fatally represented as primitive and dangerous. Then, because of her tragic death, she also became the protective goddess of women and children. It is at the end of this long process that she became, through her canonization, Lady Linshui. Those are the main periods of the cult. One could go on further and analyze other community strata. I shall give only one example.

Formerly, it is said, in the neighboring village of the Linshui temple, Zhongcun, the *bendi shen* (local gods) were two country boys, who became the tutelary divinities, Taibao. Chen Jinggu obtained her precedence over the temple at Linshui in rivalry with them. The local surroundings still retain perceptible traces of the relentless fight between the two rival communities, in which a female shaman vanquished the two strapping fellows. Local discourse integrates these events painfully and incredulously. People still show the imprint of Chen Jinggu's small foot engraved on the rock from which she took off running toward the temple, while the horseshoe prints of her rivals rest visibly in the ground, immortalizing this apparent inequality, like a last petrified denial of the result of the combat (see figure). The two Taibao, of course, are represented in the present temple: a conquering cult always offers a place, if only a secondary one, to the vanquished community. They find themselves in a side room in the main temple. People draw divination lots before these statues.[22] When I asked why, a medium of Chen Jinggu responded that the village people have never fully accepted this victory of a woman (should we accept this even for her local community?) and preferred to kneel in front of the two male gods of the locality when demanding oracles.

New episodes from the current restoration of the temple are inscribed in this same vein, and one sees how they create the "face" of such a cult, through the different facets that compose it, in space

Chen Jinggu's little foot etched in the rock at Daqiao, Gutian, Fujian. (Author photograph)

and in time. It transforms itself around the original center, the personality of the divinity, this woman, shaman and serpent, across the ages.

The Shaman as a Woman in Movement: Where the Fluid Gift System and the Rigid State Hierarchy Become Articulated

After her return from Lüshan, Chen Jinggu led a free life, not only without social constraints but also as the mistress of time and space. Constantly solicited to save people from demons who infested the country, she passed her time crossing the mountains and plains, where she fought, exorcised, healed, and purified. Vertigo sometimes seized even her, during the solitudes that are the reverse of liberty in a society where it was hardly permitted. A passage of the *Linshui Pingyao* describes her suddenly taken by this agony, calling on the Earth God to comfort her. The sensitive human elements that express these shamanic emotions are still another resonance. The place is savage and deserted. It is mountainous, the environment considered as a primitive and dangerous place, a place of regression, approaching asceticism. The vegetation is luxurious, unconquerable, and the animals are ferocious. Nobody ventures there with impunity, unless equipped with protective talismans.[23] Tudi Gong, the locality god, appears here to be the divinity of this virgin nature, with whom Chen Jinggu must deal in order to accomplish her civilizing work.

Despite the handicap of her bound feet, that social stigma, she moves without pain, knowing how to use magical techniques to "narrow space," by following the veins of the earth.[24] This is how she vanquished the two Taibao and it is not by chance that the print of her tiny foot is still shown there. This interesting point could be understood, again, as a kind of challenge to masculine Confucian society, which used to bind the feet of its women to keep them from escaping the house universe. The mythological origin of this ferocious custom is attributed to the Shang empress Daji. She was said to be a fox demon. She tried to deceive the emperor by hiding her paws. She then bound them and ordered all women to do the same, so that he could not catch on to her strangeness. Note that the legend attributes to women the origin of their alienation by men and makes an obvious analogy between all women and fox demons, well known to be sexual vampires.

Here again, this description also applies in part to Chen Jinggu's more modern initiates, *fashi* or mediums, men or women who are free to transport themselves, to travel, in contrast to the common people of both imperial and modern society. Ordinary citizens in effect have little freedom of movement. The imperial bureaucracy, like the republican structures, demanded stability of the population, an immobility that allowed constant control.[25] At all times, however, Daoists and shamans have taken travel as their privilege, following the roads of the earth as they follow its veins in ritual. They crisscross the real world, as they do the celestial regions during their shamanistic voyages "to traverse the roads and the passes" *(guo luguan)*. They are also masters of time because their rituals, individual or community, follow the rhythms of the seasonal cycles and of life and death (see Baptandier 1996b). Moreover, while their calling of souls may not revive the dead, it does at least put a universal human experience into practice: the effect of language on memory and forgetting. Like Chen Jinggu, they also come together to celebrate during the communal festivals for their tutelary divinities.

In looking over this portrait of free subjects, masters of time and space, who form communities apparently independent of state structures, one can retrieve images of Chinese society structured according to various coexisting models: the gift system of *guanxi,* the state bureaucratic system, and an emerging individual model. The *guanxi* system is based on the relationship network between parents or friends and on the exchange of gifts and services. Mayfair Yang (1989) has shown how this relational model of *guanxi*—which is also the model for cult communities—is founded on a composite subject, in perpetual construction and deconstruction, in which "face" is drawn and altered according to the principles of give and take. The subject, and thus social strata, appears in incessant movement, fluid.[26] The model of the state subject, on the other hand, appears rigidly fixed, as a family, a structure, a function from which there is no escape in time or in space, totally dependent on an official model, coming from high in the hierarchy. The observation of the cult also shows clearly how the community level is constructed and how the two structures are interdependent, which doubtless allows each to survive without destroying itself.

The Woman Chen Jinggu and Patrilineal Confucian Society

Beyond the Principle of Filial Piety: Where Lineages Appear like "Flesh Rhizomes"

The legend of Chen Jinggu thus has two extremes. Initially oblivious to all filial piety—the cardinal virtue of Confucian society—she finishes with self-sacrifice and death, in part for the very reason of filial piety.

Chen Jinggu's departure to Lüshan resembles a ravishment, in all senses of the word. When she refuses to marry—the first serious breach of filial piety—an acolyte of Guanyin literally comes to lift her up and snatch her from the red palanquin. In order to do this, she fights violently with the Chen parents who interfere, thus creating the second major fault. During the three years of Chen Jinggu's absence, her parents suffer from ulcers and abscesses on their backs and hands. On her return, Chen Jinggu will save them by grafting a piece of her own flesh, taken in advance from her arm (or leg), onto their wounds. This is surely an eloquent description of the family, conceived as one single body. Chen Jinggu, by her departure, cuts into the integrity of this body, which she reintegrates, literally, after her return. This is a crude Oedipal way, it seems to me, to deny the succession of generations.

This is a common theme in Chinese mythology. Princess Miaoshan/Guanyin, for example, offered her eyes to save those of her father, just as Nazha-Taisui gave up his bones to the paternal line.[27] Thus the flesh and bones of the patrilineal line form a certain number of bodies, male and female, apparently independent, but made of the same material, a bodily essence that appears interchangeable.[28] This is the basis of filial piety, which takes a specific form in the case of women. The Bridge of One Hundred Flowers, which Chen Jinggu watches over, is a sort of nursery garden where one can care for and make cuttings of the flowers of terrestrial women. Each woman has one individual flower there, which represents her capacity for procreation. A ritual, still very common these days, makes it possible to cultivate these flowers by cutting a new flower bud (child) taken from a particular plant (woman) and grafting it on another plant (another woman). It means, in brief, that a sterile woman can always ritually "borrow" a future embryo from another woman, in order to give it birth herself. Thus, feminine nature is also composed of a sort of primary material (flowers) that individualizes itself, certainly, but is also always susceptible of exchange. It looks like a kind of "ovule grafting." This is expressed again in the rite of passage of *guan,* specific to this tradition, conjuring one of the "nourishers" of the cult not to spirit away the soul of a living child, to "implant it" in another woman, pregnant, who would bring it into the world in her turn. Here there is a direct menace not just to the infant itself, but to its lineage, which risks being deprived of it for the benefit of another, "rhizomelike" lineage. This justifies the ritual, which is similar in part to that of recalling the soul (see Baptandier Berthier 1994b, Baptandier 1996a).

This is also evident in the field, where women actually practice this intense "traffic in children" through adoption and sworn sisterhood. They do exchange children: for instance, a woman without a son could get one from a friend, in exchange for her newborn daughter. The daughter could later be married to the adopted son. "When you are sworn sisters, the bellies should communicate," a woman told me. They put this into practice, and it is a women's affair, where men scarcely appear to take part.

Nevertheless, returning to Chen Jinggu, a girl is not made to stay in her patrilineage: she must marry out and bear children. After the return to her natal family body, Chen Jinggu was finally obliged to accept this. Yet this still would not suffice. She also had to sacrifice herself for the country, agreeing to abort to save the people from a deadly drought. Dead for country and for family, certainly. Yet she was also caught by the heartbreak of her destiny as a woman and a shaman and, paradoxically, was also guilty of having broken the rules of alliance by failing to produce a son for the patrilineage. Death in childbirth, after a fashion, is a grave breach for which a woman must endure infernal punishment in the Bloody Pond.[29] This is why Chen Jinggu is valued as a divinity.

To Give Birth or to Abort, a Social Duty: Where She Loses Her Feminine Substance for Having Seen Too Much

Chen Jinggu's story of giving birth/aborting while dancing for the rain to come lies at the heart of her legend. We see that it uses a language of life and death in the traditional society's system of representations. In effect, Chen Jinggu, having been forced to conceive an infant, found herself forced to abort, always for the fertility of the country. It seems to me that this archaic theme is also very modern.

We can find once again an equivalence between the feminine powers of conception and ritual. Here the ritual lends itself well to this since rain must be made to bring fertility to the country. In the legend, this abortion is not ordinary. Chen Jinggu somehow "exteriorizes" her infant, whom she places in a kind of symbolic maternal body, the house of her mother at Xiadu. She is ready to "reabsorb" it later and continue her pregnancy. This exteriorization of the embryo, while she dances in the ritual area of the waters of the Min (which contained Lüshan), resembles the exteriorization of breath or vital energy. This should perhaps be seen as the creation of the double ritual area characteristic of all Daoist sacrifices: an interior ritual area, secret, here the sacrificed body of the pregnant woman, and an exterior area, outwardly expressed, here the waters of the river. This constitutes the ritual metaphor (see Berthier 1988).

Still, Chen Jinggu died at the same time as her double, the serpent, who had absorbed the infant. All three form here another metaphor of the pregnant maternal body, reconstituted, and one could say sacrificed, for the well-being of the people and for the reestablishment of the cosmic order. A double sacrifice, of the two feminine entities, one sitting astride the other: the shaman, herself part and creator of the cultural order, and the demon serpent, the feminine element of savage nature. As to the infant, the ritual sublimation of its death will found the cult of Chen Jinggu, as well as its own.

We can also see in this picture—Chen Jinggu dancing on the water of the Min where Lüshan stands inverted, and where she rejoins the white serpent that has absorbed the infant—a variant on legends of the immersed village. Chen Jinggu had taken care to conceal her maternal house under a magical lake before coming to execute her ritual on the river and dying of a hemorrhage. This unhappy destiny occurred because, like all the heroines in this legendary motif, she could not resist the desire to look back and see what had been forbidden. Leaving Lüshan, she turns back at the end of twenty-four steps to see Xu Zhenjun, her master. She sees him indeed, at the threshold of the door, as if between two worlds. He then announces her destiny to her: that at age twenty-four her pregnancy will place her in great danger. Another motif of these legends involves pregnant women who are petrified, turned into trees, or, as here, die of a hemorrhage: that is, who lose all their feminine substance,[30] for having seen too much. We need only recall the mother of Yiyin or the pregnant spouse of Yü the Great, transformed into a mulberry bush for having seen the animal (bear or fish) dance of her husband (Kaltenmark 1985). Here Chen Jinggu sees her own animal double, the serpent, like her reflection in the water where the world (Lüshan) is also reversed.

Sacrifice of the female nature in its double aspect to the cosmic order, cult of an aborted embryo that has failed his patrilineage, equivalence of the power of conception and of ritual power, and example of legends of the immersed village: this episode is all these things at once, and it continues to function. We can certainly also see here, in another register, the grasp of the state and of the patrilineal structures over fertility and the female body. In contrast to what one might expect, the present family-planning campaign to have only one child has caused the cult to regain popularity. Having a son is always indispensable for patrilineages. But the chances are diminished when the women are "sacrificed" to this new social objective of birth control. Appealed to, contradictorily, by two masculine authorities (the family and the state), just as violently as in the land of Min, the help of this cult does not necessarily seem superfluous in the countryside, where temples are reconstructed and where I could see many new statues of San Sheren.

Alliance, a Destiny: Where the Natural Woman Stands Opposed to the Made-up One

Chinese patrilineal lines demand only a single thing from women: a descendant who will assure the ancestral cult. This implies that women agree to be goods of exchange and material for the alliance between two lines. This is the model that Chen Jinggu refuses. She prefers to dedicate herself to meditation, to studying rituals, and to keeping her independence as a shaman. In other words, she hopes to consecrate herself to religious practices, the only alternative to this feminine destiny, except in certain places that practiced sericulture (see Topley 1975). For some Chinese women this choice is either a matter of survival or a search and an attempt at self-preservation and self-cultivation, in a society that offers no other personal alternative.

This was also the experience of my friend Winter Perfume, medium of another goddess. Daughter of poor peasants, she loved learning to read and write, and would have liked later to teach. At eight years old—she is now in her fifties—she was given to be married as a child-wife, to a family even poorer than her own, which did not allow her to continue her studies. Searching to escape this forced marriage, she was nevertheless caught and became the mother of five children. After that she left and became a medium, founding her own cult community around her house. Her husband does not oppose her: she had given him a son for the ancestral cult. In traditional society, women have two possibilities outside of, or in addition to, alliance and the Confucian arrangement. The first model is the one chosen by Buddhist and Daoist nuns, looking to the practices of interior alchemy to sublimate their bodies.[31] This model approximates one facet of Chen Jinggu and her Daoist sisters, practicing the asceticisms of long life and studying rituals. The other model is the one mentioned earlier, which female mediums choose, or rather endorse. We should recall that the *fashi* shamans are men, even if they dress like women when officiating. Yet much like the woman I just discussed, most of the female mediums are married and are mothers. This does not prove that they must ultimately leave their homes. Nevertheless, the possession, the trance, that characterizes them and whose vocabulary is almost theatrical—one speaks of initiation as "taking a role" *(daban)*—weighs down the women with the suspicions of orthodox Confucian and Daoist structures about their powers and their sexuality. Such cults are called perverse or licentious. Split characters, these women come quite close to the double image of Chen Jinggu: shaman and wife of Liu Qi/white serpent. It is nonetheless interesting that in this context the vocabularies of marriage, theater, and trance intersect: people say that Chen Jinggu refused to "make herself up" and to "take her role" when she refused to marry. We know that the temple at Linshui in Daqiao includes a pavilion for makeup *(chuanglou)*. We should remember as well that an actor becomes the acolyte/"wife" of Chen Shouyuan. These are then the themes embroidered in the legend of Lady Linshui.

The legendary story of Chen Jinggu is undoubtedly a kind of derision of marriage. But it is also a warning of its inevitability. It is really an illustration, at the same time idealized and menacing, of those many women for whom arranged marriages, or being given in adoption as a child-wife, was standard practice. The changes that have taken place during the last half-century have only superficially modified the situation, especially in the countryside. In the legend the two family heads paint a portrait that has always been real: the fathers of Chen Jinggu and Liu Qi can think only of concluding their alliance and assuring their descendance thanks to a woman, who herself only wishes to escape them. This split conception of a woman with two faces is also real: serpent and shaman, natural and madeup, a danger yet one to whom men must resort to perpetuate the generations.

Female Insatiability and Universal Harmony: The Demon Serpent, Where Menacing Women "Nourish Life" on Their Own Behalf

Let us return to the origin of the white serpent: a hair of Guanyin, which turned white because it was touched and animated by the money/desire of Liu Qi, the future husband of Chen Jinggu, during the episode of the Wanan Bridge. Here again the sexual metaphor is evident, be it feminine or masculine. The hair in this context has always been considered as the place where vital energy and sexual power are concentrated. The man hit Guanyin on her hair knot, in the hope of marrying her. Chen Jinggu, as a shaman, performs ritual with her hair undone. Lin Jiuniang captures the demon of the Big Crevice, who tries to rape her, with one hair. This demon is the acolyte of the white serpent.

The hair of Guanyin becomes white, powerful *(ling)*, uncontrollable. The serpent thus created devours the embryo of Chen Jinggu; it devours also the flesh of the women of Min; it takes their appearance to sexually vampirize men to go on "nourishing its life" *(yangsheng)*. Transformed into a seductive woman, it bewitches young men, from whom it steals their vital energy by absorbing their semen, finally devouring them when they no longer satisfy it. Thus, the king and Liu Qi, the future spouse of Chen Jinggu, were victims just like the young apprentice of the Daoist Chen Shouyuan. For each of these fortunates who was spared a certain death, many others lost their lives. Lasciviousness and sexual addiction accompany the devouring practices.

On the other hand, when the serpent ravished the queen, Chen Jinfeng, and then changed its own appearance to take her place next to King Wang Yanjun, the health and the affairs of the kingdom were dangerously jeopardized. One does not have to look very far to see here a satire on the dissipating role of Chen Jinfeng next to this king, who enjoyed nothing better than to allow himself to be pulled away to the luxurious pavilions on the lake west of Fuzhou. This historic period of the kingdom can be described as more or less byzantine (see Schafer 1954). During its passage in the palace the white serpent, parodying the role of the queen, took charge of the royal consorts, the guarantors of fertility of the line; it devoured them, reducing them to the state of blanched bones. This is the occasion when Chen Jinggu accomplishes the *liandu* ritual to return flesh to their bones by refining them *(lian)*. The king offers them to her as her apprentices. They will later become the acolytes of the Lady, celestial nourishers charged with taking care of terrestrial children, as they had in life been in charge of the royal fertility. It is thus their processing, and then their ritual apprenticeship, that "refined" these bones and gave them access to the power to conceive—that, in sum, gave them back their flesh.[32] Femininity and ritual are rejoined once again.

Daoism considers sexuality as fundamentally necessary to the procedures of longevity and cosmic harmony. Women traditionally appear as partners, real or imagined, and as initiators, possessors of secrets. However, the fear that one of the partners may exercise a vampirism on the other quickly points to the guilt of the woman as the probable culprit because of her yin nature. This is what happens here. Chen Jinggu and her companions are certainly not the only divinities suspected of having a double nature. The Queen Mother of the West, whose double is a tigress, is the archetype of this feminine model keeping alive the masculine terrors:

> The Queen Mother of the West is a good example of a woman who obtained the path of immortality by nourishing her *yin*. Each time she had relations with a man, he fell sick, while she herself kept a polished, transparent face of the sort which *had no need of make-up* [my emphasis]. She fed herself continually on milk, and played the five-stringed lute, always keeping harmony in her heart and calm in her thoughts, without any desire. So, the Queen Mother of the West *never married*, but she loved to couple with young men. This secret could never be divulged, for fear that other women would get it in their heads to imitate her methods. (*Yufang Bijue*, cited in the Ishinpo 28:7a–b, in Despeux 1990:39)

Yet the methods of the Queen Mother of the West "were divulged" at least to her disciples, including Chen Jinggu, if one believes the tradition of a feminine Lüshan, having Wangmu as its mistress. Communities of female mediums dedicated to this goddess have also always existed in both Fujian and Taiwan. Here is a good example of one of these "licentious cults," or so it is claimed, founded on the popular mediumistic practices that orthodox Daoism had always sought to downrate, as it does a woman. Throughout her legendary life, Chen Jinggu is presented as employing herself precisely to pacify, to transform these savage practices, this savage desire, by fighting the serpent. But she finally dies with it, showing that they are one single body.

There still exists a very important cult of the python in Fujian. This python king is related to the Min and precisely to King Wang Shenzhi. According to the legend, it is the husband of a human woman, sister of a famous Daoist master of Fuqing. They gave birth together to eleven children, including twins. The Daoist brother killed eight of them. The wife of the python committed suicide and was given, after her death, the title of Smallpox Goddess by the Jade Emperor, who placed her under the orders of Chen Jinggu. Her statue is in the Gutian temple among the Thirty-six Dames, where she holds the twins.

The sexual connotations of this theme of the serpent, as well as its relations to the creation of the territory of the kingdom, become explicit here. In an important episode of the legend, Chen Jinggu is shown cutting the white serpent in three pieces on the bed of the king, where it pretended to be the queen. I have already shown (Berthier 1988) that this could be regarded as the sacrifice of the kingdom's demon—or its first occupant—on the ancestral altar of the king (become here, somewhat bluntly, his bed).

Bad Death and Mummification: Where to Keep the Flesh Appears like a Forced Passage from Pictogram to Utterance

Dying at age twenty-four from a uterine hemorrhage, Chen Jinggu had a bad death. This is why she became a deity, following the usual process of divinization in this pantheon. For this reason too they mummified her flesh, to prevent her from finally becoming a bone demon. This practice is not exceptional and corresponds to tradition. The goddess Mazu herself would have undergone the same treatment.[33] The commentary on conceptions of death, divinization, and the body made here in the legendary narrative and in the oral tradition strikes me as very interesting. Here is what they say (*Linshui Pingyao*, chap. 16:106, also published in the Daoist dictionary):

> The Lady Chen was dead. A part of her soul [*linghun*] did not lose consciousness [*bumei*]. Her real souls [*zhenhun*] did not disperse. She did not forget Lüshan. It is as if she were reborn [*ru zaisheng yiban*] and returned to Lüshan. Then a Daoist appeared to her husband Liu Qi, who was preparing the funeral rites, to give him the following directions: "Today she has attained *zhengguo*, her just reward. It is necessary to seat her and to use a piece of charcoal to preserve her flesh [*roushen*]. If she is left here at the Linshui palace of Gutian and incense burned for her for 10,000 years, she will expel demons and help everyone, dispensing her protection. She will be preserved as a relic [*guji*]. There is no need to use a coffin to bury her." Liu Qi asked an eminent scholar and a reputed lacquer master [*qijiang*] to [envelop] her body in a tissue of charcoal. On the outside, he used earth [*nitu*] to model her and to give her the appearance of the Lady riding a white serpent. Then they used a little niche to offer her sacrifices.

The story of this mummification appears to be alive today. It is difficult to say if there was ever a mummified body at the temple. Some people say yes, and that she was carried from the temple in a sack, in order to hide her. Legend or reality, in any case, it seems to me that many points merit being raised. Chen Jinggu's bad death made her a *guhun* (wandering soul). Had she been buried, her souls would not have dispersed, like those of people who have died correctly. She cannot forget. She lacks the virtue of renunciation that makes mourning possible—on the part of the living just as, projected in the system of representations, on the part of the bad death herself. This is what makes the dead into wandering souls and not ancestors: this impossibility of disappearing into the undifferentiated, which seems to regenerate death as a force in itself and thus to sterilize the bones themselves, the usual generators of vital essence.[34] At best, if the vital force of the "remnant soul" can be cultivated and elaborated, these bad deaths will become divinities. This is just what produced Chen Jinggu. Better to preserve and mummify her flesh and bones, outwardly visible, a relic *(guji)*, than to allow her souls—*hun* and *po* (the bones)—to be the only trustees of this encrypted venomous memory, invisible and unserviceable. In the same way, she thus appeased the consorts of the king, who had become blanched bones, by giving back their flesh, which disappeared once again at the death of the Lady.[35] Flesh and bone, blood and sperm are the base elements, feminine and masculine, of conception. A bad death prohibits the reintegration of the bodily essences and of the souls into the ancestral capital of the family, by creating savage elements that must be propitiated to render them beneficial, indeed fertile, and without which they risk devouring humans. This is again what we have here with "incense burned for her for 10,000 years." This is the ritual that serves as the remedy.

This also permits us once again to see the ambiguous character of this goddess in the cult. Ordinarily favorable and beneficent, she can also sometimes appear as evil—suddenly more blanched bones than goddess—through the characters of her acolytes in particular. She revenges herself on incredulous or neglectful believers by cursing them,[36] or she seeks to ravage the soul of some infant instead of protecting it (Baptandier Berthier 1994b, Baptandier 1996a). She is at the same time mother and "bad mother," maternal and menacing, flesh and bones. By nourishing her magical power *(ling)* with incense, the food of the gods, by refining *(liandu)* her, by offering her a cult, people can lead her to a more "civilized" and more humane attitude. It is as if the cult were ultimately equivalent to the lost flesh, preserved by mummifying her, or as if this perpetuation in everyone's memory alleviates the impossibility of mourning.[37] This is obvious on the fifteenth day of the seventh month, when one offers a collective banquet to all bad deaths who have neither the power nor the opportunity for a personal cult. People feed these "little brothers" for whom the entire society feels responsible. In just this same way, a single sentence notes the mummification of Chen Jinggu's body and the installation of an altar, a niche, to make her offerings. The period of her festival, between the New Year and the fifteenth of the first month, seems equivalent to the cycle of the fifteenth of the seventh. This is the moment when all come back to honor her, to feed her together, so that she will not be harmful and will be beneficent. We should recall the other venomous serpent of Linshui, which is offered incense *(jinxiang)* so that it will stop devouring the infants of the people. Feed and ritualize, make the memory evident (this is also a name for trance: "to make the spirit evident" *[fashen]*), to avoid being eaten, absorbed, and reified oneself (see Ang 1989).

It is interesting, finally, that an eminent scholar and lacquer master is in charge of the operation, even if lacquering mummies was a current practice. Chinese writing has well-known values of consubstantiality that need not be shown again. But here, this somatic inscription of not forgetting, executed by a specialist in writing and painting, offers a very strong expression of it, like a forced passage from pictogram to utterance.[38]

The Land and Maps of the Cult Today: Back to the Landscape Chart

This cult, as we have seen, is still profoundly rooted in the landscape. Nevertheless, its religious practices were prohibited for a half-century, considered to be superstition. If they are still alive, it is because their systems of representation were deeply anchored at the communal, sociological level. There are today two possible ways to rediscover the networks of the cult and to retrace the outlines of its land.

The first possibility is to traverse the archaic map by allowing oneself to be guided by the toponomies encountered in the legends (see Baptandier Berthier 1989). The place names sprinkled throughout them correspond to the first holy places, where exorcisms were accomplished by the Lady herself and where the first affiliated communities were created. These are Xiadu, Shangdu, Longtan Jiao where one finds the immersed Lüshan, the Wushi Shan where one finds the split stone of the Ladies Shijia, Loyuan, Xihe, Daqiao, and so forth. In doing this, one creates a sort of "memory palace," a map of memories of the original territory, preserved in the recollections of the present occupants of these places. One could also, inversely, consider these places, their names and their legends, as a structure that has itself preserved, as if programmed, the memory of its past reality.[39] Situated on archaic veins of the first networks of "dividing incense," these points remain as sensitive and inexhaustible language sources. Even when they remain only as imperceptible traces to a stranger, the inhabitants still recognize them and discern the elements of an ancient micro-landscape. Legends and fresh memories mix to maintain these benchmarks of other realities, intimately entangled over the years. The narrative of the high doings of Chen Jinggu intersects with the memories of processions and community festivals from the childhood of the inhabitants. These traces themselves are susceptible to evolution over the years.

Several years ago, at Xiadu, people could still show the house where, they said, the Lady was born. They recalled the legendary episodes associated with the corner of some street or some roundabout of the Min River, much as they recalled the processions between affiliated communities. By 1992 many temples had been reconstructed and a real procession had taken place with incense burners and statues of the Lady, following an itinerary modified only by the new configuration of the affiliation network. That is, as we have already seen, these different communal strata have continued throughout the ages.

The second possibility for rediscovering the land of the cult is to trace the present networks of affiliation—of the temples that divided incense from Gutian and then of those that divided incense from these temples in turn. One can observe in such a journey the present state of the temples and of their communities, and the expression of their varying local myths and rituals. One can thus draw the present map of the *fenxiang* networks, which ignore borders—those of provinces, districts, and even of China. Nowadays, throughout the land of this cult, temples are being reconstructed and their communities, often helped by returned overseas Chinese, are again taking up the activities of exchange that had been put on ice for the last half-century. The temples appear like an aspect of the market and its networks. Thus, one can see the two halves of a village, each with its own temple to Chen Jinggu, taking up business again and concretizing it by having a communal procession for the first time during the festival of the Lady. It is also moving to see the elders of a village and the heads of the incense pots of a destroyed local temple return to Gutian to do sociological work. They study the mother temple—its characters, its inscriptions, its paintings, its steles—and cross the micro-landscape so that finally they know how to reconstruct their own community temple. The founding temple plays its role well as guarantor of the memory and the orthodoxy of its cult. Soon after they have reconstructed their temple, the villagers will return in procession with their shaman, to renew their ties by dividing incense again. They carry their contributions, duly registered, and leave again with incense and a blazing coal from the founding incense pot. It is interesting also to see how written sources, such as the local annals or the *Mindu Bieji* or *Furen Zhuan,* serve as references for engraving new steles, while earlier it was the ancient steles that served as references to write these same sources. Modernity obliges hiring a local scholar—for whom, unfortunately, one must pay dearly—to consult the written literature on the Lady, which was once the oral tradition of these same communities, in order to engrave a panel or stele before a newly reconstructed temple. Time has hardly changed this point of view (see Schipper 1977).

It is edifying then, to see the overseas Chinese come back, carrying their images, statues, and votive offerings in local overseas variants. At the same time they often bring considerable gifts for the temple and for community structures. Thus, the offering of a new incense pot—truly the construction of an entire temple—will go hand in hand with the construction of a shopping arcade or factory, or with concluding an import-export marketing agreement.

Nonetheless, the temple remains what it is, what I have described, and what the State Bureau of Religions itself will restore from now on, sheltering this society of suspect shamanistic divinities. Even the rituals that punctuate communal life and its representations in space and time, accomplished by their shamans dressed as women, have reappeared. This is without doubt a transitory phase between two epochs, of which the second remains to come, after a long period of prohibition that apparently never proposed any viable alternative. Its existence is invaluable since it permits us to observe today, as if in a hologram, the lives and systems of representation of this part of China over more than a dozen centuries.

Notes

1. She is also revered under the names of Chen furen, Danai furen, Nainiang furen, Chen taihou, Ciji furen, and Shuntian Shengmu.

2. See Wei Yingqi (1969).

3. The steles of the temple of Gutian bear the names of communities coming from Malaysia and the Philippines. Moreover, some worshipers emigrated to Japan and the United States. At the temple to Mazu in San Francisco, people offer incense to nine Ladies who protect children and who play the same role as Chen Jinggu. They are also associated with the Linshui temple at Gaoxiong.

4. In geographic terms the country of Min corresponds approximately to the present province of Fujian. It was a kingdom between 909 and 945 C.E., governed by the Wang family. The king referred to here is Wang Yanjun (928–935). He proclaimed himself emperor in 935 and named his wife, Chen Jinfeng, empress. They were assassinated the same year. The *daoshi* of the Celestial Master lineage who officiated at the court and who will be mentioned below was Chen Shouyuan (see Schafer 1954).

5. Recall that anthropological theory was called the "science of civilization" *(Wenhuaxue)* by Huang Wenshan, one of the propagators of the thought of Boas and Lowie in the 1920s.

6. Zhang Yining (1301–1370) was a literatus originally from Gutian in Fujian. A bureaucrat under the Yuan (1277–1367), he was equally a celebrated statesman in the beginning of the Ming (1368–1644). Hong Tianxi was a man of Quanzhou. The report of Zhang Yining on the temple of Chen Jinggu, published in the *Cuiping Ji* (published by Siku Quanshu Zhenben), 4:48b–50a, is reproduced in the *Gutian Xianzhi,* chap. 5, 134–135.

7. This fact is related in the *Sanjiao Yuanliu Soushen Daquan* (reprinted by Ye Dehui from a Ming edition, 4:15–16) and in the *Sanjiao Yuanliu Shengdi Fozu Soushen Daquan* (n.d., woodblock edition of Tanya Tang, 2:5a–6b). The two

versions are practically identical. The oral tradition has preserved the memory of the cult.

8. This white demon serpent clearly evokes the legend of the White Serpent, which also would date from the Tang (seventh to ninth centuries) and takes place in Zhejiang. It inspired a famous short story in the style of storytelling and was often adapted to theater beginning in the seventeenth century. Several common traits unite these legends, especially the themes of animal spirits capable of cultivating their vital force. There is, of course, the theme of the serpent that transformed itself into a woman and also the theme of the flood or of the immersed village (see below). The legends also share the theme of the infant whom the mother-serpent or shaman must renounce. All these elements are again, in both cases, associated with the origin of the royal lineage. It is evident in the legend of Chen Jinggu, and it could perhaps be the case also for the White Serpent, which is sometimes associated with the origin of a royal line of Birmany (see Pimpaneau 1965). The two white serpents are nevertheless two different characters, local variations on similar themes.

9. In 1991 a troupe from the district of Xiapu, called the Minxi Tuan, inaugurated the newly restored theater. The actors performed a very brief play: *The Eight Immortals Offer Their Congratulations (Baxian Qinghe)*. At night, for the temple of the Lady in the neighboring village of Zhongcun, they performed *Baogong Weimei (Baogong Serves as Intermediary)*. Before each performance they offered incense to Tian Du Yuanshuai, the theater divinity.

10. The Temple of the Eastern Peak, the Temple of Hells in Beijing, now abandoned, included a lateral room where the queen was seated, surrounded by her ladies-in-waiting and children. This room appears to have been the privileged site of a cult for women. The Temple of Hells also honored the great divinity Bixia Yuanjun, the daughter of the god of the Eastern Peak, who holds a role in the north of China that approximates that of Chen Jinggu in Fujian. This is, without doubt, a common point of the different female communities. See also Cahill 1986, concerning the communities of Xi Wangmu.

11. See Berthier 1988 on the rituals carried out at the temple in Tainan. Most rituals are completed for women and children. Despite some interesting variations, the structures of the rituals in Fujian, as in Taiwan, remain more or less the same. See Baptandier Berthier (1994b) and Baptandier (1996a) on the rituals as performed in Fujian.

12. See *Recorded Sayings of Po Yüchan*, Harvard Yenching Index to the Taoist Canon, *Daozhang Zumu Yinde* (1296) 1:8b–9a (Beijing, 1936; reprint, Taipei, 1966).

13. The secret formula pronounced by the *fashi* for transforming his ritual appearance is the following: "I respectfully pray that Taishang Laojun rapidly obey my order and take possession of the king of the celestial demons, and that he prevent the starving demons from harming me. Celestial soldiers help on my right, the seven ferocious celestial generals are before me, the eight fierce gods protect me from behind. I wear the shoes of the Lady on my feet, the divine generals of the six *ding* help on my left with the six *jia*. The crown on my head is the headdress of the Lady. I wear the clothing of the Lady on my body. I invite my immortal, ancestral Master and the Venerable of Transformations to metamorphose my body. My body does not belong to the ordinary

world, it transforms itself and becomes the body of the Lady" (collected at Gutian in 1991).

14. Quanzhou and Fuzhou are put in opposition here in the legend as they are in history (see Schafer 1954). It seems strange a priori to place the origin of this cult at Quanzhou, where it is in the minority. There was nevertheless a temple of the Lady behind the Kaiyuan temple. It became a factory after the revolution, but an old woman perpetuated the cult there and received the faithful. Moreover, Wang Zhao was the first member of the ruling Wang family, originally from Henan, to obtain an official post in Fujian. He was named prefect of Quanzhou (886), from which place he conquered the entire province and in particular Fuzhou. The Tang emperor Zhao Zong (888–904) named him legate to Fuzhou in 896.

15. See *Linshui Pingyao,* chap. 17, and Berthier 1988. In general, I refer readers to this latter work for a more complete analysis of the legend and of the particular elements of the cult of the Lady, especially the episode of the Wanan Bridge.

16. Chen Shouyuan is sometimes credited with discovering the talismans of the first celestial master, which Tan Zixiao had known how to decode; faith in these founded the Tianxin Zhengfa. Boltz attributes this legendary discovery to Rao Dongtian in 994. The dates coincide, at any rate. This tradition relates directly to the teachings of Zhang Daoling (see Boltz 1987:33). In fact, King Wang Yanjun honored Chen Shouyuan with the title of Celestial Master (Tianshi) when Tan Zixiao was given the title of Master of Zhengyi. Three shamans were, in addition, very powerful at the court: Xu Yen, Lin Xing, and Sheng Tao. See Schafer 1954:96–98. Together they led the king to construct the Temple to the Precious August (Baohuang Gong), for which Chen Shouyuan was named Responsible Official *(Gongzhu)* in 931.

17. Chen Jinggu is represented as an empress, dressed in a brocade robe, holding her court tablet, and also as a warrior-shaman, brandishing her sword and her buffalo horn to summon the spirits and chase demons. One can see her dancing with her hair disheveled or riding a horse, or sitting on a throne or armchair, covered with tiger skins, which evokes better the seat of a medium than a court chair.

18. People often presented Maoshan to me in the field as the rival tradition to Lüshan. The first was the male tradition, the other was female. The legends of Chen Jinggu echo these beliefs, which were reported to me as much by Zhengyi Daoists as by local storytellers or shamans. Still, we know of the importance of women in Maoshan, one of whose protecting divinities is Wei Huazun (Despeux 1990, Strickmann 1981). This seems unquestionably to be a local expression of the dissensions between the different traditions, which perhaps also reflects different ritual and sexual (the search for long life) practices.

19. This passage was extracted from a *guoguan* ritual, collected at Gutian, 1991–1993.

20. The *Nüjie (Female Precepts),* written in the Han by a woman named Ban Zhao, is a manual of traditional female education treating the following seven themes: the malleability of women, relations between husband and wife, veneration and vigilance, female activities, concentration, obedience, and relations between uncles and sisters. See Despeux 1989:33.

21. This version is apparently supported by the *Sanjiao Yuanliu Soushen Daquan,* 4:15–16, which is practically identical to the *Sanjiao Yuanliu Shengdi Foshuai Soushenji,* 2:5a–6b, "The Biography of the Lady Danai." About the worship of baleful stars, see Hou 1979.

22. In reference to these divine lots, see Zhuang Kongshao 1989:97.

23. In reference to these talismans, see especially Ge Hong, *Baopu Zi,* the chapter on ascensions into the mountains. On this theme of the mountain, see Demiéville 1965, Baptandier 1996b.

24. See especially Ngo Van Xuyet 1976 and Kalinowski 1986 on the *dunjia* method. It is a matter of finding the yin moment to hide oneself in the six decades of the cycle of ten stems and twelve branches. In conjunction with the five elements—earth, water, metal, fire, wood—this method makes it possible to act on space and time.

25. The modern *hukou* system of residential certificates, which were transmitted through women until recently, limited the geographic and social mobility of the people. Marriages between people of different regions, and even of different classes, are extremely rare and in any case do not permit much mobility. In imperial China kinship structures and the structures of alliance fixed the citizens very efficiently, joined to the demands of the imperial bureaucracy.

26. Yang 1989, following especially Deleuze and Guattari 1979, envisaged two types of subjects in China: the subject of the state, created by an organization machine of centralized and rigid power—here the hierarchical bureaucracy, both imperial and modern—and a subject placed in the gift economy—here *guanxi*—based on the establishment of metonymic relations. This second model produces a molecular micro-organization, with fluid power.

27. See Dudbridge 1978 and the *Fengshen Yanyi.* See also Steven Sangren's essay in this volume.

28. This conception of the individual body as part of a whole that exceeds it corresponds well to this molecular construction of the subject at the community level of *guanxi.* It is not only the social side of the subject that is elaborated like this, but also the body of flesh and bones, whose limits are as blurred and open to change as those of social groups. Skin, where the individual destiny lies, does not separate the individual from the rest of the universe. This calls to mind two other concepts of Deleuze and Guattari 1979: the rhizome and the body without organs.

29. The Bloody Pond is a region of hell where women dead in childbirth are imprisoned, plunged in the impure blood of the menses. A ritual, including a shamanistic voyage, must be completed for a woman who has died under these conditions to allow her to find peace. During the ritual the son of the deceased "drinks the bowl of blood," a pious act that buys back his mother. The *fashi* of the Lüshan tradition complete such a ritual, as well as others involving menstrual blood, for example, the rite of propitiation of the Vagabond Shrimp *(youxia),* the demon appointed to this region and to female blood, along with the Sword Goat. Moreover, at Fuzhou, people still show with emotion the site where the Bloody Pond was formerly represented in the Temple of Hells and which is now (is it an accident?) a rice warehouse. I refer here to my own fieldwork. See also Hou 1975:80, Seaman 1981, and Ahern 1975. On representations of blood

and pregnancy, see Furth 1986 and 1987; also Berthier 1988. Note that in the legend, Chen Jinggu escapes this agony because the master of Lüshan cleanses her of all the impurities of her shed blood (*Linshui Pingyao,* chap. 16).

30. See Despeux 1990:215–219 and Furth 1986 and 1987, on blood as a female substance and on its uses. In reference to this passage, see Berthier 1988.

31. See Despeux 1990 on female practices of asceticism.

32. The ritual *liandu* as the *fashi* of the Sannai tradition offer it is really a rite of elaboration and healing for the dead, for the body as much as for the souls. They especially use lamps, which they arrange on a paper effigy in the image of the deceased. One places them, like *moxa,* on the thirty-six joints of the body and on certain organs, to make the pain cease and to save the deceased (personal communication received in the field, 1991–1993). In reference to this ritual and the Shenxiao tradition, see also Boltz 1987:28.

33. See Demiéville 1965. Note that the mummies discovered by the archeologists had been preserved with the same ingredients as those to be mentioned here.

34. Mauclaire 1991 astutely analyzes similar themes in Japan as they relate to femininity and to the real body *(benshen)* of the gods. See also Berthier 1987.

35. Many similar legends also exist. I will cite one well-known example: Meng Jiangnu, who rediscovers the bones of her buried husband in the Great Wall and brings them back to life with a drop of her own blood.

36. This story concerns the grandmother of the previous guardian of the temple at Gutian. Here is the narrative that he gave me: When his grandfather was guardian of the temple (before 1959), Chen Jinggu greatly liked his grandmother and often appeared in her dreams. One day she promised her a son. The woman could not keep the secret, and Chen Jinggu put a curse on her because she had spoken: she could have only one infant, and the same would be true for all her descendants. This occurred. The man (the grandson) who told me this story of his family wanted to leave the temple, but the curse followed him, he said. This secret, this required silence about conception and pregnancy, is also a theme of the legend of Chen Jinggu: the Lady died, reunited with the serpent, because her mother had divulged her secret (the presence of the embryo in the house). Here, the grandmother became practically sterile because she had revealed her secret (she was pregnant with a son). See Berthier 1988. It is strange also to consider that the curse sent by Chen Jinggu was equivalent to the "curse" of modern family planning: giving birth to only one child.

37. The reasons behind *liandu* and mummification thus show a great difference from Buddhism. The reasons to preserve the body in Buddhism are eschatological: they wait for the promised time of paradise in the Pure Land. In these shamanistic practices, the purpose is rather to make memory and destiny evident, via the preserved body. On this theme see Seidel n.d.

38. See Castoriadis-Aulagnier 1975, from whom I borrow this expression.

39. Here I pick up the expression "memory palace," employed by Spence (1984) for the memnonic techniques utilized by Matteo Ricci. In reference to the theater of memory and of memnonic usages, since antiquity and notably at the time of the Renaissance, see Yates 1975. In reference to the particular Chinese conception of the past and of its traces, see Ryckmans 1989.

Literature Cited

Ahern, Emily Martin. 1975. "The Power and Pollution of Chinese Women." In *Women in Chinese Society,* edited by M. Wolf and R. Witke, 169–191. Stanford: Stanford University Press.

———. 1988. "Gender and Ideological Differences in Representations of Life and Death." In *Death Ritual in Late Imperial and Modern China,* edited by J. Watson and E. Rawski, 164–180. Berkeley: University of California Press.

Ang, I. 1989. "Je te mange, tu me manges: Heurs et malheurs reptiliens." *Cahiers de littérature orale* 26:59–83.

Baptandier, Brigitte. 1996a. "Le rituel d'ouverture des passes. Un concept d'enfance." *L'Homme* 137:119–142.

———. 1996b. "A travers les chemins et les passes. Voyages chamaniques au pays du réel, voyages réels au pays des chamanes." Proceedings of the Conference Récits de voyages asiatiques: genres, mentalités et conception de l'espace. Ecole Française d'Extrême Orient. Paris, Claudine Salmon editor.

Baptandier Berthier, Brigitte. 1989. "Du bon usage des mythes en Chine, avant et après la révolution culturelle." *Cahiers de littérature orale* 26:37–59.

———. 1991. "Le pont Loyang: des mots, des humains et des dieux." *Langage et société* 57:9–43.

———. 1994a. "Le tableau talismanique de l'empereur de Jade: construction d'un objet d'écriture." *L'Homme* 129:59–92.

———. 1994b. "The Kaiguan Ritual and the Construction of the Child's Identity." Proceedings of International Conference on Popular Beliefs and Chinese Culture, 523–587. Taipei: Center for Chinese Studies.

———. 1994c. "The Interest of a French Anthropologist for the Cult of Chen Jinggu in Fuzhou." In *Research on Daoism in Fuzhou (Fuzhou daojiao wenhua yanjiu),* edited by Zhang Zhuanxing, 8–17. Fuzhou: Renmin yin cichang. "About the abortion, death and divinisation of Chen Jinggu." Idem, 17–23.

Berthier, Brigitte. 1987. "Enfant de divination, voyageur du destin." *L'Homme* 101:86–100.

———. 1988. *La Dame du bord de l'eau.* Nanterre: Société d'ethnologie, Paris X.

Bloch, Maurice. 1982. "Death, Women and Power." In *Death and the Regeneration of Life,* edited by M. Bloch and J. Parry, 211–230. Cambridge: Cambridge University Press.

Boltz, Judith. 1987. *Survey of Taoist Literature: Tenth to Seventeenth Century.* China Research Monographs. Berkeley: University of California, Center for Chinese Studies.

Cahill, S. 1985. "Sex and the Supernatural in Medieval China: Cantos on the Transcendant Who Presides over the River." *Journal of the American Oriental Society* 105(2):197–220.

———. 1986. "Performers and Female Adepts: Hsi Wang Mu as the Patron Deity of Women in Medieval China." *Journal of the American Oriental Society* 106:105–168.

Castoriadis-Aulagnier, P. 1975. *La violence de l'interprétation: Du pictogramme à l'Enoncé.* Paris: Presses Universitaires de France.

Cedzich, Ursula-Angelika. 1995. "The Cult of the Wu-t'ung/Wu-hsien in History and Fiction: The Religious Roots of the Journey to the South." In *Ritual and*

Scripture in Chinese Popular Religion, Five Studies, edited by David Johnson, 137–218. Publications of the Chinese Popular Culture Project 3. East Asian Studies. Berkeley: University of California.

Chen, C. K. H. 1974. *Biographical and Bibliographical Dictionary of Chinese Authors.* New York: Oriental Society.

Danai Lingjing (The Sacred Book of the Great Dame). Manuscript, n.d. Linshui temple in Gutian, Fujian.

Dean, Kenneth. 1993. *Taoist Ritual and Popular Cults in South-East China.* Princeton: Princeton University Press.

De Groot, J. J. M. 1897. *The Religious System of China.* Leiden: E. J. Brill.

Deleuze, G., and F. Guattari. 1979. *Mille plateaux.* Paris: Minuit.

———. 1989. *Cartographies schizoanalytiques.* Paris: Galilée.

Demiéville, Paul. 1965. "La montagne dans l'art littéraire chinois." *France Asie* 183:7–32.

———. 1989. "Les momies d'Extrême Orient." *Journal des savants* (Janvier–Mars) 144–170.

Despeux, C. 1990. *Immortelles de la Chine ancienne: Taoïsme et alchimie féminine.* Paris: Pardès.

Douglas, Mary. 1966. *Purity and Danger.* New York: Praeger.

Dudbridge, Glen. 1978. *The Legend of Miaoshan.* Oxford Oriental Monographs 1. London: Ithaca Press.

Furen Changci (The Ballad of the Lady). Manuscript, n.d. After the oral tradition. Fujian, Zhejiang.

Furen Zhuan (Biography of the Lady). Manuscript, n.d. Fujian, Zhejiang.

Furth, Charlotte. 1986. "Blood, Body and Gender: Medical Images of the Female Condition in China, 1600–1805." *Chinese Science* 7:43–66.

———. 1987. "Concepts of Pregnancy, Childbirth and Infancy in Ch'ing Dynasty China." *Journal of Asian Studies* 46(1):7–35.

Fuzhou Fuzhi (Gazetteer of the Prefecture of Fuzhou). 1877. Reprint, Taipei: Chengwen chubanshe, 1975.

Ge Hong. 1980. *Baopuzi Neipian Xiaoshi (The Master Who Embraces Simplicity),* edited by Wang Ming, 280–341. Taipei: Zhonghua shuju.

Granet, Marcel. 1959. *Danses et légendes de la Chine ancienne.* Paris: Presses Universitaires de France.

Gutian Xianzhi (Gazetteer of the District of Gutian). 1975 [1751]. Reprint, Taipei: Chengwen chubanshe.

Héritier, F. 1984. "Stérilité, aridité, sécheresse: Quelques invariants de la pensée symbolique." In *Le sens du mal,* edited by M. Augé and C. Herzlich, 123–154. Paris: Archives Contemporaines.

———. 1985. "Le sperme et le sang." In *L'humeur et son changement,* 111–123. Paris: Nouvelle Revue de Psychanalyse.

Hou Ching-Lang. 1975. *Monnaies d'offrande et la notion de trésorerie dans la religion chinoise.* Paris: Institut des Hautes Etudes Chinoises.

———. 1979. "The Chinese Belief in Baleful Stars." In *Facets of Taoism,* edited by H. Welch and A. Seidel, 193–229. New Haven: Yale University Press.

Kalinowski, Marc. 1986. "Les traités du Shuihudi et l'hémérologie chinoise à la fin des Royaumes combattants." *T'oung Pao* 72:175–228.

Kaltenmark, M. 1985. "La légende de la ville immergée en Chine." *Cahiers d'Extrême Asie,* 1:1–10.

Lauwaert, F. 1990. "Calculs des hommes, comptes des dieux: Essai sur la notion de rétribution." *T'oung Pao* 76(1–3):62–94.

———. 1991. *Recevoir, conserver, transmettre: L'adoption dans l'histoire de la famille chinoise: Aspects religieux, sociaux et juridiques*. Brussels: Mélanges Chinois et Bouddhiques.

———. 1993. "Semence de vie, germe d'immortalité." *L'Homme* 126:31–57.

Levi, J. 1985. "Le renard, la morte et la courtisane dans la Chine classique." *Etudes mongoles et sibériennes,* 15:111–141.

Linshui Pingyao (Pacification of the Demons at Linshui). n.d. Reprinted as *Linshui Pingyao Zhuan (Monography of the Pacification of Demons at Linshui).* Wujitian feng tang ed. Taizhong, 1992.

Mauclaire, S. 1991. "Serpent et fémininité, métaphore du corps réel des dieux." *L'Homme* 117:66–95.

Mindu Bieji (Historical Legends of the Min) (after the oral tradition). First publication as a book during the Qing dynasty Jiaqing period (1796–1821) Reprint, Fujian Renmin Chubanshe ed. Fuzhou, 1987.

Mindu Ji (Monography of the Min). First edition by Wang Yingshan, Ming dynasty. Reprint, Qiufang Xinzhai ed. 1831.

Ngo Van Xuyet. 1976. *Divination, magie et politique dans la Chine ancienne.* Paris: Presses Universitaires de France LXXVIII.

Picone, M. 1985. "Rights and Symbols of Death in Japan." Ph.D. diss., Oxford University.

Pimpaneau, J. 1965. "La légende du serpent blanc." *Journal asiatique* 253:251–277.

Potter, Jack. 1974. "Cantonese Shamanism." In *Religion and Ritual in Chinese Society,* edited by A. Wolf, 207–232. Stanford: Stanford University Press.

Ryckmans, P. 1989. "The Chinese Attitude toward the Past." *Papers on Far Eastern History* 39:1–16.

Sangren, P. Steven. 1987. *History and Magical Power in a Chinese Community.* Stanford: Stanford University Press.

———. 1983. "Female Gender in Chinese Religious Symbols: Kuan Yin, Ma Tsu, and the 'Eternal Mother.' " *Signs* 9(1):4–25.

Sanjiao Yuanliu Soushen Daquan (Extensive Research on the Origins of the Gods of the Three Religions). Reprint, Shanghai Guji Chubanshe, 1990.

Sanjiao Yuanliu Shengdi Fozu Soushen Daquan (Extensive Research on the Gods, the Saint Emperors, and the Buddhas of the Three Religions). First edition Ming dynasty. Reprint, Taiwan Xuesheng Shuju, 1989.

Sannai Furen Quanshi Zhenjing (Sacred Book of Exhortation of the Three Dames). N.d. Reprint, Linshui gong, Pingdong, Taiwan. Dacheng Caise ed., 1983.

"Sanshiliu Pojie Zhi" ("Biography of the Thirty-six Dames"). Manuscript, n.d. Fujian.

Schafer, Edward H. 1954. *The Empire of Min.* Tokyo: Rutland.

Schipper, Kristofer. 1977. "Neighborhood Cult Associations in Traditional Tainan." In *The City in Late Imperial China,* edited by G. W. Skinner, 665–676. Stanford: Stanford University Press.

———. 1990. "The Cult of Pao-sheng Ta-Ti and Its Spread to Taiwan: A Case Study of Fen-Hsiang." In *Development and Decline of Fukien Province in the 17th and 18th Centuries,* edited by E. B. Vermeer, 397–416. Leiden: Brill.

Seaman, Gary. 1981. "Sexual Politics of Karmic Retribution." In *The Anthropology of Taiwanese Society,* edited by E. Martin Ahern and Hill Gates, 381–397. Stanford: Stanford University Press.

Seidel, Anna. n.d. "Uncultivable Bodies." Unpublished conference paper, Stanford University.

Shahar, Meir. 1992. "The Lingyin Si Monkey Disciples and the Origins of Sun Wukong." *Harvard Journal of Asiatic Studies* 52(1):193–224.

Soushen Ji. First edition by Gan Bao, n.d. Reprint, Shanghai Guji Chubanshe ed., 1990.

Spence, Jonathan. 1984. *The Memory Palace of Matteo Ricci.* New York: Viking Penguin.

Strickmann, Michel. 1981. *Le Taoïsme du Maoshan: Chronique d'une révélation.* Paris: Collège de France, Institut des Hautes Etudes Chinoises.

Taiwan Xianzhi (Gazetteer of the District of Taiwan). 1958. Institute of Economic Research of the Bank of Taiwan. Taiwan Yinhang Jingji Yanjiushi.

Ter Haar, Barend J. 1990. "The Genesis and Spread of Temple Cults in Fukien." In *Development and Decline of Fukien Province in the 17th and 18th Centuries,* edited by E. B. Vermeer. Leiden: Brill.

Thompson, Stuart. 1988. "Death, Food and Fertility." In *Death Ritual in Late Imperial and Modern China,* edited by J. Watson and E. Rawski, 71–108. Berkeley: University of California Press.

Topley, Marjorie. 1974. "Cosmic Antagonism: A Mother-Child Syndrome." In *Religion and Ritual in Chinese Society,* edited by A. P. Wolf, 233–249. Stanford: Stanford University Press.

———. 1975. "Marriage Resistance in Rural Kwangtung." In *Women in Chinese Society,* edited by M. Wolf and R. Witke, 67–88. Stanford: Stanford University Press.

Verdier, Y. 1979. *Façons de dire, façons de faire.* Paris: Gallimard Sciences Humaines.

Watson, James L. 1985. "Standardizing the Gods: The Promotion of T'ien Hou ('Empress of Heaven') along the South China Coast, 960–1960." In *Popular Culture in Late Imperial China,* edited by D. Johnson, A. Nathan, and E. Rawski, 292–325. Berkeley: University of California Press.

Watson, Rubie. 1986. "The Named and the Nameless: Gender and Person in Chinese Society." *American Ethnologist* 13(4):619–631.

Wei Yingqi. *Fujian Sanshen Kao (Research on Three Gods of Fujian).* 1969 [1929]. Reprint, Taipei: Zhongshan University. *Minsu Congshu* 28.

Weller, Robert P. 1987. *Unities and Diversities in Chinese Religion.* Seattle: University of Washington Press.

Wolf, Arthur P. 1974. "Gods, Ghosts and Ancestors." In *Religion and Ritual in Chinese Society,* edited by A. Wolf, 131–182. Stanford: Stanford University Press.

Wolf, Arthur P., and Chieh-Shan Huang. 1980. *Marriage and Adoption in China, 1845–1945.* Stanford: Stanford University Press.

Xu Xiaowang. 1993. *Fujian Minjian Xinyang Yuanliu (Historical Records on Popular Cults of Fujian).* Fuzhou: Fujian Jiaoyu Chubanshe.

Yang, Mayfair. 1989. "The Gift Economy and State Power in China." *Comparative Studies in Society and History* 31(1):25–54.

Yates, F. A. 1975. *L'Art de la Mémoire (The Art of Memory)*. (1st edition, 1966.) Paris: Gallimard.

Ye Zhongwu. 1985. *Chen Shisi Qizhuan (Strange Story of Chen Shisi)*. Zhejiang: Wenyi Chubanshe.

"Yulin Shunyi Dutuochan Ruozhenjing" (Authentic Book on the Abortion of Yulin Shunyi). Manuscript, n.d. Collected at the Linshui temple in Gutian, Fujian, 1987.

Zhuang Kongshao. 1989. "Fujian Chen Jinggu Zhuan Qijiqi" (Field Research on Extraordinary Beliefs about the Legend and the Cult of Chen Jinggu in Fujian). Beijing, *Zhongguo Wenhua* 1.

Zhuan Shengbo. "The Great Dame Chen Aborts." Manuscript, n.d. Collected in Fuzhou, Fujian, 1991.

Zhuang Zhuanxing, Zhu Meitan, and Weng Huiwen, eds. 1993. *Chen Jinggu Wenhua Yanjiu (Research on the Cult of Chen Jinggu)*. Fuzhou.

Myths, Gods, and Family Relations

P. Steven Sangren

THIS CHAPTER PROPOSES a preliminary approach to a genre of Chinese mythologies and stories concerned with tensions intrinsic to the Chinese family system. It constitutes part of a more extensive on-going study and analysis in which I intend to link readings of such stories informed by psychoanalytic and structuralist methods to an immanent critique of interpretive techniques from the viewpoint of anthropology. My objectives are thus more anthropological than sinologi-cal. The present paper can allude only briefly to some of the wider philosophical and analytical issues raised by such an endeavor, but even this preliminary analysis should draw attention to linkages be-tween Chinese gods and family institutions—a topic that I am convinced is well worth pursuing much further.

In particular, I shall speculate here on the stories of Nazha, Miaoshan, and Mulian. None of these figures conforms to the model of the Chinese god as a celestial bureaucrat, yet each holds a place in popular religion. Nazha is widely worshiped, while Miaoshan, conceived as an incarnation of Guanyin, also figures prominently. Mulian, though less frequently an object of cultic devotion, has earned a place, particularly in funeral rites performed for women. This is not to say that no attempts have been made to fit these personages into a broadly hierarchical and bureaucratic structuration of the pantheon in some contexts. For example, Nazha is awarded an official title in the Ming epic *Investiture of the Gods (Fengshen Yanyi;* also called *Enfeoffment of the Gods)* and Guanyin is frequently included on iconographic cosmological representations of bureaucratic form. By the same token, the general framework of *Investiture of the Gods* is a story of contesting bureaucracies, both celestial and mundane.

Yet in the cases of Nazha, Miaoshan, and Mulian the bureaucratic metaphor is salient neither in their cults nor in the mythologies that define their personages in popular consciousness. Instead, each of their stories highlights a particular intergenerational family relationship: the Nazha story recounts a rebellious son's attempts to escape paternal authority; the Miaoshan tale is about tensions between a father and a daughter resulting from her pious refusal to marry; and the story of Mulian is that of a filial son who undertakes monumentally heroic exploits on behalf of his mother. Beyond these three, there are many other gods whose traditions of earthly incarnation prominently feature family processes.

I have juxtaposed these stories in order to draw attention to a category of what might rather awkwardly be termed Chinese family-relationship gods. The idea of coining such a term occurs, of course, mainly in contrast to the notion of Chinese gods as celestial bureaucrats. I have addressed elsewhere some of the limitations of the "bureaucratic metaphor" as a general model of Chinese notions of divine power (Sangren 1983, 1987). In brief, in my view it is useful to focus on the social processes that *produce* representations of power—including such obviously "religious" activities as private worship, public testimony, and collective ritual—as well as to note correspondences between such representations of power (including gods) and other culturally constituted categories, such as "officials," "kin," and "outsider-bandits." Although such correspondences are obvious and explicit, many departures evident in the ethnographic record are inassimilable to this model. More to the point, noting correspondences between categories of supernatural beings and their real-world equivalents still leaves us the problem of accounting for why people imagine supernatural beings to possess particular forms of power.

In more recent papers (Sangren 1988, 1991, 1993), I have attempted to illuminate the logic of production of representations of power that "alienate" productive power by attributing it to sources (gods, for example) other than the "real" producers (individual worshipers, communities, the state). I have also attempted to show how representations of power of various supernatural entities are sustained and perpetuated by enabling productive activities in several domains (individual construction of religious autobiographical narratives, community construction of local identity, self-legitimation of the state through ritual) to draw upon the same symbols in what I term rhetorics of mutual authentication. (In different terms, Baptandier's essay in this volume makes a similar point.) Such processes result in symbols and mythologies that, as the editors of this volume emphasize, are susceptible to multiple interpretations.[1]

The present paper addresses these issues tangentially. In concocting a category of "family-relationship gods," I intend to suggest that institutional forms other than the state or the bureaucracy—in this case, the family conceived as a culturally specific structure of production of engendered subjectivities—contribute to the production of representations of divine power. Moreover, analysis of the linkages between such representations and the institutions that spawn them allows us to undertake what I hope to show is a productive comparison of these figures. In particular, such a comparison puts into vivid relief the dramatically different emotional consequences for sons and daughters (and, less dramatically, for mothers and fathers) of the patrilineal, patriarchal, virilocal Chinese family system.

Productive agency, in terms of both ritual and social authority, is culturally located in the "subject position"[2] of "son."[3] Daughters are denied recognition of legitimate agency in patrilineal ideology, especially in ritual.[4] My argument assumes that mythic narratives register the differing emotional consequences for sons and daughters of the institutionalization of this ideology in family processes.[5] I wish to emphasize the term *emotional* in the preceding sentence, because the structural consequences of the Chinese family system are well documented in ethnography. As an ideal type,[6] the Chinese family is defined by patrilineal inheritance and descent; patrimony is divided roughly equally (with some exceptions) among sons; daughters marry virilocally "out" of their natal families, joining the families (and patrilines) of their husbands.[7] Produced within and reinforcing this family system is a highly developed tradition of behavioral norms and explicitly elaborated values that can be summarized as "filial piety."[8]

The emotional costs of this marriage/descent/inheritance system for young brides (and, less obviously, for their mothers-in-law) are also well documented in the anthropological literature. I am thinking particularly of the works of Margery Wolf (1968, 1972, 1975) that have so vividly conveyed the pathos of the situation of daughters-in-law and mothers-in-law in Taiwanese families of the 1950s and 1960s, and also of Arthur Wolf and Chieh-shan Huang's (1980) exemplary analysis of forms of marriage and their differing consequences in terms of divorce rates and fertility. Such studies align for the most part with what Chinese popular culture (traditional laments, drama, modern movies, television) conveys in less systematic ways regarding the unenviable costs of the patrilineal-virilocal family system borne by women. Baptandier's contribution to this volume and her earlier work (Berthier 1988) add significantly to our understanding of the vexed nexus of values surrounding female gender and its assimilation to a patrilineal, virilocal society. In comparison, the emotional costs for men have occasioned less frequent comment—an oversight that attention to the Nazha story might allay to some degree.

Mythologies such as those discussed here may thus be seen to add to an extensive Chinese repertoire of forms expressive of emotions and tensions arising from family relations. I am convinced that there is something in the mythic quality of these stories that hints of desires and resentments of a sort more primal and less overtly expressible in other genres of representation. As Freud's classic analysis of Oedipus argued, such stories may reveal dimensions of the costs, in terms of unfulfilled (perhaps unfulfillable) desires, borne by Chinese individuals in the processes of their production as encultured and engendered persons.[9] In other words, like the incidences of divorce and fertility revealed in Wolf and Huang's analysis, such stories may provide insights into Chinese culture unaddressed by normative convention in the more self-conscious self-representations of Chinese culture familiar to us in Chinese philosophy and elite literature.[10]

Myth and Religion

This is not the place to attempt a thoroughgoing justification of the foregoing assertions. Nonetheless, methodological issues warrant some discussion here. Important linkages among forms of popular literature, myth, and religious practice in what for present purposes can be termed "late imperial" China[11] have relatively recently begun to receive attention from anthropologists (see Seaman 1987, Grootaers 1952) and historians (Dean 1993, Johnson 1989). The three figures of interest here—Nazha, Miaoshan, and Mulian—have all been the objects of important recent studies from which I have drawn in this paper.[12] In varying degrees, all of these studies have linked their respective stories to Chinese family issues. The common assumption, one that I share, is that this linkage is justified by the overt content of the stories themselves. I believe that subsequent discussion will help strengthen this assumption, but some of the correlates of this assumption require elaboration.

Anticipating my argument, I believe that interpretation of the mythologies in question is best accomplished by focusing on what they seem most obviously to be about: the processes of production of generational and gender roles as constituent or intrinsic elements of the reproduction of the Chinese patrilineal, virilocal family.[13] I am assuming that the basic patterns of Chinese domestic culture observed by recent ethnographers do not differ radically from those extant during the historical development of these tales.[14] I shall not attempt to justify this assumption here except to suggest that its plausibility is enhanced to some degree by the very salience of the mythological themes that I attempt to understand with reference to these domestic institutions. In other words, I am assuming that there has existed a long-standing fit between the meanings I claim to perceive in the myths, on the one hand, and the experiences that make these meanings accessible to significant numbers of Chinese people.

I open my analysis here to the criticism that it assumes too much homogeneity across class, time, and space in what I am glossing as the Chinese family. I acknowledge this problem as a legitimate one; the degree to which adherence (either behaviorial or ideological) to the basic parameters of the set of institutions—patriliny, virilocal residence, equal inheritance among sons—varies across time, space, and class is still an important research question. Clearly, significant variation exists. Nonetheless, as Wolf and Huang's (1980) study shows, even such apparently divergent forms as "minor marriage" (marriage between adopted "little daughters-in-law" and their foster brothers) and uxorilocal marriage are generated by much the same set of underlying concerns and values—patrilineal continuity and preservation of control by elder generations of younger ones—that generate the more familiar "major" form of marriage (see also Sangren 1982). On the one hand, the consequences of departures in overt family form upon the quality of family relationships—as, for example, the mitigation of mother-in-law/daughter-in-law rivalry in "minor" marriage—are clearly significant; on the other hand, one cannot assume that differences in family form necessarily lead to profound differences in the gender, generational, and descent values that generate them.[15]

Another methodological issue concerns the fact that, although my argument focuses on emotions and sentiments, myths clearly belong to the domain of public or shared culture. In other words, myth is a "collective representation," evolving over time. Myth is even less clearly the product of any individual author than are other narrative forms. Consequently, to suggest as I do that myth is very much about individual experiences as they are produced in institutional context might be viewed as problematic. In other words, I am projecting meanings upon these stories based on my understanding of what would be a common ground of experience and assumption in Chinese audiences. Perhaps one might imagine strengthening my argument by linking narrative life histories or psychoanalytic case studies of individuals to their own interpretations of myths. I do not propose to provide such case studies or life histories here. Consequently, the degree to which my analysis corresponds in a statistical sense to the experiences of Chinese individuals remains an open question.

Nonetheless, I am convinced that the stories constitute representations *produced*—cumulatively and over time, in the telling, in the hearing, and in the retelling—by individual Chinese experiences of important processes and contrasts immanent in the cultural production of the Chinese person. How could things be otherwise? More-over, given the widespread currency these and similar stories enjoy in Chinese popular culture, it does not seem unwarranted to suppose that they do more than reflect or represent such experience. As recent trends in literary theory insist, readers and audiences are not merely passive consumers of texts and narratives; the act of consumption is also dialectically an act of production. In their choices of texts to read and in their imputation of meaning to text or narrative, readers (or listeners) use text to their own ends (or, if one prefers, "meaning construction"), conscious and unconscious.

I should hasten to add, however, that the constructive participa-tion of readers or audiences does not mean that narrative or text is merely an inert material for whatever constructions its consumers might wish to make of it. Although we cannot know with any abso-lute certainty what individual Chinese make of these stories (and there is no doubt a wide spectrum of variation in this regard), I believe that the stories do constrain plausible interpretations (includ-ing such analyses as the present one) by virtue of their overt content and less obvious structures.

Consequently, one might suppose the stories to exercise some pro-ductive power in their own right. In dramatic cases, some enthusiasts modeled their lives on those of mythical characters; more commonly, such characters might give form and sanction to otherwise inarticu-late or even illegitimate sentiments and values—for example, in the case of Miaoshan, resistance to conventional female roles,[16] or in the case of Nazha, autonomy and freedom from overbearing patriarchal authority.

I should also mention briefly a final methodological point. My analysis is informed by issues that have evolved largely in the context of Western social science and psychoanalytic traditions. There is, of course, an important argument to the effect that such arguments and analyses cannot be applied uncritically to non-Western cultures. It would be too cumbersome to attempt here to review such critiques and to justify fully my own analysis with regard to such issues. I shall, however, attempt to clarify the ways in which I view this anal-ysis as culturally specific to Chinese society, despite its invocation of categories of analysis developed in other contexts.

The foregoing methodological premises, I am quite aware, demand of informed readers more than the usual suspension of standards of evidence. Yet even if readers are unconvinced by the specifics of my analysis, I hope that the analysis justifies such suspension by suggest-ing that linking analysis of expressive culture and religion to family processes is a useful vantage point from which to consider issues of gender and the social production of the person in Chinese context.

My interest in these issues was initially provoked by the very colorful story of Nazha. I first encountered Nazha as a kind of guardian god—Zhongtan Yuanshuai, "guardian of the central altar"—a minor figure present in almost all the territorial-cult temples that were the object of my dissertation fieldwork.[17] In particular, I was struck by Nazha's overt rebelliousness. It was difficult to see in Nazha an exemplary figure comparable to, for example, Guandi, Guanyin, or any of myriad other Chinese personages said to have been deified for their filial or other virtues. In attempting to comprehend the Nazha story's messages, I found striking parallels with the other myths I shall describe, which soon convinced me that its interpretation could be strengthened by comparing it with such stories. While the Nazha story focuses on the father-son relationship, other stories emphasize other primary dyads. This paper argues that, considered together, these myths constitute a rich field for analysis of Chinese gender and personhood as they relate to the family.

Nazha: Fathers and Sons

The immensely popular Ming epic *Fengshen Yanyi (Investiture of the Gods)* accounts for much of the popularity of the Nazha story. *Investiture of the Gods* has exercised a considerable but relatively unstudied influence on Chinese popular culture.[18] Its popular appeal approaches that of the *Journey to the West (Xiyou Ji)*, a narrative much better known to Western sinologists; several Chinese friends and acquaintances have told me that they read *Investiture of the Gods* as adolescents and enjoyed it more than the more sermonizing *Xiyou Ji*. Writing about the *Investiture of the Gods* in 1899, Garritt emphasized the readable style and popularity of the book: "In the lithographed copy I have, [the work] forms a compact set of ten volumes, with some very striking illustrations. The approved plan of the novelist at home is found here; as you near the end of a chapter and think to lay the book down, you are told to look at the next chapter and to find how it comes out. Many a fire in Chinese cities has resulted from apprentices reading such books into the 'wee sma' hours,' and not being able to lay them down till overpowered with sleep."

In addition to the popularity of the epic, its influence on popular religion in China has been widely recognized. For example, Liu Ts'un-yan (1962:159) asserts that "most of the deities who are outside of the hierarchy formed in the book are almost forgotten." Although this assertion certainly neglects important cult figures, it is clearly the case that the book has played an important role in sustaining Chinese mythology in popular consciousness. (I might add that stories like *Investiture of the Gods* have had an obvious and direct influence on Chinese martial arts movies. Martial arts movies, in turn, play an important role today in continuing and further developing mythical tradition. This is a connection worthy of further scholarly attention.)

In Taiwan today, modern media (illustrated comic-book-style adaptations for children, television series, and so forth) contribute to the popular dissemination and transformation of stories such as those of *Investiture of the Gods*. In July 1992 (after drafting an early version of this paper), I visited the semiannual publishers' exhibition in Hong Kong. There I obtained several versions of *Investiture of the Gods,* as well as a hot-off-the-press English translation by China Books. I also noted several current editions from various Chinese provincial presses. In addition, I purchased a comic-book version of *Modern Nazha* (in which Nazha's journey to the present is the pretext for science lessons for children, something like Donald Duck's well-known visit to "Mathemagic Land"), a videotape of a full-length opera performance of *Nazha Slays the Sea-Dragon,* and several old and new iconographic representations (wooden images, woodblock prints, a baby's washbasin, an image in dough). I have also in my possession a videotape of a popular feature-length animated film from mainland China (1979) entitled *Nazha Disrupts the Sea (Nazha Naohai).* These materials constitute important collaborative evidence for the continuing popularity of the epic, and the modifications they introduce to the tradition are worthy of study in their own right.

Without doubt the story from the *Investiture of the Gods* that has most captured the Chinese imagination is that of Nazha.[19] The Nazha story—like those of Miaoshan and Mulian to be considered presently—is the basis (at least in part) of cultic worship widespread in present-day Taiwan. In Taiwanese popular religion, Nazha is identified with the divinity San Taizi ("The Third Prince," in reference to Nazha's status as the third of general Li Jing's sons), Taizi Ye (more simply "the Prince"), or Zhongtan Yuanshuai (Guardian of the Central Altar).

In brief, in *Investiture of the Gods* Nazha is a divinely conceived trickster who defies both his earthly father and heaven. As a seven-year-old, he playfully and unintentionally provokes a confrontation with the dragon-king of the oceans,[20] killing one of the dragon-king's sons. This episode is the first of a series of similar ones that lead to another series of attempts by his father to control the unruly boy. Nazha's destructive rebelliousness eventually places his father in an extremely awkward position, as the dragon-king demands divine justice. In what is represented as an act of filial self-sacrifice, Nazha commits suicide, returning his flesh and bones to his parents. This act releases Nazha's father, Li Jing, from the threat of punishment by the Jade Emperor. Even though this act violates the filial injunction against harming one's body, because Nazha does so to protect his parents, up to this point in the tale his behavior is consistent with filial convention.[21]

Desiring a new body, Nazha's spirit appears to his mother in her dreams and convinces her to defy her husband and secretly to erect a temple altar to him. Because the temple is so efficacious, never failing to respond to worshipers' requests, it attracts increasing numbers of pilgrims. Eventually, however, Nazha's father discovers the temple's existence and destroys it and its image of Nazha. But because Nazha's souls had received nourishment from pilgrims' offerings and incense, his yang (material) body is partially reconstituted. Nazha's Daoist immortal mentor, Taiyi Zhenren, reconstitutes his body from a lotus flower *(lianhua huashen)*. In a vengeful rage against Li Jing, Nazha attempts patricide and subsequently must be restrained, at the behest of Taiyi Zhenren, by Randeng Daoren, another Daoist immortal. Thus tamed, Nazha goes on in the epic to become a supernaturally gifted hero in Jiang Ziya's campaign against the evil emperor Zhou, last of the Shang.[22]

The story has obvious Oedipal overtones: the son's patricidal desire for vengeance, the father's murderous intentions toward his son, and the rivalry between them for the affection of the wife/mother. Overt expression of such sentiments, largely inexpressible in other contexts of Chinese existence, no doubt accounts in part for the popularity of the story. In other words, the story's long-standing and widespread popularity may be attributed in part to the expression it provides for otherwise strongly repressed emotions. Indeed, this is an interpretation readily accepted by many Chinese familiar with the tale, with whom I have discussed it.[23]

Although I do not wish to suggest a straightforwardly Freudian interpretation here,[24] nonetheless one need not delve too deeply into the culture of Chinese family life to find sources for such Oedipal tensions. Not only do Chinese fathers possess strongly sanctioned authority, but also, in Marxist parlance, they control the means of production. Even adult sons with sons of their own do not achieve full maturity or autonomy until "family division" *(fenjia),* when they receive their shares of the patrimonial estate. Vigorous Chinese fathers characteristically resist this division, if possible, until their deaths. (By vigorous, I mean fathers fortunate enough to be possessed not only of good health and strength of will but also of productive resources or wealth sufficient to exercise control over their sons. Poor fathers, no matter how strong of body and character, were in a much less advantaged position to attempt to control their sons.)

Under such circumstances, it is quite understandable that some sons come to resent patriarchal authority and that some fathers come to view their sons' maturation as a sign of their own imminently diminishing powers if not as a harbinger of their own deaths. One need not locate the sources of this hostility in libidinal competition for the mother, as does Freud, to see the makings of a classic Oedipal rivalry in the situation.[25]

Mothers, of course, even if they are not objects of sons' libidinal desires, are not irrelevant. Recent ethnographic research (especially Wolf 1968, 1972, 1975; Wolf and Huang 1980) confirms Chinese popular understandings of the extremely strong emotional bonds between mothers and sons fostered by overbearing patriarchal authority sometimes exercised by domineering fathers. Moreover, the pattern of virilocal residence that makes of young wives alienated outsiders in their families of procreation, at least until the births of their own sons, motivates mothers to cultivate and even to manipulate their sons. (The notion that sons, as in the case of Nazha, might be in a position to manipulate their mothers has yet to be explored, to my knowledge, in the literature.) In sum, just as in the Nazha story, in the ethnographic record alliances between Chinese mothers and sons are a characteristic locus of subversion of patriarchal authority.

One should not overlook, however, what might be seen as the analogue of the Oedipal tensions between fathers and sons in the ways in which this alliance between mothers and sons sets up a rivalry between mothers and their sons' wives. The classic tragedy for Chinese women is that, as young wives, they are stereotypically subordinated to their mothers-in-law, but as older women just beginning to enjoy the power and security associated with the maturation of their sons, their ties to their sons are threatened by the conjugal relationship between their sons and their daughters-in-law. In other words, daughters-in-law embody impending loss of a woman's power, vitality, even life, just as sons do a man's.

The Nazha story highlights the tensions in the father-son relationship, but as the analysis proceeds, the contextualization of all these other dimensions of the classic pattern of the reproduction of family and its generational and gender roles must be kept in mind.

Mulian: Mothers and Sons

Mother-son alliance figures more prominently in the well-known story of Mulian, the focus of a series of papers produced by the Chinese Popular Culture Project (Johnson 1989).[26] Mulian, in the popular story, is a disciple of Buddha who, learning of his mother's confinement in purgatory, undertakes arduous adventures and journeys to hell to win her freedom.[27] The religious significance of this story in popular consciousness is vividly evident in its explicit association with women's funerals. Seaman (1981, 1989) describes how operatic performances of the story reinforce the obligation of sons to wipe out the stain of pollution borne by all women as a means of repaying their mothers for the gift of life.[28] This debt is repaid in the ritual "Breaking the Blood Bowl":

> For women's funerals, the drama-cum-ritual called "Breaking the Blood Bowl" is an adaptation of the story of Mu-lien's descent into hell to save his mother. In the ritual, the sons and daughters of a dead woman mime a descent into hell. A set is built representing the fortress in hell where their mother's soul is imprisoned, and a bowl of wine, dyed red, is placed in the fortress to symbolize the pool of blood in which she is drowning. After the actor who plays the part of Mu-lien vanquishes the jailers of hell (who would keep the woman's soul imprisoned), the bowl of red wine is portioned out to the children of the dead woman. Each of them drinks, wipes the bowl clean, then presents it to Mu-lien for a final purification. Indeed, it is highly suggestive that in some Chinese dialects the word for "blood bowl" (*hueq-phun;* Mandarin, *hsüeh-p'un*) also means "placenta." (Seaman 1981:388–389)

Seaman also provides a compelling interpretive contextualization for the juxtaposition of filial devotion and horror of polluting blood (and, more generally, of women's biological functions) evident in such rituals:

> In societies like China, where descent is based almost exclusively on the male line, women's rights and the way women are incorporated into their husbands' lines [via virilocal, "major" marriage (Wolf and Huang 1980)] are fraught with danger, threatening male solidarity. To preserve the solidarity of the male-oriented agnatic line, a rationalizing ideology develops that subordinates the role of women to that of men. After all, a reproductive unit is formed by people from alien and potentially hostile agnatic lines. For husbands, who are parties to the difficult political negotiations involved in taking brides, the absence of "wives' rights" in the agnatic line is not difficult to rationalize. However, for sons, who owe their very being and consequently their membership in the line to their mothers, the implicit mistrust and hostility towards all women (including their mothers) is much harder to explain. (Seaman 1981:382)

I believe that Seaman's linkage of the story to the consequences for women of their place in the structure of Chinese patriarchal/patrilineal families is right on target.[29]

In a similar vein, in an earlier publication (Sangren 1983) I contrasted the negative evaluation of female gender apparent in pollution beliefs (see also Ahern 1975) to the unambiguously positive values symbolized in mother goddesses such as Guanyin, Mazu, and the Eternal Mother. I argued that female goddesses are not modeled on women in general, but are rather embodiments of motherhood—that is, they are symbols of "unifying" and "mediating" aspects of women's social roles. Roles threatening to the solidarity of patrilineally organized domestic groups—i.e., young wife/daughter-in-law—are also, not incidentally, more immediately associated with biological reproduction.[30] I further argued that beliefs and symbolizations of women's polluting, destructive powers are linked to these divisive roles. Chinese goddesses are thought of more or less as virgin mothers; sexually attractive or active women appear in Chinese popular culture mainly as evil fox spirits and the like whose classic role is to lead men to their destruction. (Significantly, one classic example is the fox spirit [hulijing] Daji, the villainess who bewitches Emperor Zhou and causes the fall of the Shang dynasty in the Investiture of the Gods.)[31]

The Mulian story, like that of Chen Jinggu (Baptandier, in this volume),[32] attempts to come to grips with this contradiction in the feelings Chinese have toward women. In other words, it manifests the Chinese recognition of the fact that one person's beloved, unifying mother is another's threatening, divisive daughter-in-law. By "the feelings Chinese have toward women," I mean those revealed in stories like that of Mulian, not that all Chinese have feelings toward others stereotypically determined by kin relationship or even gender. Moreover, although I am arguing that iconography, myth, and popular literature express emotions and vexed relationships stemming from the characteristic structure of the patrilineal, virilocal family, one should not assume that these emotions are felt only by men.

Some additional discussion of the linkage between female gender and Chinese notions of death, pollution, and decay is relevant here. As several scholars have emphasized (Ahern 1975, Seaman 1981, Sangren 1987, Martin 1988), Chinese conceptions regarding biological reproduction link female processes with pollution, decay, even death. I have argued that there is a clear association between these beliefs and the structurally problematic role assigned women in the patrilineal, virilocal family. In China as elsewhere (Bloch and Parry 1982), cultural representations of the sources of productive (and reproductive) power are linked to theories about death. Chinese are not unusual in their tendency to represent "the negative aspects of death . . . as inseparable from other biological phenomena (like copulation and parturition); that in common with other biological processes, decomposition and decay are . . . pre-eminently associated with women; and that this world of biology is elaborately constructed as something to be got rid of so as to make way for the regeneration of the ideal order" (Bloch and Parry 1982:27). The power to regenerate order and life is ideologically represented as originating ultimately from the patriline (Sangren 1983, Watson 1982, Bloch and Parry 1982). Women's sexuality may be necessary, but it is represented as subordinate to male productive fertility.

I shall not attempt to rehearse here my arguments justifying this assertion; instead I shall suggest an additional line of interpretation. I believe that the linkage in Chinese culture between women's powers of procreation, on the one hand, and pollution, death, and decay, on the other, is more than a simple manifestation of an ethnobiology of human procreation with unfortunate consequences for women's value and self esteem (Ahern 1975, Seaman 1981, Sangren 1983). This association and these consequences are not in dispute; the question is why the association should exist.

Inspired in part by Mary Douglas' well-known argument (especially 1966), Emily Martin [Ahern] believes that the association of women's biological capabilities with pollution and decay is largely consequent upon the unsettling transgressions of bodily boundaries (birth, menstruation) they constitute. She has argued (Martin [Ahern] 1988) that women's experiences (both of their bodies and of their social roles) foster in them a more holistic, life-affirming "women's ideology" that contrasts with the categorizing, divisive, hierarchical, death-valorizing "male ideology."

I shall argue instead that, although the cultural construction of bodily processes—and hence the reasons Chinese associate women's biological functions with pollution and decay—constitute an ethnobiology demeaning to women (at least in some contexts), this ethnobiology is itself validated—and in this sense, produced—by what I shall term the social organization of gender. While Martin suggests that biophysiology plays an important role in producing an ideology of gender, I would place more emphasis on how the subject positions posited for individuals by the Chinese family system produce such representations. In brief, my hypothesis is that an androcentric ideology of production defines positive productive agency as a prerogative of men—in the Chinese case, particularly sons. This ideology is the foundation not only of patrilineal kinship but also of ancestral sacrifice (what Zito [1987] terms "filial action"). But the ideology is a product as well as a premise of Chinese social life. Women's productivity, both social and biological, is an embarrassment to the fantasy of filial omnipotence instituted in Chinese kinship and expressed and produced in ancestor worship.

My argument is premised on the conviction that invocation of "cultural" constructions (or representations) in one semantic domain (in this case, ethnobiology) as an explanation for cultural constructions in another (gender) is less compelling than linking cultural constructions to their production and validation in social activities and institutions. By "linking" cultural categories to social institutions, what I have in mind is that there exists a totalizing process of social production (and reproduction) in which both institutional forms (in this case, the family) and cultural categories (the generational and gender roles and the ethnobiological ideas associated with them) emerge as mutually constitutive manifestations immanent in this encompassing productive process. This temporally dynamic productive process that links representations or cultural categories and social institutions or structures is thus in this sense a dialectical one. Stated less abstractly, the fact that both the Mulian and Miaoshan myths specifically juxtapose issues surrounding female pollution to stories that are first and foremost about family relationships seems to me to favor my interpretation over Martin's.

I do not intend to imply that representations (of male or female gender, or of ethnobiologies of reproduction) are simply reflections of social structure; insofar as they correspond to the taken-for-granted premises of social actors, representations play an important role in producing intentional action. But by the same token, such representations are also (largely unintended) products of such social action. One cannot take culture and representations as transcendent causes of social structure and action any more than one can assume that culture and representations are merely reflections of a more materially "real" social structure. In other words, the pollution associated with women's biophysiology may be a result of the poignancy of the position of the young bride in the Chinese marriage system (I have argued essentially this position in Sangren 1983 and shall not rehearse the argument here) and, just as important, of the poignancy of the position of daughters in their natal families.

Miaoshan: Fathers and Daughters

In this regard, let us take up the story of Miaoshan.[33] Born a princess, she defied her father's wishes, refused to marry, and retreated to a life of Buddhist contemplation, whereupon her father (according to later versions of the tale) had her killed. During her sojourn in hell, Miaoshan's true identity as Guanyin was revealed. The power of her great virtue enabled her to win salvation for the tortured souls there. Later, she returned to earth, assuming the guise of a mountain recluse. Hearing of her father's life-threatening illness, she cured him by offering her own eyes and arm to concoct a magic potion.[34]

Thereafter she was made miraculously whole again, and having shown her father the true path, she entered Nirvana.[35]

Miaoshan's salvation of her father and Mulian's of his mother at first glance appear as closely analogous. There is a provocative symmetry in the notion that mothers be saved by sons and fathers by daughters. However, in Miaoshan's case, her father kills her (metaphorically in some versions, literally in others) and sends her to hell, while Mulian journeys to hell voluntarily to save his mother. While in hell, Miaoshan experiences an apotheosis and saves the anonymous masses of tortured souls. This episode may reinforce Guanyin's central role in rites of universal salvation *(pudu)* typically held during the seventh lunar month on behalf of all lonely spirits *(guhun)*. In contrast, Mulian figures in funerals for specific women.

The foregoing comparison suggests that Miaoshan's murder by her father parallels the experience of marriage for Chinese women— in the view of Martin [Ahern] (1988), a kind of death. My initial inclination was to view this element of the story as figuring, particularly, an association between what in effect is an "expulsion" of daughters from the family effected by major marriage and death. But as an anonymous reviewer of this paper points out, this interpretation neglects the fact that Miaoshan's sisters are married uxorilocally. The reviewer proposes instead that conflict results from Miaoshan's desire to *leave* home to be a nun and her father's desire to use her to obtain an uxorilocal son-in-law to continue his line.

This alternative warrants serious consideration, especially in terms internal to the texts. It is nonetheless still plausible to propose that Chinese family life (at least, in late imperial times) would evoke audience *responses* to the story that align with their *own* experiences— experiences in which daughters' destinies, to marry out, are taken for granted. In other words, to be a Chinese "daughter" includes the expectation of separation from one's natal patriline and family. Moreover, one should also keep in mind that Miaoshan explicitly justifies the desire to leave the home in terms of the pollution that associates marriage and childbirth with death and decay, characteristic of patrilineal, *virilocal* family systems.

There is, in my view, overwhelming comparative evidence from other cultures for the association between patrilineal, virilocal marriage systems and ideologies of female impurity (Jay 1992, Delaney 1991, Bloch and Parry 1982). Although Miaoshan's rebellion clearly expresses a conflict between Buddhist values and filial piety, both are products of Chinese family life. Buddhist escapist desire, *in Chinese context,* is as much a consequence of patrilineal family processes as is filial piety.[36] In other words, the ritually "polluted" status that prevents women from achieving Nirvana is part and parcel of the *same* set of ideas and institutions that defines the subject position possessed of productive agency as that of the "son."

In these terms, uxorilocal marriage as a strategy to continue patrilines makes of uxorilocal husbands the equivalent of "male daughters-in-law" without, however, really making of their wives "female sons" (Wolf and Huang 1980). Uxorilocally married men are thus dispossessed of the culturally crucial privilege of ancestor worship as filial sons. The instability that arises in this ambiguity of roles manifests, for example, in high divorce rates (Wolf and Huang 1980). In the Miaoshan legends, it manifests in her sisters' husbands plotting against Miaoshan's father. One might even propose that this subplot highlights the inadequacy of the uxorilocal "solution"[37]— either in terms of providing for patrilineal continuity or as a means of obtaining for daughters the privileged (in the terms of the current argument, "integrated") position of "son" (Zito 1987).

In sum, one can see in Miaoshan's desire to renounce the world and "leave the home" a desire to imagine a "subject position" for daughters endowed of agency and power equivalent to that of a son.[38] I believe that one episode in the story may be construed to lend some support to this interpretation. When Miaoshan's father's life is threatened by illness, curable only "by one free of anger" (Dudbridge 1978:31), it is she who cures him by sacrificing her own arm and eye. Her two married elder sisters refuse. Their loyalties having transferred to their husbands, Miaoshan's sisters are in no position to obviate these obligations and make the sacrifice demanded by their father.

In Dudbridge's (1978:42) translation of one version of the story, Miaoshan's father, deeply moved by her sacrifice, "humbly besought heaven and earth to make her whole again. In a short while the holy elder had arms and eyes by the thousand . . . And then Guanyin bowed before him, and to their utter delight they expressed to one another the feelings proper to father and child. She urged him to practise good works, and he did so, cleansing his mind and changing his ways, so that finally she was able to soar aloft together with the king."

In my view, this passage imagines a reintegration of father and daughter, one that figures more closely the identifications between fathers and sons sanctioned by kinship ideology and ancestor worship. In other words, I believe that the Miaoshan story combines a daughter's fantasy of producing for herself the subject position of a Chinese son and (to a lesser extent) a father's of imagining that a daughter might occupy such a role.

Myth, Ideology, and the Cultural Construction of Gender and Person

The preceding brief characterizations and interpretations of the Mulian, Miaoshan, and Nazha stories relate them to tensions internal to the reproductive structure of Chinese families. I believe it advantageous to push the analysis further, however, and to see in the stories mythical commentary on the processes of production of Chinese male and female subjectivities—that is, selves. I emphasize *Chinese* male and female subjectivities to draw attention to the cultural constructedness of gender categories. Yet I shall depart from some ethnopsychological approaches by suggesting that it is insufficient merely to explicate or, broadly, to translate explicit gender categories into terms intelligible to us (Sangren n.d.b). It is also necessary to show how such cultural categories are produced in Chinese institutional context. I *include* this institutional context in my understanding of "culture"; as an analytical concept, "culture" is not usefully limited to the linguistic categories it produces!

In brief, my hypothesis is that the structures of social production of Chinese families—the whole constellation of gender, generational, and conjugal roles as they develop and reproduce through time— are the constitutive frame within which Chinese subjectivities are produced. At this level of abstraction the hypothesis is quite conventional. However, again in contrast to some interpretivist approaches,[39] I believe that it is important not only to recognize but also to incorporate into one's analysis the fact that explicitly elaborated cultural categories systematically misrecognize the principles of their own production. Gender, personhood, and kin roles are represented and their consequences for individuals explored in mythical narratives, but there is little overt recognition in myth that these categories and the values they imply are themselves products of social activity. Such categories and values are taken-for-granted premises; in this sense, such categories constitute what I would term "ideology."

Because "ideology" in the analytical sense I intend here is in some disrepute (especially in interpretivist and poststructuralist treatments),[40] a brief defense of my position is called for. If, for example, we are willing to criticize those in our own society who "essentialize" gender (who believe gender to be a natural, culturally unmediated attribute of persons), we thereby make an implicit claim to the effect that our own cultural categories, produced and reinforced in our society, are not only "ideological" in the sense that they are based on opinion, but also that they misrepresent some "truth." An example of such a truth that seems to me a premise of much anthropological speculation is that gender is the cultural appropriation or construction of biological sex differences (Rubin 1975). From the perspective that I am advocating, the interesting anthropological question then becomes how one accounts for the systematic reproduction of misrecognition: what is it in the institutions of our society—family, workplace, economy—that validates and reproduces such misrecognition?

Analysis of mythical narrative becomes interesting in such a context because, as Piaget (1962) notes of dreams and children's play, myth is a genre of symbolic production and representation in which the boundaries of the ego or self are relaxed. In the Nazha and Miaoshan stories, for example, both normative role models and sentiments and the transgression of such norms in the desires and behaviors of the protagonists are liberally expressed. More subtly, insofar as the stories are about the *production* of engendered subjectivities, they entail role transformations, such as child to adult.

In the parlance of literary criticism, it is not so much that the voices in the stories subvert stable subject positions as that the stories themselves constitute an encompassing, unselfconscious, transcendent perspective upon the more consciously represented positions expressed in the voices of their protagonists. By the same token, although the stories have obvious protagonists, I do not believe that they express solely the egocentric perspective of anyone in particular. It is in this transcendence of stable ego-centered boundaries that myth is dreamlike. (Conversely, any narrative is mythlike to the degree that ego boundaries are relaxed.) The absence of ego-centered self-consciousness in a speculative narrative precisely about the production of gendered selves is what makes these stories so valuable as culturally generated commentary (as well as fantasy) about culturally produced subjectivities, largely *unaware* of itself as such. I would hypothesize further that it is the reiterative, collective process of myth formation alluded to above that accounts for this relaxation of stable ego-boundaries.[41]

The fact that mythical narratives speculate upon transgression of orthodox values and role categories—in cases such as those of Nazha and Miaoshan, they may even be said to valorize such transgression —should not be taken as evidence that they escape ideology. Although one might plausibly argue that Nazha's rejection of the role of submissive son and Miaoshan's of that of wife and daughter constitute models legitimating resistance to conventional models of social personhood, the stories fall short of developing a dialectical critique of ideology that reveals how such roles and values are products or effects of social activities and institutions as well as legitimating premises. Nazha and Miaoshan may reject the roles of son and of wife, but the essential, given, transcendental nature of such roles is not really questioned. In addition to fantasizing escape from the undesired emotional consequences of such roles, the stories convey the message that short of becoming a bodhisattva or a bodiless Daoist immortal, such escape is really inconceivable. In the end, neither Miaoshan nor Nazha becomes a properly social, engendered person; both become *gods*.

By the same token, despite the eloquence of Miaoshan's story on the degradations of marriage for women, no alternative marriage system is envisioned.[42] If, as I have argued, the attribution of pollution to women is immanent in the marriage-kinship system, it is not surprising that the myth also fails to call into question the negative assessment of women's productive powers. Indeed, Miaoshan's refusal to marry and Guanyin's popularity among "marriage resistance cults" in nineteenth-century Guangdong (Topley 1954, 1975) can be taken as evidence that even in such rejection of women's culturally conceived biological roles, the notion that women's biological functioning is polluting is unshaken (Sangren 1983).[43]

The foregoing issues are perhaps better framed by saying that the stories manifest contradictions immanent in the engendering production of male and female subjects. This is an analytical suggestion that I can only outline here. That the Chinese kinship system does not foster the production of a stable female "subject position" seems evident in the mythical elaboration of the ambivalence toward women revealed in the foregoing discussion of the ceremony of the blood bowl. Women are defined by the Chinese kinship system as outsiders attempting to become insiders (mainly through marriage and incorporation into their husbands' descent lines). The ceremony of the blood bowl may be read as an example of a ritual attempt to effect this integration. But as with all ritual, its ultimate efficacy is implicitly in question. In other words, the fact that the ritual must be performed at all might be interpreted as indicating the ambiguity of women's state of being with regard to subjectivity.

I believe that there are also ambiguities with regard to the production of Chinese male subjectivity, but that these ambiguities are of a somewhat different order than those affecting women. For men the issue focuses on whether one is to be the agent/subject of one's own desires or the instrument/object of the desire of some "other"—specifically one's son or one's father. Stories like that of Nazha focus on this struggle for the empowered (male) subject position.[44] In contrast, stories like that of Miaoshan seem less to manifest a struggle for power over another (as an instrument in the production and definition of one's own subjectivity) than to register a struggle to gain recognition by the "other" (in Miaoshan's case, her father) of one's own subjectivity. If, as I am arguing, the Chinese kinship system in effect imagines full subjectivity/agency as male, then this struggle is ultimately futile in *the terms defined by that system.*[45]

I must hasten to add that in all of the preceding one should not confuse "subjectivity" and "subject position" with real people. For example, one might argue that it is in the struggle to gain recognition of their subjectivity in a system constrained to deny it to them that Chinese women are formed as *persons.* For Chinese women, the struggle to gain the recognition of others necessarily entails recognition on their own part of others' subjectivities or desires. For Chinese men, this recognition is not at issue; the issue is rather whether one's own will or desire will dominate or be subservient. Thus, for Chinese men, subjectivities abstractly defined by the kinship system seem to align more closely with personhood as experienced in life. In both domains the struggle for power seems more narcissistic or egocentric than is the case for women precisely because recognition of one's subjectivity is taken for granted and because the game then becomes one of dominance and subordination.

Some support for the foregoing suggestions can be found in the salience of issues of recognition in both the Miaoshan and Nazha stories. The struggle between Nazha and Li Jing reaches its apparent "resolution" when Nazha is forced to acknowledge Li Jing as his father. The dénouement of the Miaoshan story might be seen in what amounts to her father's coerced recognition *of her.* The asymmetry is striking and figures quite clearly the very different kinds of subjectivities figured for sons and daughters in the Chinese marriage/kinship system. For sons, recognition is assumed, autonomy must be achieved; for daughters, the struggle is rather an effort to gain recognition.

I would like to return here to the objections to my analysis noted earlier: that it inappropriately applies Freudian categories that emerged historically in analysis of Western family systems and that Nazha's and Miaoshan's self-mutilation, in contrast to Oedipus's patricide, preserve an important cultural difference consistent with Chinese filial values. I agree with my critics that Freud's classic analysis of the "Oedipus complex" is not directly transferable to Chinese culture. Even in the context of Western culture, there is much to dispute in orthodox Freudian theory. Nonetheless, I would argue that at a more abstract level, what is more generally termed the "Oedipal situation"—which I take to be the entire nexus of processes by means of which individual desire, self-consciousness, and gender are produced in the context of culturally specific socializing institutions and roles —can provide a useful comparative analytical vantage point. Indeed, by linking my analysis of these stories to Chinese family institutions, I have attempted precisely to show how desire as manifest in myth is culturally specific.

I would also agree with my critics that both Nazha and Miao-shan violate their own bodies (and not, as in the case of Oedipus, those of their fathers or mothers) and that this violation is represented as an act of filial devotion. In both cases, however, this self-violation is on behalf of a father whose interests and desires are clearly represented as at odds with those of his child. Although it is true that both stories go to some effort to represent the children's actions as containable within the norms of filial behavior, the fact remains that both are led to such self-violation by this conflict of their desires with those of their respective fathers.[46] In Nazha's case, the scene can even be interpreted as a reproach of Li Jing's abandonment of him in the face of divine authorities; in Miaoshan's case, her sacrifice is also a statement of self-vindication against the errors of her father.

Alternatively in Lacanian terms, both stories might be said to speculate upon the imagined utopia of an ego freed of the separations imposed by "the law"—by the "desire of the other"—that enjoins the socialization of subjectivities.[47] Notice, however, that this speculation expresses an unachievable desire born of Chinese social institutions rather than a critique of those social institutions. Nonetheless, one might easily imagine circumstances under which such speculation might foster actual resistance to institutional arrangements. The example best known to anthropologists is probably the "marriage resistance cults" of Guangdong, which according to Topley (1975) specifically invoked Miaoshan as a behavioral model. Nazha, in a less obvious fashion, is sometimes invoked as exemplifying justifiable defiance of patriarchal authority. I have seen, for example, in the writings of an advocate of Taiwanese independence an analogy drawn between Taiwan's relations to mainland China and Nazha's attempt to establish his autonomy (Lin 1988).

Instances of such behavioral resistance inspired by mythic figures, although perhaps not uncommon, seem to me to be secondary to what rather imprecisely might be termed their expressive qualities. Nazha's resentment of his father and more subtly his father's reciprocal feelings, Miaoshan's abhorrence of marriage and her father's reaction to her rebellion are sentiments immediately intelligible to Chinese readers and audiences. Indeed, I would argue that such sentiments are part and parcel of what it means to be a Chinese father, son, or daughter. In this regard, myths such as these might be said both to express and to give form to the affective content of Chinese kinship and, consequently, to constitute an important element of Chinese kinship understood as the institutional framework within which Chinese persons are produced.

Notes

The first public presentation of elements of my interest in Nazha and similar stories was at the conference "Learning the Rules: Schooling, Law and the Reproduction of Social Order," Department of History, University of Minnesota, 9–11 May 1991. The analysis was advanced in a paper entitled "Myths of Self-Production, with Special Attention to the Story of No-cha from the *Feng-shen Yen-i*," presented at a session, "Chinese Gods: Beyond the Bureaucracy," organized by Robert Weller and Meir Shahar, at the Annual Meeting of the Association for Asian Studies, Washington, D.C., 3 April 1992. An earlier version of the paper, entitled "Gods and Familial Relations: No-cha, Miao-shan, and Mu-lien," was presented at the International Conference on Popular Beliefs and Chinese Culture, Center for Chinese Studies, Taipei, 25–28 April 1993; it appeared in the two-volume published proceedings of the conference (*Minjian Xinyang yu Zhongguo Wenhua*, 1:33–74 [Taipei: Hanxue Yanjiu Zhongxin]). I am grateful to the Center for Chinese Cultural Studies for granting permission to publish the revised version here. Research for the paper was supported in part by an NEH Summer Stipend and by the Hu Shih Memorial Fund, East Asia Program, Cornell University. I first read *Investiture of the Gods* on a sabbatical leave at the Interuniversity Center for Chinese Language Studies in Taipei (1986–1987). My ongoing research on Nazha has benefited by suggestions from Victor Mair, James Watson, Chan Hok-lam, Bill Nienhauser, Chao Yengning, Terence Turner, Avron Boretz, Wong Kam-ming, Wang Ch'iu-kuei, and Whalen Lai. Special thanks are due Gary Seaman, Bob Hegel, and K. C. Liu for pointing out several errors of rendition and guiding me toward useful source materials.

1. I might emphasize more than do the editors the ways in which the admittedly complex and varied Chinese pantheon—rife with contradictory values linkable to all the social collectivities that constitute what we might term "Chinese society"—can still be viewed as products of processes of representation that manifest remarkable similarities precisely as alienated representations of productive power in one domain draw upon representations produced elsewhere in these rhetorics of mutual authentication. Duara 1988 seems to have a similar point in mind. I find myself more in sympathy with Freedman's (1974) call for seeking out the "underlying" structures in Chinese religion, with the important qualification that these "structures" should not be understood in the structuralist terms of, for example, Lévi-Strauss—that is, as static semantic systems like the "bureaucratic metaphor"—but instead as the structures of social production (for Bourdieu 1977, the "structuring structures"; for Giddens 1979, the processes of "structuration") that produce such representations. Among such processes of social production are the interpretive activities of various Chinese sectional interests and individuals.

2. By "subject position" I mean to indicate a rhetorical or discursive place (in relation to others) logically posited by language, ritual, or "kinship" conceived as a symbolic system. This sense, I believe, is broadly consistent with that employed in Lacanian psychoanalysis. It is important to keep in mind that individuals occupy different subject positions as social and discursive contexts shift. See Mitchell 1983, Rose 1983, Lacan 1983, and Smith 1988.

3. My argument here draws from the analysis of "filial action" by Zito 1987

and the discussion of the father-son relation in Confucian philosophy by Tu 1985.

4. To achieve that measure of orderly immortality offered by Chinese notions of afterlife and in the rituals of ancestor worship, a daughter should marry out. There is no place for spinsters in the lineages of their births, only in those of their descendants and husbands. One might even go so far as to say that there is no female "subject position" recognized in Chinese models of patrilineal, eternal, transcendent order. Sons' consumption of the blood of the pollution of childbirth symbolized in the ceremony of the blood bowl described below strikes me as collaborative argument in favor of this suggestion. To become ancestors, to achieve a stable subject position in afterlife, women must in effect be purified of that which makes them such. I think it is plausible, although quite speculative, to suggest that in the filial act of taking upon themselves their mother's female pollution, sons in effect "produce" or "reproduce" their mothers' eternal spirits as male, thus inverting the productive relations of biological procreation. Such an interpretation would be consistent with a general penchant in patrilineal societies to represent men's production of the social and spiritual as encompassing women's production (e.g., Bloch and Parry 1982, Jay 1992).

5. I am currently working on a more thoroughgoing analysis of, in particular, the Nazha story, which elaborates in more psychoanalytic terms what I characterize as the symbolic constitution of subjectivity.

6. This depiction of the Chinese family is an "ideal type" both in the Weberian sense and as a culturally sanctioned form.

7. Daughters thus know that, no matter how successfully they win the affections of their parents, structurally speaking, they are destined to be separated from the natal family. Perhaps paradoxically, I believe that these circumstances foster a desire among girls almost the reciprocal of that manifested by rebellious sons like Nazha. Instead of rejecting the subordinated integration into their natal families that is the destiny of boys, daughters may seek to reject their impending rejection from it. Salaff's ethnography of young working women in Hong Kong provides some justification for such a hypothesis. As she puts it (1981:95), "despite being taught they did not belong to their natal family, they unconsciously desired to be considered as intimate members."

8. Jordan 1986 provides a useful analysis of filial piety as manifest in popular culture, where understandings differ significantly from what one might derive from reading Confucian philosophy.

9. Spiro 1987 makes a strong and explicit argument for the universal relevance of Oedipal situations as bases for cosmology and myth. One can agree with Spiro's contention that structures of authority and socialization in domestic groups universally influence religion and ideology without seeing in this fact an explanation for religion and ideology. What seems insufficiently developed in Freudian treatments is a sense of the dialectical character of alienation (repression) as a simultaneously social and individual psychological process that continues to be produced in social activities throughout the life course of the individual. With Freud, Spiro assumes a fundamental conflict between filial emotions and filial values enjoining that the former be repressed in the interest of social order (1987:266). By locating alienation and, hence, repression in the systemic structure of the processes of self and collective production and repro-

duction—the family—one can avoid the functionalistic problems of Freud's argument and its problematic grounding on a theory of instincts (Sangren 1991).

10. Of the Miaoshan legend, for example, Dudbridge (1978:9) writes: "Study of these matters takes us deep into the corpus of popular writings which span the uncertain boundaries between religion, literature and entertainment: stories, plays, liturgies and ballads which, important or not in themselves, often articulate for us the mythological and ritual themes more dimly implied in conscious literary creations." I also agree with Grant 1989 that the fact that such stories ramify into many differing versions is attributable to the ultimately unresolvable tensions or paradoxes in social life that they register.

11. I must acknowledge the simplifications associated with this term. In particular, anthropological fieldwork on Chinese local religion postdates the fall of the Qing. Yet the main outlines of present-day Chinese cosmology, ritual, and practice still seem most intelligible when viewed as a component of a Chinese imperial system that obviously is no longer extant in its fully integrated form. That local (or "popular") religion often posits a cosmology linked to an imperial metaphor is cause for serious reflection beyond the scope of this paper. For some thoughts on this score, see Sangren 1987.

12. Particularly important are the study of the historical origins and development of the Miaoshan story by Dudbridge 1978, the work on the cult of Guanyin by Yü 1992, the brief but insightful analysis of Nazha by Ho 1988, and the studies of Mulian in Johnson 1989.

13. I am inspired in this regard by the analyses of Kayapo mythologies by Turner 1977, 1985. Turner constructs a compelling model of narrative structure in myth that points out important shortcomings in Lévi-Strauss's structuralism. Turner argues for a more dynamic and syntactically sensitive structuralist method that can account better for the narrative, sequential, storylike qualities of myth than can Lévi-Strauss's synchronic, paradigmatic, primarily semantic analyses. The subject matter of myth, for Turner, includes the processes of social production of "cultural subjects"—that is, of the socialization of individuals to their appropriate social roles. This subject matter is modeled in the generative structure of the narrative. Although I do not propose to undertake such a structural narrative analysis here, Turner's linking of mythical content to the immediate social milieu that generates myth seems essential.

14. The history of the Miaoshan legend by Dudbridge 1978 documents the story's probable origins in popular religion (including attribution to divine revelation [1978:13]), entry into more literate traditions (again, sanctioned by divine authority), and elaborations via such media as baojuan. His study is exemplary in showing how a local cult ramified through time into one of China's most important religious movements, in the process serving as an important medium of China's appropriation and transformation of Buddhism. I am not qualified to emulate such philological methods with regard to the other myths I shall discuss, but each of them is worthy of a study like Dudbridge's.

15. In this respect, I am less inclined than are the editors of this volume to suppose that the unity of Chinese religion is a "disorganized" or an "unruly" one, although I do agree that it is diverse and productive not only of widely and sometimes wildly variant forms and interpretations but also occasionally of opposed ones. The "unity" that I would propose exists rather in the processes

that produce both integration and variation (Sangren 1984, 1987). With regard to religion, one would expect to find manifestations of this unity in the ways in which social institutions, ranging from families and communities to wider regional collectivities and the state, are both unintended products of and dialectically producers of what Bourdieu 1977 terms the "doxic" taken-for-granteds that define the limits of both expressible orthodoxies and heterodoxies. Among these doxic taken-for-granteds, one might include various assumptions about the ultimate origins of natural and social order and of productive power. I would argue that the multivocality of imageries and interpretations embedded in most cults can be accounted for best if, in addition to noting that different kinds of participants bring different perspectives and interests to bear, one also notes the interlinking, potentially mutually authenticating rhetorics that embed various socially constituted subjectivities in more encompassing ones. To be sure, such interlinkages are unstable and rife with contradictions, but insofar as Chinese culture can be said to exist at all, it would seem useful to suppose that the logic of cultural production that accounts for the multivocalic potential of cultic phenomena is a reflexive product of the processes of social production of Chinese society itself. In other words, the social processes that produce whatever degree of social integration Chinese society possesses (and this is obviously locally and temporally variable; witness, for example, how local elites' devotion to bureaucratic or imperial metaphors waxes and wanes with what Skinner would term "local system integration") also produce the forms of cultic multivocalities.

16. The studies of marriage resistance in Guangdong by Topley 1975 support this suggestion. See also Sangren 1983.

17. In Daxi, Taiwan, 1975–1977.

18. The most important study is Liu Ts'un-yan 1962. Liu's main concern is the identity of the work's author, but his argument includes considerable discussion of elements of the narrative of interest to anthropologists and religious historians. He also translates sections of the novel and the entire text of its predecessor, the much shorter *Wu Wang Fa Zhou Pinghua*. Parts of *Investiture of the Gods* have been translated into German by Grube. Doré's encyclopedic study (1914–1933) drew greatly from *Investiture of the Gods*. He provides a lengthy synopsis of the Nazha story in vol. 6, part 2 (1931:111–122). Other standard works on Chinese cosmology, including de Groot 1892–1910 and Werner 1922 and 1932, also relied on it. Wan 1987 provides additional philological argument and some analysis of narrative structure. Wan provides synopses for all 100 chapters as well as an analysis of sources and some interpretive argument. Gary Seaman of the University of Southern California has translated 37 of the 100 "chapters" of the epic, including the Nazha story, which he has generously provided me, along with useful information on sources. After this paper had been written in draft form, a full English translation appeared (Gu 1992). Although it lacks the scholarly apparatus of, for example, the authoritative translation of *The Journey to the West* by Yu 1977, it suffices to make the basic narrative available to the reader of English. For a short summary and additional sources, see Nienhauser 1986:384–386.

19. The story's popularity precedes *Investiture of the Gods,* with traceable antecedents in Sanskritic, Central Asian, and perhaps Persian mythologies (Liu Ts'un-yan 1960–1961 and 1962, Chan 1987 and 1990, Ho 1988). I would like

to thank Victor Mair for alerting me to these linkages. According to the studies by Chan 1987 and 1990, Nazha was worshiped in north China primarily for his association with (and power to control) dragons, water, and rain. This is an element of his cult that is not emphasized to my knowledge in present-day Taiwan. I would speculate that the emphasis on father-son tensions in *Investiture of the Gods* has pushed this latter theme to the foreground in more recent cultic developments. It should also be noted that Nazha plays a role in Chinese Buddhistic hagiography and appears in *Journey to the West*. I would like to thank K. C. Liu for alerting me to this fact and for suggesting several sources pertaining to Nazha's appearance in Buddhistic tradition, in White Lotus sectarian religion, and in cults associated with a guild in Beijing that dealt in silk trims and sashes (personal communication 1993). I would speculate that the consistency of the association of Nazha with *Investiture of the Gods* in present-day Taiwan stems in part from a convergence in the generally Daoistic (or syncretic) sympathies of local religious cosmology with those of the author of *Investiture of the Gods*.

20. That Nazha is seven years old at this juncture is significant; at seven a child is expected to begin to let reason control his emotions. Earlier tolerance of uncouth outbursts ceases, and serious training and self-cultivation should begin. Fathers ideally play the key role of teacher in this process; sons should submit to the father's authority in their own production as fully socialized men. My thanks to Whalen Lai (personal communication 1993) for pointing out the significance of Nazha's age to me.

21. I would like to thank K. C. Liu (personal communication 1993) for emphasizing this point, overlooked in an earlier draft of this paper.

22. K. C. Liu (personal communication 1993) provides important context here. "*Fengshen Yanyi*, taken as a whole, is concerned with the dilemmas posed by Confucian obligations: loyalty to the monarch as well as filial piety. Just as, in Nazha's case, the novel invites sympathy for him in contrast to his brother Muzha, who cites Chu Hsi, the entire novel is an affirmation of the Mandate of Heaven, the benevolent cosmic will that overrides the conventional obligation of loyalty to the monarch. The author is considerate in his treatment of earnest officials still loyal to the utterly decadent Shang court. Yet such loyalty was in the end to be superseded by the higher claims of the Chou rule by virtue, embodied in the rather dull and self-effacing personality of Chou Wu-wang."

23. The analysis by Ho 1988 emphasizes this interpretation. I should also acknowledge that several of those attending the International Conference on Popular Beliefs and Chinese Culture (Center for Chinese Studies, Taipei, April 1993), at which I presented an earlier version of this paper, objected to my argument that the Nazha and Miaoshan stories convey sentiments inconsistent with the norms of filial piety, insisting that because both Nazha and Miaoshan harm their own bodies rather than those of their parents, filial values are confirmed rather than contradicted in these stories. I have attempted to respond to this important objection below.

24. One of the motives for my interest in the story is to develop a critique of Freudian and Lacanian psychoanalytic readings through analysis of it.

25. I am developing an analysis that proposes an important contradiction within patrilineal ideology between the role of patriarchs—that is, authority figures—in real life and the symbolic function of father *figures*. In rites of filial

sacrifice, transcendent father figures (ancestors in domestic cults, heaven in imperial rituals) seem to function as symbolic projections in practices whose effects are to produce sacrificers—that is, *sons*—as producers or agents (Zito 1987). The reading of the Confucian father-son relationship by Tu 1985 also, although to very different effect, locates agency in the role of the son; the father figure is, in his view, best conceived as a projection of the son's "ego ideal." Sons gauge their own efforts at self-cultivation against this transcendent ideal. The contradiction (or paradox) lies in the fact that what is represented as sons' filial subordination to a transcendent, but absent, father figure legitimates the authority of "sons" as real-world patriarchs who exercise authority over their own subordinates. Real fathers are not father figures, a reality that in my reading animates the Nazha story.

26. See also Teiser 1988 and Mair 1983.

27. The research by Hsiung n.d. on mother-son alliances in the testimonies of filial sons affirming their debts to their self-sacrificing mothers is consistent with the line of analysis I am suggesting here. Particularly noteworthy in Hsiung's research is the depth of the gratitude that sons express for the efforts of their mothers to support the development of their careers. Although such testimony should not be accepted uncritically (in a sense, it is only through their sons' testimonies that Chinese mothers "speak"), I believe that it nonetheless constitutes a genre of recognition of the costs to women exacted by the Chinese family system akin to that of myth. Deprived of opportunities to establish careers of their own, Chinese mothers identify strongly with the careers of their sons. Moreover, this identification produces a corresponding sentiment in sons, especially when the mother's burdens are increased by the early demise of her husband.

28. Seaman 1981 implies that this ceremony is performed for all women; Baptandier, elsewhere in this volume, associates the ceremony with women who die in childbirth. One suspects considerable variation in practice.

29. To avoid any hint of functionalism—that is, the notion that ideology develops *in order* to legitimate a presumably more fundamental kinship system —I would add that the ideas manifest in such rituals and their associated mythologies are *producers* as well as products of the kinship system. In other words, any implication that the *ideational* level in culture is in some unidirectional sense caused by a presumably more material *social* level should be avoided. Yet I agree with Seaman that the linkages in this case—between the kinship system and ritual/mythology—are very close and that the ideology undoubtedly has the *effects* of legitimation Seaman notes. To spell out more clearly what I mean by "very close" would require a lengthy discussion of social reproduction (Sangren 1987, 1991). One key point to emphasize is that analysis should aspire to account not only for the ways in which ideology legitimates social arrangements, but also for how both social arrangements and the ideas they instantiate are produced and reproduced.

30. See Seaman 1981, Ahern 1975, Topley 1974 for descriptions of Chinese folk theories regarding biological reproduction.

31. Pomeranz, n.d., argues that the goddess Bixia Yuanzhun associated with the cult of Taishan embodies elements of female sexuality and that it is precisely for this reason that her cult was never fully assimilable into official religion. The analysis of the cult of Chen Jinggu by Baptandier, elsewhere in this volume, suggests that both elements contribute to her aura.

32. Grant 1989 provides a thorough philological study and insightful analysis of another very evocative figure, Huang Guixiang. In some respects, the story of Woman Huang aligns more readily with my argument that women desire to constitute themselves in the subject position of agency (or filial action) than does that of Miaoshan. (As part of her "purification," Huang Guixiang is reincarnated as a man.) I read Grant's analysis after writing this article.

33. I rely mainly on the account of the history of the tale by Dudbridge 1978. I read Baptandier's contribution to this volume after writing my paper. The parallels between her analysis of Chen Jinggu and mine of Miaoshan are obvious and striking: both figures resist marriage; both engage in what Baptandier would term "shamanic" healing practices; both tales center upon the difficulties produced when a patrilineal society attempts to assimilate women's procreative powers. Moreover, I find compelling her argument that female gender seems to entail both positive (reproduction of the patriline) and negative elements. Indeed, in line with earlier arguments (Sangren 1983, 1987), I would argue that the "vampiristic" associations might be linkable to the threat to the myth of patrilineal immortality and the indivisibility of the male line constituted by ancestor worship. I also find compelling her suggestion that bad deaths prevent the reintegration of the soul into the ancestral capital of the family (or, as I would phrase a similar point, a bad death interrupts the attempt of the patriline to assert the derivative status of female procreative power) because such deaths create destructive forces that must be propitiated. Ritual propitiation transforms this destructive power into useful fertility. Unless prescribed rituals are performed, however, malevolent spirits may devour their survivors (Baptandier, in this volume).

34. Note the elaboration of this point by Baptandier, in this volume. One might speculate about the significance of Miaoshan's self-mutilation on behalf of her father. Of course, such defilement of the body's integrity is a common trope in Chinese representations of acts of filial piety, but clearly more needs to be said. Perhaps in this instance her father's ingestion of parts of her body represents, quite literally, a form of reintegration into the natal family. In the Miaoshan story, the eyes and arms have special significance in cult iconography; Miaoshan, like Nazha, is reborn with a magically augmented body—in her case with a thousand eyes and a thousand arms. This reconstituted body enhances her ability to perceive *(guan)* the suffering of her supplicants and to aid them. Thanks to Whalen Lai (personal communication 1993) for making this point.

35. There are many striking parallels between the Miaoshan and Mazu (Lin Moniang) legends. Both are goddesses said to have been virtuous, religiously minded daughters who intervened miraculously to save the lives of their fathers. Indeed, a version of the Lin Moniang legend published in a pamphlet distributed by the Chaotian temple in Beigang (the most important cult center in Taiwan where the story is still current) tells of her divine conception. Her mother and father, having six daughters and only a weakling son, pray to Guanyin for another boy. Guanyin appears to Mrs. Lin in a dream and gives her a magic pill. Shortly thereafter Mrs. Lin gives birth to Moniang (so named because she never cried). Many Taiwanese assert quite explicitly that Lin Moniang (i.e., Mazu) is Guanyin's reincarnation *(huashen)*. See also Boltz 1986, Sangren 1988 and n.d.a, Watson 1985. The parallel here with Taiyi's appearance in Nazha's mother's dream before his birth is one worth exploring.

36. These are debatable assertions, of course, which leave unaddressed the complex historical and cultural issues of China's assimilation of Buddhism.

37. I gratefully acknowledge Ding Nianci, a student in one of my courses, for this suggestion.

38. Again, I gratefully acknowledge another student, Sara Friedman, for this suggestion.

39. I have in mind studies epitomized by Clifford Geertz's influential "Person, Time, and Conduct in Bali" (Geertz 1973 [1966]).

40. This resistance is grounded in the perception that notions of ideology as false consciousness seem to deny the real efficacy of people's understandings of reality in constituting social reality. For example, Geertz 1973 and Foucault 1978 and 1980 have both polemicized against ideology on such grounds. My view is that one must recognize that ideology plays an important role in constituting social reality *as the analyst comes to understand it,* but that this latter reality necessarily differs from the understandings constituted as ideology by those we analyze or interpret. An unfortunate legacy of ethnopsychology—shared more widely by interpretivist, poststructuralist, and postmodernist intellectuals—is precisely a lack of forthrightness with regard to justifying its own implicit truth claims (Sangren 1988, 1989, n.d.a, n.d.b). The analyst's interpretation, insofar as it differs from the self-presentations of an object/other, cannot avoid positing/representing a reality that makes relative truth claims—i.e., to the effect that the analyst understands the object/other's social reality at a level of integration or transcendence that exceeds that offered in such self-representations. Lamentably, it has become fashionable to avoid defending realist transcendentalism (which I understand to be the positing of natural and social realities that include but are not limited to our understandings and representations of them) and the relative truth value of one's own analyses by disparaging realism itself as manifesting a positivist delusion of objectivity. I believe that rather than self-servingly seeking refuge in self-contradictory disavowals of realism, totalizing, and objectivity, social critics and social scientists should accept the responsibility to defend their representations of social reality (and critics of realist pretensions do not escape their own critique). This does not, as many critics assume, entail the claim that our own analyses represent some final or absolute truth: particular analyses are obviously always contestable. It does entail the conviction that there are realities that exist beyond our representations of them (it is in this sense that realism is transcendental). For an eloquent defense of ethnographic realism, see Anspach 1992.

41. It may be objected that having been written down and disseminated, in part, in books like *Investiture of the Gods,* stories like that of Nazha can no longer be considered myth, strictly speaking, even if they originated as such. I would argue, however, that because such stories continue to be an important part of oral tradition and because their personages figure prominently in new locally produced "miracles" (see Sangren 1984, 1987, 1993), they retain a mainly mythical quality.

42. In this context, uxorilocal marriage does not constitute an alternative marriage system; it is an attempt to cope with an absence of sons consistent with the values that animate the preferred "major" (that is, virilocal) form (Wolf and Huang 1980).

43. It should be noted that neither Nazha, a Daoist adept, nor Mulian, a Buddhist monk, marries. However, this fact is not itself an issue to the degree that it is in the story of Miaoshan. I suspect that having severed lineal ties, having achieved immortality, and being possessed of an indestructible body, Nazha has no need of descendants. In Mulian's case, the issue of his mother's pollution is so prominent that its mythical absolution would be called into question were her son not celibate. Obviously, there is more to explore regarding these parallels and the issues they raise.

44. I believe that the analyses of filial piety, ancestor worship, and the logic implicit in imperial sacrifice by Zito 1984 and 1987 are highly suggestive in this regard. She argues, for example, that very much at issue in ancestor worship is the production of sons as empowered sacrificers; fathers are effectively relegated to transcendent instruments of sons' desires. Inspired in part by this line of argument, I am working on a more detailed analysis of Nazha's relations with his father, his Daoist mentor, and the dragon-king.

45. In making this argument, I am inspired in part by Mitchell 1983 and Rose 1983.

46. Ho 1988 argues plausibly that Nazha's conflict with Aoguang (the dragon-king) expresses his primal conflict with a father figure before the emergence of open conflict with his own father. The latter can occur, according to Ho, only after elaborate justification—that is, after Li Jing's destruction of Nazha's temple. Ho implies that Chinese sympathies can remain with Nazha only if his rebellion can paradoxically be represented as justifiable in terms of filial piety. Dudbridge 1978 argues in a somewhat similar vein that the Miaoshan story attempts to reconcile Buddhist celibacy with the exigencies of filial piety.

47. Baptandier's description, in this volume, of the "freedoms" enjoyed by the female shaman might be construed in a similar vein.

Literature Cited

Ahern, Emily Martin. 1975. "The Power and Pollution of Chinese Women." In *Women in Chinese Society,* edited by Margery Wolf and Roxanne Witke, 193–214. Stanford: Stanford University Press.

Anspach, Mark Rogin. 1992. "When American Anthropologists Go 'Postmodern.' " *Stanford French Review* 15:81–102.

Berthier, Brigitte. 1988. *La dame du bord de l'eau.* Paris: Société d'Ethnologie de Paris X.

Bloch, Maurice, and Jonathan Parry. 1982. "Introduction: Death and the Regeneration of Life." In *Death and the Regeneration of Life,* edited by Maurice Bloch and Jonathan Parry, 1–44. Cambridge: Cambridge University Press.

Boltz, Judith Magee. 1986. "In Homage to T'ien-fei." *Journal of the American Oriental Society,* Sinological Studies Dedicated to Edward H. Schafer, Paul W. Kroll, ed., 106:211–232.

Bourdieu, Pierre. 1977. *Outline of a Theory of Practice.* Cambridge: Cambridge University Press.

Chan, Hok-lam (Ch'en Hsüeh-lin). 1987. "Yuan Dadu Cheng Jinzuo Chuanshuo Tanyuan" (Legends Surrounding the Building of Dadu: The Nazha City of the Yüan Dynasty). *Han-hsüeh Yen-chiu (Chinese Studies)* 5(1):95–127.

————. 1990. "A Mongolian Legend of the Building of Peking." *Asia Major,* 3rd series, 3:63–93.

Dean, Kenneth. 1993. *Taoist Ritual and Popular Cults of Southeast China.* Princeton: Princeton University Press.

Delaney, Carol. 1991. *The Seed and the Soil: Gender and Cosmology in Turkish Village Society.* Berkeley: University of California Press.

Doré, Henri. 1914–1933. *Researches on Superstition in China.* Translated by M. Kennelly. Vols. 1–10, 13. Shanghai: Tusewei.

Douglas, Mary. 1966. *Purity and Danger: An Analysis of the Concepts of Pollution and Taboo.* London: Routledge and Kegan Paul.

Duara, Prasenjit. 1988. "Superscribing Symbols: The Myth of Guandi, Chinese God of War." *Journal of Asian Studies* 47(4):778–795.

Dudbridge, Glen. 1978. *The Legend of Miao-shan.* London: Ithaca Press.

Foucault, Michel. 1978. *The History of Sexuality, Vol. 1: An Introduction.* Translated by Robert Hurley. New York: Vintage.

————. 1980. *Power/Knowledge: Selected Interviews and Other Writings, 1972–1977.* Edited by Colin Cordon. New York: Pantheon.

Freedman, Maurice. 1974. "On the Sociological Study of Chinese Religion." In *Religion and Ritual in Chinese Society,* edited by Arthur P. Wolf, 19–42. Stanford: Stanford University Press.

Garritt, Rev. J. C. 1899. "Popular Account of the Canonization of the Gods, Illustrated." *Chinese Recorder* 30:162–174.

Geertz, Clifford. 1973 [1966]. "Person, Time, and Conduct in Bali." In *The Interpretation of Cultures: Selected Essays,* 360–411. New York: Basic Books.

Giddens, Anthony. 1979. *Central Problems in Social Theory: Action, Structure and Contradiction in Social Analysis.* Berkeley: University of California Press.

Grant, Beata. 1989. "The Spiritual Saga of Woman Huang: From Pollution to Purification." In *Ritual Opera, Operatic Ritual: "Mu-lien Rescues His Mother" in Chinese Popular Culture,* edited by David Johnson, 224–311. Publications of the Chinese Popular Culture Project 1. Berkeley: Institute of East Asian Studies Publications.

Groot, J. J. M. de. 1892–1910. *The Religious System of China.* Reprinted 1969. Leiden: Brill.

Grootaers, Willem A. 1952. "The Hagiography of the Chinese God Chen-Wu (The Transmission of Rural Traditions in Chahar)." *Folklore Studies* 11(2):139–181.

Gu Zhizhong, trans. 1992. *Creation of the Gods.* Beijing: New World Press.

Ho Kin-chung. 1988. "Nezha: Figure de l'enfant rebelle?" *Etudes chinoises* 7(2): 6–26.

Hsiung Ping-chen. n.d. "Emotional Bonds between Mothers and Sons in Early Modern China." Unpublished paper.

Jay, Nancy. 1992.*Throughout Your Generations Forever: Sacrifice, Religion, and Paternity.* Chicago: University of Chicago Press.

Johnson, David, ed. 1989. *Ritual Opera, Operatic Ritual: "Mu-lien Rescues His Mother" in Chinese Popular Culture.* Berkeley: Publications of the Chinese Popular Culture Project.

Jordan, David K. 1986. "Folk Filial Piety In Taiwan: The Twenty-four Filial Exemplars." In *The Psycho-Cultural Dynamics of the Confucian Family: Past and Present*, edited by Walter H. Slote, 47–106 (summary of discussion, 107–112). Seoul: International Cultural Society of Korea.

Lacan, Jacques. 1983. *Feminine Sexuality: Jacques Lacan and the "Ecole Freudienne"*. Edited by Juliet Mitchell and Jacqueline Rose, translated by Jacqueline Rose. New York: Norton.

Lin Yangmin. 1988. *Taiwan Ren de Lianhua Zaisheng (The Lotus Flower Rebirth of Taiwanese People)*. Taipei: Qianwei.

Liu Ts'un-yan. 1960–1961. "Buddhist Sources of the Novel Feng-shen Yen-i." *Journal of the Hong Kong Branch of the Royal Asiatic Society* 1:68–97.

———. 1962. "Buddhist and Taoist Influences on Chinese Novels, Vol. 1: The Authorship of the Feng Shen Yen I." Wiesbaden: Kommissionsverlag Otto Harrassowitz.

Mair, Victor H. 1983. *Tun-huang Popular Narratives*. Cambridge: Cambridge University Press.

Martin [Ahern], Emily. 1988. "Gender and Ideological Differences in Representations of Life and Death." In *Death Ritual in Late Imperial China*, edited by James L. Watson and Evelyn S. Rawski, 164–179. Berkeley: University of California Press.

Mitchell, Juliet. 1983. "Introduction—I." In *Feminine Sexuality: Jacques Lacan and the "Ecole Freudienne"*, edited by Juliet Mitchell and Jacqueline Rose, translated by Jacqueline Rose, 1–26. New York: Norton.

Nienhauser, William H., Jr., ed. and comp. 1986. *The Indiana Companion to Traditional Chinese Literature*. Bloomington: Indiana University Press.

Piaget, Jean. 1962. *Play, Dreams and Imitation in Childhood*. New York: Norton.

Pomeranz, Kenneth. n.d. "Protecting Goddess, Dangerous Woman: Power, Gender, and Pluralism in the Cult of the Goddess of Taishan." Unpublished paper.

Rose, Jacqueline. 1983. "Introduction—II." In *Feminine Sexuality: Jacques Lacan and the "Ecole Freudienne"*, edited by Juliet Mitchell and Jacqueline Rose, translated by Jacqueline Rose, 27–57. New York: Norton.

Rubin, Gayle. 1975. "The Traffic in Women: Notes on the 'Political Economy' of Sex." In *Toward an Anthropology of Women*, edited by Rayna R. Reiter, 157–210. New York: Monthly Review Press.

Salaff, Janet W. 1981. *Working Daughters of Hong Kong: Filial Piety or Power in the Family*. Cambridge: Cambridge University Press.

Sangren, P. Steven. 1982. "Recent Studies in Chinese Kinship." *American Anthropologist* 84:628–632.

———. 1983. "Female Gender in Chinese Religious Symbols: Kuan Yin, Ma Tsu, and the 'Eternal Mother.' " *Signs* 9:4–25.

———. 1987. *History and Magical Power in a Chinese Community*. Stanford: Stanford University Press.

———. 1988. "Rhetoric and the Authority of Ethnography: 'Post-Modernism' and the Social Reproduction of Texts." *Current Anthropology* 29:405–435.

———. 1989. Comment on "Ethnography without Tears" by Paul A. Roth. *Current Anthropology* 30:564.

182   P. STEVEN SANGREN

———. 1991. "Dialectics of Alienation: Individuals and Collectivities in Chinese Religion." *Man* 26:67–86.

———. 1993. "Power and Transcendence in the Ma Tsu Pilgrimages of Taiwan." *American Ethnologist* 20:564–582.

———. n.d.a. "The Vicissitudes of Power: Chinese, Foucauldian, and Anthropological Conceptions of Power." Forthcoming in *Cultural Anthropology.*

———. n.d.b. "Person, Self, Subject: Philosophical Deconstruction vs. Social Production." Unpublished paper.

Seaman, Gary. 1981. "The Sexual Politics of Karmic Retribution." In *The Anthropology of Chinese Society,* edited by Emily Martin Ahern and Hill Gates, 381–396. Stanford: Stanford University Press.

———. 1987. *Journey to the North: An Ethnohistorical Analysis and Annotated Translation of the Chinese Folk Novel "Pei-yu-chi."* Berkeley: University of California Press.

———. 1989. "Mu-lien Dramas in Puli, Taiwan." In *Ritual Opera, Operatic Ritual: "Mu-lien Rescues His Mother" in Chinese Popular Culture,* edited by David Johnson, 155–210. Berkeley: Publications of the Chinese Popular Culture Project.

———. n.d. "Translation of Thirty-seven Chapters of the *Feng-shen Yen-i* (including the Nazha story)." Unpublished paper.

Smith, Paul. 1988. *Discerning the Subject.* Theory and History of Literature 55. Minneapolis: University of Minnesota Press.

Spiro, Melford E. 1987. *Culture and Human Nature: Theoretical Papers of Melford E. Spiro.* Edited by Benjamin Kilborne. Chicago: University of Chicago Press.

Teiser, Stephen. 1988. *The Ghost Festival in Medieval China.* Princeton: Princeton University Press.

Topley, Marjorie. 1954. "Chinese Women's Vegetarian Houses in Singapore." *Journal of the Malayan Branch of the Royal Asiatic Society* 27:59.

———. 1974. "Cosmic Antagonisms: A Mother-Child Syndrome." In *Religion and Ritual in Chinese Society,* edited by Arthur P. Wolf, 233–250. Stanford: Stanford University Press.

———. 1975. "Marriage Resistance in Rural Kwangtung." In *Women in Chinese Society,* edited by Margery Wolf and Roxanne Witke, 67–88. Stanford: Stanford University Press.

Tu Wei-ming. 1985. *Confucian Thought: Selfhood As Creative Transformation.* Albany: State University of New York Press.

Turner, Terence. 1977. "Narrative Structure and Mythopoesis: A Critique and Reformulation of Structuralist Concepts of Myth, Narrative and Poetics." *Arethusa* 10:103–163.

———. 1985. "Animal Symbolism, Totemism and the Structure of Myth." In *Animal Myths and Metaphors in South America,* edited by Gary Urton, 251–284. Salt Lake City: University of Utah Press.

Wan, Pin Pin. 1987. "Investiture of the Gods *(Fengshen yanyi)*: Sources, Narrative Structure, and Mythical Significance." Ph.D. diss., University of Washington.

Watson, James L. 1982. "Of Flesh and Bones: The Management of Death Pollution in Cantonese Society." In *Death and the Regeneration of Life,* edited by

Maurice Bloch and Jonathan Parry, 155–186. Cambridge: Cambridge University Press.

Werner, E. T. C. 1922. *Myths and Legends of China*. London: George G. Harrap.

———. 1932. *A Dictionary of Chinese Mythology*. Shanghai: Kelly and Walsh.

Wolf, Arthur P., and Chieh-shan Huang. 1980. *Marriage and Adoption in China, 1845–1945*. Stanford: Stanford University Press.

Wolf, Margery. 1968. *The House of Lim: A Study of a Chinese Farm Family*. New York: Appleton-Century-Crofts.

———. 1972. *Women and Family in Rural Taiwan*. Stanford: Stanford University Press.

———. 1975. "Women and Suicide in China." In *Women in Chinese Society*, edited by Margery Wolf and Roxanne Witke, 193–214. Stanford: Stanford University Press.

Yu, Anthony C., trans. and ed. 1977. *The Journey to the West*. 4 vols. Chicago: University of Chicago Press.

Yü Chün-fang. 1992. "P'u-t'o Shan: Pilgrimage and the Creation of the Chinese Potalaka." In *Pilgrims and Sacred Sites in China*, edited by Susan Naquin and Chün-fang Yü, 190–245. Berkeley: University of California Press.

Zito, Angela. 1984. "Re-Presenting Sacrifice: Cosmology and the Editing of Texts." *Ch'ing-shih Wen-t'i* 5:47:78.

———. 1987. "City Gods, Filiality, and Hegemony in Late Imperial China." *Modern China* 13(3):333–370.

Vernacular Fiction and the Transmission of Gods' Cults in Late Imperial China

Meir Shahar

"A Chinese religion exists": this view expressed by Maurice Freedman (1974:20) is shared by most students of religion in China regardless of their specific disciplines. It is generally accepted that, notwithstanding regional differences, a body of religious beliefs and practices—variously referred to as Chinese religion or Chinese popular religion—is shared by the overwhelming majority of the Chinese people throughout the vast Chinese state. However, the question of how these religious beliefs and practices were transmitted still awaits an answer. Chinese religion had neither an organization nor a body of sacred scriptures. It is therefore difficult to explain how its rituals and myths were spread. A case in point is the Chinese pantheon. Even though many deities are worshiped only in specific localities, a substantial number of gods are worshiped throughout China, or at least through vast areas of it. They include such figures as Guangong, Zhenwu (Xuantian Shangdi), the Eight Immortals (Baxian), Sun Wukong, Nazha (known also as Nazha Santaizi), Guanyin, and Mazu (Tianhou). How were the cults of these deities transmitted, both temporally from one generation to another and geographically across regional (and linguistic) barriers?

As yet, no systematic attempt has been made to explain the transmission of the Chinese pantheon. The scholars who have addressed this question have generally assumed that the state must have played a leading role in spreading gods' cults. The state enhanced the cult of popular deities by granting them divine titles and, in some cases, by instructing officials to build temples in their honor and worship them. The state thereby gained legitimization as well as control, and in the process it further spread the cult of the gods in question. Nevertheless, I will argue that the impact of the state on the transmission of gods' cults was probably limited. First, many deities, particularly of the eccentric or rebellious type, never enjoyed state recognition and yet their cult spread throughout China; Sun Wukong, Nazha, and Jigong (known also as Jidian, "Crazy Ji") are three examples. Second, even in the case of deities who enjoyed state patronage, their official and popular cults often remained separated. For example, in Taiwanese cities there were usually two temples for Mazu: one, administered by the state, was hardly frequented by the local population, the other, administered by local businessmen, served as the center of the deity's popular cult (Watson 1985:300–302).[1] Third, and most significant, the state could sponsor the *ritual* aspect of a deity's cult: it could construct temples, prescribe offerings, and so forth. But it could not spread the *myth* underlying the cult. To transmit myths literature was needed, whether written or oral. By and large, the state did not produce such literature.

Literati of the Qing period often felt that fiction, oral and written, spread gods' cults. They saw fiction *(xiaoshuo)* as the repository of popular myths and argued that it had played a crucial role in the transmission of the pantheon. Interestingly, fiction writers were themselves aware of fiction's role in spreading gods' cults. Cao Xueqin (1715?–1763), author of the *Dream of the Red Chamber (Honglou Meng)*, voices his recognition of fiction's religious impact through his protagonist Baoyu. The character does not believe in the reality of popular gods exactly because fiction has served as the vehicle that spread their cults. Baoyu exclaims:

> I hate the silly, senseless way in which vulgar people offer worship and build temples to gods they know nothing about. Ignorant old men and women with too much money to spend hear the name of some god or other—they've no idea who it is, but the mere fact that they've heard some unfounded tale or piece of fiction [*yeshi xiaoshuo*] seems to them incontrovertible proof of the god's existence—and go founding temples in which these fictitious deities can be worshiped. (Cao 1985:43:599; slightly altered from Hawkes's translation [Cao 1973–1986:2:357])

Some fiction writers even noted the possibility that the products of their imagination might unwittingly become the object of popular cults. They observed that once a fictional character caught the readers' fancy it could—contrary to its creator's intentions—be worshiped as a deity. A character named Xu Sheng in one of Pu Songling's (1640–1715) tales arrives in Fujian province where, to his astonishment, the local people worship the simian protagonist of the *Journey to the West (Xiyou Ji),* Sun Wukong. Xu Sheng shares Baoyu's disdain for ignorant people who worship fictitious creations:

"Sun Wukong is nothing but a parable [*yuyan*] invented by [the novelist] old Qiu," he protests. "How can people sincerely believe in him?" (Pu 1962:11:1459; Zeitlin's translation [1993:167]). The narrator points out in the tale's epilogue that fictitious characters, once created, are independent of their creator's will. Deities exist because people believe they do, and fictional characters can thus be transformed into *real* gods, once they are conceived of as such by readers. (The narrator's argument for the reality of fictional creations is similar to William James' pragmatic argument for God's existence: God exists since we are convinced that he helps us [James 1982 [1902]: 515–519].) The epilogue reads: "A gentleman once passed by a temple and painted a mandolin on the wall. By the time he came to the spot again, the efficacy [*ling*] of this mandolin was renowned, and incense was being burned there nonstop. Certainly, it isn't necessary for someone [like Sun Wukong] to actually exist in this world: if people believe someone to be efficacious, then he will be efficacious for them" (Pu 1962: 11:1462; Zeitlin's translation [1993:167–168] slightly altered).

Some literati mention the impact of specific novels on religious life. Tao Chengzhang (d. 1911) attributed the success of the White Lotus sect in north China and that of the Heaven and Earth Society in the south to the influence of the novels *Enfeoffment of the Gods (Fengshen Yanyi)* and *Water Margin (Shuihu Zhuan)* respectively. He writes: "Throughout the area of Shandong, Shanxi and Henan [that is, the north] there is no one who does not believe [*zunxin*] in the *Enfeoffment of the Gods* story. Throughout the area of Jiangsu, Zhejiang, Fujian and Guangzhou [the south] there is no one who does not venerate [*chongbai*] the book, *Water Margin*" (Tao 1965 [1935]: 1a). The famous eighteenth-century literatus, Qian Daxin (1728–1804), made a particularly strong statement regarding the significant role of fiction in transmitting religious beliefs. Qian, a prolific historian, held several high-ranking educational posts, including that of tutor to Emperor Qianlong's twelfth son (Hummel 1943:152–155). He saw fiction and religion as so inextricably linked that he chose to name the latter "fiction" *(xiaoshuo)*. (The amorphous body of religious beliefs that is referred to nowadays as Chinese religion did not have a name in late imperial times.) Qian Daxin observes:

> Of old there were three religions [*jiao*]: Confucianism, Buddhism, and Daoism.[2] Since Ming times [1368–1644] there has been one more, called *xiaoshuo* [fiction]. Works of fiction and historical romances [*yanyi*] do not proclaim themselves a religion. Nevertheless, among literati [*shidafu*], peasants, workers, and merchants alike, there is no one who is not familiar with them. Even children,

women and illiterate persons have all heard [these stories] or seen them [performed]. This [fiction] is their religion, and compared with Confucianism, Buddhism and Taoism, it is more widespread. (Qian 1989:17:282)

The term *xiaoshuo* denotes a wide variety of literary genres ranging from the classical tale to the vernacular novel. Which literary genres did the Qing literati have in mind when they discussed the role of *xiaoshuo* in the transmission of religious beliefs? The above examples suggest that they were referring to vernacular fiction—written and oral—and in particular to novels, which were always written in the vernacular. Qian Daxin discusses a literary genre that emerged during the Ming and was closely related to oral literature as well as to drama (he uses the verbs *hear* and *see*). He must be referring, therefore, to vernacular fiction. Qian Daxin further mentions "historical romances" *(yanyi),* which are novels. Cao Xueqin is referring to oral literature. (He too uses the verb *hear.*) Finally, Pu Songling and Tao Chengzhang single out specific novels for their religious impact; Pu Songling mentions the *Journey to the West,* and Tao Chengzhang notes the *Enfeoffment of the Gods* and *Water Margin.* All four authors thus single out vernacular fiction, particularly the novel, for its importance in the transmission of gods' cults.

Is it true that deities figure prominently in vernacular fiction, particularly in novels? As early as 1952 Grootaers noted the significance of the late Ming novel *Journey to the North (Beiyou Ji)* in the dissemination of Zhenwu's cult (Grootaers 1952; see also Seaman 1987), and more recent studies have revealed that such popular deities as Guangong, Huaguang, Guanyin, Mazu, and Zhong Kui all figure prominently in vernacular fiction (see respectively Huang 1967:100–122, Cedzich 1995, Dudbridge 1978:51–58, Li Xianzhang 1970:3–33, Eliasberg 1976:49–74). My own study of the god Jigong suggests that the emergence of his nationwide cult followed the publication of popular novels in which he was the primary protagonist (Shahar 1992a, 1994). These studies, however, are but a beginning; the overwhelming majority of novels concerned with the supernatural have not yet been studied. This vast literature, classified by Sun Kaidi as *lingguai xiaoshuo* (fiction on the supernatural), is as yet uncharted (Sun 1932:chap. 5).[3] Some of the most important novels in question, such as the *Enfeoffment of the Gods* (early seventeenth century?), have not even been dated.[4] Future studies may well reveal that this literature features most of the popular gods in late imperial China. (See table for a few examples of deities who figure in novels.)

Some Deities and Some of the Novels in Which They Figure

Deity	Novel(s)	Type
Guanyin	*Nanhai Guanyin Quanzhuan* (Wanli period, 1573–1619) *Journey to the West* (1592)	female
Mazu	*Tianfei Niangma Zhuan* (Wanli Period)	female
Guangong	*Romance of the Three Kingdoms* (late Yuan) and antecedent	martial
Xuantian Shangdi (Zhenwu)	*Journey to the North* (Wanli period)	martial
Jiang Ziya	*Enfeoffment of the Gods* (early 17th century)	martial
Sun Wukong	*Journey to the West* (1592) antecedents and sequels	eccentric/ martial
Nazha Santaizi	*Enfeoffment of the Gods* *Journey to the West*	eccentric/ martial
Huaguang	*Journey to the South* (Wanli period) *Journey to the North* (Wanli period)	eccentric/ martial
Eight Immortals (as group or individually)	*Journey to the East* (Wanli period) *Feijian Ji* (Wanli period) *Han Xiangzi Quanzhuan* (1623) *Lüzu Quanzhuan* (1662) and sequels	eccentric
Jigong	*Jidian Yulu* (1569) and sequels	eccentric
Zhong Kui	*Zhong Kui Quanzhuan* (Wanli period) and sequels	failed literatus

The little we know about *lingguai* novels suggests that they can be divided into two types. The first is hagiographic novels, which focus primarily on one deity. They outline the deity's career (which often has a human stage followed by a divine one), describe his or her supernatural powers, and recount the miracles he or she has performed on behalf of humanity. During the Wanli period (1573–1619) a group of publishers in Jianyang, Fujian, published several novels that belong in this category. They portray such deities as Zhenwu, Huaguang, Guanyin, Mazu, Zhong Kui, Damo (Bodhidharma) and the Eight Immortals (Dudbridge 1978:52–54, 60–61). The Jianyang novels are closely interrelated; some of the deities who are the subject of one novel appear as secondary characters in others. Huaguang, for example, is the subject of a novel entitled *Journey to the South (Nanyou Ji)*, but he figures also in a novel dedicated to Zhenwu, *Journey to the North (Beiyou Ji)* (von Glahn 1991:672–675). Several deities have been the subject of an entire series of hagiographic novels, the study of which can help us unravel the deity's history. Zhong Kui, the Eight Immortals, and Jigong are three examples.

The earliest novel on Jigong was published in 1569. It was followed by two novels in the seventeenth century and a plethora of novels in the nineteenth and twentieth centuries, the latest of which was published in 1987. Jigong novels tend to be longer than most hagiographic novels; one nineteenth-century novel contains 240 chapters.

The second type of *lingguai* fiction consists of large-scale novels that portray an enormous cast of supernatural characters, even if they focus on only a few of them. Of course, the two prime examples here are the *Journey to the West* (1592) and the *Enfeoffment of the Gods,* both of which were published, like the Jianyang novels, during the late Ming. The *Journey to the West* has a Buddhist bent, even though it features many deities of Daoist origins. Conversely, the *Enfeoffment of the Gods* is oriented to Daoism, but it also celebrates many deities of Buddhist descent. Between them, the two novels describe almost every god in the pantheon of late imperial China.[5] Thus, these two enormously popular novels alone could have served as a vehicle for the transmission of almost the entire pantheon. It is noteworthy that many deities who are the subject of a hagiographic novel are also portrayed in one of these larger scale works of mythology. Guanyin, for example, is a subject of a Jianyang novel, but her appearance as the tutelary deity of Xuanzang and his fellow pilgrims in the novel *Journey to the West* probably played an even greater role in the spread of her cult.

Novels on the supernatural *(lingguai)* were not the only ones to spread gods' cults. A novelist did not have to portray his subjects as deities for his novel to serve as a vehicle for their veneration. As Henri Maspero has noted, in China "every god, great or small, is a man who, after death, was promoted for various reasons to the dignity of a god" (Maspero 1981:86). Thus, if the *human* personality portrayed in a novel left a deep impression upon the readers, they could worship it as a deity. Here, the two notable examples are the *Romance of the Three Kingdoms (Sanguo Yanyi)* (probably late Yuan) and *Water Margin* (probably Yuan-Ming), neither of which is classified as *lingguai* fiction. The two novels celebrate the loyalty, courage, and martial prowess of mortal men. By and large, they depict their heroic protagonists—Guangong in the former, Song Jiang and his band of robbers in the latter—as humans.[6] Yet both novels played a significant role in the spread of their protagonists' cults. Fiction on human affairs, like fiction on the supernatural, had a significant impact on the transmission of the pantheon.

The Reach of Novels

Thus, deities figured prominently in Ming and Qing novels. How wide was the readership of these novels? Was it wide enough for them to serve as a vehicle for the transmission of their protagonists' cults? There are three reasons for the novel's widespread dissemination. First, novels enjoyed a relatively large readership because of the vernacular language in which they were written. Writings in the vernacular were probably accessible to larger segments of Chinese society than writings in the classical language. To read the former, one needed to learn a system of notation, while to read the latter, one needed to learn essentially a new language (Hanan 1981:10). Only those who had received a classical education could read the classical language, but some forms of the vernacular were probably accessible to those who had received only a modicum of education. Among the latter were "some boys,   women, and [members] of the less lettered classes—merchants, shopkeepers, shop assistants, lower functionaries, and the like" (Hanan 1981:11). For example, as a young boy, Mao Zedong (1893–1976) read the *Romance of the Three Kingdoms* and *Water Margin,* and was deeply impressed by their heroic protagonists. Jin Shengtan (1608–1661) notes that even "peddlers and yamen runners" read the latter novel (Snow 1938:115–116, Chin 1990:145). Jin Shengtan may be engaging in hyperbole, but it does appear that some Ming and Qing novels, which celebrated the deities of the amorphous Chinese religion, were accessible to wider segments of late imperial society than Confucian, Buddhist, and Daoist canonical scriptures, which were written for the most part in the classical language.

A second, and more significant, reason for the novel's widespread dissemination was its relationship to oral literature. Vernacular fiction can be likened to an iceberg of which only the tip—the written vernacular—is visible. The bulk of this literature was transmitted orally and is hidden from us. Oral and written fiction borrowed from each other; most novels derived from oral literature at the same time as they served as a source for it. Thus, for example, tales narrated by the Beijing storyteller Shi Yukun (fl. 1870s) served as the source for the nineteenth-century novel celebrating Judge Bao (Baogong) and his martial disciples *Sanxia Wuyi (Three Heroes and Five Gallants),* and this same novel continues to inspire storytellers to this day (Blader 1978, 1983). Similarly, we know that the eccentric god Jigong was a popular topic with the blind storytellers of Hangzhou before the publication of the first novel about him, the *Jidian Yulu (The Recorded Sayings of Crazy Ji)* (1569), which indeed evinces the influence of oral literature (Shahar 1992a, 1994). In later generations Jigong novels served as a source for a vast oral literature, in a variety of regional styles. H. Y. Lowe fondly remembers how, as a child in Beijing of the early republican period, he enjoyed listening to Jigong stories: "Of the stories he heard, those which appealed to him the

most were from the *Jigong Zhuan,* or the 'Life of Abbot Jigong'
... The stories made such an impression on the young mind that he
was noticed to refer to them on many an occasion at home and
abroad. It was also discovered that one of the reasons behind his
industry during his first school days later was that some day he might
be able to read the *Jigong Zhuan* in the original" (Lowe 1983 [1940–
1941]:158).[7]

It is not surprising, therefore, that both Cao Xueqin and Qian
Daxin chose the verb *to hear* in their discussion of fiction's impact on
the transmission of the pantheon. Oral fiction brought the novel to
every section of late imperial society. The significance of the written
texts lies in controlling the growth of the oral traditions. The written
novels served as a unifying source for oral fiction across regional, linguistic, and temporal barriers. While oral fiction, narrated in the
local dialect, was by definition regional, the written novels crossed
regional boundaries.

The third reason for the novel's widespread dissemination was its
relation to drama, which, like oral fiction, brought the novel to the
unlettered masses. Popular novels were intimately related to a vast
body of dramatic representations in a wide variety of regional styles.
Those who could not read the *Journey to the West* saw Sun Wukong
somersaulting on stage, in Beijing opera, Cantonese opera, Fujianese
opera, and many other forms of local drama. Likewise, those who
were unable to read *Enfeoffment of the Gods* saw Nazha, on stage,
"Wreaking Havoc at Sea" *(Nazha Nao Hai).* Written fiction had a
relationship to drama that was in some ways similar to its relationship to oral literature. Borrowings were mutual; in the case of some
deities, dramatic representation preceded written fiction. The Eight
Immortals, for example, were a popular topic in the Yuan-period
zaju drama long before the earliest known novel about them was
compiled. In other cases, such as that of Jigong, novels preceded dramatic representation. Fiction served as a source for local drama, as it
did for oral fiction, and it controlled its growth in a similar manner
too (though, of course, some forms of drama, unlike oral fiction,
were written down).

The divine protagonists of the novel were represented on stage by
both actors and puppets: hand puppets, rod puppets, shadow puppets, and marionettes. The puppet theater, like other forms of traditional drama, drew heavily on the novel, thereby propagating the
cults of its supernatural protagonists. For example, Guangong, the
Eight Immortals, Jigong, Sun Wukong, and Nazha figured as prominently in the puppet theater as they did in regional opera. Interestingly, in the case of the novel's dramatic representation, the religious
significance of the plot was often matched by the ritual function of

the performance. Most forms of regional drama, including puppet theater, were performed during religious festivals. Sometimes the performance had an exorcising function. During the ghost festival, for example, Zhong Kui, represented by an actor or a puppet, would exorcise the malignant spirits roaming the earth. More commonly the performance was considered an offering to the gods, who were invited to watch it. Plays were performed in temple courtyards, with the stage facing the altar. The gods watched the plays, of which they were often the protagonists, alongside the human audience. The content and the context of the performance were thus both religious. The plays narrated the myths of the deities in whose honor they were performed (see, among others, Schipper 1966, van der Loon 1977, Ward 1979, Johnson 1989).

In modern times, traditional novels have also become the subject of film and television adaptations. These may be animated, enacted, or, in the Taiwanese case, televised puppet shows. *The Journey to the West* and *Romance of the Three Kingdoms,* for example, have been the subject of several movies and television productions in both mainland China and Taiwan. Nazha's adventures are the topic of a charming animated movie produced on the mainland, and Zhenwu and Mazu have been the subject of Taiwanese television serials. A Taiwanese dog-spirit cult, known as the Eighteen Lords cult, illustrates the significance of cinema and television in disseminating the deities' veneration. The cult, a relatively recent craze in Taiwan, achieved its peak in the mid-1980s, at which time its canine protagonist became the subject of a television serial and a movie, both of which capitalized on the cult's popularity at the same time as they spread it further (Weller 1994:157–164, and his essay in this volume). As to Jigong, his supernatural powers have been celebrated in numerous movies and television serials on the mainland, in Taiwan, and in Hong Kong. In the Taiwanese case, the religious importance of Jigong's television entertainment shows is evinced by the great similarity between them and his spirit-medium seances. The actors portraying him on television serials wear exactly the same colorful clown garb as do his possessed spirit-mediums, and both enact exactly the same character. In 1986–1987, when I was doing fieldwork in Taiwan, I asked several mediums whether they watch Jigong on television. Their answers were firmly negative. "We do not need to learn how to enact him," they protested. "We are possessed by him!"

Because the novels were written in the vernacular and because their plots were narrated by storytellers and enacted on stage, they reached practically every segment of late imperial society—just as Qian Daxin had argued. "Among literati, peasants, workers, and merchants alike, there is no one who is not familiar with them." Thus, the novels' audience was wide enough for them to serve as the vehicle that standardized gods' cults throughout Chinese society. ("Standardization" means, in this context, that a certain number of gods are *worshiped* through vast areas of China. It does not necessarily mean that they are *understood* in the same way by all members of society.) However, the religious function of the novel raises questions that only a thorough study of novels on the supernatural would be able to answer. I will here raise several of these questions, for which I will offer not definite answers but hypotheses, which need to be tested by future research.

Some Implications of Novels' Religious Function

First, did the written novels transmit already existing cults, or were the deities themselves the products of the novelists' imagination? That is, which came first? The few case studies we have suggest that the *written* novel generally appears rather late in the deity's cult. Most novels celebrate deities who were already worshiped in one locality or region, where their myths had been transmitted orally. The significance of the written novel lies in its spreading the deity's cult across regional and linguistic boundaries and in controlling future adaptations of the myth.[8] In some cases the deity in question was already worshiped through several regions before the novel's compilation. Here the novel amplified the cult and, again, contributed to its temporal transmission to future generations. It is interesting to note in this respect that several novels themselves indicate that their protagonists were the subject of worship at the time of their composition. They mention temples built in honor of their protagonists, and they elaborate upon the proven efficacy of worshiping in them. This is the case, for example, with the *Jidian Yulu* regarding Jigong, the *Journey to the North* concerning Zhenwu, and the *Journey to the South* in respect of Huaguang.[9]

Even though the divine protagonists of most novels were not the novelist's invention but rather the subject of historical cults at the time of the novel's composition, the novels did, of course, transform the gods' images. Different novels on the same deity may even portray him or her in varying lights. The earliest novel on Jigong, the *Jidian Yulu,* for example, was probably pieced together from two different texts: one, reflecting a Buddhist understanding of his image, portrays him as an enlightened monk in the Linji style; the other, mirroring his popular cult, describes him as an uninhibited miracle-worker (Shahar 1992a, 1994). In some cases the novel's transformation of its divine protagonist was so profound, and its impact on the

shape of its cult so great, that the novelist could be considered the
deity's creator. A notable example is Sun Wukong. The cult of this
divine monkey in late imperial times cannot be separated from his
image as shaped by the successive *Journey to the West* novels.[10] In
this respect he is indeed their authors' creation, and Pu Songling's
complaint, voiced through his protagonist Xu Sheng, is justified:
"Sun Wukong is nothing but a parable invented by [the novelist] old
Qiu. How can people sincerely believe in him?"

Novels on the supernatural raise a second question: their purpose.
Are they meant to provide entertainment or religious education?
Were they published for profit, or are they marked by a proselytizing
zeal? By and large, novels on the supernatural, like most fiction in
the vernacular, are works of popular art that provide entertainment.
Even the most devout hagiographic novels garnish their religious tales with intricate plots, colorful characters, and, almost invariably, a dash of humor.[11] Furthermore, the little we know about the
authors, editors, and publishers of this literature suggests that most
of them were professional writers who were in the business for
profit. They did not specialize in religious literature; rather, for the
most part, they dealt in a variety of types of popular fiction. The
publishers of the Jianyang hagiographic novels, for example, also
published court case *(gongan)* stories, and a celebrated author of
"scholar and beauty" *(caizi jiaren)* romances, Tianhua Zang Zhuren
(fl. 1658), wrote the preface to one of the most widely read Jigong
novels (Shahar 1992a:126).

Nevertheless, entertainment and religious education are not
incompatible, profit and merit not mutually exclusive. While some
novels on the supernatural—the 100 chapters of *Journey to the West,*
for example—are sophisticated works of art in which the implied
author's view of his divine protagonists is hard to ascertain, others
are lowbrow publications, in which the narrator approaches his
divine characters without any ironic distance. The implied authors of
the Jianyang hagiographic novels, for example, appear convinced of
their protagonists' divinity and of the usefulness of worshiping them.
One novel, on Zhenwu, is even followed by a ritual appendix pre-
scribing the "rules of worship" (Seaman 1987:20). Thus a proselytizing purpose probably underlies at least some of the novels on the
supernatural. It is interesting to note in this respect that quite a few
novels whose initial publication was financially motivated were in
later generations distributed by temples as religious literature. Both
the *Journey to the South* (celebrating Huaguang) and the above-
mentioned novel on Jigong, whose preface was written by Tianhua
Zang Zhuren, are distributed nowadays in Taiwanese temples, the
latter with a commentary attributed to Jigong himself, which was

composed in spirit-writing séances (Cedzich 1995:141, n. 8, Shahar 1992a:126–127).

I have argued that vernacular fiction served as a vehicle for the standardization of the pantheon in late imperial China. This is not to say that other mediums played no role in the transmission of gods' cults. "Precious scrolls" *(baojuan)* and morality tracts *(shanshu)* are concerned primarily with religious and moral doctrine, not with myth. Nevertheless this literature, too, includes some biographies of deities. (It was occasionally related to novels).[12] Likewise, visual art shaped gods' images, and merchants, pilgrims, and travelers all contributed to the spread of gods' cults, as did government control (see the introductory essay by Shahar and Weller in this volume). Conversely, of course, not all vernacular fiction served as a tool in the dissemination of the pantheon. Many novels are not concerned with the supernatural and played no role in shaping it. Furthermore, even some novels that did contribute to the spread of deities' cults were understood differently by various readers. This is especially the case with literary masterpieces, such as the *Journey to the West,* which are saturated with different layers of meaning. The *Journey to the West* is simultaneously an exuberant mythology and a profound allegory. Some readers were captivated by its vivid description of the supernatural, others conceived of it as a psychological journey to enlightenment. While the former venerated its supernatural cast of characters, the latter—including Xu Sheng of the above-mentioned Pu Songling tale—refused to accept their existence.[13]

The role of vernacular fiction in the transmission of the Chinese pantheon is reminiscent of the role of epic poetry in the shaping of the Greek and Hindu pantheons. Epic poetry, like vernacular fiction, cannot be narrowly construed as a religious genre. It was authored for the most part by poets, not clerics, and its multifarious meanings defy doctrinal purposes. Nonetheless, the significance of epic poetry in molding popular conceptions of the divine outweighs that of doctrinal religious writings. In the Greek case, "religious texts in the narrow sense of sacred texts are scarcely to be found: there is no holy scripture and barely even fixed prayer formulae and liturgies . . . [Rather], interweaving tales of the gods with heroic narratives, epic poetry, preeminently the Homeric *Iliad,* set its seal on the way the gods were imagined" (Burkert 1985:4). Furthermore, epic poetry, like vernacular fiction, reached every segment of society due to its relationship to oral literature and drama. For the most part, epic poetry derives from oral narratives at the same time that it serves as a source for storytellers and playwrights. Thus, for example, the sixteenth-century epic of Tulsidas, the *Rāmcaritmānas,* is continuously reinterpreted in northern India in a large variety of oral and dramatic genres (Lutgendorf 1991).

The significance of vernacular fiction in the standardization of the Chinese pantheon offers us a vantage point from which to examine why Chinese religion did not have a name in late imperial times. The body of religious beliefs and practices now called Chinese religion was inseparable from Chinese fiction and drama, which served as vehicles for its transmission. Thus, this religion did not exist as an entity independent of Chinese culture, and for this very reason it did not have a name. (Similarly, from a sociological perspective, the amorphous Chinese religion—unlike Buddhism, Daoism, and sectarian movements—had no institutions independent of secular organizations, such as the family, the clan, or the guild [Yang 1961:294–298].) Other religions that are inseparable from a given civilization similarly lack names: Greek religion and Hinduism are two examples; the term Hinduism was coined by British writers in the nineteenth century and it denotes both a religion and a culture. Both the Greek and Hindu religions resemble the Chinese one in that a literary genre that cannot be narrowly defined as religious has served a crucial role in the transmission of religious beliefs.

The religious dimension of vernacular fiction has implications not only for the study of Chinese religion but also for the study of Chinese fiction. It reminds us that the application of the term *novel* to lengthy narratives in the *xiaoshuo* genre is in one sense misleading. The term *novel* has been applied in the West primarily to works whose subject matter is human experience. Of course, many *xiaoshuo* narratives are concerned with the human realm, but as we have seen, the subject of many others is the supernatural. Their protagonists are deities, whose religious powers are never questioned, even when they themselves are portrayed humorously. While in the West the human and the divine realms are strictly separated, in China they intermingle. It is exactly because most Chinese gods were originally humans that the same literary genre, *xiaoshuo,* can be applied to both.

The Chinese Supernatural as an Upside-down World

The role that vernacular fiction played in the transmission of gods' cults has had significant implications for the gods' social traits. Vernacular fiction occupied an ambiguous position in late imperial culture. "Although it was avidly read, fiction was largely disregarded by society" (Hanan 1981:12). Some notable exceptions notwithstanding, most novels in the vernacular were not deemed worthy of collection or preservation, and their authorship remained anonymous. Whereas respected literary genres, such as poetry, philosophy, and history, were written in the classical language, vernacular fiction, partly because of its immense popularity, was usually considered an inferior art form. It was disregarded not only for artistic but also for ideological reasons. Possibly because of its ambiguous position in Chinese culture, vernacular fiction highlighted aspects of Chinese life that the classical tradition left in the shade. Physical heroism and sex, for example—two topics that were only rarely discussed in classical literature—are the subject of many novels. The protagonists of vernacular fiction, whether approved of or condemned by their narrators, often deviated from accepted norms of behavior. Be it the sensitive Baoyu of *The Story of the Stone* (ca. 1760), the sexy and dangerous Pan Jinlian of the *Jin Ping Mei* (ca. 1600), or the heroic Song Jiang of the *Water Margin,* they rarely fulfilled socially accepted roles. Thus, as Patrick Hanan has pointed out, vernacular fiction "frequently served as a vehicle for criticizing the culture's dominant values" (Hanan 1981:13).

Vernacular fiction was appreciated in small avant-garde circles. However, many educators were keenly aware that its protagonists, many of whom were the subjects of religious cults, deviated from the Confucian ethos they preached. Essays, memorials, and petitions lamented the corrupting influence of fiction, which leads to banditry, debauchery, and wantonness. Girls were often warned not to read the *Romance of the Western Chamber* lest they become promiscuous, and boys were forbidden to read the *Romance of the Three Kingdoms* lest they form illegal brotherhoods and embark upon a rebellious path. The government, for its part, periodically banned the publication of novels such as *Jin Ping Mei* and *Water Margin,* which were considered pornographic and seditious (Wang 1958). Qian Daxin, who argued that fiction was a religion more widespread than Confucianism, Daoism, and Buddhism, illustrates the austere Confucian approach to this literary genre:

Buddhism and Daoism still teach people to act morally. But fiction leads them solely in the evil path. Topics such as adultery and banditry, which Confucian, Buddhist, and Daoist texts would not dare openly discuss, are described in great detail and elaborated upon with relish in this type of literature. It glorifies murderers as heroes [*haohan*] and portrays adulterers as sensitive romantics. There is no form of madness that this literature shuns. Many of our youngsters receive no education whatever and spend their days in idleness. Having fiction as well to lead them astray, no wonder they are not much better than wild beasts. . . . Those whose responsibility it is to enlighten and guide the people would do better to annihilate this literature by burning it, so that it would no longer be propagated. (Qian 1989:17:282)

An examination of popular deities as portrayed in vernacular fiction reveals that the Confucian suspicion of the genre was to a large extent justified. I will argue that many deities deviated from the Confucian ethos of the Chinese cultural elite, which—to borrow a term from Antonio Gramsci—occupied a "hegemonic" position within society as a whole.[14] Most deities as they appear in vernacular novels can be characterized as belonging to one of three groups: women, martial figures, and eccentrics, and all three groups occupied a marginal or problematic position in the usually accepted conception of society. In general, Confucian ideology, as practiced in late imperial times, placed men above women, old above young, learning above physical heroism, and etiquette above spontaneity. At the apex of the social and cultural pyramid stood the literatus: a male who had achieved his exalted position of official and moral exemplar by virtue of his learning. By contrast, the Chinese pantheon as mirrored in vernacular fiction comprised women instead of men, children instead of adults, uncouth warriors instead of scholars, and clowns instead of reserved literati. The Chinese supernatural was thus, to a large extent, an upside-down image of the Confucian ethos that guided late imperial society. I will illustrate this point by a few examples of female, martial, and eccentric deities, all of whom are the subject of novels (see table). My comments on the deities in question, based primarily on their portrayal in vernacular fiction, do justice neither to their complex personalities nor to their intricate histories; they merely highlight the aspects relevant to my discussion.

Female Deities

The Chinese pantheon includes a large number of female deities, ranging from the Eternal Mother (Wusheng Shengmu), who figures prominently in sectarian movements, to the goddess of the toilet, the Purple Maiden (Zigu) (see also Brigitte Baptandier's and Steven Sangren's essays in this volume). Two female deities occupy particularly important positions in the pantheon: Guanyin and Mazu. The former is worshiped throughout China, the latter in the eastern and southern coastal areas. In Taiwan, for example, Guanyin ranks second in number of temples (557), and Mazu third (509) (Qiu 1985:214, 103). (The largest number of temples is dedicated to the semi-demonic plague gods, the Wangye.) Both Guanyin and Mazu are the subject of Wanli-period hagiographic novels,[15] and Guanyin, in addition, figures prominently in the novel *Journey to the West*. Steven Sangren has pointed out that the gender of these deities alone "disqualifies them from being officials," and he concludes that "the counterculture embodied in the worship of female deities . . . should not be underestimated in anthropological studies of Chinese religion" (Sangren 1983:6, 25).

The cults of Guanyin and Mazu defy the hierarchical structure of late imperial society not only because of the two deities' gender but also because of their refusal to fulfill the roles assigned them by society (see Baptandier's and Sangren's essays in this volume). The myths of both deities highlight their stubborn resistance to their fathers' orders that they marry. Both prefer death to marriage: Guanyin is executed by her father, and Mazu wills herself to death. The deities' premarital deaths guarantee their ritual purity; they were not tainted by sexual intercourse or by childbirth. In this respect, their premature deaths serve the same function as the immaculate conception in Christian mythology: both provide for "virgin mothers." Guanyin and Mazu, like Mary, are referred to by their devotees as "mothers" *(ma)* (Sangren 1983:10, 14). Guanyin's and Mazu's defiance of paternal authority is particularly relevant to our discussion here: not only are they women, they are unfilial women.[16] Thus, their cults represent a sharp departure from the Confucian world view, which considered filial piety a cardinal virtue.

Martial Deities

The Confucian ethos placed the literatus at the apex of the social and the cultural pyramid. Ever since Confucius himself, Confucian ideology saw learning as intimately related to moral perfection and spiritual self-cultivation. In late imperial times social and cultural prestige as well as political power, at least in theory, were gained by learning. This is not to say, of course, that in practice military commanders did not achieve great political power—all dynasties were founded by the sword. Nevertheless, the Confucian canon of education usually placed greater emphasis on learning than on martial skills. To the degree that the cultural elite venerated martial figures, these were usually not heroic soldiers noted for their physical strength, but brilliant strategists whose military accomplishments were closely related to their learning. A fine example is Zhuge Liang, who, as portrayed in the novel *Romance of the Three Kingdoms,* succeeded in his role of supreme commander by virtue of his vast learning, which enabled him to be in tune with the forces underlying human and natural history.

In light of the enormous significance of the literatus in Confucian ideology, it is striking how few historical literati have been worshiped posthumously as deities. By contrast, the Chinese heavens are populated with warriors. Furthermore, the latter are usually not accomplished strategists but rather simple soldiers noted for the their raw courage and strength. Thus, for example, of the protagonists in *Romance of the Three Kingdoms,* it was not the wise Zhuge Liang but rather the rash Guangong who became a popular deity. Guangong is probably the most widely worshiped male deity in China. Another martial deity whose cult is very widespread is Xuantian Shangdi, who is the protagonist of the Wanli hagiographic novel *Journey to the North*.[17] Xuantian Shangdi's other name, Zhenwu (True Warrior), testifies to his military qualifications. Guanggong and Xuantian Shangdi are not the only martial deities celebrated in vernacular fiction. The vast pantheon transmitted by the *Enfeoffment of the Gods*, for example, is almost entirely martial. The latter novel even transforms into warriors such figures as Laozi, who according to early accounts had nothing to do with the military.

The military occupation and rough mannerism of martial deities distinguish them from the literatus. In addition, most of them pose a threat to the state, for they are portrayed as outlaws and rebels (though invariably their cause is just). *Enfeoffment of the Gods* is the story of the military overthrow of the Shang by the rebellious Zhou dynasty. The protagonists of *Water Margin*, who later figure in spirit-medium cults, are all outlaws, and Guangong becomes a fugitive after killing an abusive magistrate. It is noteworthy that in the case of many martial deities military skills are closely related to the mastery of magical arts. A tradition that dates back to the early-Ming novel *Pingyao Zhuan (The Quelling of the Demons)* portrays warfare as a battle of magic and counter-magic. Fanciful weaponry and the art of transformation are major tools, for instance, in Xuantian Shangdi's battles with his arch-enemies the Turtle and the Snake Demons. The combatants transform themselves at will into whatever form they choose, in order to subdue or evade their rivals. Interestingly, magic warfare still figures in modern fiction, as in the widely read novels of Jin Yong, which are the subject of numerous film and television adaptations.

Eccentric Deities

A vast gallery of clownish eccentrics, some with a Daoist bent and others with a Buddhist leaning, garnish the Chinese pantheon with color and humor. On the Buddhist side of the spectrum there are such deities as Jigong, whose nickname Crazy Ji (Jidian) attests to his eccentricity, and the obese Cloth-Bag Buddha (Budai Heshang), who came to occupy a prominent position in the pantheon as the incarnation of the Buddha Maitreya. On the Daoist side we find a group of insouciant poets and drunkards, the Eight Immortals, among whom the lascivious Lü Dongbin is the most popular object of worship (see Paul Katz's essay in this volume). Budai Heshang figures in Yuan drama; Jigong and the Eight Immortals have been celebrated in numerous novels since the sixteenth century.[18] (In the case of the Eight Immortals, some novels deal with the group as a whole, while others are dedicated to individual members.) Budai Heshang, Jigong, the Eight Immortals, and other eccentric deities, such as the God of the Marionette Theater, disregard accepted norms of behavior and, in some cases, violate cardinal moral laws.[19] Their eccentricity is revealed in their dress: they are clad in rags or in colorful patches, their hair is disheveled, and they often walk barefoot. Nazha and Sun Wukong (the protagonists of the *Enfeoffment of the Gods* and the *Journey to the West,* respectively) are even more conspicuous: the former as an oversized baby, the latter as a monkey.

Some eccentric deities share with martial ones military skills as well as, more significantly, a rebellious spirit. Nazha, Sun Wukong, and Huaguang (the protagonist of the *Journey to the South)*[20] are all warriors, and each carries an emblematic magic weapon: Nazha hurls a golden bracelet like a boomerang; Sun Wukong wields an iron rod, which can be transformed into a tiny needle hidden behind his ear; and Huaguang employs a golden brick, which enables him to transform himself at will. All three rebel against human as well as divine authority. Nazha kills the dragon-king's son and makes a belt out of his sinews. Then, as if to prove the universality of Freud's Oedipus complex, he consciously attempts to commit the most serious crime in the Chinese social context: patricide (see Sangren's essay in this volume). Sun Wukong audaciously proclaims himself "The Great Sage Equal to Heaven" (Qitian Dasheng) and embarks upon a revolt against the entire heavenly hierarchy, headed by the Jade Emperor. As to Huaguang, his cult derives from that of the noxious one-legged goblins, the Wutong, who were notorious for seducing and raping women (Glahn 1991, Cedzich 1995). It is not surprising, therefore, that in his fictionalized biographies Huaguang is repeatedly banished to earth after quarreling with almost every figure of authority in heaven.

Interestingly, it is the rebellious aspect of eccentric deities that readers and audiences most enjoy. On stage, the most popular episodes in Nazha's and Sun Wukong's careers are those in which they "wreak havoc" (at sea and in heaven, respectively). Sun Wukong is even worshiped under his mutinous title, "The Great Sage Equal to Heaven," rather than under his Buddhist name, Wukong (or Sun Xingzhe). The cult of some eccentric deities—Sun Wukong and Jigong, for example—sometimes takes on a different form from that of more respected deities, such as Guangong. In Taiwan there are not many large temples for Sun Wukong and Jigong (though there are some). Rather, the two eccentrics appear more frequently as accompanying deities in the temples of other gods. More significant, they are also the subject of spirit-medium cults. These mediums generally practice not in big temples but in small shrines *(tan),* which are often located in the medium's own house and are not registered. It is therefore hard to find evidence of such cults in historical sources. Spirit-medium shrines are not listed in gazetteers, and the historian has to rely on anecdotal literature to assess the eccentric deity's popularity.

The large number of eccentric deities in the Chinese pantheon reveals a striking characteristic of Chinese religion: its humor. The Western monotheistic experience of the divine has often been characterized by "fear and trembling" (Kierkegaard 1945 [1843]). Western thinkers have even considered solemnity or gravity a defining characteristic of religion. William James, for example, circumscribes the divine as follows: "The divine shall mean for us only such a primal reality as the individual feels impelled to respond to solemnly and gravely, and neither by a curse nor a jest" (James 1982 [1902]:38). In Chinese religion, however, the divine and human realms are much closer than in the West, and they resemble each other much more, too. Thus, many Chinese deities are humorous: they display a sense of humor, and they themselves may be the object of jokes and pranks. However, their humor does not diminish their religious efficacy in the least. The Taiwanese opera *Jigong Huofo (The Living Buddha Jigong)*, which is usually performed in temples, culminates with the two divine protagonists, Jigong and Lü Dongbin, cursing each other: "You are crazy," cries Lü Dongbin. "And you behave like a madman," retorts Jigong, to the great delight of the audience, at least some of whom probably worship them both. As to Jigong spirit-mediums, they must entertain their clients with jokes and witticisms, or else the latter would not be convinced of their authenticity. Humor is Jigong's defining, and most cherished, trait.[21]

*   *   *

I have commented briefly on three types of deities, female, martial, and eccentric, as portrayed in vernacular fiction. What is common to all three is not what they are, but what they are not: none of them is a literatus, none of them belonged to the elite. The fictionalized biography of Zhong Kui, a deity who almost joined the literati class, illustrates further the inherent marginality of many Chinese deities. Zhong Kui is the subject of a Wanli hagiographic novel *(Tang Zhong Kui Quanzhuan)* and of three Qing-period sequels. He is worshiped as a demon-queller, and as such he plays an important role in the ritual of the ghost festival. According to his fictionalized biographies, Zhong Kui traveled to the capital to take the highest civil service examinations in the imperial palace. The quality of his essays was such that he should have passed in first place. However, due to his physical ugliness, the examiners unjustly failed him, whereupon, in front of the emperor, he committed suicide. (In one version he did so by smashing his head against the palace pillars.) Then Yama—

in another version the emperor himself—appointed him a national demon-queller (Éliasberg 1976:63,161). Zhong Kui failed the exams unjustly, because of his hideous appearance. Most Chinese stood no chance in them, because they could not afford the necessary education. Thus, it is possible that the uneducated masses read in the Zhong Kui legend their own frustration with the examination system, which provided them only a slim chance, if any, of ever joining the elite. (Members of the elite who failed the exams could have found in this legend an outlet for their frustration as well.)

The Chinese supernatural emerges from vernacular fiction, which played such an important role in its transmission, as largely an upside-down image of society's dominant ideology. Female, martial, and eccentric deities all defy in significant ways the Confucian ethos of the elite, which guided society as a whole. As portrayed in novels, many deities deviated from the Confucian ideology of late imperial times both socially and culturally. While the Confucian social order placed men above women, scholars above soldiers, and old above young, the Chinese pantheon included women, soldiers, and youngsters, even children. While Confucian culture emphasized learning, refinement, and restraint, the pantheon celebrated martial accomplishments and unbridled humor. The supernatural, as mirrored in vernacular fiction, thus functioned in much the same way as the carnival culture of the European Middle Ages and Renaissance. In Bakhtin's terms, it provided the people with a "second life," in which the social codes of everyday life were reversed. Bakhtin's description of the carnival is applicable to many Chinese deities: "A boundless world of humorous forms and manifestations opposed the official and serious tone of medieval ecclesiastical and feudal culture. . . . We find here a characteristic logic, the peculiar logic of the 'inside out'. . . . A second life, a second world of folk culture is thus constructed; it is to a certain extant a parody of the extracarnival life, a 'world inside out' " (Bakhtin 1984:4,11).

I have argued that the Chinese supernatural, as mirrored in vernacular fiction, was to a large extent an upside-down image of society's official ideology. To what extent is this image characteristic of Chinese deities as worshiped in practice by diverse social and religious groups, across vastly different geographical regions? The answer is that a carnival tone is *not* always characteristic of Chinese deities. A significant number of deities, some of whom figure in novels, do not defy the Confucian ethos. For instance, the God of Literature, Wenchang, who guarantees success in the examinations, is, unsurprisingly, himself a literatus, and Judge Bao is depicted in Ming short stories as an austere Confucian, even though the stories about him contain an element of social protest (Hanan 1981:73).

Furthermore, a substantial heavenly bureaucracy mirrored the structure of the earthly Chinese state. This heavenly bureaucracy figured most prominently in the state religion and in Daoism, but it occupied a significant position also in the popular conception of the divine (see Shahar and Weller's introductory essay in this volume). Indeed, it is against this heavenly order that mischievous deities such as Sun Wukong and Nazha rebel.

It is also noteworthy that deities who are depicted in novels as eccentrics or rebels can emerge from other sources in a completely different light. A deity's representation in vernacular fiction often differed significantly from his or her image as understood by Buddhist monks, Daoist masters, and members of the literati elite. Prasenjit Duara has shown, for example, that the state bureaucracy attempted to mitigate the rebellious aspects of Guangong's personality. State-sponsored literature depicted this martial deity as a filial son and scholar well versed in the Confucian classics (Duara 1988:782–785). Another deity, Wen Qiong, appears in the novel *Journey to the North* as a bean-curd vendor, but he is portrayed as a Confucian scholar in a stele inscription by a Yuan literatus (Katz 1990:194, 206). As to Jigong, even though novels and plays invariably depict him as a drunkard, the Unity Sect (Yiguan Dao) downplays his love of wine. Informants from this sectarian movement generally contend that, contrary to popular belief, the clownish god carries medicine, not wine, in his gourd. Novels reached a wider audience than most Daoist, Buddhist, and sectarian writings, as well as hagiographic collections written in the classical language by members of the elite. Thus, the impact of vernacular fiction on the popular understanding of the supernatural was probably larger than that of any other literary genre. Nevertheless, the examples given above show that not all deities shared the eccentric and rebellious traits characteristic of deities' portrayal in novels.

I have suggested that, as portrayed in vernacular fiction, many deities defied the Confucian ethos, which guided late-imperial society. Female, martial, and eccentric deities tended to deviate from accepted social and cultural norms. How should this upside-down dimension of the Chinese supernatural be understood? Did eccentric and rebellious deities operate like a safety valve, allowing society to let off steam, so that it accepted the existing order? Or did the upside-down facet of the gods prompt real questioning of the existing order? Studies of the carnival in Europe show that it could function in both ways. On the one hand, carnival offered all members of society, high and low, a festive respite from the constraints of the existing order. On the other hand, under certain circumstances, as in Romans, France, in 1580, theater and reality merged as carnival turned into a bloody revolt (Le Roy Ladurie 1980, Burke 1978:199–204). Preliminary studies suggest that the Chinese pantheon, like the European carnival, could function as a safety valve and also offer symbolic resources for revolt. Female, martial, and eccentric deities were worshiped throughout society, even though their cults could assume different forms in varying social milieus. Thus, the pantheon, like the novels that transmitted it, offered literati and commoners alike a temporary liberation from the Confucian ethos, without necessarily endangering the social prestige of the ethos itself. But given the right historical circumstances, the upside-down dimension of the supernatural could also provide the ideological resources for organized banditry and revolt, just as Confucian educators had suspected. The triads, for example, conducted their initiation rights in front of a Guangong altar (Yang 1961:62), and the Boxers sought invulnerability by spirit-medium rituals, in which they became possessed by the protagonists of the *Enfeoffment of the Gods, Romance of the Three Kingdoms,* and *Journey to the West,* particularly by Jiang Ziya, Guangong, and Sun Wukong (Esherick 1987:294, 329). Likewise, even the Red Guards attempted to manipulate the defiant simian, Sun Wukong, into a rallying symbol for their Cultural Revolution.

Anthropologists have pointed out significant similarities between Chinese ritual and the bureaucratic process of the Chinese state. Written petitions to the deities resemble official memorials. The gods are dressed in official robes, carried in sedan-chairs like officials, and enshrined in temples fashioned after a magistrate's official residence (Ahern 1981:2). However, a study of the pantheon as portrayed in vernacular fiction reveals that, even if deities are treated like officials, their personalities may still be very different from those of typical officeholders in late imperial times. The awesome power of the gods was sometimes imagined in bureaucratic terms, but their character and training were for the most part radically different from those of traditional bureaucrats. The bureaucratic metaphor may apply to the power wielded by the gods, but not necessarily to their personalities.

Notes

1. Watson 1985 argues that the state played a crucial role in the promotion of Mazu's cult, but he emphasizes that this did not prevent varying interpretations of her figure in different social milieus.

2. Paul Ropp (1981:53) translates *jiao* here as "teaching," which lends this passage a different thrust: as a "teaching," fiction shapes moral values and behavioral patterns, not religious beliefs. Indeed, Qian goes on in the following

passage to lament the corrupting influence of fiction on the youth. However, as Confucianism, Buddhism, and Daoism evince, *jiao* as religion and *jiao* as teaching are not mutually exclusive.

3. Many *lingguai* novels are becoming available in typeset editions as part of the series *Zhongguo Shenguai Xiaoshuo Daxi,* ed. Lin Chen and Duan Wengui (Changchun: Jilin Wenshi Chubanshe, 1991–).

4. Liu 1962 suggested that the *Enfeoffment of the Gods (Fengshen Yanyi)* was written by Lu Xixing, whose dates he established as 1519–1578/9. However, Koss 1979 has shown convincingly that the novel must have been written after 1592.

5. For a comparison of the protagonists of *Enfeoffment of the Gods* with the deities currently worshiped in Taiwan, see Zeng 1985.

6. Admittedly, Guangong and Song Jiang displayed supernatural powers following their deaths; the authors note that they responded to worshipers' requests. However, throughout the larger part of the narratives they are depicted as humans.

7. H. Y. Lowe is referring to his protagonist in the third person, but his work is most likely autobiographical.

8. Ursula-Angelika Cedzich has shown that the god Huaguang, under his earlier name Wutong, had been the subject of religious worship for centuries prior to the compilation of the novel *Journey to the South.* Yet once this novel was written it exerted a significant influence on the development of his myth, especially in the regional drama of South China (Cedzich 1995:216–218).

9. *Romance of the Three Kingdoms* and *Water Margin* portray their protagonists, Guangong and Song Jiang respectively, as human. Nevertheless these novels, also, indicate that the two protagonists were historically the subject of worship; see note 6 above.

10. On Sun Wukong's origins, see Dudbridge 1970 and Shahar 1992b; on his cult see Sawada 1982 [1979] and Elliot 1981 [1955]:74–76,80–109,170–71.

11. It is enlightening to compare a novel's treatment of a deity's career to a *baojuan* treatment of the same. The former would be much richer in narrative detail (Dudbridge 1978:54–55).

12. The Wanli-period Guanyin novel was influenced by a *baojuan* text (Dudbridge 1978:44–50,56–58).

13. A distinction could be drawn between written masterpieces, such as the *Journey to the West,* and the folk traditions from which they derive and for which they serve as sources. It could be argued, for example, that most of those who venerated the protagonists of the *Journey to the West* did not read the written novel, which has a complex allegorical dimension, but instead were exposed to oral and dramatic adaptations of it, where such an allegorical level is for the most part lacking. Andrew Plaks suggests that the written novels *Journey to the West, Three Kingdoms,* and *Water Margin* ironically revise earlier folk narratives. He argues, for example, that in *Water Margin* "the ironic dimension comes into play in the deflation of heroic myths and stereotypes from the popular tradition" (Plaks 1987:499). However, these three novels themselves served as sources for a vast body of oral literature and drama, where an ironic attitude— even if apparent in the written novels—is probably lacking. In other words, even if the implied author of the written novel *Water Margin* approaches Song Jiang with ironic distance, his novel could still have fostered the latter's veneration.

Thus, Pu Songling's observation—that fictional characters may become gods contrary to their creators' intentions—may be historically accurate.

14. Gramsci used the term *hegemony* to denote the authority or prestige of the upper classes that enables them to guide society as a whole *without* the use of force (Gramsci 1971:12).

15. See respectively *Nanhai Guanshiyin Pusa Chushen Xiuxing Zhuan (Chronicle of the Incarnation and Self-Cultivation of the Bodhisattva Guanshiyin of the Southern Sea)* (Wanli edition, 1990 reprint) and *Tianfei Niangma Zhuan (Biography of the Heavenly Consort and Mother)* (1990).

16. In the Guanyin myth there is an attempt to mitigate the deity's unfilial behavior; following her death, Guanyin saves her ill father by offering him her own eyes and arms.

17. *Beifang Zhenwu Zushi Xuantian Shangdi Chushen Zhizhuan (Chronicle of the Incarnations of the True Warrior of the North, Patriarch, and Emperor of the Dark Heavens)* (Wanli edition, 1990 reprint).

18. The earliest novels on Jigong and the Eight Immortals, respectively, are *Qiantang Huyin Jidian Chanshi Yulu (Recorded Sayings of the Recluse from Qiantang Lake, the Chan Master Crazy Ji)* (1569 edition, 1990 reprint) and *Baxian Chuchu Dongyou Ji (The Origin of the Eight Immortals and Their Journey East)* (Wanli edition, 1990 reprint).

19. On the God of the Marionette Theater (Tian Du Yuanshuai) see Dean 1994 and also Schipper 1966.

20. The earliest edition of the novel, published during the Wanli period (1990 reprint), was entitled *The Biography of the Heavenly King, Huaguang (Huaguang Tianwang Zhuan)* and not *Journey to the South.*

21. Humor plays an important role in Chinese ritual drama as well. Li Fengmao 1991 pointed out that comic elements figure both in Daoist *gongde* (merit) funerary rites and in "Change of Fortunes" *(gaiyun)* rituals performed by Taiwanese ritual masters *(fashi).*

Literature Cited

Ahern, Emily Martin. 1981. *Chinese Ritual and Politics.* Cambridge: Cambridge University Press.

Bakhtin, Mikhail. 1984. *Rabelais and His World.* Translated by Hélène Iswolsky. Bloomington: Indiana University Press.

Baxian Chuchu Dongyou Ji (The Origin of the Eight Immortals and Their Journey East). 1990. Wanli edition. Photographic reprint in *Guben Xiaoshuo Jicheng (Collection of Ancient Editions of Fiction)*, vol. 70. Shanghai: Guji Chu-banshe.

Beifang Zhenwu Zushi Xuantian Shangdi Chushen Zhizhuan (Chronicle of the Incarnations of the True Warrior of the North, Patriarch, and Emperor of the Dark Heavens). 1990. Wanli edition. Photographic reprint in *Guben Xiaoshuo Jicheng (Collection of Ancient Editions of Fiction)*, vol. 71. Shanghai: Guji Chubanshe.

Blader, Susan. 1978. "*San-hsia wu-yi* and Its Link to Oral Literature." *Chinoperl Papers* 8:9–38.

———. 1983. "'Yan Chansan Thrice Tested': Printed Novel to Oral Tale." *Chinoperl Papers* 12:84–111.

Burke, Peter. 1978. *Popular Culture in Early Modern Europe*. New York: Harper and Row.

Burkert, Walter. 1985. *Greek Religion*. Translated by John Raffan. Cambridge: Harvard University Press.

Cao, Xueqin. 1973–1986. *The Story of the Stone*. Translated by David Hawkes (vols. 1–3) and John Minford (vols. 4–5). Harmondsworth: Penguin Books.

Cao, Xueqin, and Gao E. 1985. *Honglou Meng (The Dream of the Red Chamber)*. 3 vols. Beijing: Renmin.

Cedzich, Ursula-Angelika. 1995. "The Cult of the Wu-t'ung/Wu-hsien in History and Fiction: The Religious Roots of the *Journey to the South*." In *Ritual and Scripture in Chinese Popular Religion: Five Studies*, edited by David Johnson. Publications of the Chinese Popular Culture Project, no. 3. Berkeley: Institute for East Asian Studies.

Chin, Sheng-t'an. 1990. "How to Read *The Fifth Book of Genius*." Translated by John C. Y. Wang. In *How to Read the Chinese Novel*, edited by David L. Rolston, 124–145. Princeton: Princeton University Press.

Dean, Kenneth. 1994. "Comic Inversion and Cosmic Renewal: The God of the Theater in the Ritual Traditions of Putian." In *Minjian Xinyang yu Zhongguo Wenhua Guoji Yantaohui Lunwen Ji (Proceedings of the International Conference on Popular Beliefs and Chinese Culture)*, 2:683–731. Taipei: Han-hsüeh Yen-chiu Chung-hsin.

Duara, Prasenjit. 1988. "Superscribing Symbols: The Myth of Guandi, Chinese God of War." *Journal of Asian Studies* 47(4):778–795.

Dudbridge, Glen. 1970. *The Hsi-yu chi: A Study of Antecedents to the Sixteenth-Century Chinese Novel*. Cambridge: Cambridge University Press.

———. 1978. *The Legend of Miao-shan*. Oxford Oriental Monographs 1. London: Ithaca Press.

Éliasberg, Danielle. 1976. *Le Roman du Pourfendeur de Démons: Traduction annotée et commentaire*. Paris: Collège de France, Institut des Hautes Etudes Chinoises.

Elliot, Allan J. A. 1981 [1955]. *Chinese Spirit-Medium Cults in Singapore*. Reprint. Taipei: Southern Materials Center.

Esherick, Joseph W. 1987. *The Origins of the Boxer Uprising*. Berkeley: University of California Press.

Freedman, Maurice. 1974. "On the Sociological Study of Chinese Religion." In *Religion and Ritual in Chinese Society*, edited by Arthur P. Wolf, 19–41. Stanford: Stanford University Press.

Glahn, Richard von. 1991. "The Enchantment of Wealth: The God Wutong in the Social History of Jiangnan." *Harvard Journal of Asiatic Studies* 51(2): 672–675.

Gramsci, Antonio. 1971. *Selections from the Prison Notebooks*. Edited and translated by Quintin Hoare and Geoffrey Nowell Smith. New York: International Publishers.

Grootaers, Willem A. 1952. "The Hagiography of the Chinese God Chen-Wu." *Folklore Studies* 11(2):139–181.

Hanan, Patrick. 1981. *The Chinese Vernacular Story*. Cambridge: Harvard University Press.

Huaguang Tianwang Zhuan (The Biography of Heavenly King, Huaguang). 1990. Wanli edition. Photographic reprint in *Guben Xiaoshuo Jicheng (Collection of Ancient Editions of Fiction)*, vol. 70. Shanghai: Guji Chubanshe.

Huang Huajie. 1967. *Guangong de Renge yu Shenge (Guangong's Human and Divine Personality)*. Taipei: Shangwu Yinshuguan.

Hummel, Arthur W. 1943. *Eminent Chinese of the Ch'ing Period*. Washington, D.C.: Library of Congress.

James, William. 1982 [1902]. *The Varieties of Religious Experience*. Harmondsworth: Penguin Books.

Johnson, David. 1989. "Actions Speak Louder than Words: The Cultural Significance of Chinese Ritual Opera." In *Ritual Opera, Operatic Ritual: "Mulien Rescues His Mother" in Chinese Popular Culture*, edited by David Johnson, 1–45. Publications of the Chinese Popular Culture Project 1. Berkeley: Institute of East Asian Studies.

Katz, Paul. 1990. "Wen Ch'iung—The God of Many Faces." *Hanxue Yanjiu (Chinese Studies)* 8(1):183–219.

Kierkegaard, Søren. 1945 [1843]. *Fear and Trembling: A Dialectical Lyric.* Translated by Walter Lowrie. Princeton: Princeton University Press.

Koss, Nicholas. 1979. "The Relationship of the *Hsi-yu chi* and *Feng-shen yan-i.*" *T'oung pao* 65(4–5):143–165.

Le Roy Ladurie, Emmanuel. 1980. *Carnival in Romans*. Translated by Mary Feeney. New York: Braziller.

Li Fengmao. 1991. "Taiwan Yishi Xiju Zhong de Xiejue Xing: Yi Daojiao, *Fajiao* Weizhu de Kaocha (The Humorous Dimension of Taiwanese Ritual Drama: An Investigation Based Primarily on Daoism and *Fajiao*)." *Minsu quyi* 71:174–210.

Li Xianzhang. 1970. "Yi 'Sanjiao Soushen Daquan' yu 'Tianfei Niangma Zhuan' Wei Zhongxin Lai Kaocha Mazu Chuanshuo (Using the 'Compendium of the Three Religions' Deities' and 'The Biography of the Heavenly Consort and Mother' As Primary Sources for the Investigation of Mazu Lore)." Translated by Li Xiaoben. Reprinted in *Huitu Sanjiao Yuanliu Soushen Daquan (An Illustrated Compendium of the Biographies of the Three Religions' Deities)*, edited by Wang Qiugui, 3–33. Taipei: Lianjing chubanshe.

Liu Ts'un-yan. 1962. *Buddhist and Taoist Influences on Chinese Novels. Vol. 1: The Authorship of the Feng-shen yen-i*. Wiesbaden: Kommissionverlag.

Loon, Piet van der. 1977. "Les origines rituelles du théâtre chinois." *Journal asiatique* 265(1–2):141–168.

Lowe, H. Y. 1983 [1940–1941]. *The Adventures of Wu: The Life Cycle of a Peking Man*. Reprint. Princeton: Princeton University Press.

Lutgendorf, Philip. 1991. *The Life of a Text: Performing the Rāmcaritmānas of Tulsidas*. Berkeley: University of California Press.

Maspero, Henri. 1981. "The Mythology of Modern China." In *Taoism and Chinese Religion*, 75–196. Translated by Frank A. Kierman. Amherst: University of Massachusetts Press.

Nanhai Guanshiyin Pusa Chushen Xiuxing Zhuan (Chronicle of the Incarnations and Self-Cultivation of the Bodhisattva Guanshiyin of the Southern Sea). 1990. Wanli edition. Photographic reprint in *Guben Xiaoshuo Jicheng (Collection of Ancient Editions of Fiction)*, vol. 76. Shanghai: Guji Chubanshe.

Plaks, Andrew H. 1987. *The Four Masterworks of the Ming Novel*. Princeton: Princeton University Press.

Pu Songling. 1962. *Liaozhai Zhiyi (Liaozhai's Records of the Strange)*. Edited by Zhang Youhe. Shanghai: Guji.

Qian Daxin. 1989. *Qianyan Tang Ji (Collected Writings from the Qianyan Hall)*. Edited by Lü Youren. Shanghai: Guji.

Qiantang Huyin Jidian Chanshi Yulu (Recorded Sayings of the Recluse from Qiantang Lake, the Chan Master Crazy Ji). [1569] 1990. Photographic reprint in *Guben Xiaoshuo Congkan (Reprint Series of Ancient Editions of Fiction)*, series 8, vol. 1. Beijing: Zhonghua Shuju.

Qiu Dezai. 1985. *Taiwan Miao Shen Zhuan (Temple Deities in Taiwan)*. Douliu: Xintong Shuju.

Ropp, Paul S. 1981. *Dissent in Early Modern China: Ju-lin wai-shih and Ch'ing Social Criticism*. Ann Arbor: University of Michigan Press.

Sangren, P. Steven. 1983. "Female Gender in Chinese Religious Symbols: Kuan Yin, Ma Tsu, and the 'Eternal Mother.' " *Signs* 9(1):4–25.

Sawada Mizuho. 1982 [1979]. "Songokū shin (The Deity Songokū)." Reprinted in *Chūgoku no Minkan Shinkō (Chinese Popular Beliefs)*, 86–102. Tokyo: Kōsaku Sha.

Schipper, Kristofer. 1966. "The Divine Jester, Some Remarks on the Gods of the Chinese Marionette Theater." *Bulletin of the Institute of Ethnology: Academia Sinica* 21:81–96.

Seaman, Gary. 1987. *The Journey to the North: An Ethnohistorical Analysis and Annotated Translation of the Chinese Folk Novel Pei-yu-chi*. Berkeley: University of California Press.

Shahar, Meir. 1992a. "Fiction and Religion in the Early History of the Chinese God Jigong." Ph.D. diss., Harvard University.

———. 1992b. "The Lingyin Si Monkey Disciples and the Origins of Sun Wukong." *Harvard Journal of Asiatic Studies* 52(1):193–224.

———. 1994. "Enlightened Monk or Arch-Magician? The Portrayal of the God Jigong in the Sixteenth-Century Novel *Jidian Yulu*." In *Minjian Xinyang yu Zhongguo Wenhua Guoji Yantaohui Lunwen Ji (Proceedings of the International Conference on Popular Beliefs and Chinese Culture)*, 1:251–303. Taipei: Han-hsüeh Yen-chiu Chung-hsin.

Snow, Edgar. 1938. *Red Star over China*. New York: Random House.

Sun Kaidi. 1932. *Zhongguo Tongsu Xiaoshuo Shumu (Catalog of Chinese Popular Fiction)*. Beiping: Guoli Beiping tushuguan.

Tang Zhong Kui Quanzhuan (The Complete Biography of Zhong Kui of Tang). 1990. Wanli edition. Photographic reprint in *Guben Xiaoshuo Jicheng (Collection of Ancient Editions of Fiction)*, vol. 68. Shanghai: Guji.

Tao Chengzhang. 1965 [1935]. *Jiaohui Yuanliu Kao (Researches into the History of Religious Sects)*. In Xiao Yishan, *Jindai mimi shehui shiliao (Materials on Modern Secret Societies)*. Reprint. Taiwan: Wenhai Chubanshe.

Tianfei Niangma Zhuan (Biography of the Heavenly Consort and Mother). 1990. Shanghai: Guji.

Wang Xiaochuan. 1958. *Yuan Ming Qing Sandai Jinhui Xiaoshuo Xiqu Shiliao (Materials Concerning Forbidden Fiction of the Three Periods: Yuan, Ming and Qing)*. Beijing: Zuojia Chubanshe.

Ward, Barbara E. 1979. "Not Merely Players: Drama, Act and Ritual in Traditional China." *Man,* new series 14(1):18–39.

Watson, James L. 1985. "Standardizing the Gods: The Promotion of T'ien Hou ('Empress of Heaven') along the South China Coast, 960–1960." In *Popular Culture in Late Imperial China,* edited by David Johnson, Andrew J. Nathan, and Evelyn S. Rawski, 292–324. Berkeley: University of California Press.

Weller, Robert P. 1994. *Resistance, Chaos and Control in China: Taiping Rebels, Taiwanese Ghosts and Tiananmen.* Seattle: University of Washington Press.

Wolf, Arthur P. 1975. "Gods, Ghosts and Ancestors." In *Religion and Ritual in Chinese Society,* edited by Arthur P. Wolf, 131–182. Stanford: Stanford University Press.

Yang, C. K. 1961. *Religion in Chinese Society.* Berkeley: University of California Press.

Zeitlin, Judith. 1993. *Historian of the Strange: Pu Songling and the Chinese Classical Tale.* Stanford: Stanford University Press.

Zeng Qinliang. 1985. *Taiwan Minjian Xinyang yu Fengshen Yanyi zhi Bijiao Yanjiu* (A Comparative Study of Taiwanese Popular Beliefs and the *Enfeoffment of the Gods*). Taipei: Huazheng Shuju.

Zhongguo Shenguai Xiaoshuo Daxi (The Big Series of Chinese Fiction on the Supernatural), 1991–. Ca. 30 vols. Edited by Lin Chen and Duan Wengui. Changchun: Jilin Wenshi Chubanshe.

Transmission in Popular Religion: The Jiajiang Festival Troupe of Southern Taiwan

DONALD S. SUTTON

WHILE THE TRANSMISSION of the main surviving schools of Daoism can be traced to canonical sources through lineages of masters and pupils (Schipper 1985b), it is far harder to understand, even in principle, how the seemingly protean forms of popular religion have evolved. Broad unities have often been remarked on (Freedman 1979, Wolf 1974, Weller 1987, Sangren 1987, Watson 1985 and 1988, Feuchtwang 1992), but there is no agreement on how far they go or on what brings them about. Does myth, iconography, or ritual provide essential continuity? Local gods in China have neither the mythic structure supplied by scriptural canon nor the fixed liturgy and iconography enforced by a centralized church. What, then, acts to limit the elaboration and variegation of myths and ritual forms? A fruitful approach in accounting for standardization and its limits may be to examine closely the forms and sources of innovation within a particular local tradition. The case of the Taiwan Jiajiang, a performative troupe of dramatic exorcistic dancers, is relatively accessible. Its institutional history is brief, and its spread and artistic development, especially since the 1950s, have been rapid.

The study of such a troupe can shed light from an unfamiliar angle on the popular understandings of Chinese deities. The Jiajiang[1] are not fully gods but by nature move between the categories of god, ghost, and human performer. Their common titles "general" *(jiangjun)* or "great god" *(dashen)* should not disguise the fact that everyone regards them as minor gods. They exist to serve important military gods that protect communities, and they are extensions of those gods' power and dignity on the occasion of periodic *jiao* (grand offerings) or pilgrimages on gods' birthdays: escorting them in processions, exorcising demons and bad influences for local people and their shops and houses, and performing before gods and people alike. They are petitioned not in their own right but only for the power delegated from the god. They originate as ghostlike creatures in bad deaths or bad lives. The face-painted dancers represent these demigods, who may on occasion wildly possess them. Currently, the dancers are usually teenagers, and like many of the gods discussed elsewhere in this volume, they convey the sense of unruliness even as they go about their duties of bringing order and harmony to communities. As I shall show, the uncertain, liminal position of the Jiajiang is their essential characteristic.

Almost all informants insist that their troupes are more traditional than others, and that there is a single legitimate way to march, dance, paint faces, do exorcisms, and so forth. One has only to look at several troupes and traditions (or schools) to be convinced of their diversity. My purpose is not to decide on the question of legitimacy but to explain how variation or replication occurs; to suggest how in spite of appearances they constitute a single tradition that is at once organizational, mythic, and performative, each aspect affecting the others; and to uncover the changing social context and the neglected role of institutions.

The Main Phases of Jiajiang History

In their general idea, the Jiajiang are ancient, but their particular history dates back to the eighteenth century, and their mature forms were reached only in Taiwan in the twentieth century. Exorcists, performers, and god's escorts, the Jiajiang (Hokkien: Kacheong) are deeply rooted in the mythic notion of the underworld and its ten courts for judging the newly dead, in the conception of underworld gods serving as place-gods responsible for the protection of this-worldly territories, and in the practice of periodic processions for local renewal and purification in which local gods are paraded like imperial officials. Face-painted or masked exorcistic dancers can be identified as far back as Han (Bodde 1975) and Song times, but the Jiajiang's immediate prehistory is the Wuchang (Life-Is-Transient) character. This is the messenger who escorts the newly dead to purgatory and serves as assistant in the courts, at times doubled to a yin and a yang figure, Heiwuchang and Baiwuchang (Lu Xun 1976). In the lower Yangzi City God temples, these become the paired yin/yang hollow figures responsible for day and night jurisdiction, which were taken out to escort the god in his ritual inspection of the local territory (Maspero 1981). In the next stage of the Jiajiang's prehistory, in both Fujian and Taiwan, the doubled Wuchang appear as short and tall figures, known already in the nineteenth century as Seventh and Eighth Masters, Qiye and Baye (Doolittle 1865).

These two contrasting images are still indispensable in the Wangye and City God temples in Taiwan and have a standard explanatory myth concentrating on their difference in height. Fan and Xie were bailiffs or policemen and sworn brothers. During a rainstorm Xie offered to go for help, or fetch an umbrella, and Fan promised to wait for him beside a bridge. The water rose and loyal little Fan was drowned. Xie returned, saw his friend's body, and hanged himself in remorse.

The legend is strongly associated with Fuzhou, where two expressions still current in the 1930s testified that the story was a local favorite: "Dying clinging to the bridge, you cannot lose faith and go back," and a literary version, "Don't cling to the bridge yet lose faith" (Huang 1940; cf. Ye 1993:87–88, citing the Xiapu county gazetteer of 1929). Early versions of the tale associate it with Nantai Bridge near the walled city of Fuzhou. Whether myth precedes or follows iconic form is here unclear. The tall/short distinction may have been introduced by the demands of performance, to accentuate and dramatize the contrast between the two light and dark figures. The mythic explanation of the two friends may have been developed later, under the influence of the details of Wuchang iconography (the tongue stuck out, the umbrella still held by some hollow temple figures), with the detail about Nantai and its bridge added for verisimilitude. Thus, iconography may have given rise to myth, or the reverse.

In any case, there can be no doubt about the aptness of this myth on several levels. The legend of the dying friends at the bridge almost invents itself by giving tangible form to the principal ideas already associated with the Wuchang tradition. First, by the forms of their death the two became feared ghosts of the drowned and hanged variety propitiated by many Chinese communities as lost, unworshiped spirits *(wanghun)* (Weller 1987). Second, by dying in water and air respectively they recall the yin/yang distinction of the Wuchang tradition. Third, most powerfully the myth evokes the idea of transition at the root of the Wuchang characters—transition from life to death, from earth to purgatory—for which the bridge must stand as a symbol. These resonances may account for the long currency of this myth and the absence of alternative explanations of the tall Qiye and the short Baye.

The Jiajiang center on the Wuchang pair, but they are an iconic confection. The tall and short Wuchang figures, now known as Generals Xie and Fan, or simply as Daye and Erye,[2] are joined by two other characters from the underworld: a pair of stave bearers invariably called Gan and Liu, to make up the first and second ranks (sometimes called the Four Generals); by the Four Seasons, who are drawn from the Fuzhou festival round (Doolittle 1865) and have no connection with the underworld; and by two this-worldly messengers, civil and military, who go out in front of the troupe. These are paralleled by the Civil and Military Justices who are added at the end of the Ten Generals (Shijiajiang), but not in most Eight Generals troupes (Bajiajiang). Each character has a distinctive conventional implement, color of dress, and style of face paint (see below). The whole troupe is preceded by a usually unpainted figure, the punishment bearer *(xingju)*, carrying model instruments of torture mounted on two boards slung over his shoulder and deriving from official processions.

Why this chaotic combination in place of uniformly dressed guards? The inspiration is clearly from the day-to-day world of sub-bureaucracy in imperial China (Shi 1986),[3] but in a vague and schematic sense. The performers seen on the march—excluding the Four Seasons—represent a process, though it is never ritually played out: arrest by yamen underlings. In principle the punishment bearer warns, the messengers search out, the stave bearers pursue, Erye and Daye take into custody, and the justices at the rear interrogate and record. The Four Seasons fit a different logic; the strange objects they carry (see below) may have once represented the variety of harms or plagues that the troupe in procession was supposed to exorcise.[4] Although converted into seasonal names with appropriately matching colors to communicate harmony and order—a typical Daoist transformation of popular, more literal demonic forms—the Four Seasons may be in origin specialized forms of harm, just as the other generals are specialized means of attacking it.

For the sake of performance, these iconically diverse elements were combined, but they were not immediately integrated. Only the development of more active dances and the experience of collective movements gradually, by fits and starts, created the familiar Taiwan Jiajiang iconography of the twentieth century. A stele of 1781 at the Fuzhou Bailongan (White Dragon Shrine)—the main temple of the Wufudadi or Wulinggong, the Fuzhou Plague Gods—lists seventeen generals, including all those most commonly used today.[5] They carry their implements not in their right hands but in their inside hands, which suggests that the outside hands might well have carried feather fans like those carried by the troupes of today. Without the fans, this variously equipped and dressed troupe would resemble a baggage party following an army or opera actors searching for their stage. Fans added a certain unity, softened the troupe's martial air, and gave the standard pacing, called Ruyibu (As-you-like-it step), its stately and dramatic character.

It is likely, then, that a version of the Jiajiang—though not yet in its standard twentieth-century Taiwan form—did exist in the Bailongan in the eighteenth century when the stele was carved. Evidence of a continuous performative tradition is lacking. The missionary Justus Doolittle (1865), who described the festivals of the city in great detail, notes elements resembling parts of the Jiajiang, but no Jiajiang in the Taiwan sense. As already noted, the Four Seasons whose faces were painted existed as a separate group, as did Fan and Xie in their more common form as hollow figures, but not incorporated within a larger Jiajiang group.[6] But other Eight Generals (Bajiang) existed elsewhere in the Fuzhou suburbs and in neighboring counties (Ye 1993:73–77,87–88).

It was probably in the 1870s that military men posted from the provincial capital of Fuzhou brought incense and images of the Wulinggong of the Bailongan along with the Jiajiang tradition onto the island prefecture of Taiwan (Shi 1986). A series of plague epidemics occasioned regular processions of these Plague Gods with their "Shijiajiang before the Sedan." The personnel was no doubt reduced from the unwieldy number of seventeen and may have consisted in its most common form of the six pairs of men still present in Ten Generals (Shijiajiang) troupes today.

The late development of the Jiajiang is suggested by a painting of the Taiwan Bailongan[7] dating probably from the last decades of the nineteenth century, when the Jiajiang were still very different from those of the present. This is a traditional-style painting of actors, not a visualization of gods. They are seated in pairs, but face paint and dress are not yet integrated: instead of painted designs, Daye and Erye wear huge eyebrows and a bare inside shoulder, very much like the unmodified hollow temple figures, their namesakes. The stave bearers lack bare inside shoulders and the hats of today, and Liuye wears the face-paint pattern now worn by Daye, a double bat design. The single messenger (absent from the 1781 stele) is hatless and shoeless, thus not appearing to be an integral part of the troupe, and there is no sign of the character of punishment bearer. They do look like off-duty soldiers, these heavy-set, overdressed men dancing in their large boots. It is hard to picture Daye and Erye playing the vigorous role of today without risking the indignity of unstuck eyebrows. They could certainly look impressive as escorts of Wufudadi, but despite the fans they still seem a somewhat random group, unsuited to complex choreography.

Probably this is the precursor troupe of all southern Taiwan troupes. The others seem to have branched out (with or without permission) from the Bailongan or its various offshoots in Taiwan and do not appear to predate the twentieth century. The face-painted

Bajiang (Eight Generals) troupes in counties just south of Fuzhou did not directly influence the Taiwan versions. In spite of the fact that Taiwanese (except the Hakka) are overwhelmingly from the far south of Fujian, most Jiajiang today look to the Bailongan as their place of origin, and many have the Fuzhou Wulinggong (now called Wufudadi) as their patron god.

The Bailongan hall (Ruyitang, "As-You-Like-It Hall") was originally in the Qing constabulary headquarters. When the Japanese took over after the forced cession of Taiwan in 1895, they closed down the hall, but Taiwanese water carriers saved the gods' images and took them to a little temple, the Yuanhegong (Palace of Primal Harmony), less than a mile to the north, which was dedicated to a different god. The tradition of the Jiajiang was observed, but mostly in the breach: when the Wuling gods went out, it was the custom for each sedan to have its Jiajiang escort. Training continued under the auspices of local inhabitants, groups of whom were designated to pay and man either a Jiajiang troupe or a sedan. Sometimes the Jiajiang would dress for a god's birthday, but the procedure was so cumbersome and expensive that they rarely went out in procession.

Perhaps this was why their spread from Tainan was surprisingly slow. There were other difficulties as well: the expense of setting up a new troupe, the Yuanhegong's lack of interest in sharing the Jiajiang, and particularly the absence of other Wufudadi temples in Taiwan, resulting from the virtual absence of Fuzhou natives among the settlers. The fairly primitive stage of artistic and ritual development must also be emphasized. In the early part of the century, face-painting conventions were being gradually established. The earliest dances appear to have emphasized, as they still do, the Taiji boxing tradition of martial poses and slow movements that must have appealed to the soldiers from Fuzhou. They could not have been as attractive in performance as some of their successors.

Four more schools[8] were eventually established in other southern towns. The earliest troupe outside Tainan was probably one set up in Jiayi before 1907, at a temple dedicated to Wangye, the Plague God of southern Fujian. Around that time, when an earthquake destroyed the temple, a cake maker from Madou returned home and trained a troupe for the annual Night Arts, a competitive extravaganza lasting several weeks in which two ritual halves of the town vied with new and old troupes of all kinds recruited from a wide surrounding area. Two rival groups of Jiajiang served the chief god of the event, Dizangwang, the merciful God of Hell, and came out only with the sedans on the last night. This was the ideal forum for the development of elaborate choreography, and this tradition spread to Jiali and the Xigang triennial festival and still dominates central Tainan County.

Jiajiang troupes were established in the 1920s and later at other prosperous places with regular large-scale festivals. Former members of the Bailongan troupes started two more rival troupes at Jiayi, a boom town north of Tainan at the foot of Ali Mountain, whose sandalwood forests were being felled to meet demand in metropolitan Japan. They also established one each in the large center of Fengshan east of the newer port of Gaoxiong and the fishing port of Donggang farther south. Fengshan and especially Jiayi had the highly competitive temple environment that spurred the development of new choreographic forms.

During the Japanese period the Jiajiang troupes outside Tainan all appear to have been dependent on temples engaged in regular processional activities. Competition was an important source of innovation, but when they competed, it was not in a marketplace where their services were freely bought and sold. A further characteristic was that their contacts were quite limited, each being focused on activities in a single town and its surrounding villages. Consequently, the schools developed separate styles of choreography and ritual practice.

The replacement of Japanese by Kuomintang rule led to a spurt of local interest in the Jiajiang as a native Chinese folk art, most noticeably in certain schools in Tainan; one man who went to a public boys' junior school in the early 1950s near the Yuanhegong recalled that he and his classmates could all do the steps. But the temple still did not authorize the establishment of tributary troupes, and growth was at first slow. Jiayi proved the most active of the old centers, counting two main schools in many variations. By the 1960s a few Jiajiang were hiring themselves out for the use of the increasingly common *jiao* festivals and pilgrimages conducted by community temples, and the practice spread with Taiwan's economic miracle and the improvement of communications. A new type of semiprofessional or professional troupe had appeared alongside the traditional troupes, calling itself Bajiajiang (Eight Generals) (most of the traditional troupes were Shijiajiang, Ten Generals). Some of these troupes (which I shall call commercial troupes) were essentially dancers; others in upland Gaoxiong (equally commercial in intent) developed a new style of self-mortification. To the present the three categories have persisted—traditional, commercial, and self-mortifying—though they are not sharply distinguished from each other[9] or equally represented in the various regional schools. Relations among them can be strained, but all have flourished.

Modern communications, particularly to and from pilgrimage sites, continue to have an effect. The birthday celebrations of Wangye at Nankunshen (Taiwan's premier pilgrimage site) and to a lesser extent Madou have helped spread the custom of mortification. At the same time they have helped to standardize certain customs from school to school.

It is plain that now a market exists throughout southern Taiwan, affecting even the traditional troupes. Market demand was crucial for a dramatic increase of self-mortifiers in the late 1970s and 1980s. Knowing the appeal of controlled violence and spilled blood to spectators, temple committeemen are willing to pay an extra NT$10,000 per day (say NT$30,000 instead of NT$20,000) if mortification is promised.[10] The costs, on the other hand, are not very different. Usually these performers are better paid than most traditional troupes, and more paid helpers are required to assist the self-mortifying rituals. On the other hand, self-mortifying troupes can afford to neglect training, can save money on dress and paint, and earn quite as much in exorcisms.

Though tentative, this historical sketch refutes the notion of a popular tradition without history, sprung fully formed from some mainland model and not appreciably changed in Taiwan. New questions must now be posed: How did the Jiajiang organizations spread, what was transmitted and altered, and what determined the forms of innovation and their acceptance?

Dynamics of Jiajiang Troupe Organizations

The clientele that a troupe builds determines whether the troupe flourishes or dies, but the leader has different options in the three types of troupe.

Founding a new troupe requires expensive props (implements, hats, fans, uniforms) and learned or purchased skills (face painting, training in footwork and dance, and exorcism). In the central Tainan County school with its complex choreography, one hall leader helped train six or seven other halls for NT$10,000 a time. Commercial and self-mortifying troupes have energetic entrepreneurial leaders, who in some cases perform themselves. Many commercial leaders are *fashi* (ritual masters) or spirit-mediums, who can mobilize their esoteric ritual and knowledge in a form of charismatic leadership useful in motivating their young charges and in impressing the troupe's clientele. Self-mortifiers more often are led by pure entrepreneurs.

Links with one or more local temples are essential. The temples' periodic processions present the main occasions to use the troupe. Their precincts are the most suitable home for the little images of these gods' defenders, their locked cupboards a safe place to store the equipment, their courtyards a convenient location for evening training, and their rear or side chapels the ideal place for early-morning face painting on days of performance. Perhaps the best situation is for the Jiajiang to be organizationally inseparable from the temple, as at Donggang, where the traditional-style Gongyitang is within the Gongshantang, the principal temple in one of the seven precincts *(jiaotou)* that organize the big temple's triennial grand offering *(jiao)*. Some commercial-style troupes are also lodged in or beside a temple, but most establish their own hall *(tang)* on the ground floor of the house occupied by the leader's family and hire themselves out to temples with which he has connections.

Commercial and especially self-mortifying troupes can collaborate with other troupes with similar styles, lending drumming groups, providing face-painting services, and exchanging performers or equipment.[11] These types of troupes are unstable, with a normal life of perhaps six or seven years. Most are formed from teenagers, who continue until military training starts at twenty sui (age eighteen or nineteen by Western count). In this process the rigors of after-school coaching for national school examinations *(buxiban)* virtually ensure the withdrawal of the academically successful students except in the traditional troupes, which perform infrequently. Where job opportunities were few, as in Jiayi in the 1980s, many eighteen- to nineteen-year-olds made the troupes a social center and sometimes earned enough to regard themselves as professionals.

Military service at twenty *sui* makes the continuous infusion of new performers a necessity, because few veterans want to return to be Jiajiang after the two- or three-year break. Most long-established troupes can depend on a number of former Jiajiang to pass down their skills to younger performers. In the traditional Boxing-style troupes, with their differentiated steps and paired poses, each role must be taught by an experienced performer: a former Daye will train a new Daye, the stave bearers Gan and Liu will train their successors and so on. In the most thorough case, the Donggang Gongyitang, as many as fifty performers are trained in pairs and as a group for a month before the triennial festival. This is enough to keep a full team in reserve, essential for the four grueling days of procession, and has the effect of guaranteeing the persistence of this particular tradition. In a second pattern, the members graduate from role to role, say from diminutive messenger to squat Erye and during their teens to Liuye. This more flexible method suits a commercial troupe, where gaps need to be filled at short notice. Self-mortifying troupes, whose steps are simpler, switch roles even more readily and can make do with little training.

The troupes lacking a single temple affiliation may have a precarious existence. The first troupe in one northern Tainan town was set up in association with the Mazu temple in about 1973, when a committeeman there invited a teacher from nearby Jiayi. This was a curious arrangement, in that Mazu is a female deity lacking any rationale for a troupe of martial guardians, and it was unpopular with some Mazu temple committeemen from the start. Opposition became open three years later when self-mortification made its appearance in the town. Since that time the troupe has never had a hall of its own, either separately or in a local temple. "We feel like vagrants," one of the organizers told me. Land prices are rising too fast to make a separate hall feasible. For a time several new troupes were started in a middle school, but recently the task of managing the troupe, which still goes out at least six times a year, rotates among four or five men in their thirties, several of whom serve as amateur ritual masters *(fashi)* and amateur mediums. The troupe itself was indirectly embroiled with the law when the brother of a member was jailed for possession of amphetamines. In such conditions (and in the general distaste for the self-mortifiers, who are more dominant in the Jiayi region than elsewhere), the many senior men who know the steps do not wish to give moral or financial support, and the troupe survives from hand to mouth. Its twelve face-painted men and boys and eight helpers net only NT$1,000 each outing and a few thousand more to bank for uniform replacement and other costs.

Effective leadership and good management are essential for a troupe's survival. Negotiating with sponsoring temples can be difficult, and there are often tales of fees cut after the fact, of a trip canceled on the grounds that a god "had decided not to invite the Jiajiang after all." The leader must worry about his troupe's morale. A day on the roads can be exhausting, since it starts with face painting at 4:00 or 5:00 A.M. (see figure) and finishes with the late-night entry to the main temple and the return home; the usual fee of NT$700 to $1,200 is not high pay: it is about the usual amount to hire unskilled male labor for a day. Members of troupes perform without pay in the case of their own outings, and traditional troupes are expected to perform free also for a friendly temple. The leader must be concerned with the appearance of the troupe, which costs money, and with their training unless they have few steps and perform regularly as do the mortifiers. He must keep uniforms, hats, and implements in proper condition. He must hire face painters, if he does not do it himself, and coordinate with the host temple and its sedans. He must avoid offending friendly temples who expect his troupe to perform without pay. No wonder one veteran leader, whose traditional-style troupe was dubbed the "best managed" in Jiayi by an old rival, told me he had advised his three sons, all trained as Jiajiang, not to succeed him as troupe leader: "Too many headaches."

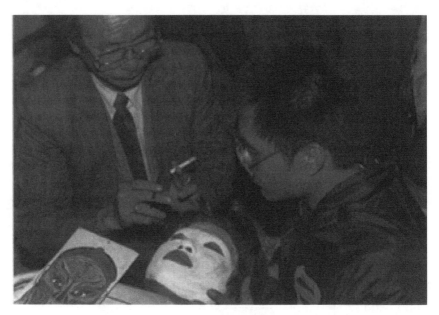

The retired troupe leader of Jiayi Gongjitang gives an apprentice painter advice on applying the water-based face paints this troupe uses. (Author photograph)

What happens to the Generals when a troupe is dissolved or suspended? Statuettes normally fastened during festivals in two ranks to the front of the god's sedan may be retained in front of the main altar, keeping alive the memory of the local tradition, as in Jiayi before the revival of the 1950s. They are not worshiped, or handled with particular reverence. This is because magical effectiveness *(ling)* is achieved not through a consecrated image and spirit-mediumship as with an important local god, but in the face paint, gesture, and dance of trained performers. Somewhat more important seem to be the implements, which tend to be taken off and kept in the household of the last trainer, sometimes in the hope of reestablishing the troupe at a later date.

The survival of the three types of troupe reflects the different emphases of each: the traditional (which are closely linked to a particular temple) emphasize the escorting of its god; the commercial troupes stress performing and frequently separate themselves from the sedan they are hired to protect; and the self-mortifying stress exorcising, which brings in more money.

The different histories of the three types of troupe—traditional/escorting, commercial/performing, and self-mortifying/exorcising—reflect different organizations' response to the changing market. The first has escaped serious alteration to the extent that it has remained attached to large temples committed to periodic festivals, but troupes of this type will hire themselves out for a price. A few earn such local prestige that members volunteer their services. The second type flourished in the 1960s and early 1970s, before color television was introduced, at a time when the cosmological resonances of the dances were still grasped by many Taiwanese, and when a teacher's authority was rarely questioned in any part of the educational system. Troupes of the third type, self-mortifiers, are spectacular enough to rival television images and make the best use of the modernized road system of Taiwan today. With easy-to-learn techniques based on those familiar from the Taiwan spirit-medium, they offer financial support to those teenagers who drop out of the last years of the school system. The increasing shift to self-mortifiers reflects a more modern spirit (see below); these rarely have disciplined leadership but are easy-going and attuned to the market. Temple committeemen are willing to pay half as much again if mortification is promised. Two new pilgrimage centers at Nankunshen and Madou, dedicated to the Plague Gods informally styled Wangye, have played a big role in standardizing some troupe forms and spreading mortification, especially with the help of modern roads north of Tainan.

Myths Invented and Transmitted

The historical sketch suggested a performative origin of the troupes. Thus, although they share the unruliness of many minor gods, they do not have a single master legend or a developed story like the divine heroes of popular fiction (see the essays by Steven Sangren and Meir Shahar in this volume). The legends, consistent with this, are very varied. Yet they all have the same surface functions to explain iconographic peculiarities, usually face paint, and to account for their service as escorts "Before the Sedan" (jiaqian) to a particular god, invariably the god of the temple supplying the legend.

One legend elaborates on the standard tale of the Fuzhou Plague Gods, who were originally five scholars. They learned in a dream that the Jade Emperor had sent down the five Poison Gods to punish Fuzhou people at the only local well. They decided to throw themselves in the well to warn the people not to drink the water. The Jade Emperor forgave them and deified them as Wufudadi to protect the people from plague. "The Generals had been the officials' armed subordinates [buxia] and also sacrificed themselves. They have face paint because some were horribly mutilated by the poison in the well."[12] Another spells out the connection with the Fuzhou Wufudadi differently: "Pirates disguised with face paint attacked the Emperor's ship when he was traveling incognito off Fuzhou. They surrendered when the characters Wulinggong appeared over its masts. Having identified these gods, the Emperor installed them at the White Dragon Shrine [Bailongan] as the Wufudadi and allowed the pirates to stay in their service."[13]

A story widely related at Jiayi and Tainan Wangye temples enlarges on the Fuzhou Seventh and Eighth Masters' legend but links the troupe with Wangye, the Plague God of southern Fujian.

> The Generals were captured bandits under escort by the bailiffs Fan and Xie. Passing near their homes, the bailiffs generously gave them leave to visit their families. When they failed to return on time, Fan and Xie committed suicide together. The bandits arrived to find their bodies. Overcome by remorse, they too committed suicide. The Jade Emperor heard of this and took pity on these unfortunate victims. With Fan and Xie they were placed under the command of Wangye and charged to protect his sedan on his periodic visits of inspection from the underworld.[14]

Another legend, from mountainous Qishan, shifts the setting to the mountains and fastens on the iconography of the four seasons. "These had been transformed into spirits of lotus, gourd, Peng bird, and black tiger respectively, and occupied Pine Mountain, which they used as a lair and covered with the bones of people they preyed on. Gan, Liu, Xie, and Fan and the Civil and Military Justices were defeated by Wufudadi with the help of the Black Flag of the Emperor of the Dark Heaven [Xuantian Shangdi], and incorporated into Wufu-dadi's escort."[15] This version accounts for the Qishan school's practice of using a black flag immediately behind the troupe.

A rather similar version from Donggang applies this explanation to all the Jiajiang:

> The twelve astral bodies [shier xingsu] had a very wild character. As a punishment, the Jade Emperor sent them down to earth. They did many bad things to people in their new incarnations. The Jade Emperor ordered Wufudadi to take them in as his escorts. They had never been fully transformed into people, so their deformed faces are painted and partly hidden with fans. Because of their background they are expert in capturing lonely spirits and wild ghosts. That is also the reason we offer them binlang [betel nut] and cigarettes—kinds of wild fruit and wild grass.[16]

This myth also explains the fans, as well as the Generals' assigned task of capturing wrongdoers.

A Jiayi myth says the Four Worthies (as the Four Seasons are called there) were goblins (yaomo or yaojing) redeemed by Guanyin to be her servitors, each taking the form of her icons: the *hulu* gourd face represents her purifying bottle, the lotus forms her seat, the beaked character is a bird-spirit who bears her reciting jewel *(nian-zhu)* in its beak, and the tiger guards the Purple Bamboo Monastery (Zizhusi) in the Southern Ocean (Nanhai). Here specific iconic elements seem to have inspired their own myth.[17]

In spite of the absence of a single mythic explanation for the troupe as a whole, the myths have a common structure. As we have seen, all the variants account for the troupe's attachment to particular gods, its composite nature, and its curious iconography. At the same time they validate the troupe's work as exorcists deriving power from movement to and from the underworld. Specifically, each myth plays on the transition between yin and yang, taking the terms to refer not only to the other world and this, but also to the harmful and the beneficent. Three shifts take place. First, a fault in the Generals' original human nature, or their suffering an unjust death, moves them to the yin realm as ghosts/evil spirits. Second, the Jade Emperor (or another god) redeems them. Third, obedient to a subordinate martial god, they escort him on visits to this world to punish the bad and reward the good. Although the Generals finish by being associated with beneficent yang forces, they still have yin power clinging to them, the dangerous power of ghosts, and still habitually move between yin and yang realms. Their shifts between order and disorder and between earthly and divine realms, consistent with their wandering between realms as gods' escorts, give them power as exorcists.[18]

These myths or origin stories, passed down by the troupe trainers,[19] are relatively sparse and undeveloped, and derivative of ritual and iconographic practice. Still, they have an important organizational logic. As I have shown, they explain how the troupe was composed, why it escorts a particular temple god, and why it has exorcistic powers. Since little emphasis is given to a troupe's myth (the performers concentrate on learning the steps and usually are ignorant of specific myths of origin), there is little pressure to reconcile these myths with each other.

At the same time such myths reflect (and help to sustain) the mythic core of belief in underworld lore and its connection to the living that is present everywhere in local Chinese religion. Again and again, Jiajiang ritual and iconographic and mythic elements, in all their variety, reiterate the same notions: of posthumous recompense and punishment, of unhappy ghosts and their appeasement, of the trials awaiting the newly dead in the underworld courts at the hands of their denizens, of the localized protective powers of community gods at the lower level of the divine hierarchy that culminates in the

Jade Emperor, of the link between relations among gods and those among communities, of the calendrical and periodic responsibilities of communities to escort their protective gods' images and make appropriate offerings, of the capacity of involuntary and voluntary possession to represent the gods and make them present, of the numerological and color correspondences in the Five Phases scheme, of yin-yang theory, and, not least, of the exorcistic, renewing, and harmony-bringing power of face-painted dancers.

All these concepts, which form a kind of diffused mythology distinct from myths about particular gods or cults, are linked in too many ways to spell out here. They are far from abstractions; instead, they are action oriented, receiving expression in countless individual, family, and community rituals.[20] They are reinforced by temple iconography and by popular entertainment, notably Taiwanese opera and television serials. They are found specifically in spirit-mediumship, Daoism, opera, and funeral practice—a circumstance that helps account for the Jiajiang leaders' disposition to borrow from these local genres.

Performative Elements: Icons, Rituals, Choreography

Performance, like myth, is marked by variation and fluidity. This appears to be in flat contradiction to the conservative stance maintained by each school: "We follow tradition faithfully, our methods are orthodox, how could we change what our forefathers [or masters] handed down to us?" To an extent, however, that stance is justified by a common core of meaning.

Icons

Although iconic interpretations vary, icons themselves are passed down or copied from troupe to troupe (implements, surnames, face-paint forms) and are the most stable performative elements. Face-paint traditions all plainly stem from the same source, though the school of central Tainan (Madou, Xigang, Jiali), which split off first, shows the largest changes, and even paints its punishment bearer. The traditional troupes emphasize face paint most strongly; the self-mortifiers are the sloppiest, sometimes only two or three pairs being painted, and sometimes being painted after their own design. The self-mortifiers usually replace the Four Seasons with duplications of the front four Generals, and only the traditional troupes retain the Justices at the rear, for they process and do not perform, let alone (with their long cloaks) self-mortify.

Even in the traditional Tainan version (see table), the Four Seasons have undergone modification, departing from a tradition long predating the Jiajiang.

The Jiajiang as Marching Escorts (Front First)

Instruments of Punishment (xingju)   Bears the "eighteen instruments of punishment" on two wooden boards. Face painted in central Tainan school, otherwise preformed in succession by two or three unpainted performers.

(yang *side, right seen from the front, all carry fans in their left hands, an instrument in their right*)

(yin *side, left seen from the front, all carry fans in right hands, an instrument in their left*)

Civil Messenger   Various facepaint, dress matching military messenger. A tablet *(lingpai)* of the god of their tang or temple.

Military Messenger   Pair of black fins and tails pointing to the bridge of the nose. Yellow tiger-pattern gown. A flag *(lingqi)* or trident (also called *lingqi*).

Gan   Yinyang face, red background on his right side, black on other; white striations, geometric "longevity" design on forehead. White gown leaving right upper arm bare. Split-bamboo stave.

Liu   Asymmetric black striations diagonally resembling two Y-shaped cangues. Black gown, bare left shoulder. Split-bamboo stave.

Daye   White ground on face, down-tilting mouth; double bat-face with long vertical wings broadened through eyes, body out over eyes. Tall white hat with the legend *yijiandaji* (Great happiness as soon as I appear). A stylized cangue with a Y-shaped end.

Erye   Short performer, dark face. Black gown, bare left shoulder. Squat hat, squarish tiger board *(hujia)* in left hand, usually reading *changshanfa'e* (reward the good, punish the violators).

Spring   Heye. Red forehead with dragon horns or hulu gourd shape, lower face in contrasting green or blue. White dress. Bucket.

Summer   Zhangye. Red ground on face, white firelike design or *lianhua* on forehead. Hat similar to Spring's. Red, usually scarlet dress. Fire pot.

Autumn   Xuye. Birdlike feather design on face, beak lips. Black or dark green dress. Club, usually wooden.

Winter   Zaoye. Tiger-pattern face, tail-end on red forehead. Dark green or black dress. Snake (metal, rubber, or live).

Civil Justice   No facepaint. Traditional black gown with ring belt. Book and brush.

Military Justice   Various facepaint styles. Variously colored long gown. Short staff.

Note: The four generals (Gan, Liu, Erye, Daye) often have Qing-style pigtails or loose hairpieces. The four seasons are given different sets of surnames with some overlap in the various schools.

The phases may have originally been copied in the implements and the creatures in the face designs, but no two troupes are alike today. Spring more often has a gourd face, its sinuous lines perhaps evolving from an earlier attempt to draw a dragon. Spring may also carry a gourd or else a metal bucket rather than a wooden one, with flowers stuck in it. Summer's face has what may have been flames transformed into a lotus on its forehead (see figure). Though carrying a

A Gaoxiong version of Summer, scarlet on white, lotus shape on forehead. Note the charm pasted on the turkey-feather fan. (Author photograph)

canonical firepot, Summer may stick flowers into it, for fire resembles flowers in design and also in Taiwanese pronunciation (Hokkien *hui*). Autumn's face has taken Summer's bird, and the once metal club is wooden. Winter in turn has borrowed the tiger-face pattern from Autumn and has made its water-associated creature into its instrument, a metal or rubber model of a snake. Colors are also switched in many cases. This iconographic deterioration reflects the negligible effect of the written tradition and the preference of teachers to have pupils copy forms instead of learning meanings. It is noticeable that troupe masters strive to keep their own tradition rather than to seek intellectual consistency, though most are aware of the rough correspondences. In a few cases the Four Seasons are explained by a separate myth, as in the case of the Jiayi link with Guanyin (the feminized Chinese Avalokitesvara, Goddess of Mercy). (For the standard Han associations for the Four Seasons, two millennia ago, see table.)

Iconic elements may also inspire choreography. At Donggang the pairs (Spring and Summer, Autumn and Winter) actually use their weapons in confrontation, an attempt being feigned to pour water on fire (or flowers) and the club raised as if to strike the snake. This is an effective development of the boxer style originated at the Yuanhegong, one that graphically expresses yin-yang relationship, since the two sides dominate alternately, yang temporarily finishing in the ascendant. Here the icons have inspired innovation.

All the schools have made percussive innovations, evidently to keep time as the dances grew more difficult. The martial boxing style of the Bailongan made accompaniment unnecessary. In Jiayi both main schools and their offshoots adopted the small cymbal, one or two of which are struck in two timbres in a series of distinctive beats, along with a small drum. Central Tainan with its complex choreography uses the quicker beat of the tray-drum, clearly adopted from the numerous Songjiang martial troupes of that region. The postcolonial self-mortifying Qishan school has added the Daoist lads' troupe of handle-drums along with black flag, in a hypnotic rhythm with a slower pace well suited to possession, which (real or faked) is neces-

The Four Seasons, Han-Dynasty Associations

Season	Phase	Color	Creature
Spring	wood	green	dragon
Summer	fire	red	small bird
Autumn	metal	white	tiger
Winter	water	black	tortoise/snake

sary in such troupes as a prelude to self-mortification (though it is found in all three types). Choreographic needs have found an iconic solution. Once percussive instruments had been added, they became essential ritual props: "We would never go out without the drums," said the leader of a Gaoxiong troupe.

The straw shoes and operatic hats used now by the great majority of Bajiajiang are iconic features drawn from mourning practice and regional opera, and caution is needed in evaluating their novelty. Although neither is worn in the early painting of the founding Taiwan troupe at the Yuanhegong, both are so entirely appropriate and familiar in local culture that they may well be traditional. Besides unifying the disparately equipped performers, the hats remind us that the troupe members are below-stage actors, for the sake of harmony making all the world a stage. The shoes of straw (actually rice stalks) are identical with those worn by mourners in the standard funeral and precisely capture the liminal sense of passage to purgatory that is intrinsic to the troupe and indeed the entire Wuchang tradition. The Yuanhegong trainer claims that straw shoes have never been used in his now inactive troupe, but we cannot be sure that they were not present on the mainland. Indeed a contemporary Bajiang troupe I have seen in a recent video shot in the Fuzhou region is clearly wearing straw shoes.[21] If one can rule out any reverse Taiwan connection in that part of Fujian, as I think one can in view of the rudimentary face paint and awkwardly idiosyncratic steps and dances of this troupe, this means that straw shoes were part of the traditional mainland Bajiang repertoire. Conceivably this Jiajiang practice may have crossed the straits to Taiwan independent of the Bailongan/Yuanhegong tradition.

One can be more certain, however, that the implements of the self-mortifying troupes are genuine Taiwan innovations: they are, after all, adapted from the spirit-medium native to the southern Fujian cultural area, who generally moves in Taiwan processions between the god's sedan and the Jiajiang. Some self-mortifying troupes use the spirit-medium's standard instruments, but more common are the two-foot-long ice axe and the small prick ball. Both can be easily stacked in a small metal trolley in case all the members take up their weapons simultaneously.

In sum, iconic innovations are performative, reflecting the different needs of the three types of organization in the market.

Rituals

Ritual innovation is very common in the Jiajiang, but like the myths of origin and iconographic additions, new rituals grow out of the constitutive triple function of the Jiajiang as escorts, performers, and exorcists. They fit what I have called the diffused popular mythology. The new rituals come to be considered as essential and legitimate.

A good example of new practices bearing the stamp of tradition are the exorcistic charms tucked in at the performers' waistbands and handed to individuals and families along the route of march. The charms are of yellow paper. They have the standard "thunder-command" *(leiling)* heading of Zhengyi (Black Head) Daoism, and below that are the names of the hall and the god flanked with narrow columns with matching phrases (six armed men, six infantry, and so forth). Paired exorcistic phrases complete the "tail" of the charm. The charms can be very elaborate indeed, and knowledge of them is highly prized.[22] But how old are such charms? The most recent leader of a troupe now in abeyance (the Zhenyutang of Jiayi) set before me the three carved wooden blocks for printing the charms used by three generations of leaders: himself, his teacher, and his teacher's teacher. The first, dating from the 1920s or 1930s, had only three characters in its inverse inscription: "Bajiajiang," the Eight Generals. The second bore an Eight Trigram sign and the legend Jiayi Cijigong Zhenyutang Bajiajiang. The third added exorcistic phrases and was covered with figures and characters (see figure). Public demand, he said, produced the change. No doubt competition among the halls encouraged the elaboration as people came to expect a more and more complex form of charm. The uniformity of the charms, instead of being proof of a common early Jiajiang tradition, simply reflects borrowing from troupe to troupe and the widespread influence of lesser-ritual *(xiaofa)* Daoism, usually channeled through the Black Head tradition.

The profusion of ritual forms can only be suggested here. The Bailongan tradition has no remembered repertoire of exorcistic spells, but some troupes have borrowed those of lesser-ritual Daoist texts.[23] The Bailongan did have its special inauguration, with chairs laid out for the Generals' costumes in front of the temple to prepare for the troupe's coming out. Central Tainan has none, but the other schools have introduced their own procedures from lesser-ritual texts summoning the gods, and in some troupes of the Qishan school the Jiajiang have their own invocation chanted to drum beat.[24] Other troupes have adapted spirit-medium inauguration (literally *dianyan*, "eye marking" or "eye opening") using blood and a sword. Then there is a large variety of confusingly inconsistent taboos from troupe to troupe, concerning whether to abstain from sex and meat eating before and during the procession days, and whether to raise the fans protectively when passing cemeteries, gods of certain levels, other Jiajiang, and so forth. In these rituals (exorcistic spells, inauguration,

Three woodblocks for printing charms of the Jiayi Zhenyutang, used over a fifty-year period. The oldest block is at the left; note their progressive complexity. (Author photograph)

taboo) what is important is plainly the fundamental idea, not the form. There must be exorcism because this is how the Jiajiang help the inspecting god purify and renew his assigned territorial community. There must be an inauguration because the Jiajiang come as petty gods who will stand beside the performers during the days of performance. There must be taboos to underline the special status of the actors. All three rituals are well developed because they are in the interest of the troupe organizer in a competitive market situation— not only to make his troupe's ritual more impressive to others, but also to improve its members' morale and discipline. Organizational goals encourage ritual development and variegation.

The forms that new or modified ritual takes are not arbitrary. Ritual is always consistent with Jiajiang ideology. Its purpose is to represent and manifest the Generals' power and varies according to each troupe's conception of whence that power derives. The traditional-style troupes, in their inauguration, are seated and addressed in official Qing terminology and are formally named Daguan; the commercial-style troupes tend to use Dajiang, and the mortifying troupes, Dashen. These terms of address may have historical causes: ordinary soldiers of the traditional Yuanhegong could scarcely have been called generals. But too much should not be made of whether the metaphor is bureaucratic or nonbureaucratic, civil or military, human or divine. These idioms are part of a linguistic repertoire that owes its effect as a transcendent medium (these are not everyday generals) to its deliberate archaism.[25] The organizers select the idiom that best suits the particular organization and history of their troupe.

Choreography

There is a similar complexity in choreography and a similar core of shared meaning. The picture is of extraordinary variation. Three common features can be noted, the first two very cursorily. The first is the basic step and gesture of greeting, always done pair by pair and involving a triple deferential thrust downward with the fans before the altar. In its varied forms the distinctive step and greeting distinguish the Jiajiang from all other festival troupes; it is imitated by schoolboys and rehearsed gracefully at the drop of a hat by octogenarian ex-performers. For many it, along with the icons, is the essence of what is transmitted. The second is a single dance, immensely varied, reflecting the Fuzhou Seventh/Eighth Masters' myth, in which the staves of Liuye and Ganye represent the bridge where both suffered death.[26] The third is the common nomenclature, such as the "four gates" *(simen)* or "eight trigrams" *(bagua)* or "seven star" *(qixing)* pattern. I have room here only to discuss the third feature, with reference to a single dance, the Four Gates. The term is avoided by traditional troupes, whose masters prefer the name Four Corners and claim that Four Gates is a late invention. It was very likely drawn from the local opera, which frequently stages a Four Gates dance when immortals are represented. But like opera itself, it is plainly under the influence of the Daoist altar space, also on occasion paced out as a square with diagonals (Schipper 1982, Lagerwey 1987).

In spite of the lateness of its development, the Four Gates is popular, extremely widespread, and extraordinarily varied. As informants themselves suggest, military defense is the subject of the movement. The invisible city can be readily identified in the successive squares (walls) parallel to the temple façade and the diamonds (gates) formed by the performers as they move out from close-in positions. At the Yuanhegong in Tainan, which claims the oldest tradition, it is done by Liuye, Ganye, Erye, and Daye, who approach the four gates after each has visited a different corner (see figure). A variant Tainan version begins with the four Generals entering from outside the city and successively covering the opposite gates and the corners in two

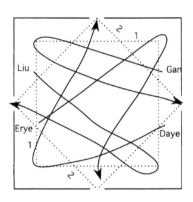

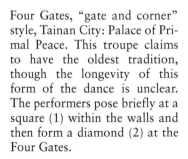

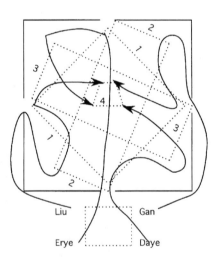

Four Gates, "gate and corner" style, Tainan City: Palace of Primal Peace. This troupe claims to have the oldest tradition, though the longevity of this form of the dance is unclear. The performers pose briefly at a square (1) within the walls and then form a diamond (2) at the Four Gates.

Four Gates, "gate and corner" style, Tainan City: A recent Tainan version, my proposed reconstruction. Note that Erye and Daye stay in the same position for (1) and (2), and Gan and Liu occupy the same positions in (1) and (3).

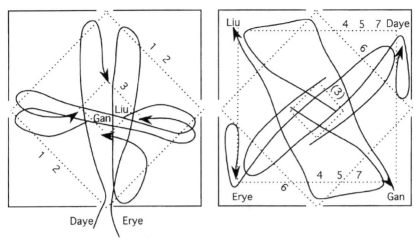

Four Gates, "crossed exchanges" style, Qishan: Five Dragon Belvedere, Qishan (reconstructed dance).

A. The four players (identified at start) move between opposite gates, forming a diamond shape twice, Erye and Daye at north and south gates, Liu and Gan at east and west gates. They finish at a small diamond in the center.

B. The four (here identified at end before return to a small square, omitted) now successively form two large squares (for which Liu and Gan stay in the same positions), a large diamond and a large square, each pair again crossing to opposite corners of the city and visiting one of the gates.

rectangles (see figure). Both have the form of "gate and corner." In others (which I call the "four walls patrol"), the four gates are ignored, and the performers move in a square within the walls, each pair always at opposite points: at Donggang, counterclockwise with all four Generals; in Tainan and Jiali, the front pairs in opposite directions. A third form consists of repeated "crossed exchanges." The Qishan version had the performers exchanging across and then shifting clockwise, forming a square, two diamonds, and then a second square, so that they finish opposite their first position (see figure). A Gaoxiong version (the "ruler" style) also has circling and crossing, with alternations of the square and diamond. As Daye and Erye pass inside Ganye and Liuye, the four players form a straight line, repeated at every crossing in a different plane (see figures). This by no means exhausts the existing variations.

Although these forms are widely divergent, they follow the same unspoken rules. Most important is an emphasis on the cardinal directions, continuing an ancient preoccupation with proper cosmic orientation (Wheatley 1971). Since cities were conventionally aligned on a north-south axis, north-south is prior to east-west, and the first in

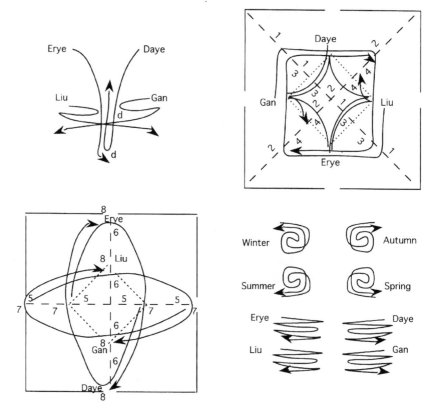

Four Gates, "ruler" style, Gaoxiong: Belvedere of Prestigious Brightness.

A. The starting diamond is reached via the Staveseat *(zuopai)* with dominance poses by Daye over Erye, who kneels at points (d) (performers identified at starting point).

B. Performers (identified at starting point) begin at the arrow points in (A), and straight lines (1–4) are successively formed. The performers also describe a diamond, all covering each corner once. Two bow-and-arrow poses are struck at each corner, and a double backpace is done at each line. Note that line (4) pivots to become line (5) in stage C.

C. Four further lines (5–8) are formed running between the gates (performers identified at concluding point). Three diamonds are fleetingly created between each of them at the inner box. A double backpace is done at each line. In stages B and C the lines may be taken to point respectively to the corners and the gates. In all, seven triangles and eight lines are formed.

D. In the "crossing" routine, the Four Generals cross in pairs, while the Four Seasons cross each other in a circle; my sketch represents each player's movements separately for the sake of legibility. Crossings are done with this tradition's double backpace, and with dominance poses for the Four Generals when one performer kneels and the other stretches his fan vertically and then leaps over to the other side. Thus Daye dominates twice, Gan and Liu once each. Gan and Liu, during the dominance poses, hit their staves six times and add a final blow that "opens the gate."

At a pilgrimage stop, watched by a Song Jiang boxer troupe, a Gaoxiong offshoot of the central Tainan school does the "crossing" routine in its Four Gates. Gan and Liu are in front, Daye and Erye (as often, hatless) are behind, the Four Seasons at the rear. (Author photograph)

each pair is also prior to the second, the following order of priority results: N, S, E, W. This is reflected in every Four Gates routine because the Daye and Erye pair is understood to dominate Ganye and Liuye, and the yang side to dominate his yin partner. Consequently Daye will spend more time at the south gate facing the temple, Erye will occupy the north gate with his back to it, while Ganye and Liuye gravitate to the east and west gates respectively. A further rule is followed by all these troupes, stemming from the notion of complementarity in yin-yang thinking: if they move separately, the first moves must be made by the subordinate pair or partner. So Ganye and Liuye will move first of the front four, and Erye frequently will dash forward alone, after which the more leisurely Daye restores his natural dominance.

Like the two-by-two marching order, the Four Gates is military in inspiration, depicting the Generals as protectors and escorts of the gods visiting for the periodic festival. Since a Chinese city must be an administrative center, generally the only city permitted to have walls, the message is maintenance of the established order, specifically of constituted civil authority ultimately based on force. Again market competition plays its part. This is the kind of message that must have appealed to those who hired troupes in the 1950s, 1960s, and 1970s, when almost all the Four Gates varieties were developed.

The 1980s have seen a shift from elaborate dances as commercial and self-mortifying troupes have become more numerous. Choreography has become less valued by temple committeemen. The crowds at pilgrimage sites since the 1970s have put a premium on briefer and more dramatic temple entrances over the hour-long performance of some 1960s troupes. Self-mortification had a particularly large effect on dance. Before the self-beating starts, fans and implements must be replaced by weapons; headgear and upper dress have to be removed. Thereafter the performance takes on the idiom and ideology of spirit-mediums (see Sutton 1990b). The divine general is represented no longer by his characteristic implement and by occasional possession, but by mortification, which gives dramatic proof of divine presence and supplies the red (lucky, yang) blood for exorcistic purification. The standard Jiajiang method of approaching, dancing, and then greeting at the god's altar is modified, in one of five common forms: (1) complex dances followed by mortification by all in front of the temple; (2) mortification one by one beginning in the march up to the host temple; (3) two or four using weapons while the rest dance and greet the gods; (4) some using the weapons on the approach to the temple, but recovering to join the dance and greeting; (5) unpainted helpers in ordinary dress, sometimes also called Jiajiang or *tangki* (spirit-mediums), mortifying themselves before the temple, leaving the painted Jiajiang to do their own dance and greeting. A further change may occur in the troupe's divine composition. In some troupes the rather passive Four Seasons, with their heavy clothing and unmenacing weapons, are replaced with duplications of the four Generals, perhaps bearing different surnames, or with such characters as Niuye and Maye (Horsehead and Oxface) from the repertoire of City God's underworld helpers. Taboo and inauguration rites are largely dropped, with organizational as well as religious implications. There is less discipline on the march and a freer atmosphere. In some cases (e.g., Jiayi in 1986–1987), some Bajiajiang became involved in shady activities, acquiring "underworld connections" in a quite different sense from the Wuchang figures in the courts of hell.

This change is substantial but, like other innovations, not so complete as it first appears. Occasional possession is found in all kinds of troupes, and mortification by the spirit-medium is a familiar practice to all festival participants. Even the new personages are drawn from the same underworld mythology out of which the troupes originally sprang.

Conclusion

We now know enough about the Jiajiang and their development to situate them with respect to other gods. The gods whom the sub-bureaucratic Jiajiang principally serve are themselves not fully respectable, like so many of the gods discussed in this volume. As noted above, the most common myth of the Wufudadi of Fuzhou has them only as would-be officials—scholars in Fuzhou for the examination. Dreaming the same dream, they learn that a plague has been sent down on the people of Fuzhou through the five wells of the city. They make the extreme sacrifice for the people by drowning themselves in the wells to make the water undrinkable. Becoming gods, they continue to protect the people as gods in charge of the plague department, receiving the title of "great emperor" which vaults them over the entire bureaucracy. Yet their bad deaths make them a little fearsome, like ghosts.

Note that the kind of power exercised by these gods, like that of other principal gods in local temples, is not at all the delegated power enjoyed by replaceable officials, and in every case the departures from the secular pattern serve the interests and convenience of worshipers. The gods' power is permanent. Unlike earthly officials, they are not promoted, demoted, or transferred, with very few exceptions, and they are always middle-aged. Their identification is local: their effectiveness reflects, represents, and enhances the state of the community. Although serving collectively, as a group they have a dual personality, alternately passive and active, but always under temple control. The image represents the passive side, being moved almost at will about the community to protect its members in times of special trouble. The spirit-mediums (and Infernal Generals where these exist) represent the gods' active side, intervening with predictable cyclicity in local affairs, that is to say, in seances at least once a week and in annual birthdays and less frequent periodic jiao. In short, they have none of the limits on their power that curb officials, and they are vastly more available to worshipers. What is "bureaucratic" about them is their appearance: their dress, demeanor, and means of transportation. In this way they can appropriate the awesomeness of an official without assuming any of his inaccessibility and unpredictability.

The mental construct of bureaucracy is, then, hardly applicable to such deities.[27] Not only do these heroes fail to become officials, in some accounts they actually swear brotherhood after the manner of bandits and rebels. More useful may be an analysis based on the gods' practicality. It is the practical usefulness of gods that determines conceptions of their power. If this is true, it follows that people are likely to resort to various kinds of authority, to various idioms besides the bureaucratic one. For example, the term enfeoffment does not suit the delegated hierarchical powers of bureaucracy but suggests an emperor endeavoring to establish a personal ascendancy over foreign princes on the borders of Chinese civilization. This is exactly the metaphor that fits a powerful local ghost who is coopted and divinized to serve the community: a spirit that must be humored and flattered but which cannot be ordered about because its source of power remains partly demonic[28] and autonomous.

How do the gods' retainers, the Infernal Generals, fit into this understanding of Chinese gods? They too are conceived in practical terms, not understood in some consistent bureaucratic analogy. We have seen that their terms of address (god, general, or official) are variable, even in the same troupe, depending on local tradition and on which idiom appeals to the organizers. Personal (not bureaucratic-style) attachment to the gods they serve, as well as to each other, is pronounced, whatever higher gods may have redeemed them, with the effect that their attachment to the locality is unconditional. They are represented in every way as similar but subordinate to the local gods they serve. The standard myth of the Fuzhou Seventh and Eighth Masters—whose likenesses, Daye and Erye, dominate the troupe—is of the comrades who die for each other, a parable of loyalty yet without the humanitarian, socially responsible element of the Wufudadi sacrifice. Because they are more lowly, and more human, their actions can be seen. Their marching, greeting, dancing, and exorcistic rites can give visual form to the purifying, devil-scaring role of the procession in which the Plague Gods are the central elements. Their power, though derived likewise from "bad deaths," is also delegated from these gods. Their permanence depends not on icon carvings or incense splitting but on the transmission of gesture and dance from one generation or cohort to another. Their identification is not only local but also with the youth who form most troupes. Indeed we may say that performative demigods like the Jiajiang—and like the essentially performative gods Nazha (see Sangren's essay in this volume) and Jigong—represent youth, as contrasted with the main gods who represent age. The relationship of big and little gods repeats the relationship among the men of the community, in which the middle-aged control affairs and younger men work more actively, behave more wildly, and are not yet considered socially responsible enough to take over the reins of the community.

Can the conclusions I have drawn about transmission be generalized to full gods, and to those who do not invariably perform? I have shown that what is transmitted is not so much a story—neither the Jiajiang nor the Plague Gods are linked to a novel[29]—but the performance, along with its icons and mannerisms and particular dances. Could that not be true of some of the livelier gods described elsewhere in this volume (see the essays by Sangren and Shahar in this volume)? The idiom of gesture may be what counts even for gods about whom novels have been written. People rarely watch opera closely in the chaotic atmosphere of a festival and, today at least, can rarely tell you what is going on. One may doubt whether close familiarity with gods' stories is what makes the gods who figure in novels so popular. Instantly recognizable to everyone at an open-air performance are those characters whose dress, implements, or condition give them an entirely idiosyncratic way of moving: this is true of the tipsy Jigong, the mischievous Sun Wukong, and the playful Taizi Ye with his twirling golden ring. In southern Taiwan at least, impersonation of these figures—and incidentally the main characters of the Jiajiang—is part of the stock in trade of the more versatile spirit-mediums, another active instrument of transmission. Gestures refer to very few incidents, and it may be wondered whether any of these little gods would ever have won their popularity without the characteristic gestures and icons of performance. Their transmission, I would argue, was achieved less by the reprinting of books than by the memory and imitation of gestures. Although only the written record survives, it is not necessary to neglect the many centuries of popular storytelling (storytellers don't communicate just with their mouths), temple engravings (see Paul Katz's essay in this volume: these also are iconic and gestural in emphasis), shaman dramatizing, and temple performance.

As a performative genre, the Taiwan Jiajiang have evolved more rapidly than could be expected of established gods or "textualized" gods—those with full-length printed stories in circulation. The picture is of innovative form and broadly standardized content. Innovations are designed to improve performative effect and therefore competitive value, but their dissemination and effects vary. Some innovations, such as the spread of face paint (along with some of the identifying designs) to all players and of operatic hats to the rear four dancers, have become universal and some, such as the doubling of messengers, virtually so. Other innovations, such as the adoption of charms and spells, have been disseminated into individual troupes across several different schools. Another category of innovations has remained peculiar to a particular school or troupe, such as the newly choreographed dances and new accompanying percussive instruments. Still another kind of innovation, self-mortification, has led to a new kind of Jiajiang practice.

These innovations are rarely claimed as new but are asserted to be traditional and legitimate by the troupes that have adopted them. Like Confucius, the troupe leaders say they are only passing on what they have been taught, and indeed the majority of leaders do exactly that, trying to limit change and passing down the work of an exceptional (and perhaps unknown to them, innovating) teacher as hallowed by tradition. But even the reluctant may find themselves innovating: like Confucius again, teachers teach one corner and expect their pupils to grasp the other three, so there are gaps that must be filled by invention: "He didn't teach me everything." "He taught us the rough outlines." Such changes will invariably be represented as insignificant.

What makes innovations easy to accept is familiarity and fit. They resonate with what I have called the diffused mythology of local religion, have the veneer of well-known names (the Four Gates dances), and as noted may be drawn directly from local practices of spirit-mediumship, funeral practice, opera, and, not least, the minor rites of Daoist liturgy. At the same time they fit with and often reinforce the central idea of the Jiajiang as liminal figures with the power to exorcise and protect.

Although there is a tendency in explaining changes in popular belief and practice to look to educated elites and the state, sometimes very plausibly (Watson 1985), we have found little trace of such influence, except in the sense that the troupe leaders convey yin-yang and the Five Phases concepts in choreography or adopt Daoist texts and charms for ritual uses. Under Kuomintang martial law, the controls on the *jiao* involved irksome paperwork by temple leaders but did not affect the form or content of the troupes' activities. Nor more recently has the effect of governmental sponsorship of popular festival arts been much felt in this troupe tradition: Jiajiang do not like to perform on such occasions, and the organizers of such festivals now seem less inclined to count them as popular custom *(minsu):* "Those are religious organizations, so we didn't include them."

If officialdom does not standardize in post-Qing Taiwan, what does? Why does change keep within fixed bounds, even when in myth, iconographic interpretation, ritual, and choreography, innovation and fluidity are the rule? What, in other words, keeps innovations consistent with the underlying logic of the Jiajiang described above? The deliberate traditionalism of local religion, asserting old ways in spite of modernity, is only part of the answer; after all, participating alongside the Jiajiang at festivals are comic troupes that show heavy influence from modern commercial and industrial values (Liu 1986, Sutton 1990a). What is specifically traditionalist about the Jiajiang is that they are not just performers before the gods but also escorts and exorcisers on their behalf. As divine agents they must keep their actions and appearance ritualized in order to convey the requisite weight and importance. To persuade, ritual has to remind us of what we already know in our bones. Locally elaborated forms consequently cannot afford to stray from accepted religious ideas but must remain rooted in fundamental Chinese notions of the human/cosmic order. The demands of ritual, above all, are what standardizes.

I have suggested that the mechanism by which old notions are reproduced and new forms kept within bounds is the marketplace of troupes and local festivals. The agent of standardization and innovation alike, to put it differently, is the relationship between community temple and troupe leader, the former as a financial organization and social center, and the latter as purveyor of services for local influence and reputation or money. These three institutions—the community temple, troupes with their masters, and the festival market—are certainly powerful in southern Taiwan today and deserve closer scrutiny than I have been able to give here. Chinese religion may not be strongly institutionalized in the sense of possessing central religious organizations, but that does not mean strong institutions have not given it shape. Temple, troupe, and festival continue to produce new forms and to elaborate standard religious meanings, even in the absence of important state interference.

Notes

1. The formal name is Bajiajiang or Shijiajiang, "The Eight [or Ten] Generals." The term *jia* (household) may originally mean "personal" generals, that is to say, bodyguards or retainers of a particular god, but its absence in the Fuzhou region (see note 7 below), where the name Bajiang is standard, suggests that the *jia (ka)* is added for euphony in Taiwanese. The name Jiajiang or Jiajiangtuan (troupe) is often used by temple committee people. Because of their association with the underworld, I have called them Infernal Generals (Sutton 1990a).

2. *Ye* is a suffix denoting a mixture of informality and respect, somewhat like uncle.

3. Using the phrase "divinized constabulary," which points correctly to the composite nature of the Generals, Shi Wanshou has ingeniously identified their function and duties with the lower level county officers in Qing Taiwan, but there are difficulties with this historical/functionalist interpretation. From his description, the local officers' roles do not seem precisely parallel with roles plausibly assigned to the Jiajiang, except in the sense that local government anywhere in the premodern world was similarly staffed. Nor according to the oldest memoirs (there are no other sources) did official roles match certain roles assigned to specific members: for example, the Xiaochai (messenger) at the Yuanhegong used to be sent out to catch miscreants identified by the temple spirit-medium, in contradiction to Shi's version of his duties. Furthermore, the Jiajiang would be a most inefficient constabulary in any literal sense of the term. Not to mention the expense and time needed for dressing and painting a troupe, these generals direct their energies inward, performers facing each other, pointing only a fan at spectators, carrying instruments on their inside hand that are unsuited—especially in the case of the Four Seasons—to cause harm. Before the invention of ice-axe mortification weapons in the 1960s, the most menacing weapon, a trident, was held in the Military Messenger's left hand. The realm of activity of the early troupe is also inconsistent with a paramilitary role. If the

Qing had intended the role of constabulary for the Generals—a notion unsupported by written records or popular myths and legends—why was it not extended over the countryside and smaller centers? In fact, only the Bailongan just outside the city had Jiajiang troupes in the decades before Japanese takeover in 1895. Besides, if oral history is correct that the Bailongan group was a voluntary off-duty pastime of the military, it could not add to constabulary strength in Tainan. The intermittent appearance of the Jiajiang (annually in the late nineteenth-century Tainan plague festivals) made them unsuitable as an official instrument of force. I agree with Shi that the Jiajiang are a ritual, paramilitary troupe. Their ritual and performance styles could be frightening, and they were certainly a powerful symbol of the forces of local order. A document I secured in Chiayi, copied from the stele in the Bailongan at Fuzhou in 1981, supports the theory that the troupe originated in Fuzhou; it proves to be almost identical with a document discredited by Shi and his informants. It makes clear that essentially the same characters danced for the Wufudadi in Fuzhou.

4. Compare Ye 1993 on the Badajiang played by beggars in Jian'ou, north-central Fujian.

5. Text in possession of the author, from 1981 copy.

6. Ye 1993 has surveyed the Bajiang tradition in Fujian. Most troupes appear to be centered on the Qiye, Baye characters, accompanied by Oxhead and Horseface and several civil justices. First, in Houban village in the suburbs of Fuzhou region, eight face-painted performers go out on the ninth of the ninth month to escort and exorcise in the procession of the Dongyue Taishan god. They are not iconically paired, and their movements are not collective. But note that Horseface (bearing an iron cudgel) is Liu (Willow) Dudu, the surname on the Bailongan stele. (The paired figure Oxhead is surnamed Yan, however, and holds an iron fork.) Second, in northern Fujian (Shaowu Prefecture in villages to the south of the capital), a group of eight dancers wore masks for plague exorcism. Third, in north-central Fujian (Jian'ou County), the so-called Badajiang were gathered at short notice from among beggars painted as bad demons, holding respectively a snake, a toad, a rat, a weasel, a scorpion, a bucket of blood, and so forth. Here there were three Wuchang characters separate from the Generals. Fourth, in Chaozhou (Guangdong), contiguous to southern Fujian and close to it in culture, there was a custom for dancers dressed as demons and barbarians *(guiman)* to "parade the eight parts of Min [*you ba Min*]," possibly a corruption, Ye suggests, for *you ba man,* "parading the eight barbarians." Fifth, in the former Funing prefecture, linguistically and culturally close to Fuzhou, the City God's processions included seven or eight Eight Generals *(bajiang)* with demons' faces.

On available evidence the characteristic Taiwan split-bamboo stave figures (Gan and Liu), the punishment bearer, the Four Seasons, and the civil and military messengers (which make an actual eleven players) all seem absent. Iconographic pairing is at best incomplete. While the Taiwan Jiajiang seems, then, to have followed its own line of development stemming from the Fuzhou Bailongan, it is clearly from the same tradition and "diffused mythology," deriving roughly common features from the standard temple figures assisting gods supervising the underworld, such as the City God and Dizangwang, using their fearsome and demonic aspect to curb the demonic, exorcising communities, and escorting their gods in procession. The earliest association seems to be with the five Plague Gods of Fuzhou.

I am grateful to Wang Chiu-kui and Kenneth Dean for bringing Ye's article to my attention.

7. Stored at the Yuanhegong, Tainan city.

8. The research on which this statement is based is set out in a longer manuscript nearing completion.

9. Most traditional troupes are willing to sell their services, and most give their members some daily fee or "red packet" containing money.

10. All dollar figures are in new Taiwan dollars. In the summer of 1988 the exchange rate was NT$27 or NT$28 to the U.S. dollar; in 1991 to 1992 it moved between 26:1 and 24:1.

11. Two troupes on the outskirts of Gaoxiong that split off from the Temple of Hell in Gushan lent each other a drumming group and provided face-painting services on different occasions in 1992. Two recently established troupes in Pingdong that had the same teacher regularly exchange performers if one is lacking, and this is done elsewhere in similar cases. Two rural troupes in Gaoxiong exchange equipment, the brothers in charge of one having been taught by the other's leader. Relations with Jiajiang troupes from different traditions tend to be cautious and distant, no doubt a reflection of the esprit de corps each develops and of the competitive market.

12. Interview with Mr. Wang, former head of the Zhongzetang troupe, 6 or 7 June 1988.

13. Interview with committee head of Yuanhegong, 4 July 1992. An alternative version simply has the pirates sneaking with face paint into Fuzhou during a festival procession. On capture they are pardoned and put in Wufudadi's service, and accompany them on future tours of inspection.

14. I was told this by a senior helper on a Jiayi troupe pilgrimage to Madou in June 1987.

15. Information from Mr. Li, the former organizer of the Qishan Bailongan, on 28 June 1992.

16. Information from a senior helper at the Donggang Tongantang, 24 October 1991.

17. Information from Mr. Zhang, former organizer of the Ji'antang, 14 March 1992.

18. The yin-yang theme of the myth echoes the iconography, with Daye playing yang to Erye's yin: light:dark::promising:threatening::tall, dominating:short, submissive. It also prepares for choreographic pairing, which is extended to all the performers (see below).

19. Although trainers do insist that their mythic story is authentic and others bogus, I have heard two alternative myths of Jiajiang origin from the same committeeman ("We do not know which one is true"). The majority of performers are unaware of their troupe's myth, if it has one.

20. I do not mean here to deny that Taiwan Chinese views on religion have changed in the past few decades, a topic that needs closer study. The areas commanded by these notions are now far smaller, even in the countryside, but it seems that Taiwanese who have lived in big cities and return to their native villages act nostalgically as if they were in a world where this diffused mythology applied.

21. I am grateful to Michael Szonyi for showing me his unedited video of the Bajiang, now revived in the area around Nantai long associated with the Daye/Erye tradition.

22. "You should study charms," said one troupe trainer to me during a discussion I had sought about dances, and he spent fifteen minutes reconstructing from memory the standard charm used by his former group at Qishan.

23. Note the following (in the possession of the author): "Worshipfully request the master to command the salt and rice for us, the patriarch [zushi] to command the salt and rice for us, the [Fourth City God] to command the salt and rice for us, change the salt into bronze bells, change the rice into iron bullets, the unlucky gods and bad curses just get back ten thousand miles to where they belong, the earth curses and the earth barriers, the unpropitious gods and evil curses together get back to the western quarter where they belong, press them to retreat far away; the divine soldiers quick as fire are commanded to do as ordered. First, strike open the gate of heaven, second, make the thunder peal, third, strike for people to have long life, fourth, strike to destroy the unpropitious gods and evil curses. We receive the [Fourth City God's] order for the divine soldiers quick as fire to do as ordered." The Fourth City God is the patron god of several Jiayi temples with an attached Jiajiang hall. The brackets around the Fourth City God (in the original) indicate that he may be replaced by other gods, depending on the festival the hall is participating in.

24. In possession of the author. The text, added in this copy immediately after the Wufudadi invocation, fits the Qishan myth of the Jiajiang origin cited earlier:

> Respectful petition to the Ten Generals [Shijiajiang], these great gods,
> Whose divinity pervades far and wide to save the myriad people:
> Once they were top generals at Pine Mountain,
> And followed our masters to be used as guards before the sedan.
> Our masters brought them to distinguish the good and the bad
> They received the imperial command to take in the five poisons on
>   Tainan commandery.
> An awe-inspiring garrison, the Linggong conferred help with true
>   manifestations
> They expel harms and control sickness, extending their awe-inspiring
>   power
> They are ordered to take in the Ten Generals [Shijiang] bearing tallies
>   of command
> Our masters' troops and horses are a million strong.
> Minister Lei [Leibu] our master has the power to expel harm.
> Powerful charms spread upwards, startling the ghosts and spirits
> We are personally charged by Linggong
> To supervise affairs in both the yin and yang realms
> In one hand we grasp the bird-feather fans,
> In the other we hold close to us the instruments of punishment
> If people worshipfully request us we respond accordingly
> Through the diviner's tool we descend to help the words of truth.
> The disciples with all their hearts worshipfully request

The ten great gods to quickly come down.
Divine soldiers quick as fire are ordered to obey!

25. The persistence of the imperial and bureaucratic metaphors eight decades beyond the republic can largely be explained in these terms. I return to the question of the "bureaucratic" metaphor in the conclusion.

26. I argue this in an unpublished paper, "Iconography of the Taiwan Jiajiang."

27. The Western notion of bureaucracy seems too specific and rigid for the Chinese "pantheon" (probably itself a misnomer too, insofar as the commonest Chinese equivalent is the shapeless and fluid *zhongshen,* the "mass of gods"). We know very little about the gods, people often say. This is what makes their doings open to different idioms of divine power and subject to inventive elaboration in a quite unbureaucratic spirit. One spirit-medium in a small Tainan city temple, whom I know, switched from Wufudadi to Jigong, as some might say stepping outside the bureaucracy. After a year had passed and Jigong still had not won over old constituents, he was once again possessed exclusively by Wufudadi. Although the reversion was greeted with relief, it was the idiom that had displeased: people were choosing awe and dignity over frivolity, not a bureaucratic over a nonbureaucratic god. Then there are the spirit-mediums who declare themselves above bureaucracy: another Tainan medium (a woman) is regularly possessed by the mother of the Jade Emperor. (A third, outdoing the Buddhist canon, is the teacher of the Buddha Sakyamuni.) The reality is far more nebulous than bureaucracy, in spite of what we hear from the rare rationalizing, systematic informant. The Western term *bureaucracy* is a useful analogy if not taken literally, but reified as a model it leaves out of account the flexible nature of Chinese popular religious conceptions.

28. For a stimulating treatment of the demonic element in Chinese religion, see Feuchtwang 1992. I believe people do see the Infernal Generals as demonic in origin and appearance but understand them to be unambiguously on the side of the common good and community order.

29. An apparent counterexample is the Songjiang troupe, a sort of boxer militia common in the southern Taiwan countryside that is inspired by a novel: *Shuihu Zhuan (Water Margin)* (Sutton 1990a). A troupe of thirty-six, the standard number, corresponds to the main heroes of the novel, and there are even troupes where specific links are made to these characters through face painting. But what is striking is the dominance of Li Kui in most troupes of Songjiangzhen: not because of his importance in the novel but because of the spectacular solo displays that are possible with his assigned weapons, a pair of axes. Again, performance is what tends to dictate development, not the mythic story.

Literature Cited

Ahern, Emily Martin. 1973. *The Cult of the Dead in a Chinese Village.* Stanford: Stanford University Press.

Bloch, Maurice. 1989. *Ritual, History and Power: Selected Papers in Anthropology.* Atlantic Highlands, N.J.: Humanities Press.

Bodde, Derk. 1975. *Festivals in Classical China.* Princeton: Princeton University Press.

Chen Xiaoling. 1975. "Bajiajiang." *Zhongguo Funü Zhoukan (Chinese Women)* (January):72–75.

Dean, Kenneth. 1993. *Taoist Ritual and Popular Cults of South-East China.* Princeton: Princeton: Princeton University Press.

Doolittle, Justus. 1865. *The Social Life of the Chinese.* New York: Harper.

Feuchtwang, Stephan. 1974. "Domestic and Communal Worship in Taiwan." In *Religion and Ritual in Chinese Society,* edited by Arthur P. Wolf, 105–129. Stanford: Stanford University Press.

———. 1992. *The Imperial Metaphor: Popular Religion in China.* London: Routledge.

Freedman, Maurice. 1979. *The Study of Chinese Society.* Edited by G. William Skinner. Stanford: Stanford University Press.

Granet, Marcel. 1975. *La pensée chinoise.* Reprint. Paris: Albin Michel.

Huang, Fengzi (Ōshi Hōshi). 1940. *Shichiya Hachiya (Seventh Master, Eighth Master).* Taipei.

Jordan, David K. 1972. *Gods, Ghosts and Ancestors: Folk Religion in a Taiwanese Village.* Berkeley: University of California Press.

———. 1984. "The Repression of Hostility and the Representation of Hell in South Taiwan Religious Processions." In *Concepts of Hell in Asia,* vol. 1, 18–20.

Kang, Bao (Paul Katz). 1991. "Pingdong Xian Donggangzhen de Yingshen Jidian: Taiwan Wenshen yu Wangye Xinyang zhi Fenxi" (The Rites of the God's Festival in Donggang Township, Pingdong County: An Analysis of Beliefs in the Taiwan Plague Gods and Wangye). *Minzu Xue Yanjiusuo Jikan (Journal of the Institute of Ethnology, Academia Sinica)* 70: 95–210.

Lagerwey, John. 1987. *Taoist Ritual in Chinese Society and History.* New York: Macmillan.

Liu Huanyue. 1986. *Taiwan Minsu Zhi (A Record of Taiwan Popular Customs).* Taipei: Luocheng.

Lu Xun. 1976. *Dawn Blossoms Plucked at Dusk.* Peking: Peking Foreign Languages Press.

Maspero, Henri. 1981. *Taoism and Chinese Religion.* Translated by Frank A. Kierman, Jr. Amherst: University of Massachusetts Press.

Qiu Dezai. 1985. *Taiwan Miaoshen Daquan (Compendium of Taiwan's Temple Gods).* Jiayi: Fenglin.

Sangren, P. Steven. 1987. *History and Magical Power in a Chinese Community.* Stanford: Stanford University Press.

Schipper, Kristofer M. 1982. *Le corps taoïste.* Paris: Fayard.

———. 1985a. "Seigneurs royaux, dieux des épidémies." *Archives de sciences sociales des religions* 59(1):31–39.

———. 1985b. "Vernacular and Classical Ritual in China." *Journal of Asian Studies* 45(1): 21–57.

Shi Wanshou. 1986. "Jiajiangtuan—Tianren Heyi de Xunbu Zuzhi" (The Divine Guardians: A Constabulary Organization to Unify Heaven and Humanity). *Tainan Wenhua (Tainan Culture)* 22:48–65.

Smith, Richard. 1991. *Fortune-Tellers and Philosophers: Divination in Traditional Chinese Society.* Boulder: Westview.

Sutton, Donald S. 1990a. "Ritual Drama and Moral Order: Interpreting Tainan God's-Festival Troupes." *Journal of Asian Studies* 49(3):535–554.

———. 1990b. "Self-Mortification and the Temple Community: Taiwanese Spirit-Mediums in Comparative Perspective." *Journal of Ritual Studies* 4(1): 99–125.

Tambiah, Stanley. "A Performative Approach to Ritual." In *Culture, Thought, and Social Action,* 123–166. Cambridge: Harvard University Press.

Teiser, Stephen F. 1988. *The Ghost Festival in Medieval China.* Princeton: Princeton University Press.

Turner, Victor. 1968. *Forest of Symbols.* Chicago: University of Chicago Press.

Watson, James L. 1985. "Standardizing the Gods: The Promotion of T'ien-hou ('Empress of Heaven') along the South China Coast, 960–1960." In *Popular Culture in Late Imperial China,* edited by David Johnson, Andrew J. Nathan, and Evelyn S. Rawski, 292–324. Berkeley: University of California Press.

———. 1988. "The Structure of Chinese Funerary Rites." In *Death Ritual in Late Imperial and Modern China,* edited by J. L. Watson and Evelyn S. Rawski, 3–19. Berkeley: University of California Press.

Weller, Robert P. 1987. *Unities and Diversities in Chinese Religion.* Seattle: University of Washington Press.

Wheatley, Paul. 1971. *Pivot of the Four Quarters.* Chicago: Aldine.

Wilhelm, Hellmut. 1960. *Change: Eight Lectures on the I Ching.* New York: Pantheon.

Wolf, Arthur P. 1974. "Gods, Ghosts, and Ancestors." In *Religion and Ritual in Chinese Society,* edited by Arthur P. Wolf, 131–182. Stanford: Stanford University Press.

Yang, C. K. 1961. *Religion in Chinese Society.* Berkeley: University of California Press.

Ye Mingsheng. 1993. "Lun 'Bajiang' zai Fujian de Liubu, Bianyi ji Nuo Wenhua Yiyi" (On the Spread and Variation of the Eight Generals and Its Meaning in No [Festival] Culture). *Minsu Quyi (Popular Dramatic Arts)* 85:63–103.

Matricidal Magistrates and Gambling Gods: Weak States and Strong Spirits in China

Robert P. Weller

CHINESE GODS tempt us to think of them as staid and sober imperial bureaucrats. Most of them dress in official-looking robes, live in guarded yamens, spend their time reading formal petitions, and respond by giving stern orders to their underlings while glancing over their shoulders at their superiors. Like all proper bureaucrats, they flaunt their ranks and titles, and proudly display encomia from higher officials in front of their offices.[1] No one has argued that the idea of bureaucracy exhausts the interpretive possibilities of Chinese gods, or even of the imperial system as a metaphor. Nevertheless, the image of gods as bureaucrats captures one of their major themes and has guided much Western thought on the topic.

Yet as we learn more about these exemplars of authority, we keep seeing hints of dark pasts and hidden inner lives. Gender immediately raises problems for the bureaucratic image of some of the most important deities: several of the most popular are female. As Shahar shows elsewhere in this volume, popular tales and local operas about many gods reveal personal lives far from the formalities of official life; the nurturing female deities are only the most obvious exception. Origin stories thus often leave clues of religious retreat, military prowess, self-mutilation, suicide, and other nonbureaucratic behavior. Worse still, all kinds of quite unbureaucratic spirits command worship in the cracks between more respectable community temples. Many areas harbor temples to stones, foxes, turtles, or dogs; to the pitiful corpses of unwed virgins or the mangled remains of battlefield victims; to inebriated priests or executed thieves. Hidden beneath the folds of their dragon robes, many gods harbor unbureaucratic traces of death and desire.

Communities occasionally seem to abandon the bureaucratic façade completely, letting death and desire step out from their hid-ing places. This paper explores two such cases, one in east-central Guangxi in the 1840s and the other in Taiwan in the 1980s. The Xunzhou region of Guangxi offered very few temples to officially recognized bureaucrats. The most respectable deities were three Daoist hermits, who bore little figurative or literal relation to any bureaucratic hierarchy. King Gan (Gan Wang) rivaled them in importance. He had murdered his mother as a stepping-stone toward official position and was known during the period for extorting large payments from the local magistrate. The Tai-wan case features the popular apotheosis of humble ghosts—some of them anonymous victims of violent ends and others known crimi-nals—into powerful patrons. They tend to favor seedy requests from gamblers, prostitutes, and gangsters. One such temple in the 1980s developed into a clear rival of the island's most famous and important temples to imperially honored deities such as Mazu. It attracts thou-sands of visitors every day to offer cigarettes to seventeen dead bodies and a dog.

The altered images of gods in these two cases suggest that we take a close look at the times when the bureaucratic metaphor falters. As a first hypothesis, we might expect that bureaucrats themselves would strongly promote the metaphor of an equally bureaucratic heaven for popular consumption. Gods might therefore shed their official cover-ing when there is a decrease in state power over religion, or at least when the local elites that control major temples and rituals distance themselves from the state. This occurred in both Guangxi and Tai-wan, although in very different ways.

Matricide

East-central Guangxi spawned the Taiping Heavenly Kingdom (Tai-ping Tianguo) in 1850. One of the fortunate side-effects of the upheaval was a fuller description of the area than we usually see for peripheral parts of China. Many Taiping sources supplement the local gazetteers, and scholars have done oral histories since the early twentieth century.[2] It is now possible to outline a general picture of god worship in Thistle Mountain (Zijing Shan), a distant hinterland in Guiping County, in the years just before it became one of the early Taiping base areas.

Strong Gods

The most important community temples in the entire region hon-ored the Three Generations (San Jie). These were three members of the Feng family, scattered over several centuries, each of whom reached the heights of Daoist perfection. The most recent beatification occurred in the seventeenth century, and the cult began soon thereafter with a temple in neighboring Gui County. Temples to the Three Generations soon spread throughout the region (*Guiping Xianzhi* 1920, *juan* 15:10). People I interviewed remembered six temples in the Thistle Mountain region alone.

The Three Generations are as close as Thistle Mountain came in the 1840s to the model of community bureaucrats that anthropologists and historians have described for more central parts of China. They sponsored community rites of renewal *(jiao)* every few years, and local elites probably controlled their temples. When one wealthy landlord created an early self-defense force in the 1840s to stem the rising tide of banditry and unrest, he placed his headquarters in the Three Generations temple at Daxuanxu, a major market town near Thistle Mountain (Guangxi Shifan Xueyuan . . . 1981:272).

Yet as a rule Daoist saints are miracle-dealing mountain hermits, not paper-pushing bureaucrats. The Three Generations had a purely local following with no ties to officialdom either through their origins or through any imperial deification. They recall an earlier Chinese tradition in which most gods were purely local saints and worthies, before the state began systematically to promote and coopt local deities in the Song Dynasty, enlisting them as parts of local government (Hansen 1990:160–166). Although these temples functioned much like bureaucratic community temples, their roots grew firmly in local history, not national hierarchy.

In contrast, the Three Generations' main rival for community authority did draw on the bureaucratic metaphor, but only to undermine its legitimacy. King Gan had indeed earned high office when he was alive, and at least five local temples honored him. His cult centered in Xiangzhou, just to the north of Thistle Mountain. Another major branch temple thrived in Sanjiang, a major river port for Thistle Mountain people. King Gan also held *jiao* rites of renewal, and the local gazetteer mentions no other deities besides King Gan and the Three Generations who performed this major community function (*Xunzhou Fuzhi* 1897, *juan* 54:67). In some ways his popularity even surpassed that of the Three Generations. I was told that worship of King Gan had revived at some temples, but the standing Three Generations temples remained empty shells in 1985.

Both King Gan's origins and his actions, however, mock any claims to bureaucratic respectability. A geomancer identified a burial site that would guarantee high office for King Gan, but only if he used it immediately. Lacking any convenient corpses, but anxious to answer when opportunity knocked, he slaughtered his mother and buried her in just the right spot. This sacrifice of filial piety to personal ambition worked perfectly, and he quickly rose to secular success as an official and then to heavenly success as a god.

King Gan's actions further enhanced his image. The local magistrate once passed near his temple. King Gan seized a young boy and, speaking through the child's mouth, demanded that the magistrate step down from his sedan-chair and worship in the temple. The magistrate complied, and he even went along when King Gan demanded an extremely expensive set of official robes as a gift. The god again emphasized his official position by abusing the system whose authority he claimed. He acted like the local strongmen who sometimes usurped state authority and ran their own little empires where the state grew weak. The local gazetteer also accused the temple of inspiring people to sing obscene songs.[3] Instead of legitimizing government through the bureaucratic metaphor, King Gan made it ludicrous.

No other temples rivaled those of King Gan or the Three Generations in community standing, but several had major followings, and none made the least pretense to bureaucratic propriety. The most infamous was the Liuwu temple, because Hong Xiuquan, the Taiping leader, had denounced it for corrupting the population. Local legend tells that a failed candidate for official degree fell in love with a woman singing on Liuwu Mountain. They sang together for seven days and nights. When they suddenly died on the seventh night, ants buried their bodies. Like King Gan, they would also extort worship out of people, sending anything from snake attacks to stomach aches to plague people who showed too little respect (Guangxi . . . 1962: 49). The paired singing reflects local Zhuang minority tradition, and the legend clearly fits Han repugnance at what was viewed as profligate sexual license. Much like the temple of King Gan, this temple combined images of improper death, reliance on threat and extortion to command worship, origins tied to strictly local history, and dark hints of sex.

Informants also told of a Thistle Mountain temple to Grandaunt Liu (Liu Dagupuo). She was the spirit of a girl who had died young and childless, and who performed many good deeds in both life and death. Such stories are familiar to us from other parts of China. Dead virgins pose a problem for ancestor worship: they have no descendants to worship them, but they may behave as angry ghosts if left unworshiped. As Baptandier points out elsewhere in this volume, the transformation to goddess "civilizes" these marginal female spirits, who would otherwise stand as unincorporated threats to patrilineal responsibility and filial piety. Far more eminent deities than Grandaunt Liu—from Lady Linshui to Mazu—began as just such marginal women.

Taiwanese often resolve this problem by building small girls' temples *(guniang miao)* where passers-by may stop to burn a little incense (Wolf 1974:149–150.). These resemble ghost temples both architecturally and in the nature of their spirits. The names of the dead may be known, unlike true ghosts, but they suffer similarly from the lack of a proper place on an ancestral altar. Unlike Mazu or Lady Linshui, Grandaunt Liu never had any state recognition and maintained more of the ghostly aspects of a girls' temple. Yet unlike those little shrines, she had a major local following of her own. Neither exactly a ghost nor a local religious worthy, she was clearly no bureaucrat in any sense.

Temples to Pangu (sometimes called Panhu or Panwang) also dot the region, with at least five in the area around Thistle Mountain. Many Chinese know Pangu as a legendary creator of the world. Yet these local temples instead have close ties to origin myths of the Yao minority, although my informants said that members of all ethnic groups worshiped there, at least in the early twentieth century. The local Pangu tradition stems from a confusion of names with Panhu, a dog described in the *Hou Han Shu* (Lü 1982:1–7). The emperor offered his daughter in marriage to anyone who could quell a powerful bandit force. When the dog Panhu showed up one day with the bandit general's head in his jaws, the daughter insisted on keeping the promise. The odd couple's six sons and six daughters fathered the Yao.

This tale may contain elements of Han chauvinism, but Pangu/Panhu is quite clearly a central Yao deity. Yao informants in Guangxi told tales of Pangu helping them on legendary migrations through southern China, and they showed me several ritual texts featuring Pangu. No version of Pangu resonates at all with the bureaucracy, and this one instead conjures up images of dog worship and totemic ancestors. The inevitable contact with non-Han groups in peripheral areas was one factor undermining the orthodox image.

One other odd story rounds out the group. The Qiansa temple, an important nearby shrine, commemorated a vagrant who had thrown cow dung into a river. The dung transformed itself into rocks, making a passage over the river.[4] Temples and stories like these were not unique to Thistle Mountain. Unlike Thistle Mountain, however, more central areas never allowed such temples to develop on such a large scale, at least not without first undergoing a transforming rectification. Such acts of rectification need more study, but we already have some examples. Dean (1993:154–159), for example, shows the Confucian sponsorship of the Reverent Lord of Broad Compassion; some local elites promoted ritual at the grave of the god's parents as a memorial to his filial piety. At the same time, they condemned or simply swept under the rug conflicting versions of the deity, including one tale of the murderous geomantic revenge of the future god (then a cowherd) against his master that resonates with King Gan's story

(Dean 1993:135–137). Baptandier, in this volume, shows a similar attempt when local party authorities sponsored a bowdlerized version of a play about Lady Linshui in 1993. Local followers of the cult generally disapproved.

These attempts to control meaning probably never succeeded entirely.[5] In Guangxi during the 1840s, however, even the attempt appears to have ended. Gods brazenly displayed their purely local loyalties (not one of the major popular deities had state recognition), their willingness to use brute force to compel worship (like King Gan demanding a gift of official clothes), and their close ties with death and desire—from matricidal King Gan to suicidal lovers to dead virgins. The processes that helped push such stories into dark corners in other parts of China had weakened here.

Weak States

The consistent undermining of the bureaucratic metaphor at this place and time suggests that the local secular bureaucracy itself was struggling for control. Indeed, the mechanisms that might ordinarily allow the state to tighten the reins on local worship were collapsing in peripheral Guangxi in the 1840s. Thistle Mountain shared many of the characteristics of Chinese internal peripheries that sapped official power, and the events of the time had further weakened the state.

Like many comparable parts of China, east-central Guangxi had large populations of non-Han minorities. A large population of Yao, practicing swidden agriculture high in the mountains, maintained many of their own traditions. An even larger group of Zhuang had been largely sinicized by the mid-nineteenth century but still spoke Zhuang. They also retained some Zhuang traditions, like that of the paired singing of young couples that had inspired the story of the Liuwu temple. There were also some Cantonese-speaking Chinese (or perhaps fully sinicized Zhuang) and a large group of fairly recent Hakka immigrants. As usual in such situations, exchange among these groups accompanied their inherent tensions.[6] Yao spirit-mediums and curers, for example, had a broad influence, as did their Pangu temples. Many people were bilingual: Hakka and Zhuang people communicated in Cantonese (*Xunzhou Fuzhi* 1897, *juan* 54:77). By the 1840s the pax sinica that had kept ethnic tensions down to a simmer began to break down in the area, providing further evidence of weakening state control. Large-scale ethnic feuding became endemic during this decade, with battles sometimes involving thousands of people (Kuhn 1977).

Typically peripheral, the area itself was cut off even from the nearest county seat. When I went with modern transportation in 1985, the trip still required almost half a day, beginning with a ferry ride (there are no bridges in the area), a long drive until we abandoned the car where it stuck in the mud, a wet walk to a rickety little ferry, and a final walk to the local settlement. In the 1840s the county seat (itself considered a backwater) had little direct control over areas like Thistle Mountain. The lack of significant inland naval force further weakened the chances for control, as the state often ceded domination of the main water transport routes to pirates.

Indeed, local gazetteers lamented a startling increase in river piracy and bandit attacks during this period. With names like Bighead Goat, Big Carp, and Wild Boar Arrow, bandit leaders led gangs numbering in the hundreds and more (*Xunzhou Fuzhi* 1897, *juan* 55; *Pingnan Xianzhi* 1883, *juan* 18; Xie 1950). One disheartened contemporary suggested that 30–40 percent of the population of the province were bandits by 1854 (Yan 1962 [1854]). The sudden surge in river piracy and other banditry in the 1840s resulted indirectly from the Opium War, which had put many inland water workers out of business by opening up new ports. Many of these people put their old skills to new uses, moving from the economic trade routes of Guangdong to the safer bandit havens of peripheral Guangxi (Xie 1850, Wakeman 1966:126). At the same time, the reopening of some played-out silver mines brought another group of rootless and hardened vagrants into the area (Liang 1981, *Guixian Zhi* 1893, *juan* 1:12). The inexorable rise of the Taiping rebellion at the end of this decade, trampling over feeble state attempts to stop them, illustrated just how weak the state really was by then.

As these changes increasingly immobilized state control over the area in the 1840s, new local strongmen arose to exercise their own alternative authority. The first references to what local sources called "rice lords" *(mifan zhu)* appeared at the beginning of this decade (Zhong 1984, Xie 1950:32–35). They offered examples of the much broader pattern of Chinese peripheral strongmen that Meskill described (Meskill 1979:88–91). Usually wealthy and well-connected to begin with, such strongmen controlled private forces of armed braves, serving as both local patrons and plunderers. They managed local institutions at the same time as they preyed on their enemies. The strongest ran private empires, controlling both armed force and wealth, and effectively replacing civil government in some places.

This coincidence of timing, where a feeble officialdom accompanied a rising panoply of unexpected gods, suggests that the bureaucratic metaphor thrives mostly where the state itself is strong and effective. Alternative secular powers instead fostered the sides of Chinese deities that owe little to bureaucratic respectability. Although the data from Guangxi on the eve of the Taiping rebellion will never reveal much detail about how this actually worked, they point in fruitful directions. This material suggests—at least as an initial and tentative hypothesis—a kind of Skinnerian regional variation in gods (Skinner 1977).[7] Core areas, which had a strong state presence closely integrated with local elites, helped shape gods toward the bureaucratic model. Peripheral areas, however, with their non-Han influences, difficult transport, and alternative authorities, left the field open to gods beyond the bureaucracy.[8] Dean sees a similar pattern in Fujian, where cults with the closest ties to official Daoist and government circles thrived closest to administrative centers, while strictly local cults instead prospered in more peripheral regions (Dean 1993:32).

Although regional variation cannot explain all the permutations of Chinese deities, as I show for Taiwanese ghosts below, it does begin to suggest how religious alternatives relate to social and political contexts, and to focus attention directly on how the state or other authorities can influence interpretation. At the same time, however, peripheral religion in nineteenth-century Guangxi offered little true innovation. Even its strangest features existed as hints lying in the chinks of more central religious practice elsewhere in China. Thus, an important national deity such as Lü Dongbin (see Katz's essay, elsewhere in this volume) or a major community deity in a core area, such as Lady Linshui (in Baptandier's essay, elsewhere in this volume), has multiple layers of resonance, some of which closely recall these Guangxi cases.

Although some of the deities in Guangxi (like a dung-tossing beggar or dead lovers) abandoned the bureaucratic metaphor, the most important gods carried on a hidden dialogue with the idea of bureaucracy. The localism of the Three Generations and the criminal/official career of King Gan grew significant only by contrast to more official deities. This was no new language of religion, incomprehensible to more central areas, but instead a very different proportioning of ideas with a broad base throughout China. The keys to the variation lay both in sources of political authority and in an unsystematic but widely shared set of ideas.

Money

Taiwan in the 1980s was no economic periphery, nor was the state at all weak by any standard definitions. Yet that decade also saw skyrocketing worship of another set of spirits that undermined the idea of bureaucracy. Popular religion in Taiwan had increased hand in hand with economic development, quite in contrast to the prescriptions of earlier modernization theories (Qu and Yao 1986). Especially in the 1980s, however, when Taiwan stood on the verge of recognition as a fully "developed" country, the fastest growing segment of popular religion involved spirits of bandits, drunkards, unknown corpses, and others who offered little to bureaucratic propriety (Li 1992). Hardly any place in China could be more different —socially, politically, and economically—from 1840s Guangxi, but both pushed religion in directions that seem far from our usual model.

Mischief and Biased Wealth

Perhaps a century ago, or perhaps much longer (no one really knows), a fishing boat washed up on the shore at the northernmost tip of Taiwan. The local people had no idea who the seventeen corpses on the boat might be, nor did they recognize the dog that somehow remained alive. They followed the usual tradition when one stumbles across bodies or unknown bones in Taiwan: they buried the men in a common grave and erected a tiny shrine so that people might make occasional offerings to these otherwise unworshiped and pitiful spirits. The only odd bit of the story was the dog, whose unbreakable loyalty to his masters caused him to leap into the grave along with the bodies, to be buried alive by the villagers. The dog was the eighteenth of what the local people politely (and euphemistically) named the Eighteen Lords (Shiba Wanggong).

The little shrine followed the fate of most such ghost temples, gradually deteriorating over the years and receiving only occasional worship. By the 1960s it was little more than a vague mound with a gravestone and an incense pot, occasionally worshiped by a lonely soldier standing coastal sentry duty. A decade later, however, its transformation began. Taiwan broke ground for its first nuclear power plant not far away, and the grave was slated for destruction as the bulldozers reinforced the cliffs along the shore. When several accidents happened on the site, some of the workers began to worry about ghosts. Their fears were confirmed one day when a backhoe, just poised to tear up the Eighteen Lords' grave, suddenly froze and defeated all attempts at repair. At this point, workers and local inhabitants mobilized in defense of the shrine. The government finally gave in, agreeing to "respect local customs" and recreate the shrine at the new, higher ground level.

Not only had the previously forgotten shrine brought the state itself to do its bidding, it had done so in front of an audience of workers from all over Taiwan. The newly rebuilt temple was larger and fancier than any other ghost temple ever built in Taiwan, and within a few years it rivaled the island's most important god temples in popularity, attracting thousands of people every night and thoroughly tying up traffic on the coastal road for hours. Although ghosts have turned into gods in the past (Harrell 1974), these instead continued to celebrate their ghostliness on a grander scale than ever before, often brazenly inverting the usual practices of community god temples.

Even though half of the new temple had god images of the Eighteen Lords, the main center of worship remained the grave mound and two larger-than-life bronze statues of the dog that flanked it (see figure). The dogs themselves attracted most attention, as members of the invariably raucous crowd would stroke them and empower amulets by rubbing them over the dogs. Worship peaked in the small hours of the morning (the *yin,* ghostly time) instead of the daylight of the *yang* gods. Even more unusual, the original grave had been preserved as an underground room, directly below the replica with its dog statues. Those who knew about the basement room would go down there to experience the Eighteen Lords' power even more strongly. The necessities of the reconstruction meant that the original grave and its incense pot now pushed up directly against the wall, leaving no room where worshipers would normally stand or kneel. To top it off, instead of offering sticks of incense in the pot, everyone instead erected a burning cigarette. With worshipers attending underground and late at night, fondling a bronze dog, and offering slightly disreputable cigarettes instead of the pure and spiritual smell of incense, the Eighteen Lords' cult turned bureaucratic god worship on

The images of the Eighteen Lords (including the dog) in the background on the "god" side of the temple in northern Taiwan; another image of the dog has been placed in front of them. (Photograph by Meir Shahar)

its head. It is an extreme example of the kinds of carnivalesque inversions that Shahar discusses in his essay in this volume.

Ghosts will do anything in exchange for worship, quite unlike those proper bureaucrats who will not deal with improper requests. Ghost shrines always have the reputation of pandering especially to those, such as gangsters, gamblers, and prostitutes, who cannot go to the god-officials. The Eighteen Lords played up this reputation. In fact, so many people went that they could not all have been underworld figures, but clearly people found a thrill in going to a temple that claimed this element of danger. Visitors are always warned about pickpockets, who frequent the place both to worship and to ply their trade in the thick crowds. The very carnival atmosphere at this temple plays up the contrast to other gods; there are even real carnival attractions on the way from the parking lot to the temple.

Relations with the Eighteen Lords resembled contracts with mobsters more than the respectful petitions to proper gods. The Eighteen Lords would do anything at all, but punishment for not paying them was quick and dire. Typical community gods, on the other hand, act out of goodness (although they are happy to accept appropriate gifts in return), but act only when they consider a request appropriate. Many of the requests to the Eighteen Lords concerned profit (to which even the stuffiest gods have no objection in China), but especially profit from gambling on an illegal lottery, or from the stock-market craze that swept Taiwan in those years, or from less than strictly respectable business practices.

This temple was the largest and most famous of its kind, but it was far from unique. Several other ghost temples also achieved some prominence at roughly the same time, and a great many saw increased worship because of their success at stock-market and gambling advice. At least three tombs to typically ghostly violent deaths became quite important. The closest to respectability was that of Li Yong, a general killed fighting aborigines in the nineteenth century. More typical was that of Liao Tianding, a sort of Robin Hood during the Japanese occupation of Taiwan. He was murdered in his sleep by a brother-in-law who wanted the reward. A similar shrine honors a mainland soldier who turned to bank robbery, supposedly to support a friend's child. He was shot by a firing squad. While each of these has a generous side that has no part in the story of the Eighteen Lords (whose respectable bit was instead the loyalty of the dog), each also died a ghostly death, thrived beyond official control, and maintained a very ghostly flexibility about honoring all kinds of requests.

The same decade also brought a sudden popularity to a handful of gods—invariably those who were least bureaucratic and most mischievous. As I was paying my bill at a restaurant one evening, the small altar near the cash register (typical of many Taiwanese businesses) caught my attention. An image of the Cloth-Bag Buddha (Budai Heshang) sat in the middle: the fat, jolly character with a big bag of goodies slung over his shoulder, ready to hand out to people. He appears widely in Taiwan, but more as a decoration than as an important object of worship. Although some people say he was an incarnation of the future Buddha, Maitreya, they treat him more like Santa Claus. This image, however, had a burning cigarette hanging from his lips, strongly reminiscent of those cigarettes for the Eighteen Lords. One also finds burning cigarettes stuck in the mouths of ceramic dog images bought at the Eighteen Lords temple.[9]

The Cloth-Bag Buddha with his sack of presents provides an easy symbol for the idea of quick wealth falling into your lap. The woman who took my money in the restaurant described him as the God of Biased Wealth (Piancai Shen), an innovative term to my knowledge, contrasting with the well-known God of Wealth (Cai Shen). *Biased wealth* is a technical term in Chinese fortunetelling and refers to unearned gains. The Cloth-Bag Buddha hands out wealth willy-nilly, while the Eighteen Lords demand a contractual payment. Yet both celebrate sources of wealth outside the formal economy, and those burning cigarettes clearly unite them. Not coincidentally, the Eighteen Lords' temple's next most popular sales items after the ceramic dogs are images of the Cloth-Bag Buddha.

Other gods have not been left out of the resurgence of popular religion in Taiwan, but a handful stand out from the rest for their rapid growth. In each case, the deity undermines the bureaucratic metaphor. The most important beneficiaries also appear in other papers in this volume: Jigong (the wine-besotted monk), Taizi Ye (Nazha, the patricidal child), and Sun Wukong (popularized in the West as the mischievous Monkey) (Hu 1986). Officially registered Jigong temples, for example, increased from 12 to 120 between 1981 and 1986 in Taiwan (Hu 1986). It is safe to assume that a great many more remain unregistered. Like the Eighteen Lords and other ghostly temples, and like the God of Biased Wealth, these deities thrived in the 1980s because they would not be held to the moralities of the bureaucratic metaphor.

This entire set of unbureaucratic deities happily gave stock-market tips, illegal lottery advice, and help in the shadier sides of the capitalist market. From executed bank robbers to unidentified corpses to a monk who mocks his own (already unbureaucratic) discipline, this group stands out for its challenge to bureaucratic order. Most of them are eccentrically individualistic, and none of them has the associations with community morality that typify our images of most gods. These particular gods' shrines rarely functioned as community temples, and those of ghosts never played such a role. Their followers constituted neither congregation nor residential community, as the deities themselves stood idiosyncratically independent from secular or heavenly lines of power.

Gambling and Modernity

Like east-central Guangxi in the 1840s, Taiwan in the 1980s lavished its worship on a collection of quirky and ominous characters, at least in comparison to those upright bureaucrats. The deteriorating state in Guangxi provided a pivot for an explanation there, but Taiwan's political system certainly showed no similar signs of weakness (unless one somehow takes increasing democracy for weakness). The explanation instead lies in the specific nature of Taiwan's economy during that decade and in the inability of a modernizing government to maintain its influence over religion.

This embodiment of religious individualism in Taiwan—where community gods lost ground to deities with no community basis, serving the selfish ends of isolated individuals—grew at exactly the same time as Taiwan's small enterprise-based capitalism was thriving. The relationship of the individual to the marketplace in capitalism, with its associated breakdown of communal ties, has been recognized since the writings of Marx on alienation and of Durkheim on anomie. The situation grew particularly intense in Taiwan in the 1980s, when many people felt that rising labor costs and a changing world market threatened the small, labor-intensive enterprises on which they had built their wealth. While they recognized the threat, they saw no plausible alternative kinds of investment. The result was a huge increase in unproductive investment: the booming illegal lottery, an exploding stock market, and skyrocketing land prices. The boom in unearned wealth finally went bust in 1990, when the stock market lost 75 percent of its value.

For much of the 1980s profit appeared less as a product of hard work and smart decisions than as a result of luck, greed, and insider connections. At the same time the crisis of economic confidence accentuated the tooth-and-claw image of the economy always implied as one side of petty entrepreneurial competition. With small business under pressure, and with the stock market and gambling dens booming, success appeared increasingly as the result of self-serving utilitarianism rather than of community morality. That is, it fit desperate ghosts and idiosyncratic gods better than moralizing bureaucrats. These capricious deities matched the capricious nature of profit itself. What had been an odd undercurrent in popular religion flooded the more standard gods in the unusual conditions of that one decade.

China had long had a developed commodity economy and clear ideas about individual competition, along with its more Confucian ideas of hierarchy and order. Yet a strong state and traditional elite apparently held the religious side of the market economy in check, at least in more central parts of China. It burst its bonds in modern Taiwan because the state had given up almost all control over religious interpretation, although it was in no sense politically weak like the state in Guangxi a century earlier. From the founding of the Republic of China in 1911, its leaders had been dedicated modernizers, as much in the cultural as in the economic sense. Their resulting dedication to "rationality" over "superstition," along with their Western-style guarantees of religious freedom, resulted in their sanctioning only organized textual traditions as religion, while most popular practice was damned as superstition and discouraged (Duara 1991).

The official approval of religious freedom and discouragement of "irrational" ideas led to numerous halting and ineffectual attempts at religious control after the Nationalist Party regained the island from Japan. None of this, however, was systematic enough to cause any real transformation, and the real increase of civil liberties in the 1980s undercut all attempts at religious control. By renouncing a religion of its own and embracing Weberian rational bureaucratic principles, a modernizing state like Taiwan finds it very difficult even to attempt to influence religious interpretation. Unwilling by the 1980s to suppress popular religion, its only real option was to ignore popular beliefs. While state and elite control over religion had been weak in late imperial times, it collapsed completely in modern Taiwan, and the absence allowed a new proportioning of religious practice.

The general questioning of political legitimacy that occurred along with the broadly increasing freedoms of that decade further undermined state control. Contrary to the predictions of many development theorists, the modernizing state has actually fostered more openness for religious development by abdicating its right to determine religious meaning. At the same time, by basing its legitimacy on bureaucratic rationality, such a state undermines claims about ultimate values, leaving a void that religion has stepped in to fill. In a very limited but important sense, then, Taiwan's state in the 1980s was just as weak as Guangxi's in the 1840s: both had lost any significant control over popular religious practice.

Conclusions

These two cases of how unusual deities rivaled, and even overshadowed, their staid and bureaucratic colleagues occurred in two places as different as they could be and still be Chinese. Guangxi in the 1840s was a peripheral frontier with a collapsing social and political order, about to be torn apart by one of the largest rebellions in history. Taiwan in the 1980s was a political center with a thriving modern economy. Yet both places embraced spirits of questionable Confucian morality, known more for sex, drunkenness, gambling, and murder than for dedication to bureaucratic order. Could the same processes really have been at work in both places?

The collapse of political control over religion in both Guangxi and Taiwan brought the hidden side of religion strongly to the surface. The Guangxi case suggested that a Skinnerian regionalization of China might also map variation in the power of the bureaucratic metaphor, where peripheral areas encourage gods beyond the bureaucracy. Adding the Taiwan case, however, allows us to focus more clearly on just one aspect of regional variation: the nature of political control. Nineteenth-century Guangxi resembled modern Taiwan only in the frailty of state control over religion and not in other major features of regional variation, such as geographic marginality or economic system. Such political weakness may develop more easily on peripheries, but the periphery is only one form of weakness. Peripheries themselves will vary historically along these lines, with the 1840s marking a low point for central Guangxi. At the same time, Taiwan shows how a very comparable weakness can develop from quite different roots: the secular politics of modernity in a strong state rather than the strongman politics of a collapsed state.

Not surprisingly, these two examples suggest that the bureaucratic metaphor dominates hidden desires especially where the bureaucracy itself dominates alternative social and political arrangements. Weak though state and local elite control over religion was in China, especially by comparison with Catholicism in medieval Europe, these cases suggest that it did manage to keep alternative gods on the sidelines when it held the upper hand. Where other forms of power began to take over, from local strongmen to a fickle market, the mechanisms of attempted control faltered. Although a great deal of further research remains to be done on this kind of variation, these cases clearly suggest that gods beyond the bureaucracy thrived especially where the state began to lose the struggle for overarching control.

The variation in state power over religion is not the only influence over how thoroughly Chinese deities developed the bureaucratic image. Gods and goddesses also reflect social tensions that cut across cores and peripheries, or imperial and modernizing regimes. As Sangren explains, elsewhere in this volume, the most important of these may have been internal family dynamics: the conflicts between fathers and sons, and the contradictory position of women as sexual threats and nurturing mothers. This exists throughout China quite independent from state politics. The state never tried to remove goddesses entirely from the pantheon. Rather, it happily accepted many of them, even though real women were never bureaucrats. Yet there was political pressure even on the goddesses. Cleaned-up versions of goddesses can lose their troubling ambiguities, appearing as nurturing mothers holding babies, with no mention of their fundamental breaches of filial piety in not bearing sons or in refusing marriage (see also Baptandier's essay in this volume). Grandaunt Liu, on the other hand, could achieve prominence in her relatively threatening form only in a place like peripheral Guangxi in the 1840s.

The situation is complex and involves more than just bureaucratic versus unbureaucratic gods. The two cases I have discussed, after all, were very different from each other, although neither featured bureaucratic gods. Guangxi developed its own versions of community cults to major gods, preferring hermits and a matricide to take over the usual role of bureaucrats. Even the Taiping Christian god, who showed up in the 1840s, was another unbureaucratic god who oversaw a communitarian congregation.[10] In Taiwan, on the other hand, upright community gods held their own, while the newly popular deities catered to individual followers with no claims over any residential community. Guangxi experienced an unbureaucratic self-definition of community, while Taiwan played up idiosyncratic gods and hungry ghosts who never defined communities. In Guangxi the state had collapsed and left the field open for new community identities. In Taiwan, however, state power in communities was as strong as ever, but a kind of capricious capitalism had thrived. Ghosts and pariah gods fit neatly with the idea of an amoral individualism that saw greed as held back only by the threat of enforcers to carry out contracts. The particular nature of weak state control over religion thus relates closely to just how gods move beyond the bureaucracy, leading to very different patterns in Guangxi and Taiwan.

Do any of these alternatives to our usual understanding of bureaucratic gods constitute a kind of counter-hegemony? Although the apparently systematic rejection of bureaucracy makes the claim tempting, neither case allows a simple affirmative answer. Guangxi not only retained the usual structure of community god temples, but also many of its deities derived their significance by contrast with bureaucrats, thus relying on the system they questioned. King Gan certainly undermined the bureaucracy, yet he also drew his power from it: gaining legitimacy by humiliating a real official and working as an official himself. In Taiwan the bureaucratic gods continue to thrive; the explosion of interest in gods beyond the bureaucracy supplements the system without challenging it.

Yet the very existence of these alternatives at least provides the kernel of an entirely new view of the world. Taiping ideas (such as monotheism, egalitarian economics, and even a ban on sexual intercourse), which were certainly radical by Chinese standards, thrived in the same fertile fields as King Gan. By redefining community values, Guangxi planted the seeds of possible alternatives. Taiwan's innovations, however, involved individuals each out for his or her own gain, and it is much harder to see how an organized movement for change might grow out of alienated ghosts. Nor does any radical change in religion seem likely unless bureaucratic gods themselves begin to disappear. These religious variants thus do not simply reflect political and economic changes; rather, the religious form itself also shapes future political potentials.

Notes

I am especially grateful to Liang Ken and Liu Bingzhen for their assistance in the field; to Cai Shaoqing, Hsiao Hsin-Huang, Li Yulin, and Mao Jiaqi for their intellectual companionship and practical help; and to my various hosts during this research, especially the Department of History at Nanjing University, the Guiping County History Museum, and in Taiwan the Institute of Ethnology at the Academia Sinica.

1. Ahern 1981 has developed this side of the gods in the most detail.

2. I conducted interviews there in 1985. I am especially grateful to Li Yulin and other scholars and officials of Guiping County for their time and help, and to Liang Ken for invaluable assistance.

3. This description is based on the *Taiping Tianri* (in Michael 1966–1971:73–76), Hong Rengan's confession (in Michael 1966–1971:1519), Hamberg (1854:36–37), *Xunzhou Fuzhi* (1897, *juan* 54:87), and my own interviews.

4. Personal communication, Zhong Wendian, Department of History, Guangxi Normal University.

5. The essays by Katz and Baptandier in this volume show especially clearly how multiple levels of meaning permeated even cults that had long histories of ties to the state and to Daoism. See also Weller 1987 and 1994 on the general failure of such attempts to achieve full control.

6. For examples involving religious ideas in Taiwan, see Shepherd 1984 and Seaman 1978:114.

7. Skinner divided China into major regions, largely based on watersheds and thus ease of transport. Each region in turn has a core and a periphery, with the core characterized by higher population density, better transport, a more developed economy, and so on. East-central Guangxi falls into the periphery of his Lingnan region.

8. One might argue that the minority influence in this case is unique, because specifically Yao and Zhuang elements were important here and would not have been reproduced in other peripheral areas. Nevertheless, minorities of one sort

or another characterized nearly all Chinese peripheries, and other non-Han influences on religion could equally have discouraged elaboration of the bureaucratic metaphor.

9. Note that the ghost-god Jiajiang in Sutton's essay in this volume also receive offerings of cigarettes and that the individuals who perform those roles may have underworld connections.

10. See Gernet 1985:221–232 for evidence of how Jesus appeared troubling to Confucians: an illegitimate child who died the humiliating death of a criminal.

Literature Cited

Ahern, Emily Martin. 1981. *Chinese Ritual and Politics*. New York: Cambridge University Press.

Dean, Kenneth. 1993. *Taoist Ritual and Popular Cults of Southeast China*. Princeton: Princeton University Press.

Duara, Prasenjit. 1991. "Knowledge and Power in the Discourse of Modernity: The Campaigns against Popular Religion in Early Twentieth-century China." *Journal of Asian Studies* 50(1):67–83.

Gernet, Jacques. 1985. *China and the Christian Impact: A Conflict of Cultures*. Cambridge: Cambridge University Press.

Guangxi Shifan Xueyuan Shidixi 72 Ji. 1981. "Taiping Tianguo Qiyi Jige Wenti de Diaocha" (Investigation into Several Questions Concerning the Taiping Heavenly Kingdom Uprising). In *Taiping Tianguoshi Yanjiu Wenxuan (Selected Research on the History of the Taiping Heavenly Kingdom)*, edited by Guangxi Taiping Tianguoshi Yanjiuhui, 271–290. Nanning: Guangxi Renmin Chubanshe.

Guangxi Zhuangzu Zizhiqu Tongzhiguan, comp. 1962. *Taiping Tianguo Geming zai Guangxi Diaocha Ziliao Huipian (Compiled Materials from the Investigation of the Taiping Heavenly Kingdom Revolution in Guangxi)*. Nanning: Guangxi Zhuangzu Zizhiqu Renmin Chubanshe.

Guiping Xianzhi (Guiping County Gazetteer). 1920. N.p.

Guixian Zhi (Gui County Gazetteer). 1893. Compiled by Liang Jixiang. N.p.

Hamberg, Theodore. 1854. *The Visions of Hung-siu-tshuen and the Origin of the Kwang-si Insurrection*. Hong Kong: China Mail.

Hansen, Valerie. 1990. *Changing Gods in Medieval China, 1127–1276*. Princeton: Princeton University Press.

Harrell, C. Stevan. 1974. "When a Ghost Becomes a God." In *Religion and Ritual in Chinese Society*, edited by Arthur P. Wolf, 193–206. Stanford: Stanford University Press.

Hu T'ai-li. 1986. "Shen, Gui yu Dutu: Dajia Le Duxi Fanying zhi Minsu Xinyang" (Gods, Ghosts and Gamblers: The Influence of Popular Beliefs on the Everybody's Happy Lottery). Paper presented at the Second International Conference on Sinology, Academia Sinica, Taipei.

Kuhn, Philip A. 1977. "Origins of the Taiping Vision: Cross-cultural Dimensions of a Chinese Rebellion." *Comparative Studies in Society and History* 19: 350–366.

Liang Renbao. 1981 [1957]. "Taiping Tianguo he Kuanggong" (The Taiping Heavenly Kingdom and Miners). In *Taiping Tianguoshi Yanjiu Wenxuan (Selected Research on the History of the Taiping Heavenly Kingdom)*, edited

by Guangxi Taiping Tianguoshi Yanjiuhui, 50–64. Nanning: Guangxi Renmin Chubanshe.

Li Yih-yuan. 1992. "Taiwan Minjian Zongjiao de Xiandai Qushi: Dui Peter
Berger Jiaoshou Dongya Fazhan Wenhua Yinsu Lun de Huiying" (The
Modern Tendencies of Taiwan's Popular Religion: A Response to Professor
Peter Berger's Theory of Cultural Factors in East Asian Development). In
Wenhua de Tuxiang (The Image of Culture), 2:117–138. Taipei: Chongchen
Wenhua.

Lü Simian. 1982. *Lü Simian Dushi Zhaji (Lü Simian's Notes on Reading History)*. Shanghai: Shanghai Guji Chubanshe.

Meskill, Johanna Menzel. 1979. *A Chinese Pioneer Family: The Lins of Wu-
feng, Taiwan, 1729–1895*. Princeton: Princeton University Press.

Michael, Franz. 1966–1971. *The Taiping Rebellion: History and Documents*. In
collaboration with Chang Chung-li. Seattle: University of Washington Press.

Pingnan Xianzhi (Pingnan County Gazetteer). 1883. Compiled by Qiu Bin. N.p.

Qu Haiyuan and Yao Lixiang. 1986. "Taiwan Diqu Zongjiao Bianqian Zhi
Tantao" (Discussion of Religious Changes in the Taiwan Area). *Bulletin of
the Institute of Ethnology, Academia Sinica* 75:655–685.

Seaman, Gary. 1978. *Temple Organization in a Chinese Village*. Asian Folklore
and Social Life Monographs 101. Taipei: Orient Cultural Service.

Shepherd, John. 1984. "Sinicized Siraya Worship of A-li-tsu." *Bulletin of the
Institute of Ethnology, Academia Sinica* 58:1–81.

Skinner, G. William. 1977. "Regional Urbanization in Nineteenth-century
China." In *The City in Late Imperial China*, edited by G. William Skinner,
211–249. Stanford: Stanford University Press.

Wakeman, Frederic. 1966. *Strangers at the Gate: Social Disorder in South
China, 1839–1861*. Berkeley: University of California Press.

Weller, Robert P. 1987. "The Politics of Ritual Disguise: Repression and Response in Taiwanese Religion." *Modern China* 13:17–39.

———. 1994. *Resistance, Chaos and Control in China: Taiping Rebels, Taiwanese Ghosts and Tiananmen*. London: Macmillan.

Wolf, Arthur P. 1974. "Gods, Ghosts, and Ancestors." In *Religion and Ritual in
Chinese Society*, edited by Arthur P. Wolf, 131–182. Stanford: Stanford University Press.

Xie Xingyao. 1950. *Taiping Tianguo Qianhou Guangxi de Fan Qing Yundong
(Anti-Qing Movements in Guangxi around the Taiping Heavenly Kingdom)*. Beijing: Renmin Chubanshe.

Xunzhou Fuzhi (Xunzhou Prefecture Gazetteer). 1897. Compiled by Xia Jingyi.
N.p.

Yan Zhengji. 1962 [1854]. "Lun Yuexi Zei Qingbing Shi Shimo" (All about the
Guangxi Bandits and the Qing Army). In *Taiping Tianguo Shiliao Zongpian
Jianji, Vol. 2 (Selected Historical Sources on the Taiping Heavenly Kingdom)*,
compiled by Taiping Tianguo Lishi Bowuguan. Beijing: Zhonghua Shuju.

Zhong Wendian. 1984. " 'Mifan' Zhu Sanlun" (Some Thoughts on 'Rice Lords').
Paper presented at Jindai Zhongguo Huitang Wenti Xueshu Taolunhui (Conference on Scholarly Problems of Secret Societies in Modern China).

Glossary

Aoguang 敖光
Aquan 阿全

Ba 巴
Baihua qiao 百花橋
Bailongan 白龍庵
Bai Mudan 白牡丹
Baishe Zhuan 白蛇傳
Baiyun Guan 白雲觀
Bajiajiang 八家將
Bamin 八閩
Ban Zhao 班昭
baoan jiao 保安醮
baocheng 報稱
Baogong 包公
Baohuang gong 寶皇宮
baojuan 寶卷
Baopu zi 抱朴子
Baosheng Dadi 保生大帝
Baoyou 寶祐
Baoyu 寶玉
Bashiqi Shenxian Tu 八十七
　　神仙圖
Baxian 八仙
Baye 八爺
Beiyou Ji 北遊記

Beizhen 北鎮
bendi shen 本地神
benming 本命
benshen 本身
Bi 畢
bian dao 遍禱
binlang 檳榔
Bixia Yuanjun 碧霞元君
Boyu 伯玉
bu 補
Budai Heshang 布袋和尚
bumei 不昧
buxiban 補習班

Cai furen 蔡夫人
Cai Shen 財神
Cai Xiang 蔡襄
caiyin buyang 採陰補陽
caizi jiaren 才子佳人
Caoping 曹坪
Cao Xueqin 曹雪芹
changshan fa'e 償善罰惡
chaodu 超度
Chaoyuan Tu 朝元圖
Chaoyuan Xianzhang Tu
　　朝元仙仗圖

269

Chen Chang 陳唱
Chen Danai Tuotai 陳大奶脫胎
Chen furen 陳夫人
Chenghuang 城皇
chenghuang shen 城隍神
Chen Jinggu 陳靖姑
Chen Jinggu wenhua yanjiu
    陳靖姑文化研究
Chen shisi qizhuan 陳十四奇傳
Chen Shouyuan 陳守元
Chen Si 陳四
Chen taihou 陳太后
Chen Tongzu 陳同組
Chen Yu 陳玉
Chen Yuanjin 陳元晉
Chen Zao 陳早
Chenzhou 陳州
chong 冲
chongbai 崇拜
Chongxu Tongmiao Shichen Wang
    Xiansheng Jiahua 沖盧通妙侍
    臣王先生家話
Chongyang 重陽
Chongyang dian 重陽殿
chujia 出家
Chunxi 淳熙
Chunyang 純陽
Chunyang dian 純陽殿
Chunyang Wanshou Gong 純陽
    萬壽宮
Ciji furen 慈濟夫人
Cijigong 慈濟宮
Cui Fujun 崔府君
Cuiping Ji 翠屏記
Cui Yu 崔珏

daban 打扮
dafu 大浮

daguan 大官
daizhao 待詔
dajiang 大將
Dali 大曆
Damo 達摩
Danai furen 大奶夫人
Danai Lingjing 大奶靈經
Danxia Dasheng 丹霞大聖
daode tongxuan jing 道德
    通玄經
daoshi 道士
Daqiao 大橋
dashen 大神
Daxi 大溪
Daye 大爺
Deng Yougong 鄧有功
Deng Zhimo 鄧志謨
dianyan 點眼
diben 底本
Diji Zhu 地基主
dijun 帝君
ding 丁
dishen 地神
Donggang 東港
du 度
Du Dechun 杜德春

Erye 二爺

fabao 法寶
Fan (1) 范
fan (2) 反
fangzhong shu 房中術
fashen 發神
fashi 法師
Feijian ji 飛劍記
fenben 粉本
fen ci 焚詞

fenggu bufan 風骨不凡

Fenghua 奉化

Fengshan 鳳山

Fengshen Yanyi 封神演義

fengshui 風水

fenjia 分家

fenxiang 分香

fu 符

fuben 副本

Fujian minjian xinyang yuanliu
    福建民間信仰源流

Fujian sanshen kao 福建三神考

Fuqing 福清

Fuqiu 浮邱

Furen Changci 夫人唱詞

Furen Cheng 夫人城

Furen shan 夫人山

Furen Zhuan 夫人傳

Fuzhou 撫州 (Hymes chapter)

Fuzhou 福州 (Baptandier and
    Sutton chapters)

gaiyun 改運

Gan Wang 甘王

Ganye 甘爺

Gaoxiong 高雄

Gaoyou 高郵

Ge furen 葛夫人

Ge Hong 葛洪

gong (1) 工

gong (2) 公

gongan 公案

gongde 功德

Gongjitang 拱吉堂

Gongshantang 共善堂

Gongyitang 共意堂

Gongzhu 宮主

guan (1) 觀

guan (2) 關

Guandi 關帝

Guangong 關公

guanren 官人

Guansheng Si 廣勝寺

guanxi 關係

Guanyin 觀音

guanzhu 觀主

guhun 孤魂

Gui 貴

Guiping 桂平

guishen 鬼神

guji 古跡

guniang miao 姑娘廟

Guo 郭

guo luguan 過路關

Guo Shengwang 郭聖王

Gusu 姑蘇

Gutian 古田

Han Xiangzi Quanzhuan 韓湘子
    全傳

haohan 好漢

Heibai wuchang 黑白無常

He Xiangu 何仙姑

Heye 荷爺

Honglou Meng 紅樓夢

Hong Mai 洪邁

Hong Xiuquan 洪秀全

Hongzhou 洪州

Hou Yonghui 侯用晦

huaben 畫本

Huagai San Zhenjun 華蓋三真君

*Huagai Shan Fuqiu Wang Guo
    San Zhenjun Shishi* 華蓋山
    浮邱王郭三真君實事

huagong 畫工

Huagong Huapo 花公花婆

Huaguang 華光
Huainandong 淮南東
huajue 畫訣
Huangliang Meng 黃粱夢
Huang Yue 黃鉞
Hui 回
hui (Hokkien) 花，火
huishou 會首
hujia 虎枷
hukou 戶口
hulijing 狐狸精
hulu 壺蘆
hun 魂

jia 甲
Jiajiang 家將
Jiali 佳里
jianghu 江湖
Jiang Hupo 江虎婆
jiangjun 將軍
Jiang Ziya 姜子牙
Ji'antang 吉安堂
jiao (1) 教
jiao (2) 醮
jiaotou 角頭
jiaozhu 教主
jiaqian 駕前
Jiayi 嘉義
Jidian 濟顛
Jidian Yulu 濟顛語錄
Jigong 濟公
Jigong Huofo 濟公活佛
Jigong Zhuan 濟公傳
Jin 金
jingjin 淨盡
Jingxiang 淨鄉
Jinling 金陵
Jin Ping Mei 金瓶梅

Jinqi 金溪
Jin Shengtan 金聖歎
jinshi 進士
jinxiang 進香
Jin Yong 金庸
ji wo 急我
juan 卷

Kaiyuan Si 開元寺
kanban 刊板
ke 客

leifa 雷法
leiling 雷令
Li 李
li 禮
lian 煉
liandu 煉度
Liang Daocong 梁道從
Liangnü 良女
lianhua huashen 蓮花化身
Li Guangda 李光達
Li Jing 李靖
Lin'an 臨安
Linchuan 臨川
ling (1) 靈
ling (2) 令
linggu 靈谷
lingguai xiaoshuo 靈怪小說
linghun 靈魂
lingpai 令牌
lingqi 令旗
lingyan 靈巖
Linji 臨濟
Lin Jiuniang 林九娘
linshui 臨水
Linshui Furen 臨水夫人
Linshui Pingyao 臨水平妖

Lin Xing 林興

Li Sanniang 李三娘

Li Tieguai 李鐵拐

Liu Cong 劉聰

Liu Dagupo 劉大姑婆

Liu Qi 劉杞

Liuwu 六烏

Liuye 柳爺

Liu Zai 劉縡

Li Zhichang 李志常

Longtan Huo 龍潭壑

Lu 路

Lü Dongbin 呂洞賓

Luling 盧陵

Luoyuan 羅源

Lü Rang 呂讓

Lüshan 閭山

Lü Wei 呂胃

Lü Weng 呂翁

Lu Xixing 陸西星

Lü Yan 呂巖 (嵒)

Lüzu Ci 呂祖祠

Lüzu Quanshu 呂祖全書

Madou 麻豆

Ma Junxiang 馬君祥

Maoshan 茅山

Mao Xianweng 毛仙翁

Mao Zedong 毛澤東

Maye 馬爺

Mazu 媽祖

Miao Daoyi 苗道一

Miaoshan 妙善

Miao Shanshi 苗善時

mifan zhu 米飯主

Min 閩

Mindu Bieji 閩都別記

Mindu Ji 閩都記

ming 命

minsu 民俗

Minxi tuan 閩戲團

Min Zaji 閩雜記

Mulian 目連

Muzhong 穆仲

Nainiang furen 奶娘夫人

Nanfeng 南豐

Nanhai Guanyin Quanzhuan
   南海觀音全傳

Nankunshen 南鯤鯓

Nantai 南台

Nanyou Ji 南遊記

Nazha 哪吒

Nazha Nao Hai 哪吒鬧海

Nazha Santaizi 哪吒三太子

neidan 內丹

neidan bizhi 內丹祕旨

neizhuan 內傳

nianhua 年畫

nianzhu 念珠

nitu 泥土

Niuye 牛爺

Nüjie 女誡

paishi 派詩

Pan Dechong 潘德沖

Pangu 盤古

Panhu 盤瓠

Pan Jinlian 潘金蓮

Panwang 盤王

Piancai Shen 偏財神

pingyao 平妖

Pingyao Zhuan 平妖傳

po 魄

Pojie zhi 婆姐志

pudu 普渡

Pu Songling 浦松齡
Putuo 普陀

Qian Bing 錢丙
qian cang 錢倉
Qiandao 乾道
Qian Daxin 錢大昕
Qiansa 阡陌
qianshi 前世
Qifu 七富
qijiang 漆匠
Qilin Sansheren 騎麟三舍人
qingci 青詞
Qingyuan 慶元
Qinnu 秦奴
Qin Zhian 秦志安
Qiong 瓊
Qishan 旗山
Qitian Dasheng 齊天大聖
Qiu 邱
Qiu Chuji 丘處機
qixing 七星
Qiye 七爺
Quanzhen 全真

Randeng Daoren 燃燈道人
Rao Dongtian 饒洞天
renao 熱鬧
roushen 肉身
ruyibu 如意步

Sanguo Yanyi 三國演義
sanji 三己
Sanjiang 三江
Sanjiao yuanliu shengdi fozu
    soushen ji 三教源流聖帝佛祖
    搜神記

Sanjiao yuanliu soushen daquan
    三教源流搜神大全
San Jie 三界
Sannai 三奶
Sannai Furen Quanshi Zhenjing
    三奶夫人勸世真經
Sannai Jing 三奶經
Sanqing Dian 三清殿
San Sheren 三舍人
Sanshiliu Pojie zhi 三十六婆姐志
San Taizi 三太子
Sanxia Wuyi 三俠五義
Shang 商
shang 上
Shangdu 上度
Shangqing 上清
Shangqing Gusui Lingwen Guilü
    上清骨髓靈文鬼律
Shangqing Tianxin Zhengfa
    上清天心正法
shanshu 善書
shanxiao 山魈
Shao Yong 邵雍
shen 神
shenfo 神佛
Shengshou Gong 聖壽宮
Sheng Tao 盛韜
Shengzhi 升之
Shennong 神農
shi 識
Shiba Wanggong 十八王公
shidafu 士大夫
shier xingsu 十二星宿
Shijia Furen 石夾夫人
Shijiajiang 什家將
Shi Yukun 石玉崑
shoujing 收驚

Shuihu Zhuan 水滸傳
Shuntian Shengmu 順天聖母
Shunyi furen 順懿夫人
sigui 四貴
siji 四季
simen 四門
Song Defang 宋德方
Song Jiang 宋江
Songjiangzhen 宋江鎮
Soushen Ji 搜神記
Sun Deyi 孫德義
Sun Kaidi 孫楷弟
Sun Shidao 孫士道
Sun Wukong 孫悟空
Sun Xingzhe 孫行者

Taibao 太保
taiji 太極
Tainan 台南
Taiping Tianguo 太平天國
taishang 太上
Taishang Laojun 太上老君
Taishang Zongzhen Biyao
　　太上總真秘要
Taisui 太歲
Taiyi Zhenren 太乙真人
Taizi Ye 太子爺
tan 壇
tang 堂
tangki (Hokkien) 童乩
Tanya Tang 澹雅堂
Tan Zixiao 譚紫霄
Tao Chengzhang 陶成章
Tao Hongjing 陶弘景
tian 天
tiandun jianfa 天遁劍法
Tian Du Yuanshuai 田都元帥

Tianfei Niangma Zhuan 天妃
　　娘媽傳
Tiangong 天公
Tianhou 天后
Tianhua Zang Zhuren 天花藏
　　主人
Tianqing 天慶
Tianshi 天師
Tianxin Zhengfa 天心正法
tidian 提點
tiji 題記
tiju 提舉
Tongantang 通安堂
tudi 土地
Tudi Gong 土地公
tudi shen 土地神

Wang 王
Wang Chao 王巢
Wang Gonghuan 王公桓
Wang Guan 王瓘
wanghun 亡魂
Wangmu 王母
Wang Wenqing 王文卿
Wang Yanbin 王延彬
Wangye 王爺
Wang Zhe 王嚞
Wang Zhidao 王志道
Wang Zhuo 王拙
Wei Huacun 魏華存
Wenchang 文昌
weng 翁
Wengui 文貴
Wenhuaxue 文化學
Wenqing 文慶
Wen Qiong 溫瓊
Wuchang 無常

Wu Cheng 吳城
Wudang (shan) 武當山
Wu Daozi 吳道子
Wufudadi 五福大帝
Wuji Men 無極門
Wulinggong 五靈公
Wulu Caishen 五路財神
Wusheng Laomu 無生老母
Wusheng Shengmu 無生聖母
Wu Shiliang 武師亮
Wushi Shan 烏石山
Wutong 五通
Wu Wang Fa Zhou Pinghua
        武王伐紂平話
Wuxian 五顯
Wu Yuantai 吳元泰
Wu Zongyuan 吳宗元

Xiadu 下度
Xiahao 下郝
xian 仙
Xianchun 咸淳
Xiangong Miao 仙公廟
Xiangshan 香山
xiaoben 小本
xiaochai 小差
xiaofa 小法
xiao liangkou 小兩口
xiaoshuo 小説
Xie 謝
xietu 謝土
Xigang 西港
Xihe 西河
Xinghua Si 興化寺
xingju 刑具
Xi Wang Mu 西王母
Xiyou Ji 西遊記
Xuantian Shangdi 玄天上帝

Xuanzang 玄奘
xuepen 血盆
xun meng 尋夢
Xunzhou 潯州
Xu Sheng 許盛
xuwu 戌午
Xu Xiaowang 徐曉望
Xu Yan 徐彥
Xuye 徐爺
Xu Zhenjun 許真君

yang 陽
yangsheng 養生
Yanxian 彥先
Yan Yatui'er 鄂牙推兒
yanyi 演義
Yanzhou 嚴州
yaojing 妖精
yaomo 妖魔
Ye 葉
yeshi xiaoshuo 野史小説
Ye Zhongwu 葉中鳴
Ye Zuwen 葉祖文
yi 役
yichou 乙丑
yifu lanlou, xuerou gouwu
        衣服藍縷, 血肉垢污
Yiguan Dao 一貫道
yijiandaji 一見大吉
Yijian Zhi 夷堅志
yin 陰
yinbing 陰兵
yinyang 陰陽
Yin Zhiping 尹志平
Yiwu Lüshan 醫巫閭山
Yongjin 湧金
Yongle Gong 永樂宮
you ba man 游八蠻

you ba Min 游八閩

youxia 游蝦

Yu 禹

Yuan Congyi 袁從義

Yuanfu 元符

Yuanhegong 元和宮

Yufang bijue 玉房秘訣

Yuhuang Dadi 玉皇大帝

Yulin gong du tuochan
　　玉麟宮度脫產

Yulin Shunyi Dutuochan Rou-
　　zhenjing 玉麟順懿度脫產
　　若真經

Yunfang 雲房

Yushu Leigao 漁墅類稿

yuyan 寓言

zaju 雜劇

Zaojun 灶君

Zaoye 曹爺

Zeng Jili 曾季貍

zhai 齋

Zhang'an Shan 張安山

Zhang Bangchang 張邦昌

Zhang Daoling 張道陵

Zhang Sanfeng 張三丰

Zhangye 張爺

Zhang Yuanshu 章元樞

Zhang Zhide 張志德

Zhang Zhuanxing 張傳興

Zhao Daoyi 趙道一

Zhaoxian li 招賢里

Zhao Ziju 趙子舉

Zhaozong 昭宗

zhen (1) 貞

zhen (2) 真

zhengguo 正果

Zhengyi 正一

zhenhun 真魂

zhenren 真人

Zhenwu 真武

Zhenyuan 貞元

Zhenyutang 振裕堂

zhima 紙馬

Zhinan Gong 指南宮

Zhiwan 至晚

Zhiwu 支午

Zhongcun 中村

Zhong Kui 鍾馗

Zhong Kui Quanzhuan 鍾馗
　　全傳

Zhongli Quan 鍾離權

zhongshen 眾神

Zhongtan Yuanshuai 中壇元帥

Zhou 紂

zhou 咒

Zhou Bida 周必大

Zhou Xian 周顯

Zhuan Shengbo 傳生波

Zhuang Kongshao 莊孔韶

Zhuge Liang 諸葛亮

Zhu Haogu 朱好古

Zhu Quan 朱權

Zhusheng Niangniang 註生娘娘

Zigu 紫姑

Zijing Shan 紫荊山

Zixuan Dong 紫玄洞

Zizhusi 紫竹寺

zongjiao 宗教

zunxin 尊信

zuo yuezi 坐月子

Zushi 祖師

Index

Contributors

BRIGITTE BAPTANDIER is a researcher at the Centre National de la Recherche Scientifique, Laboratoire d'Ethno-logie et de Sociologie Comparative, Paris. She is also responsible for teaching courses on China at the Depart-ment of Ethnology, University of Paris–X. She is the au-thor of *La dame du bord de l'eau* (Paris, Société d'Ethno-logie, 1988).

ROBERT HYMES is professor of Chinese history at Columbia University. He is the author of *Statesmen and Gentlemen: The Elite of Fu-chou, Chiang-hsi, in North-ern and Southern Sung* (New York: Cambridge Univer-sity Press, 1986), and the editor, with Conrad Schiro-kauer, of *Ordering the World: Approaches to State and Society in Sung Dynasty China* (Berkeley: University of California Press, 1993). He has recently completed a book entitled *Way and Byway: Taoism, Local Religion, and Models of Divinity in Sung and Modern China*.

PAUL KATZ received his Ph.D. from the Department of East Asian Studies at Princeton University in 1990. He taught for two years as an assistant professor in the Institute of History at National Chung Cheng Univer-sity (Chia-yi, Taiwan) and worked two years as a visit-ing fellow at the Institute of History and Philology, Academia Sinica (Nankang, Taiwan). He is currently an assistant professor in the Institute of History at Na-tional Central University (Chung-li, Taiwan). He is the author of numerous articles and a book on plague god cults in Zhejiang and Taiwan, and is currently working on a new book about the growth of Lü Dongbin's cult at the Yongle Gong.

P. STEVEN SANGREN received his Ph.D. from Stanford University in 1980. Since then he has been teaching at Cornell University, where he is now professor of anthropology and Asian studies. He is currently working on a book on the social production of gender, power, and personhood in Chinese religion.

MEIR SHAHAR is lecturer in East Asian Studies at Tel Aviv University and received his Ph.D. from Harvard University in 1992. He is the author of "The Lingyin Si Monkey Disciples and the Origins of Sun Wukong" (*Harvard Journal of Asiatic Studies* 52 [1] June 1992). He is currently completing a book on the Chinese god Jigong.

DONALD S. SUTTON, professor of history at Carnegie Mellon University, is the author of *Provincial Militarism and the Chinese Republic* (Ann Arbor: University of Michigan Press, 1980) and has recently published articles about local religious cults, shamanism, and performance and ritual on China's southern frontiers. His current work alternates between the study of the Southwest through Qing texts and of Taiwan largely through ethnographic fieldwork.

ROBERT P. WELLER is research associate at the Institute for the Study of Economic Culture and associate professor of anthropology at Boston University. He is the author of *Unities and Diversities in Chinese Religion* (Seattle: University of Washington Press and London: Macmillan, 1987) and *Resistance, Chaos and Control in China* (Seattle: University of Washington Press and London: Macmillan, 1994).